The Balanced Homeschooler

Homeschool · T.B.H. · Titus 2:3-5 · Home Life

Helping Moms Create Their Successful Homeschool Household
Through Biblical Personal Mentoring

2019 Revised & Expanded Edition

Authored by Carol A. Gary
www.thebalancedhomeschooler.com

Published by:
Carol A. Gary
Litchfield Park, AZ
www.thebalancedhomeschooler.com
inquiry@thebalancedhomeschooler.com

Photocopies may **ONLY** be made of the forms provided in this book's Appendices sections as follows: Appendix A, Appendix B, and Appendix C for use within the family who has purchased and owns this work.

No information in this manual shall be construed as a replacement for professional advice on any topic including but not limited to relationship counseling, financial advice, tax planning, or legal recommendations.

Please also note that *The Balanced Homeschooler* is an **affiliate of the Christianbook Group**. This means that you are able to purchase most of the books referenced in this manual as well as other curriculum you may need through http://www.thebalancedhomeschooler.com/tbh-affiliate-store.html. Orders processed this way will be fulfilled by Christianbook.com. In doing so, the fees earned from these sales and *The Balanced Homeschooler* program in general go to support the development and maintenance costs associated with this program offering as well as to the **Evan C. Gary Memorial Scholarship** administered by the Grand Canyon University Scholarship Foundation.[1]

---

[1] http://gcuscholarshipfoundation.org/donor-recognition/

This work is dedicated to our sons:
Evan, Benjamin, Jonathan, and Simon.

Each one of you has truly and uniquely
blessed your parents in
countless
and
bountiful
ways.

I know that I was destined to be your mother and your father's wife.
For these purposes, I was created.

Acknowledgements

First, I am grateful to the hundreds of homeschooling families I have had the privilege of interacting with over the years and appreciate the insight I have gained from them as well as the opportunities I have had to minister to them. I am also grateful for organizations like AFHE (Arizona Families for Home Education) and HSLDA (Homeschool Legal Defense Association) whose tireless support of home education on the state and national levels make it possible for all of us to have the choice to home educate our children.

To my fellow homeschooling friends over the years, I am grateful for the way each one has touched my life. Thank you for your Godly examples of leadership and motherhood, your sense of humor, and your sincerity in fulfilling your life's calling. As we have aided and mentored each other through the sometimes challenging but always rewarding world of home education, I am privileged to call each one of you my friend.

I would also like to give a special "thank you" to the following women and long-time friends in my life who have encouraged and supported me not only through this project, but also over the past several years through many of life's tough experiences. To Krystal Koons, Cynthia Keleher, Denise Oistad, and Lisa Wynn, you have all been essential parts of my life, and I thank you for you faithful and loving support, friendship, availability, and encouragement these many, many years.

I would also like to thank my brother-in-law, Brandon Gary, for generously giving his time and expertise to help us with many of the technical aspects of getting this original project produced as well as the creative logo he designed for me. Thank you to his wife and my wonderful "sister", Karen Gary. You are my best friend and have always encouraged me at every difficult season in my life, supporting every undertaking I have pursued.

To my father, John Chrysty who passed away in 2002, I would like to say that it was from him I learned about responsibility, integrity, and perseverance. In his honor, you will see the phrase "This page is left blank intentionally" peppered throughout the manual. He worked most of his career as a senior electrical engineer with Arizona Public Service and did a great deal of additional design work at the Palo Verde Nuclear Power Plant. In his technical design specifications, he would occasionally need to include such pages, and I would say to him, "Dad, these are the only pages I understand in the whole document!" He would probably say the same thing to me today for parts of this manual if he read it today!

To my mother, Barbara Chrysty, I also want to express my love and appreciation for the unwavering support and love you have given me my entire life. No one shares my joys and helps to bear my sorrows as completely and compassionately as you do and have done. Thank you for being my lifelong friend and cheerleader.

Finally, I want to say how incredibly thankful I am to my husband, Grant. Without your ongoing support and technical help in working with me to complete this project during that initial, intensive three-month period, it never would have happened. Even more than that, you are my partner in life during all seasons, no matter how joyous or difficult. Thank you for always loving and encouraging me.

Table of Contents

> Extended Friends and Family
>   o Write a Variety of Letters
>   o Involve Them in Your Homeschool Experiences
>   o Practice Hospitality
>   o Be Available to Help
>   o Develop Adult Friendships Wisely
> Local Community
>   o Be Aware of Neighborhood Needs
>   o Carefully Choose Adult Mentors for Your Child
>   o Involve Yourself Strategically in Church Programs
>   o Be Aware of Local and State Political Involvement Opportunities
>   o Consider Other Community Programs
> National Organizations
> International Missions
> A Word of Caution

> Who Rules Your Home Anyway?
> "If It Isn't on the Calendar, It Isn't Going to Happen!"
> Embrace Flexibility by Prioritizing and Building in Margin
> Begin with the End in Mind
> Seek Out Time Savers
>   o Homeschooling & Traveling – Relates to Part I (Chapters 1-4)
>   o Spiritual Discipleship – Relates to Chapter 5
>   o Correspondence & Financial Management Duties – Relates to Chapter 6
>   o Home Management - Relates to Chapter 7
>   o Community or Ministry Activities – Relates to Chapter 8
> Creating the Family Calendar
> Detailed Homeschool Schedules

PART III – HOMESCHOOL SUPPORT GROUP OPTIONS

> Is a Local Support Group Really Necessary?
> Characteristics and Cautions of a Good Support Group
> Considerations for Leadership
>   o Should You Associate with a Church or Not?
>   o Common Considerations for Any Group
>   o One Group: Many Personalities
>   o We're All in This Together
> Building a Strong Support Group
>   o Unity of Purpose
>   o Clarity of Organization
>   o Faithful Member Commitment

This page is left blank intentionally

Introduction

      In 2000, I wrote a *"Homeschooling Resource Letter"* containing about ten pages of helpful information for homeschoolers that I used as a tool to help new homeschoolers in our local support group get started. I then updated and tweaked it into a "Top 10" list of important elements for homeschoolers to consider that covered about ten pages. As the years passed and I continued to assist a growing number of families, that "Top 10" list eventually turned into this current format: a ten-chapter mentoring program called, *The Balanced Homeschooler.*

      Since you are reading this manual, you have probably decided to take the plunge into homeschooling! Perhaps, on the other hand, you have been homeschooling for years and are looking for some new directions and fresh perspectives about homeschooling or the various home management issues we all face. Still, others of you may be only pondering the idea of homeschooling. Maybe you are not quite sure if this is right for your child and your family, but you are enticed enough to at least check it out. Wherever you fall on the scale between the confidently committed and the interested seeker, you are trying to do what is best for your child by making sure to include the homeschool option in your research process. So, welcome to you all!

      First, recognize that **regardless of how you choose to have your child educated, parents must be totally invested in the process.** This is true whether your child attends school in a public, charter, private, or home setting. If they attend school outside of your home, do you understand what the teaching goals and approaches of the school are? Do you have an opportunity to preview the curriculum they use? What kind of effort does it take to ensure that you get your child signed up with the "right" teacher or enrolled in the "right" programs only to repeat the process next term? Are you able to set a few minutes aside in the evening sometime during their two to three-hour nightly marathon of homework to try and disciple them? Maybe you make every effort you can to try and understand the "worldview" they are learning in school so that you can intercept and even counter any teachings being delivered to your child that are contrary to your family's beliefs and values. What relationships are you concerned about your child encountering and are they ready for the social variables and challenges that await them? These are just a few considerations that those who entrust their children to a public or even a private program must tackle.

On the other hand, perhaps you can just do it yourself. This manual is for those parents, particularly moms, who are considering or have already decided to just educate their children themselves. It is also for those families who may have been homeschooling for a while but just need to reboot their priorities, obtain fresh perspective, or tackle a new season. They know that the character development and discipleship of their children must take priority over every other goal and would rather spend their time constructing Godly and positive building blocks of experiences in their child's education rather than fixing and pulling down unstable ones that run counter to their family's goals and belief system.

So, this means that choosing to direct your child's education is **a matter of running offense rather than defense.** Are you driving the engine of the train or just trying to hang on to the back of the caboose? My prayer is that, by going through this mentoring process, parents will free themselves out of the caboose and make their way to the engine room where God intends them to be!

Second, recognize that **this mentoring manual is not intended to provide all of the answers for you in every conceivable area of running your school or your home.** It is designed, rather, with the idea of the words found in the book of Titus, where more experienced women are to mentor women who are at the beginning of their journey. Veteran wives and mothers are challenged to...

> *"...train the younger women to love their husbands and children, to be self-controlled and pure, to be busy at home, to be kind, and to be subject to their husbands, so that no one will malign the word of God."* Titus 2:4-5 (NIV)

Therefore, to get the most out of this experience, my prayer is that you will **go through this tool with a veteran homeschooling, "Titus 2" mom**, either on a one-on-one basis or in the context of an established and reputable local homeschool support group who can help facilitate your development in the various areas covered in this manual. Surround yourself with Godly women who can provide useful feedback and guidance that will take you beyond the bounds of "how-to-homeschool" so you can also incorporate the homeschooling lifestyle with the reality of all the other issues that we wrestle with in life. You could go through it on your own and it is written in such a way that you can certainly self-study the book. However, it is better to do it with a friend.

Remember that **when it comes to home education there really are no "experts":** only moms who have walked the path before you and have a heart to share their thoughts. That is all I have done here, and that is what your mentor or group leader can do as well. In other words, the goal is to guide you in what to consider in your research and where to go for information as you adjust your plans and approaches to homeschooling and home management over the years. It is a **balance between giving you enough "fish" to get started and teaching you "how to fish"** in the various waters of school and life so that you can continuously learn and make the best choices for your family as you all grow. For it is usually a struggle not between good and bad choices but rather between good and best choices as you strive to make it all work together as harmoniously as possible.

Most of what I have provided for your consideration is **from my own experiences** over time since 2000. However, when appropriate, I have also incorporated a fair amount of **observations from the hundreds of homeschooling families** I have worked with since 2002. Each chapter leads with an opening scripture followed by detailed topical discussions, highlighted learning points, leader callout boxes, and journal pages. After working through the "Introduction", the program is divided into the following three parts.

> ➤ **Part I (8 hours: Total Mentoring Sessions over 4 Weeks):** This part is primarily designed to encourage veteran homeschoolers to help homeschoolers who are new or still early in their journey. It is also valuable to homeschoolers who have been at it for years and need to reset their priorities or gain inspiration and support in addressing new areas of challenge. You will learn more about what home education is and what important questions need to consider as you develop your family's vision for your children. You will have an opportunity to work through those tough and sometimes confusing initial questions that new homeschoolers tend to ask while gleaning wisdom from your mentor on each topic. We will also spend some time discussing the various teaching approaches utilized by homeschoolers and the related curriculum choices available to you. You will then consider the "Four C's" of how to select the best curriculum for your child. Finally, we will look at how to specifically apply certain tools and methods in your home to make it all work together, balancing your teaching style and methods with the learning style of your child as well as with the "season" they currently occupy. Part I will then wrap up with a discussion on portfolios, recordkeeping, and transcripts. You will also have an opportunity to summarize your findings and decisions before moving on to Part II.

> ➤ **Part II (10 hours: Total Mentoring Sessions over 5 Weeks):** This part was developed to help homeschoolers discuss together the ever-changing challenges of making it all work within the landscape of the entire household structure. Moms can either continue right after

completing Part I or they can jump in just for these sessions. We will look at the critical aspects of spiritually grounding yourself and your marriage in God's Word as a prerequisite to the "seasonal", spiritual discipleship of your child. Practical topics including financial management, meal preparation duties, and physically creating a healthy home will also be addressed. In addition, your mentor will spend a good deal of time discussing communication, relationship development, grief management, and conflict resolution techniques that will serve to move you towards the fulfillment of your family's vision statement while also bringing a greater level of harmony to your home. We will look at what role the surrounding community fulfills in your family as we discuss the purpose of the local church and opportunities to work with other local, national, and international organizations. We will also discuss the importance of connecting your child to mentors who will benefit them while reinforcing your family's values. Lastly, we will end Part II by pulling it all together as we discuss the issues of scheduling and time management considerations both for your home and your school.

> **Part III (2 hours: Optional Mentoring Session):** The final section deals with participating in and/or running a homeschool support group. Whether you are interested in being involved in the leadership of such a group or just participating in one, this chapter will give you the points you need to consider when figuring out related logistics and determining whether a group under consideration is a good fit for your family or not.

Throughout the manual, you will find that there are plenty of places for you to write down your thoughts as well as your husband's and your mentor's ideas related to each topic discussed. This manual is meant to be a working tool for you so that you can use it to plan and consider adjustments to your strategies over time. As it has morphed from being a three-ring binder to a paperback book, it is now a more portable and practical tool for you to read and write in as needed. Remember, **what will make this tool most useful for you is what *you* will add to it** during your mentoring time and as you pass through your future homeschooling years.

Sessions can be tailored to your group's needs. The first meeting usually takes about three hours to complete since it includes the "Introduction" section plus chapter one's "Visions and Variables" content. The remaining ones run about two hours each and take place over a three-month period with scheduled breaks. Chapters two and three are usually combined into one session since the material is so closely related. Chapter four is quite extensive, so it is best to cover learning styles and seasons in one meeting and then complete the methods, tools, and recordkeeping session in a separate one. Moms may also cover this entire program at an accelerated pace of about five weeks by meeting twice weekly instead of spreading it out over a three-month period. The last chapter is optional and may be covered just with moms who are interested in the specifics of running or even choosing a homeschool support group.

Take time now on page twenty to **determine your meeting schedule and to exchange important contact information** in the space provided. Each person in the group should have contact information for their group leader or mentor and at least two other group members whom they can contact throughout the week for guidance and encouragement. For larger groups, consider breaking up the discussion time by "season" so that you will not have a problem covering applicable material within the given time frame.

Remember, **moms who are new to *The Balanced Homeschooler* (also referred to as TBH), receive a full year of TBH Premier Program membership for FREE.**[2] Additional support resources for TBH moms who have invested in the program and maintain their TBH Premier Program status include the following benefits. Renewed annually for a nominal fee, member moms have access to....

- o regularly offered virtual "Chapter Chats" video conference discussion with Carol (both topical and free form),
- o automatic receipt of full TBH e-Manual (PDF format) as new revisions are released,
- o extended articles, additional resources, and exclusive tools/templates,
- o private TBH Facebook community,
- o and HSLDA group discount program. Our special group code is 210313.[3]

What questions do you have about your investment in the TBH program?

_____

_____

_____

_____

_____

_____

_____

---

[2] See http://www.thebalancedhomeschooler.com/3-premier-program.html for more information regarding TBH Premier Program membership. If you have invested in the program, send your proof of purchase to Carol Gary at orders@thebalancedhomeschooler.com to receive your FREE searchable, clickable companion copy of this manual.

[3] http://www.hslda.org/join/protect.asp - Read about the benefits at this link and then click "Special Membership Offers" to route here: https://www.hslda.org/join/offers.asp. Use code for a one-year membership discount with HSLDA.

Mentoring Schedule & Group Information

Part & Chapter Covered	Scheduled Meeting Dates	Scheduled Meeting Times	Scheduled Meeting Locations	Special Instructions or Assignments
P1: C1				
P1: C2 & C3				
P1: C4A				
P1: C4B				
P2: C5				
P2: C6				
P2: C7				
P2: C8				
P2: C9				
P3: C10				

Group Contact Names	Phone numbers	E-Mail
Lead Mentor:		
Member:		
Member:		
Member:		
Member:		
Member:		
Member:		
Member:		
Member:		
Member:		
Member:		

Additional group notes: _____

_____

_____

_____

_____

_____

More introductions....

Before you begin chapter one discussions, take some time now to get to know your mentor or group leader. Every homeschooler has a "story" on what tipped the balance on their judgment scales to bring about their decision. We have even MORE stories about why we continue to homeschool, but we will get into that territory later in the process!

I will first tell you my story and then your mentor/group leader will have an opportunity to share theirs as well. Then consider to yourself what you think your story might be since it will greatly help you with some of the exercises you will encounter in the first chapter.

Though I did not know it at the time, my story began in 1998 when I was rocking my oldest child to sleep. He was only a few months old, but I remember thinking to myself, "I just can't believe I'm going to have to give him over to someone else for the better part of each day in just a few short years." I was not thinking about homeschooling or anything remotely related to education at that time. I only knew that I was NOT looking forward to him being away from me and missing out on so much of his life and development.

Fast forward to about two years later, and I remember the conversations of advice and questions that started to flow my way about school options for him. Many of our friends and acquaintances had children who were well into their grammar school years when we were just starting our family. So, I was overwhelmed to say the least! Conversations starting with, "So what are you going to do about school for him?" emerged frequently.

"What do you mean?" I would reply thinking, "Good grief, he's only two!"

"Well," they would say, "you need to start thinking about it now. That way, you can get on the right waiting list for whatever it is you are going to do."

"Waiting lists? What do I need to do?" I asked anxiously.

Then they gave me some materials to look at regarding potential private or charter schools in the area. After talking to my husband, we decided immediately that public school was not going to be an option. So, I started considering these other school choices. But as I examined what each one offered and eliminated the various possibilities for one reason or another, a light began to dawn on me. Here I was, a stay-at-home mom with a spiritual gift of teaching and I began to sense that the Lord was speaking to my heart saying, "Why don't *you* just do it?"

I had one person in the world, a relative in California, whom I knew had homeschooled their children and that was it. I had no other point of reference and knew absolutely nothing about homeschooling. But that did not matter. I had my marching orders from the Lord and I sunk my teeth into the research process like I had never done with any other initiative or assignment prior to that time. He opened door after door during and since that time, and I have never looked back. As you will also see throughout the manual and particularly noted in chapters one and seven, my husband and I are blessed to have lived a life of "no regrets" in our decision to home educate our sons.

One other important truth that I have learned from our story and I find echoed in hundreds of other homeschooling households over the years is that there is a theme of passion and dedication in most homeschooling families. **No**

matter what your background and spiritual gifts are, if the Lord has pressed upon your heart to homeschool your children, He *will* give you the resources, tools, support, and focus necessary to do it. Do not allow any roadblocks or doubts to get in your way. Instead, just know that questions will be answered, and it is a step-by-step process where He will give you the wisdom and confidence you need to obtain the next level in your journey at the right time.

What is your mentor's story?

_____

_____

_____

_____

_____

_____

_____

_____

_____

_____

_____

What is your story or what do you think your story might be?

_____

_____

_____

_____

_____

_____

_____

_____

_____

_____

_____

_____

Dear Mentor or Leader,

First, **thank you** for being willing to facilitate your friend or group through this mentoring process. One of the consistent messages I have received over the years is that many veteran homeschooling moms want to help their friends come up to speed on all the basics of getting started, making homeschooling work with home life to stay the course. However, they do not necessarily have the bandwidth or essential resources readily available that are needed to help their friend during their discussions. My prayer, then, is that this tool will help you do just that, freeing your time to support and encourage them without reinventing the wheel every time you assist a new homeschooler.

I have shared many ideas, opinions, and thoughts of my own in this manual, but that is just a starting point, and I certainly do not expect moms to agree with every perspective that I share. Rather, the manual is a way to **connect both veteran and novice homeschoolers** as a framework for discussion on a variety of topics that are of mutual concern. So, I strongly encourage each homeschooling mom to continue to refine her own philosophy and opinions about her family's priorities and homeschooling decisions as they grow and mature in their journey each day and especially each year. Remember that mentoring is not just to serve new homeschoolers but can also provide insight and direction to veteran homeschoolers who are struggling with one or more areas or even a new season in their home school.

How do you use this manual? You have choices! After going through as "TBH Mom" yourself, you can then go through it along with your group or friend for the first time, working through the various sections as directed. However, another option is to have them work through it independently and then you check in with them at periodic points. There really is **very little preparation work** needed to facilitate a successful meeting. Later, this manual will continue to serve as a tool that you, as either a support group leader or independent mentor, can utilize with new members or friends as needed. Simply direct your friend or each group member to purchase their own copy of the manual, meet with them about the introductory information, and then set a plan and a schedule for how you will help them through it.[4] Then touch base with them about questions that arise after they work through each chapter's information and "homework". Although a new homeschooler *can* read and work through the manual 100% on their own, they will gain the most out of it by discussing the topics in either a group or a one-on-one setting with at least one other veteran homeschooler. The regular "Chapter Chats" virtual session I offer to TBH Premier Program members can also fill this need when no formal group is available.[5]

While I regularly update this manual, I do not have the ability to address every issue or idea that can arise across all topics. Thus, leaders and veteran moms are encouraged to **add their own thoughts, resources, references, and recommendations** to each section, and plenty of designated space is included to

---

[4] http://www.thebalancedhomeschooler.com/1-mentoring-program.html
[5] http://www.thebalancedhomeschooler.com/2-group-mentoring.html

do just that. My hope is that moms will not just use this manual once but can add to it and use it as a **working tool** throughout their season as a homeschooling mom.

As you prepare for your meetings, realize that **there is no separate leader's book** since group facilitators have the same tool as the member moms. You will notice, however, that I have occasionally inserted a *"Note to Leaders and Mentors"* callout box as is appropriate for additional points of consideration on topics that may be useful to your mentoring meetings or to your support group. I have also included a final chapter for additional information to those who would like more information on starting or leading a support group in their area. So here are some meeting specifics that will help you to keep your mentoring sessions moving along, particularly in a group setting.

1. **Start and end on time.** Even if you have more moms that you know are coming or logging in, be mindful of the time constraints that everyone is under and honor the fact that you do have moms who were on time and ready to get going. Also make sure that your moms leave or log out on time so that their husbands can count on them being available at the time originally stated. If you are meeting virtually, make sure your moms have their technical requirements set up and tested in advance of the meeting.

2. **Encourage balanced participation** from each mom so that no one person dominates the discussions. While not every mom will want to speak on every topic, be sure that each one is given the opportunity to regularly do so.

3. **When a topic comes up that you are unsure of how to handle,** ask for input from the group or let them know that you will research the issue and follow up the next meeting. Remember that you should not feel pressured to be a content expert. Instead, focus on providing encouragement and clarification while facilitating discussions. I also welcome mentors to contact me when clarification is needed about the program contents, how to handle a difficult question, etc.[6]

4. **Above all, honor the Lord.** Make sure to pray for your group and even with them as you feel led. Allow His timing to direct the path of each discussion for a customized and relevant experience for each mom.

5. **When moms are unable to attend in-person or via video conferencing, be sure to engage them in an alternate make-up option**, either during the current session with another group or the following season. The material is also conducive for self-study.

One final point is that you will notice I have made several references to homeschooling in Arizona since this is where I reside. However, a great deal of the value of the manual is not tied to any one state since the principles discussed are

---

[6] Contact Carol via the website at www.thebalancedhomeschooler.com or via e-mail at inquiry@thebalancedhomeschooler.com.

universal. Your **moms do not need to live in Arizona to benefit from this program** and, where national resource information is available, I have included it.

For **updates** about resources, specific supplements related to each chapter, and other pieces of relevant information, you are also encouraged to visit my website at www.thebalancedhomeschooler.com. TBH Premier Program members also have access to additional resources via our private Facebook group.

I would also love to hear from you. So please feel free to contact me through the website, the public or private TBH Facebook site, or e-mail me with your stories of encouragement, questions, or comments about your personal journey or your group's experiences with this manual.[7] If you would like to submit requests for corrections or updates, I truly appreciate those as well.

Enjoy the journey!

Carol A. Gary

What other questions regarding leading or facilitating do you have prior to starting your local sessions for TBH? Ask yourself this same question if you are self-studying through this tool.

_____

_____

_____

_____

_____

_____

_____

_____

_____

_____

_____

_____

_____

---

[7] http://www.thebalancedhomeschooler.com/
https://www.facebook.com/thebalancedhomeschooler.public - Public Facebook page for easy sharing.
https://www.facebook.com/groups/thebalancedhomeschooler/ - Private Facebook group when you purchase the manual and also accessible by TBH Premier Program members.
inquiry@thebalancedhomeschooler.com

This page is left blank intentionally

Chapter 1

Getting Started: Visions & Variables

Where there is no vision, the people perish:
but he that keepeth the law, happy is he.
Proverbs 29:18 (KJV)

Without a Vision...

You may have read this scripture from Proverbs 29:18 before, reminding us that the greatest goal of a person's life must be defined to keep motivation, progress, and growth going. However, I also find it interesting that in the New International Version that very same scripture is worded like this:

Where there is no revelation, the people cast off restraint;
but blessed is he who keeps the law.
Proverbs 29:18 (NIV)

So here we find that the primary reason that the "people perish" is because they have "cast off restraint", doing what is right in their own eyes in the absence of guidance. I believe that looking at this Scripture in both translations gives a great picture of what our goal should be with our children. **It is our job as their parents to cast that vision for them when they are young and to keep it alive and adaptable as they grow.** We help them to understand what the boundaries of life are and to recognize that by working within God's "law" that we are better off than we would be without them. Our children can expect to be both "blessed" and "happy" when they "keep the law". Ultimately, in the context of the homeschooling family, we seek to keep their eyes focused ahead by teaching them the tools and truths of the "law" so that they may meet the vision God has for their life. The "law" really goes beyond the Ten Commandments or the summary of the law given to Moses when Jesus himself said this:

What is God's vision for your child?

> *"The most important one is this: 'Hear, O Israel, the Lord our God, the Lord is one. Love the Lord your God with all your heart and with all your soul and with all your mind and with all your strength. The second is this: 'Love your neighbor as yourself.' There is no commandment greater than these." (Mark 12:29-31 – NIV)*

So, how is such a vision instilled in our children? Can it be accomplished through a weekly trip to church and a few other moments of time that you try to snatch with your tired child in between this commitment and that appointment? With the number of hours U.S. students spend in school over a twelve-year period averaging nearly 14,400 hours, can parents possibly instill what is necessary and often contrary to what their child is learning and experiencing during the day?[8] In fact, students really spend more time than that either away from or isolated from their families when both parents work outside of the home all year long.

Slicing the data differently, students average 1,195 hours in school. However, that does not count the additional hours students spend engaging in related extracurricular activities or doing homework, which can easily add up to an additional two or three additional hours a day. When I worked in the corporate world, we used the figure of 2,080 hours to calculate benefits and estimate salary levels for full-time employees, which is probably the figure that is more accurate for us to use when thinking about our child's engagement in an institutional school. **Over twelve years, that becomes the staggering figure of 24,960 hours.** So, if 2,080 of a child's best waking hours *every year* are spent under the direction and leadership of adults who do not, or cannot, mention the prevalence of God's hand throughout history or His design in our world's structure and functions, can your child really catch the vision for what God has designed them to do? It has been said by other leaders in the homeschooling community that "if you send your children to Caesar's palace to be educated, you are going to get little Romans back in return." So ultimately, our vision for our children should reflect God's unchangeable standards and truths: not those of our politically correct and morally bankrupt society.

The answer, then, to the vision question is that **it is up to parents to do it**. God has entrusted your child to you and your husband and only the two of you are going to be accountable one day to Him for how you trained and discipled them. They are a gift on loan to you for a short season, and it is your blessed task to be a good steward of their lives, giving them the best opportunity for success in a lost and hurting world. Ultimately, children do make their own

---

[8] https://nces.ed.gov/surveys/sass/tables/sass0708_035_s1s.asp

choices and, sadly, they are not always the right ones even despite our best efforts. However, you are *not* responsible for the harvest of your child's spiritual walk. **Instead, you are responsible for tilling the soil, sowing the seeds, and caring for the seedlings until they are out of your home and have entered God's world for service.**

What is your own vision for your child?

So, while most new homeschoolers have a desire to jump right in and start choosing curriculum and figuring out their schedules immediately, I have found over the years that it is wise to **take a step back and first clarify the foundations of why you are doing what you are doing.** In addition, it is important that you be informed about what homeschooling is and what sets it apart from other educational choices. The differences under consideration reach far beyond just the geography of where your child spends their time learning. Finally, you will see that this first chapter will help you to acquaint yourself with other essential issues that must be addressed before "jumping in" or engaging in a serious "reboot". Accordingly, put first things first.

Start with Scripture and **identify your family's "life verse" for your initial inspiration**. Our family's verse is Proverbs 3:5-6, *"Trust in the LORD with all your heart and lean not on your own understanding; [6] in all your ways acknowledge Him, and he will make your paths straight."* For us, this illustrates "trust" and "direction" as concepts to draw from in the brainstorming process.

Now it is time to **write your family's vision statement**. It should not just be about the three "R's" or any specific strategies you want to employ in your school nor should it be too lofty or vague. In fact, the term "homeschooling" should not be mentioned at all. Instead, recognize that home education is just a tool for you and your husband to use, keeping your eyes fixed on why you are doing with your child what you are doing. The vision creation process just involves you, your spouse, and the Lord. If you have tweens or teens, fold them into the process as well for optimum buy-in and cooperative involvement.

Your family's vision statement should also be relatively **unchanging over the years**. While your strategies to meet your goals and fulfill your vision for your child must and will alter over time, the vision or mission you have crafted for your family should not.

In our family, we have varied our objectives, our methods, and our curriculum. We have even updated the wording from time to time on our mission statement for our children, but the focus and spirit of it remains constant. Here is the long and lofty version of the **"Gary Family Mission Statement" that we first developed for our children:**

"Our mission is to faithfully disciple, train, and educate our children in a way that honors God's desire for and from them: that they remain teachable, exercise loyalty, and serve His purpose with integrity, boldness, humility, usefulness, and love as He fulfills His unique plan for each one of their lives."

A great way to create the vision statement is to have both you and your spouse **write out separate ones first and then bring them together for a final synthesis.** Can you tell who contributed what words to our first draft above? I wrote thoughts that included "love", "humility, and "teachable" whereas my husband focused on the ideas of "integrity", "boldness", and "usefulness". Do you sense the differences in focus and style in our writing as well? **Now here is the shorter, more accessible version:**

> "We seek to faithfully and uniquely equip each of our children to live a teachable and loyal life of integrity, boldness, humility, usefulness, and love as they grow to fulfill God's purpose."

Notice how this second iteration is more concise and is starting to sound **unified in voice and purpose.** Although it is still a bit long, it is down to one sentence and can even be posted in our home as a banner of what it means to "be a Gary". Over the years, moms have shared many creative ways to post and continually communicate their family's vision statement. You can distribute it on notecards, make it into a customized plaque, design it on keepsake paper and display it in a centrally located frame, or stencil it around the doorframe of your home, as inspired from Deuteronomy 6:9.

There is nothing magical about the process of writing a vision statement. **The point is to just do it.** You may not like the way yours reads at first and will adjust it after a while to clarify your meaning here or there, but the heart of it will remain with you throughout your career as a parent. Say to yourself, "I want to do _____ to accomplish _____ in our child." If you review our family mission again, it basically says "We want to _____ so that _____ will happen."

Another exercise we use in our kick-off sessions to prompt the thinking process is to **make a clay creation** that reflects the first word or thought that comes to mind. This can serve as the foundation of your vision statement and may also help to provide a creative outlet to visually communicate the essence of your family's vision to your child. Similarly, you can **draw an image** that represents your key word or phrase that grounds your family vision statement. These exercises can enhance the mission-writing process by also providing a family logo to reinforce the heart of your goal, which is particularly useful when communicating intangible ideas with young children.

Note to Leaders and Mentors:

Writing a vision or mission statement for your support group is also an essential activity. Decide what the purpose of your group is and then stick to that purpose without compromise. Make sure that every activity and program you employ fits with that vision. If it does not fit or you do not have parents willing to organize a certain area, then do not do it! Also ensure that every new leader who comes onto your team understands and supports the vision of the group. To read more about this important concept, reference chapter ten of this manual.

Now take the space provided on the following pages and **write some initial thoughts** about the goals you have for your child: character qualities you want them to have, beliefs you wish to instill in them, ultimate purpose fulfilled, etc. It is good to take a few days to work on this so that it has time to sit. Then you can return to it several times until it feels right to you and reflects your and your husband's hearts. Remember, first work on them separately and then synthesize them together so that the result is as balanced and genuine as possible.

I want to do

—————————

to accomplish

—————————

in our child.

For additional biblical inspiration, identify your family's "life verse".

_____

_____

_____

_____

_____

Here are some <u>character</u> or <u>value</u> words you can use to jump start your list!

honesty, integrity, steadfastness, persistence, boldness, maturity, mercy,

generosity, considerateness, purity, usefulness, confidence, servant heart

_____

_____

_____

_____

Now write some of the <u>actions</u> necessary to meet your "purpose thought" you wrote for your child above. Work with your husband to have shared input and unity on the vision.

_____

_____

_____

_____

_____

Finally, put these two exercises together and take a stab at writing a vision statement for your family. This is your first draft.

_____
_____
_____
_____
_____
_____
_____
_____
_____

Play with it more and write it again so that it is closer to the wording that you think best reflects your thoughts.

_____
_____
_____
_____
_____
_____
_____
_____
_____

Write your final draft here:

_____
_____
_____
_____
_____
_____

Congratulations! Now you have written your final family vision statement!

If you are tempted to skip this step of writing a family vision statement, please reconsider! The fact is that **we are all either intentional or reactionary in how we parent and teach our children so choose to be intentional!** Articulate on paper what God has placed on your heart, so you have something concrete to work with. As you go through this program, keep the thoughts contained within your family vision statement in mind and ask yourself, "What is the best way to educate our child to accomplish this goal?" Does this particular curriculum or that specific strategy help or hinder this goal? Keep coming back to your vision statement and refine it throughout the process as you feel led to do, knowing that it probably will and should remain fairly static as the years pass.

Why do parents choose to Homeschool?

Years ago, I served on a panel of moms who shared various ideas with a MOPS (Mothers of Preschoolers) group about educational options for young mothers to consider. I represented homeschooling and there were three other mothers as well: one who had taught in the public schools and whose child was currently in the public system, one whose child was in a charter school, and one who was there to represent the private school option, although she had done all four options at various points in her children's lives. This last mother on the panel made a comment at one point in the discussion that warned parents against homeschooling for the unhealthy reason she did it. She said she had homeschooled because it was "fashionable" at the time, referring to the late 80's and early 90's, and that she never really "got it". I nearly dropped my microphone. I thought to myself, "You have GOT to be kidding me!" Of all the reasons for or admonitions against homeschooling, the idea of being "fashionable" has never been a concept had come across before or since that time. In that moment, I did my best to calmly reassure the attendees that if the Lord leads them to take full responsibility for their child's education that He would certainly equip them to do it, regardless of what society may think about their choice to homeschool. **We homeschool for an audience of "One"**, and our children just happen to be the beneficiaries. Fashionable or not, our choice to homeschool must be an inspired event to stay in it for the long haul.

In contrast to this experience during the first homeschooling conference I ever attended, I went to a lecture given by Marilyn Boyer, a homeschooling mother of fourteen and wife of Rick Boyer. They are the co-founders of **Character Concepts**, formerly known as **The Learning Parent.** Marilyn Boyer is one of those mothers you cannot help but be awed by with her sweet spirit, calming

> **Note to Leaders and Mentors:**
>
> *You are a natural point of contact for questions about homeschooling, so it is a good idea to understand that research supports the following facts for why most families choose to homeschool.*
>
> *"Teaching specific philosophical or religious values, controlling social interactions, developing close families, and high-level academics are the most common reasons for home schooling."*
>
> *NHERI – Home Education Research Fact Sheet*

"I want to have no regrets."

presence, and wise heart.[9] Throughout the course of her presentation, she tenderly shared how she would not trade one moment of the time she had spent homeschooling her children for anything. Her point was especially powerful when she told her listeners of the suffering that one of her teenage sons experienced as he fought and later succumbed to leukemia after an 18-month battle. She said that many people asked her during the following months if she felt anger towards God. After all, He could have provided a saving cure for her son and given him a powerful testimony. She would then ask in return, how is it that she could be angry with God for the gift He had given her for sixteen years? She viewed herself and her husband as having those wonderful, though short-lived, years with him and that his siblings were close to him as well. She saw the impact her son's life made on others both inside and outside of their family, particularly in his final months. The closeness and bonding that occurred during that time because they homeschool was precious to her and she said that, above all, **she had "no regrets".**

At that moment, I thought, "YES! That's it. That's why I want to homeschool." I knew the spiritual, relational, and academic benefits of homeschooling, but a "no regrets" mantra is what really spoke to my heart. The powerful way that God communicated through Marilyn to me in that moment is an experience that still resonates with me after all these years, especially given our own son's subsequent battle with leukemia from 2010 to 2012 that I recount in further detail in chapter seven of this program. Although we can all certainly wish we had done this or that differently in hindsight over time as parents and as our child's teacher, to know that we have "no regrets" in the investment we have made in this short period of time called "childhood" is an extraordinary privilege.

So how does my experience stack up against statistics? As previously indicated, parents typically choose to homeschool for a variety of reasons, and the best source for evaluating such statistics can be found at the **NHERI (National Home Education Research Institute)** website[10]. Dr. Brian Ray regularly publishes the *Worldwide Guide to Homeschooling* and other books and articles that provide every possible statistic you can think of to research home education. However, the motivations that parents typically have for homeschooling their child boils down to the following list: to instill godly values, to build and maintain healthy family relationships, and to customize their child's education so that they may address any developmental issues or enhance any unique gifts the child has. As it turns out, these elements were essential in our family's "no-regrets" experience.

So, rarely are academic success and well-rounded experiences alone the driving reasons why parents choose to homeschool. Rather they are the beneficial byproducts of such primary goals as creating **close and lasting family relationships**, focusing on the importance of **character development** and then exercising the opportunity to incorporate the **religious beliefs** of the family into the educational process.

---

[9] http://www.characterconcepts.com/

[10] http://www.nheri.org/

Academically, you will find that **homeschoolers typically outperform their public-school peers by an average of 15-30%.** Specifically, on standardized test scores where the average public-school student scores in the 50th percentile, the homeschooled student averages scores between the 65th to 80th percentile. Essentially, there is no equal to producing academic excellence than a one-on-one tutoring style of educating and mentoring our children.[11]

What are your reasons for homeschooling or why do you continue to homeschool?

Homeschoolers also **have opportunities to specialize and explore** a variety of interests that are often difficult to nurture in an educational setting outside of the home. In the home, parents can customize their child's educational program to help both address weaknesses and sharpen strengths. The child is neither held back from going on to other work so others may "catch up" nor are they "left in the dust" when they do not understand a concept. Families can also adjust how much time they spend on each topic of study, depending on the interests of the child and their family. It is also an ideal environment to teach children who have special needs, whether they have physical disabilities or learning issues, as we will discuss further in chapter four when we talk about the "Struggling Learner".

Now take a few moments and discuss with your mentor what some of your reasons are for homeschooling your child. List the benefits you can think of and be sure to discuss these ideas with your husband. You may even want to **rank them in order** from your most to least important reasons, which will help you later in your planning process. Another exercise that may be useful is to **distinguish some different reasons for each child.** Finally, **ask your husband** to write down some of his thoughts about why your family wants to homeschool and then compare and discuss your answers. If you have homeschooled for a while, think about what your original motivations were and how they now compare to why you continue to homeschool.

Write down some reasons you would like to homeschool or reasons that you continue to homeschool. _____

_____

_____

_____

_____

_____

_____

---

[11] http://www.nheri.org/research/research-facts-on-homeschooling.html

Now write down your husband's feedback. Highlight similarities and discuss the differences between your opinions.

_____

_____

_____

_____

_____

_____

_____

_____

Now write a consolidated summary of why you would like to homeschool or continue to homeschool that reflects BOTH your thoughts and your husband's.

_____

_____

_____

_____

_____

_____

_____

_____

_____

_____

_____

_____

_____

_____

_____

_____

_____

_____

What is a Homeschooler?

There has been much discussion in recent years as to what denotes a family who is home educating their children versus other combinations of educational choices. To add to the confusion, although homeschooling is legal in all fifty states, every state has their own statute governing the definition of a homeschooler and the related compliance requirements. This variation in the language and the depth to which each state defines a homeschooler can make it difficult to understand when a family is traditionally homeschooling or if they are engaged in something else. To address the confusion, **AFHE (Arizona Families for Home Education)** has published a clarification documents as well as legislative updates to address both the history and status of home education in AZ.[12]

Do you want your child to receive "Parent-led, family-funded, relationship-based education" in your home?

Note to Leaders and Mentors:

This is a good time to address the issue of tax credits. Many parents ask if tax credits are available to homeschoolers since their children will not be utilizing the public-school system. Those of us who own a home know that a great deal of the annual property tax burden goes to fund the local public school system, so it seems to be a sensible question to pose. However, most homeschoolers oppose the idea of pushing for any type of tax credit because when such considerations are given, strings are usually attached at some point in the form of increased governmental control over how a family's home school is being run, what testing is required, how is curriculum selected, etc. So, if your well-meaning legislator wants to kindly offer you a tax credit, simply say, "Thanks but no thanks!"

AFHE defines homeschooling as follows:

Home education is best defined as parent-led, family-funded, relationship-based education of your child at home.

Arizona Families for Home Education (AFHE) defines a "Homeschooler" as follows:

Homeschoolers are parents or legal guardians who choose to educate their own children at home in at least the required subjects of reading, grammar, math, science, and social studies pursuant to A.R.S. §15-802.[13]

Thoughts to help further clarify the definition of a homeschooler continues with former AFHE Board Member, Carol Shippy, who wrote in 2010:

A homeschooler retains complete control of their child's primary level education. Delegation of control to either a private school program or fee-based classes held outside the home for core subjects reclassifies the parents or legal guardians as something other than homeschoolers, at least in

---

[12] https://www.afhe.org/?s=not+your+father%27s+law
[13] http://www.azleg.gov/viewdocument/?docName=http://www.azleg.gov/ars/15/00802.htm
http://www.azleg.gov/arsDetail/?title=15

relation to the child/children involved in said program or classes. It is unclear what percentage of a child's education constitutes homeschooling, but the spirit of the law implies that the parent teaches the core subjects.

Additionally, fractional enrollment in publicly funded programs designed for homeschoolers may require the parent or legal guardian to withdraw the Affidavit of Intent to Homeschool with the County School Superintendent. A school district or charter school is eligible to receive the entire ADM allocation for a child taught over 15 hours per week.

Parents of secondary level students enrolled in community college classes, or utilizing other means of instruction, are still considered homeschoolers as long as the parent or legal guardian remains the primary instructor and retains complete responsibility for their child/children's education.

No matter what state you live in, this definition captures the essence of what a traditional homeschooler is in our current educational climate. Fundamentally, **it comes down to direction and control of the child's education**, both in terms of funding and content, as well as the parent's involvement with the child throughout the process. Ask yourself if you, as the parent, are funding your child's education privately, determining their course of study yourself, and directing the delivery of the content. Many families, particularly in the high school years, may have their child take a course on-line with a private institution or take a dual-credit course at the local community college. However, the family is still considered a traditional homeschooler if they fall within the guidelines previously described. The gray area can occur when homeschooled students participate to some degree in public programs, which we will address in the next section. There can also be issues if the parent gives over most of the direction of their child's education to another person or group, regardless of whether that person is paid to do so or is just volunteering.

To further enhance your understanding of how homeschooling compares to other options available in Arizona, read this article by Jon Callahan called "The Importance of Knowing Who We Are as Homeschoolers".[14] In it, he not only clarifies important questions about home education but also details six **educational options** in Arizona, although the emerging trend of hybrid schools are not covered.[15] A **hybrid school** is where parents technically enroll their child in a two or three days a week private school that uses homeschooling curriculum, and the families deliver the teaching requirements for the remaining two or three days at home.[16] Families who live outside of Arizona or are considering a move from one state to another should thoroughly research homeschooling laws and options by state via HSLDA.[17]

---

[14] https://www.afhe.org/?s=knowing+who+we+are+as+homeschoolers
[15] https://www.afhe.org/wp-content/uploads/2017/06/AFHE_six_classifications_arizona_student.pdf
[16] http://fourteensixacademy.com/about/academy-overview/ (example of a hybrid school)
[17] https://www.hslda.org/laws/

In Arizona and in a growing number of other states, another point that relates to home education that needs further discussion is called **Empowerment Scholarship Account (ESA)**.[18] Simply put, this option allows parents to contractually break from the public school system and either place their child in a private school or home education option. After spending a minimum of 100 days in a public school (virtual or typical), qualifying families agree to no longer use public programs to fulfill their child's educational and developmental needs. Originally, this choice was created for families who have a child with learning issues or physical disabilities and was not being properly served in public school. In this arrangement, parents receive 90% of what the school is allocated for their child while the state's

department of education retains 10% to administrate the program. The amount a family receives corresponds directly to the child's diagnosis and classification. The parent agrees to handle all their child's needs and to follow very strict requirements as to how and when funds may be used (i.e. curriculum, therapies, special equipment, etc.). Now that ESA continues to expand its definition to include siblings and other typical children, many traditional homeschoolers are concerned about the confusion and possible intrusion that may ensue.

However, as the ESA option continues to expand in scope, **ESA families seem to most closely resemble traditional homeschoolers than any other educational option**. Such overlap is evident since ESA home educators do indeed need to make curriculum decisions and they also closely direct their child's need for therapies and other services. Due to these two points, parent/child interaction also tends to be high. While these elements all mirror traditional homeschoolers, the main departure that ESA families make from the traditional definition is that they either in whole or in part funding their child's education with public monies. This concern of receiving governmental funding has led to a great deal of disagreement and divisiveness within the homeschooling community in Arizona and, most likely, in other states as well, which include Florida, Mississippi, North Carolina, Nevada, and Tennessee.[19]

How should an individual family or support group in the traditional homeschooling arena respond to ESA families? Without delving into the politics of the matter, **hopefully our response is "with grace and respect"**. As traditional homeschoolers, support of "school choice" must include all options and not just the ones that are as clearly defined. ESA is here to stay and there will certainly be ways that both traditional and ESA home educators can co-exist in respectful yet clearly unique ways that are both God-honoring and supportive of the concept of "school choice".

---

[18] https://www.edchoice.org/school-choice/programs/arizona-empowerment-scholarship-accounts/
[19] https://www.edchoice.org/school-choice/types-of-school-choice/education-savings-account/

Am I clear on the definition of a traditional homeschooler? What additional questions do I have?

_____

_____

_____

_____

_____

_____

What about public programs?

While ESA is a unique hybrid in the world of educational choice, there are other public programs that need to be clearly distinguished from homeschooling. Parents seeking an alternative to public or even private "brick-and-mortar" schools can often be attracted to the idea of enrolling in a virtual academy because it seems like such a great arrangement. The academy usually offers a "free" computer and other support resources to the parent while the child gets to be physically located at home to do their work. Sounds like a great deal, right?

However, if you contrast the earlier definition of a homeschooler we covered to the issue of participating in a public-school program, including charter or virtual school academies, it may not turn out to be as good of a situation as most parents hope it will be. The bottom line is that **virtual academies are still public school programs** that are just delivered in the home in front of a computer with minimal parent-child interaction and little to no input from the parent on course content. While public-school-at-home is a fit approach for certain families, parents are often confused and even, at times, misled about virtual academies, believing them to be equivalent to homeschooling. Over several years of serving in the leadership team of a large local support group, I counseled many-a-family during their time of transition from a virtual academy setting to traditional homeschooling. Without exception, the families that I have known to make this transition express their initial frustration and even anger over feeling like they were misinformed as they were told it was the same as traditional homeschooling. Many had also been led to believe that they were going to have more flexibility in controlling their child's program participation than what was experienced. The "free" computer, etc. came with a cost.

Thus, it is important that parents are clear that these are two different educational choices. While homeschoolers in many states, including Arizona, can minimally participate in a public program and still be considered homeschooling, **there is a line that can inadvertently be crossed that moves the family out of the definition of being a traditional homeschooler.** If the extent of your child's participation requires your them to be registered with the school in such a way that the district receives public funding for your child as if they were full-time students, there is probably an issue. If this is the case, then you may be in violation of state law. For example, in Arizona, a parent is required to have an affidavit on file of their "intent to homeschool" the child. So, they cannot have the child enrolled in a public program as a full-time student *and* have an affidavit of intent on file with the county. It must be one or the other but not both. Therefore, if you plan to participate in a public program to some level, please seek counsel from HSLDA (Homeschool Legal Defense Association) or some other legal support resource before filing any paperwork or making your final decision. [20]

In summary, **a virtual academy is simply public school at home**. Your child must meet the requirements set by the state and you are accountable to make sure that they perform at those levels, take all required standardized tests, and participate in any other programs set forth by that state. Parents are usually not able to incorporate their own curriculum choices, especially if it has religious undertones to it. There is also little to no parent/child interaction since students spend their time in front of the computer most of the day, and the development of family relationships that are typically so important to homeschooling families is hindered. So, while virtual academies may be a viable choice for some families who, either for medical, social, or other reasons, may need to remove their child for a time with the plan to reintroduce them to a public or private setting, this public-school-at-home option should not be equated with traditional home education.

For **further information about virtual academies as well as charter schools**, please refer to HSLDA's position paper on this subject.[21] The article and now video entitled "Exposing a Trojan Horse" is another useful resource.[22]

What are my thoughts and questions about participating in public programs?

_____

_____

_____

_____

_____

_____

_____

_____

_____

_____

---

[20] http://www.hslda.org/
[21] https://www.hslda.org/docs/nche/Issues/S/State_Charter_Schools.asp
[22] http://www.pheofca.org/CharterSchoolTrojanHorse.html

How do I make it legal?

In Arizona, **affidavits are required for children who are ages six through sixteen**, unless you will not begin instruction until they are eight. In that case, you fill out the affidavit reflecting that fact (i.e. that formal instruction will not begin until they are eight). Once the filing status is determined, the Arizona paperwork process to specify your child as a homeschooled student is quite simple. At the beginning of the given school year, if the child is six at that time, the parent must file a one-time affidavit with the Superintendent of Schools in their county for each child they will be educating at home. They need to complete the form and sign it in the presence of a local notary before they submit it to the county. Mail the documents to the county superintendent's office and then retain a copy for your records. Then follow-up with the county within a couple of weeks to ensure they have it on file. Once they process it successfully, they will send it back to you stamped with their acceptance information. You may also handle this process, including notarization, in person if you do not wish to deal with the mail process. Parents only need to fill an affidavit out one time for each child they are homeschooling. For more information about filing in Arizona's Maricopa County, contact **Homeschool Liaison at 602-506-3144**.[23] If you need to update your affidavit or wish to withdraw it, contact the county directly to adjust as needed. So, to recap the process for Arizona...

1. Download a copy of the one-page affidavit from AFHE (Arizona Families for Home Education).[24] You will need one for each child (ages 6-16). If you are withdrawing your child from a public or private institution, you have 30 days to complete this affidavit submission process.
2. Fill out the information for each child (one child per form).
3. Do not sign the form until you do so in the presence of a notary.
4. Once the form is signed and notarized, you must mail it or personally deliver it to your county's Superintendent of Schools office along with a certified copy (NOT a photocopy) of your child's birth certificate.

> **Note to Leaders and Mentors:**
>
> *It is important to understand the truancy laws in your state. If you are going to be out and about with your school-aged child in a public setting, you will usually never experience a problem.*
>
> *However, you never know if you might be approached by a police officer or city official who will want to inquire why your child is not in school. Libraries and community centers are examples of places where uninformed employees may take it upon themselves to contact authorities if they believe your child is truant.*
>
> *Having a copy of your child's accepted affidavit with you is a great way to address this. We also encourage families to have a current membership with HSLDA so that they can have access to the members-only 800 number to ask legal advice or address privacy concerns at any time.*

---

[23] For a complete list of counties and contacts in Arizona visit https://www.afhe.org/az-law/. For legal information regarding other states, visit https://www.hslda.org/laws/

[24] https://www.afhe.org/wp-content/uploads/2016/05/affidavit_of_intent_to_homeschool.pdf

5. Ensure that your affidavit was accepted and returned to you with the completed stamp of receipt to show that they have acknowledged and processed it and now have it on file.
6. You are done and ready to homeschool!

What do you do if you reside in a different state? Look at **HSLDA's state law summary website page** for your state's requirements as well as an understanding of how restrictive your state's laws are compared with others.[25] Some states, like Texas, require no action at all and do not even need an affidavit filed. Other states, like Washington, require periodic standardized testing. Still others, like Pennsylvania, require an annual review of the following: their child's progress portfolio, a psychological assessment, a log of instructional hours, and other requirements. As you can see, states vary greatly in what is required of home educators to comply with their local law.

What steps do you need to take to "make it legal"? Make notes here regarding your correspondence with the county's office for the superintendent of schools. Write any other questions you have about your state's legal requirements here.

_____

_____

_____

_____

_____

_____

_____

_____

_____

_____

_____

_____

_____

_____

_____

_____

_____

_____

---

[25] https://www.hslda.org/laws/

What about testing?

Arizona law does not require that students be tested at any time during their educational career at home. Yet homeschooling parents may choose to do so anyway. Those who oppose standardized testing say that it does not really add much value to their teaching plans for their children and that preparing children to take such exams is just "teaching to the test". In other words, it is not really a reflection of what they know or whether they met their educational goals for that year or not. However, many parents, including myself, *do* like to participate in standardized testing for a few important reasons.

> **Note to Leaders and Mentors:**
>
> *If your group is interested in testing, consider contacting a local resource center to come to your location of choice to administer the test. Many libraries allow homeschoolers to utilize their facilities for free or for a nominal fee, especially if your group is a 501c3.*
>
> *In the case of the ITBS or the Stanford 10, private homes can also administer tests if they meet the requirements, such as having a bachelor's degree. Check with the testing center first if you wish to proctor the test for others.*

As much as we may hesitate to admit it, parents generally like to participate in standardized tests to **periodically see how their child compares to their non-homeschooled peers.** I share this view and believe that homeschoolers do the homeschooling community a service when they participate in standardized testing. This is what makes it possible for the many useful statistics in support of home education to be published by organizations like **NHERI**. Such statistics are also helpful in **HSLDA** court cases that go before a judge where the value of homeschooling is called into question.

Another good reason to consider testing is that it **reinforces to you, your child, and your husband where your child's strengths and weaknesses are**. Sometimes it is useful to have an independent party provide feedback such as this on an annual basis so that you have some sense of how your child is doing outside of your own assessment. It can also point out areas that you may not have covered yet with your child but are useful and necessary skills, such as map reading, library skills, and questions about using reference materials.

It is also a useful instrument to use that will **prepare the child to take such tests in the future when ACT and/or SAT examinations are necessary for college entry,** which will be covered more thoroughly in chapter four.[26] Test taking of this type is a definite skill in discernment and time management that you will want to teach your child at some point, although I would not recommend starting the process until your child has at least finished 3rd grade and is reading well independently.

---

[26] http://www.collegeboard.com/testing/; Be aware that the Common Core has impacted these tests, which changed dramatically in 2015 and 2016. For up-to-date test prep information, do your research before your child needs to prepare for the test. James Stobaugh's newly designed *SAT Prep for the Thoughtful Christian* is a good place to start. Read Cathy Duffy's review here: http://cathyduffyreviews.com/college-preparation/SAT-prep-for-the-thoughtful-christian.htm. See also the "Jr. & Sr. High Season" section in chapter four of this manual for additional information on preparation for college testing.

Typically, there are private organizations and local resource centers that you can contact to assist you with test preparation activities and to arrange a testing date for your child in your area. If you wish to use the **IOWA Test of Basic Skills (ITBS)**, you can consider administering the test yourself in the comfort of your own home if you meet their requirements for administering the exam. [27] The results come directly to the administrator of the test and then are given to the parents, so privacy concerns are not an issue since they do not go to any local, public school system.

The same is true for the **Stanford 10** option, which has recently given homeschooling parents another at-home testing option.[28] It is like the ITBS except that each section is untimed, although students are expected to finish it within two days. Also, the Stanford 10 is completed on-line instead of by hand as the ITBS. Results come back within a day or two whereas receiving ITBS results in the mail usually takes several weeks.

Organizations like **Seton Testing Services** or **Triangle Educational Assessments** can assist parents in making the best testing choice and reviewing at-home administration requirements.[29] Local organizations, such as **Covenant Home School Resource Center** in AZ, may also administer standardized testing to homeschoolers as an alternative to taking it at the public school or administering it at home.[30] **AFHE** has a helpful section on their website about testing, including many resource centers that can help you select the test and services that are right for your child, if you live in Arizona. Please visit their website or your own state organization's site for further thoughts and resources that are useful to consider on this subject.[31]

One final word about testing in Arizona is about the **AIMS (Aptitude Inventory Measurement Service) Science, which was mostly replaced in 2014 with the AzMERIT tests**.[32] Although the state requires students to take these exams, homeschoolers are not required to do so and are generally discouraged from participating in such tests for several reasons. First, voluntary participation may serve to muddle the way for undesirable laws to surface that would undermine the present, favorable legal status of homeschooling that now gives parents autonomy from the public school system. Second, privacy issues are of concern since the results are sent to the state and not to the parents directly to be utilized or kept for an undetermined amount of time and for uncertain purposes. Third, in measuring standardized performance with peers, parents and students are better served using the more objective, skills-oriented exams like the **IOWA** or **Stanford 10** tests than the more subjective instruments conducted by the state and are often shaped by Common Core standards, which are discussed further towards the end of this chapter.

---

[27] http://www.setontesting.com/iowa-tests/ - Triangle Assessments is an example of a resource center that you can use to source various types of achievement tests, including the ITBS.

[28] http://www.pearsonassessments.com/learningassessments/products/100000213/stanford-10-online.html

[29] http://www.setontesting.com/stanford-10-online/ or https://www.triangleeducationassessments.com/

[30] https://www.chsrc.org/

[31] https://www.afhe.org/resources/faqs/

[32] http://www.azed.gov/assessment/

What are my thoughts and questions about standardized testing?

What is the difference between a co-op and outsourcing?

The word "co-op" can be a daunting term leaving many homeschoolers puzzled as to what it really means to co-op and how it compares to other options available when addressing certain parts of their child's education. In the simplest terms, **a co-op is an abbreviation to refer to a cooperative learning experience**. It involves both the parent and their child with one or more other families who have the same educational goals in mind for one or more topics. This is often accomplished informally among families who come together on their own to share teaching responsibilities and learning experiences for a particular subject and for a specific period of time. For example, two or more families may come together to do a unit study on a historical topic, form a literary discussion group, or conduct joint science labs. Not all families co-op, but most families will consider it at some point and/or for some purpose in their child's educational experience, particularly at the junior high and high school levels. It is a great way to build relationships while learning in a larger setting and digging deeper into a topic than perhaps is normally done within a single family's home school. For more information on starting successful co-ops or incorporating the concept into your support group, go to Rainbow Resource Center and order the book titled *Building Together: How to Organize and Conduct Fun and Successful Homeschool Co-ops.*[33] Carol Topp wrote a great, straightforward book on the subject as well called *Homeschool Co-Ops.*[34]

Regarding outsourcing, there are two ways to look at this concept. The first application is when a **group of homeschoolers will outsource a specific teaching responsibility to someone else.** Although some support groups may organize themselves around this idea and refer to themselves as a "co-op", they may not be a co-op in the purest sense unless *all* parents share in the teaching and organizational responsibilities. Usually a group that outsources its teaching responsibilities will offer a list of classes facilitated by paid instructors, who may or may not be some of the parents in the group. When this happens, it often occurs that other parents have little or no input or involvement in the organization and/or facilitation of the classes and it becomes an outsourced drop-off program, blurring the concept of homeschooling in the process. So, while these groups have value to offer for certain families, parents need to be careful about how much of their child's education they are really leading. In other words, are they truly home educating? If most of the child's education takes place outside of the parent's direction, they are probably engaged in something other than traditional homeschooling.

The support group I led for many years was often asked whether we operated as a co-op or not. While we did have parents sometimes organize classes for our families, we were not considered exclusively a co-op. Instead, we networked families together and encouraged them to initiate a co-op on their own terms if they felt it would benefit their educational goals. Typically, **successful co-ops have clearly defined goals and responsibilities, involvement from all parents and children, and clarity in their agreement about logistics,**

[33] http://www.rainbowresource.com/index.php; http://www.rainbowresource.com/product/sku/061304
[34] http://homeschoolcpa.com/

teaching, goals, and schedules. If such ground rules cannot be easily established, then reconsider your participation in the group since such an absence of clear boundaries can lead to poor results and frustrated friendships.

The second side of the outsourcing coin is when **parents individually decide to externally utilize a resource that supplements their child's education in a specific area**. Hiring a foreign language tutor or engaging with a private piano teacher represent examples of this type of outsourcing. Another example would be if the parent decides that the child should participate in an on-line class facilitated by a private organization. For example, **Patrick Henry College** offers on-line classes in constitutional law for high school students.[35] **Memoria Press** is another example with their on-line instruction in art, music, Latin, and logic.[36] **Institute for Excellence in Writing** offers a variety of on-line writing classes as well.[37] Parents utilizing outsourcing in this self-funded manner are still considered traditional homeschoolers since they retain control of their child's educational goals and are closely involved in understanding the content of what is being taught as well as the performance expectations for their child.

Take a moment to write down your mentor's thoughts as well as you own ideas about participating in a co-op. Discuss your ideas and questions with your mentor. Seek out advice from other moms in your group who may be currently participating in a co-op or may have done so in the past. If moms in your group have outsourced certain teaching responsibilities, find out how their experience went for them and what their recommendations are. Plan to research this option further, if necessary, and remember that options to outsource constantly change.

What do I think about co-oping or outsourcing? What else do I need to learn about it?

---

[35] http://www.phc.edu/
[36] http://www.memoriapress.com/onlineschool/index.htm
[37] http://iew.com/events-classes/online-classes

What about social interaction?

Although it is the most common concern that non-homeschoolers have about homeschooled children, ensuring positive **"socialization" for your child is rarely an issue of any real concern.** If anything, the opposite issue is true, and homeschoolers find that they need to, instead, be very particular about what their children are involved in so that they are not away from their studies too much!

Homeschooled children get to build relationships and interact with different groups children of various ages throughout the week.

Truthfully, most people who question about how *you* address the "s-word" haven't really thought about it much *themselves*. Somehow there is a false assumption that if we place our child in a room with thirty-five-plus other children who are the same numerical age, they will be appropriately trained to function in society one day. So, the next time you are asked, "What are you doing about socialization for your child?", think about these points.

First, **remember that different people mean different things when they ask about socialization.** Some are concerned about **social skills** and may define it as "the process whereby a child learns to get along with and to behave similarly to other people in the group, largely through imitation as well as group pressure."[38] If this is the concern, be confident in your response that you can say, "Actually, socialization is one of the primary reasons we are homeschooling. We know that children take on the social habits and tendencies of those they are around, and we want our children to learn how to interact with different groups of people of all ages and walks of life, not just one primary group of children who are at their own age of immaturity."

Second, others may be thinking more in terms of making sure that the child becomes a **functioning member of society.** These folks look at socialization as "the process by which a human being beginning at infancy acquires the habits, beliefs, and accumulated knowledge of society through education and training for adult status."[39] The argument here is more one of gaining the qualities of a balanced citizen, which they assume can only be gained by placing your child in a classroom setting with a large group of other same-aged children. Again, rest assured that training a child to participate as a functioning member of society is *not* tied to their education taking place in a public or private institutionalized setting. In fact, children who have been educated in the home and have had the experience of understanding how the adults around them, such as their parents, grandparents, neighbors and other adult relatives or acquaintances, handle daily life and issues that arise in the

---

[38] http://www.answers.com/topic/socialization
[39] http://www.merriam-webster.com/medical/socialization

home are truly *more* equipped to function in society as adults later on than their peers who were not homeschooled and lack the visibility of daily life challenges and community issues.[40]

Most of your concerned friends and family members have a third viewpoint, however, and are just **curious about how your child is going to "get out"** and interact with other kids. Most of the time, people raising this question are not so much doubting your decision to homeschool but are just perplexed with how your child is going to learn to "get along" with others, "live in the real world", and appropriately "communicate with their peers." Somehow homeschooling to them is equivalent to home-bound and learning in a segregated, institutionalized setting is akin to the "real world"'. Neither assumption could be further from the truth!

Homeschooled students have a large variety of options available to them to interact with other children their own age as well as children and adults of a **variety of ages**. So, picking the best ones to be involved with is really the larger issue. Homeschooled students have the freedom to interact with a variety of **different groups of children** in any given week when you consider music groups, community center classes, church groups, hobby clubs, support group activities, art programs, special interest clubs, field trips, and sports programs, just to name a few.

Also, remember that a **homeschool environment models "real life" more than other school settings**, and you have an opportunity for your kids to interact not only with other children but also with a variety of social situations involving other adults. Homeschooled children have a greater opportunity to be out in the "real world", experiencing "real life" in their communities because of the freedom that they possess to do so. Field trips, volunteer opportunities, service project options, and career exploration experiences abound for curious homeschoolers. Your child also can see firsthand how you handle your business interactions with other parties, conversations with neighbors, and difficult phone discussions on a more regular basis than their peers who live outside the home all day long. They see how to run a home, manage finances, deal with unexpected crises, and cope with illness as they watch their parents manage through those daily demands. **Now *that* is learning to live in the "real world"**.

> **Note to Leaders and Mentors:**
>
> *These days, many organizations are aggressively seeking out homeschoolers as they design classes to offer during the day when their facilities are often idle. Private studios that teach dance, karate, or drama are just a few examples of organizations who may offer discounted programs for homeschoolers willing to come during their "off-peak" hours.*
>
> *For parents who wish to organize classes with such an organization, be sure that to obtain all of the policies, costs, and requirements of the class before getting your families excited about a potential program. Also, be careful to make sure that it is a proven organization with references before aligning your group with their organization.*
>
> *Finally, caution new families to be careful about spreading their time too thin, trying to attend every field trip or program that your group offers. There is such thing as "too much of a good thing"!*

---

[40] http://www.nheri.org/research/research-facts-on-homeschooling.html

For those people you seek out to supplement some part of your child's growth and development as we discussed in the previous section, **be particular about the adults you enjoin your child to** in life: sports coach, church leader, private music instructor, etc. Be sure to have discussions with these adults in advance and share your views and expectations with them about their interaction with your child. Treat it somewhat like an interview and, even if the service-providing adult you are interviewing is great at the content of what they teach, think twice about involving your child in their program if you and he/she are far apart on teaching philosophies, moral values, and learning expectations. If you have any doubts, ask to sit in on an existing class or lesson that they facilitate and see for yourself if their interaction with other children is suitable for what you are seeking. It is better to know up front if it is not going to work rather than after several meetings or lessons where your child is already involved with them.

For more information about the issue of socialization, be sure to visit **Character Concepts** by Rick and Marilyn Boyer, as Rick is the author of *The Socialization Trap*.[41] Another great resource that addresses this and other related topics, in addition to the *Worldwide Guide to Homeschooling,* is Dr. Brian Ray's book from **NHERI** called *Home Educated and Now Adults: Their Community and Civic Involvement, Views About Homeschooling, and Other Traits.*[42] Essentially, you will find that, when it comes to homeschoolers growing up to be well-adjusted, fully functioning, contributing members of society, the "proof is in the pudding!"

What do I want out of my child's interactions with other children and adults?

_____

_____

_____

_____

_____

_____

What other thoughts does my mentor have about the idea of socialization?

_____

_____

_____

_____

_____

---

[41] http://characterconcepts.com/store/product.php?id_product=3
[42] http://www.nheri.org/

How do I handle unsupportive family members?

Dealing with unsupportive and even combative family members can be a grueling reality for some families that can nearly derail a potential homeschooler's efforts before they even begin their journey in earnest. Most objections to homeschooling that are raised by unsupportive family members or even friends and acquaintances are typically one of two smoke screens. The **first one** usually centers on their **inquiries regarding the basic questions** that we are covering in this first chapter. They want to know how you are going to make sure your child is properly "socialized", as we just covered. Or they cannot imagine that you could one day teach chemistry or algebra to your children: a job that should be left to the "experts". Some may speculate if it is even legal! For these family members, simply helping them to unpack the "mystery of homeschooling" by calmly addressing their questions is usually all that is needed to educate them about homeschooling and your confidence in utilizing this method of education to teach your children.

However, there is a **second** argument that seems to surface above all others in the Christian community that deserves some special attention. You will find this issue regularly discussed in homeschooling circles to one degree or another is what can be called the **"salt and light" argument**. We initially encountered it when our oldest was in first grade. While the verbiage can vary, the argument typically centers around a statement that goes something like this: "If all Christian parents took their kids out of public and private institutions, how will anyone ever be salt and light to non-Christians?" Then there is usually a vague reference to the "salt and light" passage found in Matthew, chapter five. However, when you look more closely at God's Word in this section, you will find a different perspective.

> *"You are the salt of the earth. But if the salt loses its saltiness, how can it be made salty again? It is no longer good for anything, except to be thrown out and trampled by men.*

> *"You are the light of the world. A city on a hill cannot be hidden. Neither do people light a lamp and put it under a bowl. Instead they put it on its stand, and it gives light to everyone in the house. In the same way, let your light shine before men, that they may see your good deeds and praise your Father in heaven. Matthew 5:13-16 (NIV)*

Notice how both passages begin by saying you *are* salt, or you *are* light. So, who is Jesus talking to? He is speaking to Christians: believers who have accepted Jesus Christ as their Lord and Savior. Often, our young children have not matured in their spiritual walk to have made this important decision in their life yet, even though we continue to guide them down that path. **Children in this situation are not equipped yet with the spiritual tools and maturity necessary to withstand a long-term exposure to a school system that is built on humanistic principles and cultivates negative peer pressure.**

Secondly, even for those children who have accepted Jesus and are walking in their Christian faith, they are not being admonished by Jesus to *do* anything here. Nowhere are Christians instructed to go out and *be* salt or to *be* light. Instead, Jesus states that we Christians *are* these things and warns us to be careful to guard our saltiness so that we are useful and not useless in our representation of Him in our walk. **As parents of new and potential Christians, then, we must be careful to guard the "saltiness" of our children's faith.** This point is further emphasized in the gospel of Luke.

> *"Salt is good, but if it loses its saltiness, how can it be made salty again? It is fit neither for the soil nor for the manure pile; it is thrown out."* Luke 14: 34-35a (NIV)

Jesus also says that we then will *let* the light of God's truth in us shine before men. Again, this is not a directive to do anything, much less to put your child into a public or private institution. Rather it is a reminder that *God* **does the work of giving off light from the Christian who truly lives the Christian life.** This passage states *who* we are but does not tell us *what* we are to do. A "city on a hill" is to be set apart as conduits of God's light. We *are* salt. We *are* light.

It is also important to continue reading through verse twenty when looking at the "salt and light" passage in Matthew.

> *"Do not think that I have come to abolish the Law or the Prophets; I have not come to abolish them but to fulfill them. I tell you the truth, until heaven and earth disappear, not the smallest letter, not the least stroke of a pen, will by any means disappear from the Law until everything is accomplished. Anyone who breaks one of the least of these commandments and teaches others to do the same will be called least in the kingdom of heaven, but whoever practices and teaches these commands will be called great in the kingdom of heaven. For I tell you that unless your righteousness surpasses that of the Pharisees and the teachers of the law, you will certainly not enter the kingdom of heaven.* Matthew 5:17-20 (NIV)

This passage highlights the seriousness of what Jesus thinks about those who will seek to violate God's law or to anyone one who "teaches others to do the same." If you know that God has called you to home educate your children to instill Godly principles and values in them and you have someone in your life who is pushing you to send them to a public or private institution where these goals will be seriously undermined, then they are encouraging you to go against what God is calling *you* to do in the life of your child. Instead, **help them to understand** that by home educating them, **you are training them up to become** Christians so that they *can possess the qualities* of "salt and light" so they may "fulfill God's Law" and positively impact others in their adulthood for God's Kingdom purposes. The best deconstruction of this argument that I have heard is by Dr. Voddie Baucham called "Thoroughly Christian Education". So, explore resources from his website below for more information as you continue to research this topic to your family's satisfaction.[43]

In the end, regardless of the reasons why your family members or others may be unsupportive, try to refrain from becoming defensive in your communications with them. Realize that even years into the homeschooling process, you will continually encounter people in your life who are mystified by the concept of homeschooling and will never quite "get it". Remind yourself that it is okay if not everyone you know "gets it". Your only job is to try to pleasantly clarify their misconceptions as you go along in your relationship with them and then also suggest helpful resources, such as **NHERI's** *Worldwide Guide to Homeschooling* previously mentioned. A good strategy is to have this or other helpful books and resources on hand that you are happy to lend out to them for further information. Typically, when you **invite them to research it further** beyond the information you have given them and begin to place some of the research responsibility back on their shoulders, they are usually satisfied with what you have said and take it no further.

Ultimately, in working with unsupportive friends and family, it is usually a matter of permitting your child's development to unfold before them, **allowing them to see the fruit of what is happening in their life first-hand.** For skeptical grandparents who do not live near you, regularly send them samples of your child's work. This can be done through video conferencing, e-mail, or even recordings. Creating video clips of your child presenting their own work or public performances can be particularly effective. You may also consider sending grandparents yearly progress reports that you write up, which we will discuss more in the latter part of chapter four. Have a "presentation night" for friends and family members in your area so your child can showcase their work and share their progress with them. You may also have your child write personal letters regularly to those people in your life that are important to you and allow their progress and spiritual development to be evident over time as they interact with your child.

Ultimately, make sure that you stay strong in your convictions and know that the important non-homeschoolers in your life will almost always eventually see the wisdom of what you are doing as time passes. Also pray that the Lord will continue to work on their hearts and soften them towards how you and your husband have decided to educate your child. Honest skepticism is almost always satiated by a look at the factual results they will observe over time as your child's spiritual, emotional, and academic maturity blossoms. Unfortunately, some families will have naysayers in their midst who will dig their heels in against your choices no matter how well your child is doing. **So be prepared, in those instances, to understand your relational boundaries and steel yourself to stick to them in defense of your family.** One other resource that can be useful to families struggling with unsupportive friends and family is the book called *Boundaries* by Dr. Henry Cloud.[44] Dr. Cloud also offers personal coaching services for those who need additional support.

---

[43] http://www.voddiebaucham.org/ - Please note that this presentation is no longer readily available.
[44] https://www.boundaries.me/

Who are the family members or important friends in our life who are unsupportive of our homeschooling and how can I respond to them in Christian love and confidence?

_____

_____

_____

_____

_____

_____

_____

_____

_____

_____

What other thoughts does my mentor have about the idea of handling unsupportive family members?

_____

_____

_____

_____

_____

_____

_____

_____

_____

_____

_____

_____

_____

What essential support resources do I need?

Regarding essential resources, each homeschooler should have a **three-pronged approach** to their external support system. First, homeschoolers should connect with their **local homeschool support group** so that they can network with other families who have similar priorities, challenges, and goals for their children. Support groups range in their focus but can generally be thought of from two perspectives. The number one consideration is whether the group is considered **Christian or secular**. Christian groups often have a "statement of faith" and a written list of common beliefs that they share so that potential members understand what is expected from their families. Conversely, secular groups tend to have families from various faith backgrounds and can sometimes come across as being more loosely organized.

The second consideration in joining a local support group is to **understand what the primary involvement structure** looks like. Groups vary in their focus across different offering options including field trips, park days, physical education classes, workshops, mom's social clubs, play groups, dad's events, or academic co-oping activities. Some try to accomplish all of these areas while others only focus on only one or two.

There is also a growing number of **virtual support groups** that are managed through a social media tool like Facebook. The key is to find a group that is right for you and your child: one that will provide both the additional support you need as a mom and teacher as well as the involvement that you desire your child to have with others. We will cover these ideas and many more details about the role and considerations of a local homeschool support group when we get to chapter ten.

The second prong in the external support system is to connect with the **state-wide support organization**. These organizations typically serve the local support groups and their leaders as well as individual families. They produce periodic newsletters and are also usually the groups that organize the state-wide conventions and curriculum fairs. Generally maintaining their own website with helpful resources and articles for new homeschoolers, they are also involved with the legislative process that governs the homeschooling laws in their state. Connecting families with a suitable local support group is also a focus for most state-wide support organizations. In Arizona, as previously mentioned, this state-wide support organization is **AFHE (Arizona Families for Home Education).** Upon joining, members of AFHE will receive a welcome packet that includes several important pieces of information including key contacts, homeschool helps/resources, and the legal information you need to know about homeschooling in Arizona. Another benefit in connecting with the state-wide support organization is that there are often archives of articles as well as speaker lectures that you can download or purchase to address whatever questions or timely topics you wish to learn more about. For such lectures from **AHFE** and other state-wide convention organizers, visit **Resounding Voice** to purchase them in either a CD or MP3 format.[45] To find your state-wide support organization, contact **HSLDA** for more information[46]. However, if your state does not have an active presence or its resources are not easily accessible, consider connecting with an online support community that maintains a Facebook presence and hosts periodic virtual conferences. Two such borderless organizations are **Home Education Council of America** and **The Homeschool Teaching Online Summit**.[47]

The final prong in the external support system is for homeschooling families to align themselves with a **national support organization**. Such an association keeps track of legislative and legal priorities for homeschoolers on a national and even international basis. They also provide essential support for state support organizations like **AFHE**. The largest and most recognized national/international support organization for homeschoolers is **HSLDA (Homeschool Legal Defense Association)**. In addition to the support mentioned already, HSLDA has a membership system where homeschooling families pay a nominal annual fee to join. This provides member families with the protection and support they need if they ever run into legal problems or discrimination issues associated with their homeschooling. They also produce an excellent quarterly periodical called the *Court Report* for their families with homeschooling articles and up-to-date legal and legislative information. Likewise, they provide additional support for families in homeschooling the early years, high school, and special needs situations through their designated consultants, extensive website resources, and regular HSLDA "@ home e-event" interactive presentations.

A current example of one very critical priority for HSLDA is to serve as a strong opponent to the **Common Core** that potentially threatens homeschooling freedoms.[48] Fortunately, many states are beginning to reject Common Core as it threatens to shift the responsibility for educational standards away from the states and into the hands of the federal government.[49] Even Arizona, who initially accepted it, has now replaced Common Core with their own state standards that proactively incorporated public input.[50] Another national priority for HSLDA is the support of a **Parental Rights Amendment** that will, among other benefits, ensure parents have an expressed—not just implied—right to direct the education of their children as they see fit.[51] Many states, including Arizona, have also taken steps to pass state-specific law protecting parental rights since the national time horizon to do so is uncertain.[52]

---

[45] http://www.resoundingvoice.com/

[46] http://www.hslda.org/orgs/

[47] http://hecoa.com/ & https://homeschoolsummits.com/

[48] Read Carol's blog article about the Common Core and what it means to homeschoolers. http://www.thebalancedhomeschooler.com/blog/what-is-the-common-core-and-should-homeschoolers-worry

[49] https://www.hslda.org/commoncore/

[50] http://www.azed.gov/superintendent/2016/12/21/common-core-repeal/

[51] https://parentalrights.org/

[52] https://parentalrights.org/states/az/

An additional national organization to connect with is **NHERI (National Homeschool Education Research Institute)**. As a research organization, NHERI works closely with HSLDA in providing reliable and scholarly research information in support of home education, both for the benefit of families and legislators.

For those interested in the plight of international homeschooling, HSLDA can also connect families with current events, issues, and plans that relate to homeschooling in other countries through **HSLDA International**.[53] Families can sign up to receive e-mail updates that will enable them to not only become aware of international issues related to homeschooling but also to devote prayer and support plans for these families who are struggling to obtain the school choice freedom we enjoy here in the U.S.

Listing of potential local support resources I will research or contact:

_____

_____

_____

_____

_____

Listing of my state-wide support resource I will research or contact:

_____

_____

_____

_____

_____

Listing of national or international resources I will research or contact:

_____

_____

_____

_____

_____

---

[53] https://www.hslda.org/hs/international/

More Chapter Notes...

Chapter 2

Researching "How to Homeschool" Approaches

The heart of the discerning acquires knowledge;
the ears of the wise seek it out. Proverbs 28:15 (NIV)

Seeking Discernment

If there is one piece of wisdom I encourage you to seek out and even pray for, it is discernment. When we are discerning, we not only have confidence in *why* we are doing what we are doing but also in *how* we are going to do it. **Discernment leads us to exercise good judgment** in how we are going to give God the room He needs to fulfill the family vision statement that He placed on our hearts. In the home education environment, then, discernment must be exercised in figuring out the most efficient and workable approach possible for achieving the vision.

There are many homeschooling families and circuit speakers who will tell you that considering and identifying your approach to home education is not an essential step in your quest to homeschool. I have attended plenty of seminars where moms are

Discernment must be exercised in figuring out the most efficient and workable approach possible for achieving the vision.

encouraged to just jump right in and get going and, certainly, there are families who succeed in their home school without this element. However, you will be more confident as you begin your journey and better equipped to adjust along the way if you **understand the broad landscape of common approaches first** and then begin narrowing down your specific choice from there.

The other benefit of considering the available approaches is that it will allow you to be familiar with other methods that you personally may not use but someone you know may. It will help you to speak to them intelligently about the successes as well as struggles they are facing. You can **discern the opportunities or drawbacks** of the various approaches more easily than if you just jump right in without knowing what other perspectives exist. You may even find yourself able to guide or coach new or potential homeschoolers about these choices and why one particular curriculum may be better for them than others.

General Research

No matter how we may want to avoid it, some amount of **general research is necessary** for new homeschoolers and may also prove beneficial to those who feel a need to "go back to the drawing board". Since there is no shortage on the amount of "getting started" book options out there to consider, I have put together a list of the ones that have stood the test of time and are useful to consider. These initial titles are broad in nature and do not necessarily subscribe to a single homeschool approach. We will get to those specific options a little later in this chapter.

The first listing of titles is not only great for parents seeking more information about homeschooling even before they commit to it, but they are particularly **helpful in speaking to your husband or even skeptical friends and family members about the benefits of home education**. Unfortunately, many husbands who are wary at first may place unrealistic measures and deadlines on their wives and children about the results they want to see without ever picking up a book to allow another Godly man to speak to them about the bigger picture. Remember that, although most moms find that "the proof is in the pudding" as mentioned in chapter one, your home school can achieve success and enjoyment so much sooner if both you and your husband are united from the very beginning of the process.

Note to Leaders and Mentors:

Many of the resource suggestions listed here are essential for new homeschoolers to read. However, it is not always practical for an individual to purchase several of them; especially when some of the titles mentioned are the type of book that is read once to get started but then is rarely picked up again. The other challenge is that, since many are Christian in nature, most are not available at the local public library.

So, consider checking with your local church regarding their lending library. If they have one, ask if they have some of these titles or would consider placing a few of them on their shelves. Another option is for the moms within your support group to pool together their general reference books and begin a lending process within the group. Moms can also source many of these titles used on the Internet, for instance through Amazon's marketplace reseller program or HSLDA's Curriculum Market, for a fraction of their original price. Remember that you can also visit our store as well: http://www.thebalancedhomeschool er.com/tbh-affiliate-store.html

General Education Resources: These titles work to build a case for homeschooling and also provide general considerations for your child's education. They are especially great for dads and even skeptical grandparents or family members to read.

1. *Homeschooling; The Right Choice: An Academic, Legal, Historical and Practical Perspective* by Chris Klicka; As a homeschooling pioneer and champion of legal rights for homeschoolers, Mr. Klicka builds a case for home education. This is considered a must-read by most homeschoolers.

2. *The Christian Home School* by Greg Harris; A great "classic" that builds a solid case for home education.

3. *No Place Like Home….School* by J. Richard Fugate; Another "classic" that builds a case for home education.

4. *Dumbing Us Down: The Hidden Curriculum of Compulsory Schooling* by John Taylor Gatto; Builds a case for home education while also addressing many modern issues within the public system.

5. *Family Matters: Why Homeschooling Makes Sense* by David Gutterson; Another title that builds a case for home education.

6. *A Thomas Jefferson Education* by Oliver Van DeMille; Excellent read for ANY parent of a school-aged child. Author recommends use of classics and mentors as the best alternative to a "conveyor belt" education.

7. *Upgrade: 10 Secrets to the Best Education for Your Child* by Kevin Swanson; This book is also helpful for ANY parent of a school-aged child. Swanson emphasizes the importance of the parent/child relationship, character development, emphasis on individuality and educational basics.

8. *Weapons of Mass Instruction: A Schoolteacher's Journey Through the Dark World of Compulsory Schooling* by John Gatto; Powerful account of the negative effects of compulsory education in our modern society.

9. *Worldwide Guide to Homeschooling* by Dr. Brian D. Ray; Excellent, objective read for those desiring more information about the national and international statistics of homeschooling benefits and results. Great for skeptical family members and also for new homeschoolers who want to acquaint themselves with the broader issues of interest in

the home education community. See the **National Home Education Research Institute (NHERI)** for the latest information and statistics.[54]

General Homeschooling and Encouragement Resources: These books are especially great for encouraging moms in a casual and open style. It is also a good idea to thoroughly research websites for your state's homeschool support organization as well as a national one. In Arizona, as mentioned earlier in chapter one, the state organization is AFHE (Arizona Families for Home Education).[55] Nationally, the best overall support organization is HSLDA (Homeschool Legal Defense Association).[56] HSLDA goes way beyond just providing legal counsel for home educating families and have countless articles and resource options for nearly any homeschooling topic.

1. *Beyond Survival* by Diana Waring; Practical peek inside a homeschooling family who uses mostly a lifestyle of learning approach. For a perspective on homeschooling high school students, see Diana's book called *Reaping the Harvest*. Another great resource by the Waring's is their reflective look back at their personal homeschooling journey called *Things We Wished We'd Known.*

2. *Carschooling* by Dianne Flynn Keith; A sign of our changing times, car-schooling, van-schooling, SUV-schooling, and the like are here to stay! Reading this resource gives homeschoolers or even potential homeschoolers a sense as to how to keep the academic journey fresh and fun during sometimes challenging logistics.

3. *The Homeschool Book of Answers: The 88 Most Important Questions Answered by Homeschooling's Most Respected Voices* by Linda Dobson; This title attempts to answer the most common questions both new and seasoned homeschoolers ask about homeschooling. Linda writes, "You now hold the results in your hand: 500 collective years-- half a millennium--of thoughts, observations, philosophies, tips, and personal stories that can lead you to the personal-empowerment of homeschooling."

4. *Homeschooling: A Patchwork of Days* by Nancy Lande; Practical and interesting look inside 30 different homeschooling families.

5. *The Homeschooling Handbook* by Mary Griffith; Though somewhat dated, it is still a good overall resource for new homeschoolers who want general guidance and a preschool-to-high school overview.

---

[54] http://www.nheri.org/
[55] http://www.afhe.org/
[56] http://www.hslda.org/

6. *Homeschooling on a Shoestring* by Melissa L. Morgan & Judith Waite Allee; Fantastic resource any home educator can use to save money!

7. *Lies Homeschooling Moms Believe* by Todd Wilson; Though this book is often used to help "talk moms off the ledge" of homeschooling, it is a refreshing option of encouragement to read before crisis hits! Though a bit emphatic at times, it is a refreshing change to read a book by a homeschooling father who wishes to encourage moms in their journey.

8. *Mary Pride's Complete Guide to Getting Started in Homeschooling* by Mary Pride; Voluminous storehouse of information that provides guidance in nearly every aspect of the homeschooling experience as well as practical "how to" information.

9. *A Mom Just Like You* by Vickie & Jamie Farris; Encouragement and practical advice from a seasoned homeschool mom; Very uplifting!

10. *So You're Thinking About Homeschooling: 2ⁿᵈ edition* by Lisa Whelchel; Former "Facts of Life" television star and homeschooling mother of three gives a lighthearted, encouraging look at various ways families incorporate home education into their lives. The book is written as a compilation of input from over 1,000 different homeschooling parents.

Approaches Defined

Though terminology may vary slightly in different homeschooling circles, the remainder of this chapter discusses the most common approaches that families adopt in their home schools. Although the lines can definitely blur, as found in the most common "eclectic" approach mentioned last, I have ordered the discussions about these approaches **in order of what I consider to be the most structured to the least structured options.** I have also tried to place resource recommendations with the approach that they most closely reflect, although a few of them could be classified as utilizing more than one approach.

Homeschoolers may also find resources available to them to incorporate using **Waldorf** or **Montessori** methods.[57] However, since these approaches originated in corporate school settings and were later adopted in some homeschooling circles, they are not the focus of the primary approaches that most homeschoolers tend to utilize, and are, therefore, outside of the scope of what we will cover here. Still, I mention them since you may find that adapting some of their ideas, particularly for young learners, may be of use.

Remember that there is **ultimately no one "right" approach**: only the one that is best for you and your child. Also, keep in mind that many families will modify their approach over time to meet the changing needs of their child as well

---

[57] http://www.waldorfhomeschoolers.com/; http://www.montessori.edu/homeschooling.html

as to accommodate moms as they become more comfortable with what and how they are teaching.

We will cover commonly related curriculum options for each teaching approach in chapter three. The mention of these options is not intended to be an endorsement of the various products but rather an explanation as to which teaching approach it most closely mirrors. In most situations, families can choose to pursue a fully developed curriculum option or create one of their own that is based on their teaching approach of choice. Still other families may use a combination of the two options that is suitable for both the student and the teacher.

What approaches are you familiar with? Which ones would you like to learn more about? What other books or resources does your mentor recommend?

_____

_____

_____

_____

_____

_____

_____

_____

_____

_____

_____

_____

_____

_____

_____

_____

_____

_____

_____

The Textbook Approach

This approach is suitable for those families who are comfortable using **traditional textbooks and workbooks**. For this reason, it is sometimes also called the "Traditional Approach". It commonly works well initially for families who are withdrawing children from a public or private setting and they want to keep the materials that the child uses to be of similar style so that transition issues are minimized. Using this approach also tends to help new homeschoolers get their bearings and feel more confident in their ability to teach since the curriculum available for this approach tends to be highly scripted and provides step-by-step instructions and schedules. Keep in mind, however, that a textbook approach is not necessarily the most rigorous program but is rather the most structured method a parent can utilize.

PROS: Easy to implement, little teacher prep time due to the variety of large publishing houses available that provide mostly scripted curriculum for this approach. Covers all ages and subjects.

CONS: Not as flexible, scalable, or creative as some families need. The potential for a lower level of parent-child interaction could lead to issues in the younger grades; can tend to bog families down with busy work.

Other thoughts and feedback:

_____

_____

_____

_____

_____

_____

_____

_____

_____

_____

_____

_____

_____

_____

_____

The Cultural Literacy Approach

Although this approach is not commonly found in most homeschools I have encountered, it is worth a mention because you will probably run across this term at some point. Emphasis on Cultural Literacy has been largely developed by Dr. E.D. Hirsch, a former educator who turned his focus to academic criticism that he hoped would change the school system to improve their results. The emphasis he developed argues that **education should not just be about collecting skills but should also include broad knowledge in several specific topics.**

Read these additional resources for more information:

1. *Books to Build On: A Grade by Grade Resource Guide for Parents and Teachers* by Dr. E.D. Hirsch; Descriptive bibliography by grade level and topic of recommended books to use for teaching with a Cultural Literacy Approach.

2. *The Core Knowledge Sequence* by Dr. E.D. Hirsch; Cultural Literacy approach to what the child needs to know when.

3. *Cultural Literacy* by Dr. E.D. Hirsch; Philosophical description of Cultural Literacy Approach.

4. *What Your Kindergartner Needs to Know*, etc. by Dr. E.D. Hirsch; Practical Cultural Literacy approach to what the child needs to know when. This is one of a series up books up to 6th Grade that can be sourced at most libraries. Though not from a Christian perspective, it encourages Bible reading and can provide a useful framework.

PROS: Resources are easily accessible and can help supplement the parent's goals with their child. Parents pulling their child from a public setting may feel initially more comfortable with this approach.

CONS: Not designed for homeschoolers so it is framed around a public school idea of "scope and sequence"; possibly building in some unnecessary, busy-work concepts. Faith-based families need to incorporate religious training separately.

Other thoughts and feedback:

_____

_____

_____

_____

Principle Approach

This approach is appealing to those families who seek out a scholarly yet Christ-centered, civic-minded approach. It works well for those families who are comfortable using traditional textbooks but wish to concentrate the **emphasis of their child's education on civic responsibilities and the role of the government** in the lives of their country and community. The "Principle Approach" provides a great deal of structure and emphasis on the "4-R" method of researching, reasoning, relating, and recording. Above all, this approach places the task of relating God's biblical principles to your child as the heart of the entire framework of their education and the foundation of every single subject. The "principles" that are reinforced in this method include the following seven points.[58]

1. God's principle of individuality
2. The Christian principle of self-government
3. America's Heritage of Christian Character
4. "Conscience – Most Sacred of All Property"
5. The Christian Form of Our Government
6. How the Seed of Local Self-Government is Planted
7. The Christian Principles of American Political Union

Read these additional resources for more information:

1. *Come Let Us Reason* by Kris Bayer; Standard, though sometimes hard to find, among homeschoolers using the principle approach.

2. *A Guide to American Christian Education for the Home and School* by James Rose; Divided into four parts, this is an essential text for Principle Approach homeschoolers and schools. It covers the rudiments of American Christian Education, Education for the American Christian Home, the American Christian School at Home, and Curriculum for the American Christian School. This is a great reference for teaching American government to your child, even if you are not using the Principle Approach.

3. *Teaching and Learning America's Christian History: The Principle Approach* by Rosalie Slater; This companion guide to James Rose's title mentioned above helps parents to design their curriculum plan for the Principle Approach. It includes three parts; Constituents of Constitutional Liberties; Teaching and Learning America's Christian History, and Key to Expanding Principles.

---

[58] http://www.principleapproach.org/?page=principle_approach

PROS: Emphasis on civic responsibly and establishment of Godly principles in problem solving. Involves homeschooling fathers more in the teaching.

CONS: Requires teacher to be comfortable with scholarly works and methods. Few mainstream curriculum providers. Since fathers are typically more involved in this approach, it may pose logistical issues for some families.

Other thoughts and feedback:

_____

_____

_____

_____

_____

_____

_____

_____

_____

_____

_____

_____

_____

_____

_____

_____

_____

_____

_____

_____

Classical Approach

This approach is one of the more mainstream methods that you will find used in the homeschooling community. However, it is also the most extensive to explain. It works well for families who are seeking an overall structure to how they will facilitate their child's education while at the same time providing flexibility to those parents regarding the actual curriculum and resource choices they make.

This approach centers heavily around history and literature as the "spine" from which the other studies stem. The classical home **views the child's school career in three separate four-year cycles**. First through fourth grade is considered the "Grammar Stage" where children are absorbing facts and information, essentially learning the "what" for each subject while their minds are most apt to sponge up information. Then the child shifts to the "Logic Stage" in fifth through eighth grade. This is the time when the child begins to make connections between the "what" and the "why". They are still learning many new facts but are now able to make cause-and-effect connections that were not accessible to them in their younger years. The final stage in high school is the "Rhetoric Stage" where they not only begin to make assessment and judgment statements about what they are learning but are also able to articulate them fluently in both written and oral forms. Adam Andrews, author of *Teaching the Classics*, explains the differences among these stages by using the example of the Civil War: the "Grammar Stage" is when they learn the facts of the Civil War, the "Logic Stage" is when they understand the main causes of the Civil War, and the "Rhetoric Stage" is when they evaluate whether or not the Civil War was necessary.

In tandem with these three stages, known as **"The Trivium"**, the child is also cycling through history in a chronological fashion three full times while also covering the related science, art, literature, and music of each period. Each time they cycle through, they cover the material in an increasingly difficult manner. See the chart below for further clarification and examples.

Grade Level	History Covered	Examples of Related Period Subjects
First, fifth, and ninth	Ancients (Creation – 400 A.D.)	Biology; Nomadic, Egyptian, Greek, and Roman Art; Related Literature written in or about that time, such as Gilgamesh, Greek Mythology or Homer's works.
Second, sixth, and tenth	Middle Ages (400 A.D. – 15th and 16th centuries)	Earth and Space Science; Scientists of the time like Copernicus or Galileo; Medieval art and architecture; Gregorian chants; Literature written in or about that time such as Beowulf, King Arthur, The Canterbury Tales, and the works of Shakespeare.

Third, seventh, and eleventh	Early Modern Times (17th – mid-18th Centuries)	Chemistry; Art and Architecture of the Renaissance; Literature of the Victorian Age, such as the works of Mark Twain, Jane Austen, Charles Dickens, and Jules Verne.
Fourth, eighth, and twelfth	Modern Times (mid-19th to 20th Century)	Physics; Scientists of the time, like Einstein; Modern art and composers; Literature or plays written in or about that time, such as Little Women, The Jungle Book, the works of H.G. Wells, The Crucible, and Oscar Wilde's plays.

The information provided in the chart above is just a small example of how a classical home could organize their plans. The main point to remember is that the child has an **opportunity to encounter the major historical periods and all that goes with it three different times at increasingly difficult levels**. Whereas in first grade you read to your child a picture book of the Odyssey, in fifth grade they can read a more advanced, but still somewhat abridged, version of it by themselves. Then by the time they encounter it in ninth grade again, they are not intimidated by it and can read the unabridged, original work.

The same is true for the work the child produces. Younger children can orally narrate to you while you write down their feedback. Middle-school children can write their own summaries without much aid, and high school students can research and write essays independently or participate in an oral debate or presentation about the same subject.

Read these additional resources for more information:

1. *Classical Education and the Home School* by Douglas Wilson, Wes Callihan, and Douglas Jones; Homeschooling standard for explaining the philosophy of the Classical Approach

2. *Recovering the Lost Tools of Learning* by Dorothy Sayers; Original essay regarding the definition and use of the Classical Approach.

3. *Recovering the Lost Tools of Learning* by Douglas Wilson, Wes Callihan, and Douglas Jones; This is the book regarding the Classical Approach that is based on Sayers' original essay.

4. *Teaching the Trivium* by Harvey and Laurie Bluedorn; Written from a Christian perspective, this is an excellent source to guide the home school who is following the classical structure. Several resource suggestions are available in the index and excellent

chapters discussing the importance of teaching Latin, Greek and Hebrew as well as logic are included.

5. *Trivium Mastery: The Intersection of Three Roads: How to Give Your Child an Authentic Classical Home Education* by Diane Lockman; The author builds a case for emphasizing language, thought, and speech towards mastery in the classical home. She also profiles several familial "case" studies to illustrate how a classical education can be administered in any home environment.

6. *The Well-Trained Mind: A Guide to Classical Education at Home, 4th Edition* by Jessie Wise and Susan Wise Bauer; This is a must-have for every classical homeschooler. Even though it is not written from a Christian perspective, the authors do emphasize the importance of religious training. It has an excellent, practical, and comprehensive scope and sequence to using the "Classical Approach" from preschool all the way through twelfth grade.

PROS: Teaches history chronologically and ties curriculum together across subjects for a holistic result. There are many resources available and there is a high level of child/parent interaction. There is a strong emphasis on literature and other classic writings.

CONS: More time consuming and complicated prep work. Although some companies are beginning to offer packages, mom usually must "put together" curriculum from a variety of sources. The scope of areas to cover can be too scholarly for some families.

Other thoughts and feedback: _____

_____

_____

_____

_____

_____

_____

_____

_____

_____

_____

Common Sense Approach

This approach is well suited for families who just want to **follow what makes the most sense to them as they go along.** They are not so much concerned with following one particular method over another and just want to take it as it comes. For parents who just wish to focus on the basics, Dr. Ruth Beechick has written several excellent materials to help homeschoolers get started in this straightforward way of teaching.

Read these additional resources for more information:

1. *Dr. Beechick's Homeschool Answer Book* by Ruth Beechick; Covers preschool through high school and the core subjects of reading, spelling, writing, math and Bible.

2. *The Complete Home Learning Source Book* by Rebecca Rupp; Covers every subject from "Arithmetic to Zoology" with listings of resources and related reviews. Though printed in 1998, it has many useful topics to consider when designing your curriculum plan.

3. *How to Homeschool: A Practical Approach* by Gayle Graham; Mrs. Graham refers to herself as using a "natural approach", which is similar to the "Common Sense Approach". She takes Dr. Beechick's ideas and puts into a step-by-step approach.

4. *Language and Thinking for Young Children* by Dr. Ruth Beechick and Jeannie Nelson; Dr. Beechick covers the importance of using stories, vocabulary, thinking skills, games, memorization, poetry, and more to solidify your child's language skills.

5. *The Three R's* by Ruth Beechick; The standard for the three R's and all that is needed in a "Common Sense Approach" to these subjects. It is an excellent and simple tool that is a staple in most homeschooling homes.

6. *You Can Teach Your Child Successfully* by Ruth Beechick; Provides similar guidance as seen in her other books but is specific to teaching children in their older middle school years.

PROS: With an emphasis on instilling a strong foundation of basics, this approach is a very accessible and easy approach to incorporate for the nervous and intimidated mom. Method works especially well with moms starting out with preschool aged children.

CONS: Can leave mom sensing that she is not "doing enough" to cover all of the necessary subjects. Some students may need more challenging material than what is typically used with this approach.

Other thoughts and feedback:

Living Books or Charlotte Mason Approach

This approach is ideal for families who want to **base their curriculum on well-written, original books and biographies that serve as the spine for their home school.** Books chosen are unabridged and varied in their style. This method is called "Living Books" because it relies on the use of great books rather than those of dry and less personal textbooks. You will also find that many homeschoolers using other methods as their primary approach also incorporate this "Living Books Approach" into their homeschooling experiences as well.

Related to this style is the Charlotte Mason method. Charlotte Mason was a British educator who lived during the late nineteenth century and **believed in the teaching principles of creating a learning "atmosphere", instilling "discipline" through good habits, and that experiencing "life" is how a child best learns.** Like the "Living Books" style, the "Charlotte Mason Approach" also centers heavily on the need for using great books. She also emphasized that rather than just learning about a subject, the child should experience it by being out in God's creation and interacting with and journaling about the subjects first-hand.

Read these additional resources for more information:

1. *A Charlotte Mason Companion* by Karen Androlea; Useful and accessible book for interpreting Charlotte's philosophy and approach.

2. *A Charlotte Mason Education* by Catherine Levison; This is also a very readable and helpful tool for applying Mason's ideas.

3. *Educating the Whole-Hearted Child* by Clay and Sally Clarkson; This is a great resource for any home school. The Clarkson's seek to combine "whole-book" education within the context of Christian discipleship.

4. *For the Children's Sake* by Susan Schaeffer Macaulay; Inspirational book of why we do what we do that also has a Charlotte Mason "flavor" to it. An inspirational must-read for homeschoolers regardless of your primary teaching approach.

5. *For the Family's Sake* by Susan Schaeffer Macaulay; This is also very inspirational and useful for keeping the focus on the family.

6. *The Original Homeschooling Series* by Charlotte Mason; Mason's philosophy is concerned with kids being able to think on their own, avoiding "twaddle", and focusing on the educational elements of a loving atmosphere, discipline in good habits, and giving a child's life/soul lots of ideas by experience and exposure. This is a very difficult read, but it is a collection of her original writings.

PROS: Gets children interacting with their world and learning through experience. It is especially great for preschool and young children in building good habits and learning how to observe God's world in detail. It works to preserve that wonderful curiosity that many children tend to lose as they get older and become more disenchanted with the learning process.

CONS: Can seem too ethereal or "touchy, feely" for parents seeking a more concrete or rigorous approach to their child's education. May present a challenge for parents when their child enters the junior high or high school years, which tend to require greater emphasize on the more technical aspects of writing, research, documentation, analysis, etc.

Other thoughts and feedback:

_____

_____

_____

_____

_____

_____

_____

_____

_____

_____

_____

_____

_____

_____

_____

_____

_____

_____

_____

_____

Lifestyle of Learning or Relaxed Approach Resources

This method is for the parent who wants **little to no structure in their home school.** Parents work with their children to learn subjects only when the child is observed to be truly ready for it. This is also related to the "Delight-Directed" or even "Unschooling" approach where parents plan a natural course of a study that sparks the child's interest and then allows that interest to direct the plans and curriculum choices as they go along.

Read these additional resources for more information:

1. *Relaxed Home School: A Family Production* by Mary Hood; Although Mary Hood's approach is a very casual "Lifestyle of Learning" and may even be considered to be an "Unschooling Approach", she emphasizes the importance of having a literate home where there is a lot of reading.

2. *The Simplicity of Homeschooling* by Jack and Vicky Goodchild; Again, there is an emphasis on the need for a literate home even though the environment is relaxed.

3. *Teach Your Own* by John Holt; Classic book about the principles of "unschooling" that are present in many "Lifestyle of Learning" or "Relaxed" home schools.

4. *Wisdom's Way of Learning* by Marilyn Howshall; Another title explaining the "Lifestyle of Learning Approach", although it is more difficult to source.

PROS: This works for families who are not necessarily concerned about having a rigorous program for their child and can be a great approach for a struggling learner. It can promote creativity and spontaneity.

CONS: Tends to be child-centered rather than parent-directed. It can also lead to boredom if the parent is not in tune with the child's academic capabilities and does not, therefore, challenge them as much as they should. Tends to minimize training in necessary study, time-management, and various other life skills.

Other thoughts and feedback: _____

_____

_____

_____

_____

_____

_____

_____

_____

_____

_____

_____

_____

_____

_____

Eclectic

This is the part of the chapter where I share with you that, in the end, we are probably all really "Eclectic" homeschoolers, borrowing a bit here and there from the various methods to come up with a single approach that works for us. **So, if you are wondering why it is necessary to be at least familiar with the various approaches we discussed if no one seems to be a purist in any of the areas, I will tell you it is important for three reasons.**

First, while most families blend, homeschoolers do tend to **lean in one primary direction** more than the others. One family could be following a "Classical" method but still blend concepts from "Lifestyle of Learning" or "Living Books" approaches as well. Second, families tend to **change their blend of approaches over time,** so it is good to be aware of the various methods as your family's needs change. Lastly, since the homeschoolers you will meet vary widely in their approaches, it is good to understand the various options so that you are **versed in what others are doing** and can balance their feedback to you or questions for you against what you know about their approach.

So now it is time for you to do some brainstorming about these approaches. Write some final thoughts down and then take some time with your mentor to look again at the brief summaries I have provided and determine one or two books that you will read as you check more thoroughly into one approach or another. Then use page 81 to make notes on what your first impression is on what you like or do not like about each approach. **Rank the top three approaches** that appeal to you from numbers one to three. This will give you a fairly good idea on which way you are leaning and which approach(es) you would like to learn more about. You will also continue to learn about many of these approaches in the next chapter about choosing curriculum.

Other thoughts and feedback:

Homeschooling Approach Planning Sheet

Approach	What I like about this approach...	What I do not like about this approach...	Rank Top 3	What more information do you need? What book(s) will you read?
Textbook				
Cultural Literacy				
Principle				
Classical				
Common Sense				
Living Books or Charlotte Mason				
Lifestyle of Learning or Relaxed				
Eclectic				

Now take your notes and findings above and attempt to **describe what you think your approach to home education might look like**. For example, in the beginning, I followed a "Classical Approach" as my spine, utilizing the *Well-Trained Mind* for a great deal of my structure. However, I have also used a "Living Books Approach", incorporating the use of unabridged literature and the teaching methods of narration, dictation, and copy work. Still more recently, as our sons are older now, we also incorporate textbook options that lend to a greater level of independent learning and college preparedness.

Look again at your approach choices and then take some notes here on what you think is the best approach to begin with for your home school. Remember, you can and will modify your view on this as time passes. Your strategies, including what approach you use to achieve your unchanging family vision for your child, will also usually change over time.

In summary, I think that the approach that will best suit our family will....

_____

_____

_____

_____

_____

_____

_____

_____

_____

_____

Here is a listing of books that I would like to read for more information on these approaches:

_____

_____

_____

_____

_____

_____

_____

_____

_____

Chapter 3

Curriculum Choices & Selection Criteria

Hear, O Israel: The LORD our God, the LORD is one. Love the LORD your God with all your heart and with all your soul and with all your strength. These commandments that I give you today are to be upon your hearts. Impress them on your children. Talk about them when you sit at home and when you walk along the road, when you lie down and when you get up. Tie them as symbols on your hands and bind them on your foreheads. Write them on the doorframes of your houses and on your gates. Deuteronomy 6:4-9 (NIV)

Where Do I Even Begin?

Run a search on the Internet regarding homeschool curriculum and you are likely to stumble away from your computer with a fearful and frustrated heart. There are so many—really too many—choices available to us. While this is great in some respects, it makes it so **difficult to "separate the wheat from the chaff"** when trying to make good selections.

If you have been around Christian homeschoolers for any length of time, you have or will hear this verse from Deuteronomy above quoted as the "homeschooler's verse". It so profoundly summarizes the idea that **discipling and training your child never stops.** It is a **24/7 task** that cannot be easily accomplished when they are away from you a great deal of the day, every day. However, I also observe an additional piece of wisdom when I look at this passage. For it is interesting how this passage from Deuteronomy is directly tied to the vision that Jesus casts for us when he took the main points of these instructions that had been originally given to the people of Israel and says we are *all* to love the Lord with all of our heart, soul, and mind and then love our neighbor as ourselves. To me, it is God saying, "Okay, I've given the heart of my purpose to you and your family in the time of Moses and my Son has reinforced this in His words to you during His time on Earth as well. Now I am going to ask you to read these words again, so I can help you clearly understand *how* to do it!"

So, while it is true that this passage in Deuteronomy does not tell you what teaching approach you should use or what curriculum to purchase, you can be sure that the **methods you select for helping your child fulfill your family vision for them will need to be something that you can deliver consistently, constantly, confidently, and comprehensively.** We know this because He says we are to have His Word "upon our hearts" and we are to "impress them" on our children. This **requires confidence in what we are teaching**. We are also commanded to talk about them when we "sit at home, walk along the road, and lie down". This **requires consistency and constancy**. Finally, we are to "tie them as symbols, bind them on our foreheads, and write them on our doorposts." This **requires a comprehensive plan and delivery method**. Therefore, with these **"Four C's"** in mind as a guideline as well as our previous discussion about the various approaches available to you, you are one step closer to determining a great starting point for which curriculum would best suit your family's needs.

> *Use the "Four C's" to help choose the curriculum that is right for you and your child.*

Which Profile Does My Family Fit?

When choosing curriculum, it is best to start simple. If you try to make it too complicated in the beginning, your frustration level will be too high to be productive. In the years I have spent working with families to help them get started in their journey, I have observed two different starting profiles.

The first profile applies to **families who have decided early on that they want to homeschool their child**. Usually these are the parents who contact me when their oldest is five or younger and they know that they want to homeschool and just need a little direction on where to start their research process.

The second profile belongs to those **parents who have decided to homeschool after their child has already been in a public or private setting for some period of time** and have transition and timing issues to deal with. These families usually sense they are running against the clock in trying to withdraw their child, file their affidavit, and figure out their curriculum plans all at once. They are often filled with a certain degree of apprehension and fear about "doing it right" and will often try to replicate in the home what their child has been used to doing at their previous school.

If your family is more closely representative of the **first profile**, you usually have the benefit of time where you can research more thoroughly the approach and curriculum you wish to use. Take advantage of that position by not feeling rushed to make any decisions just because you have friends and neighbors who are taking their three-year-olds to a program several days a week and you may be feeling pressure to just do something that "feels like school". Little ones are naturally curious, and you are probably already engaging them in many training activities without even realizing it. In our home, this is the profile that we came from, and I really took my time trying to figure out what was going to work for us. I started very slowly with some basic phonics and math instruction and then focused mainly on character training and reading: lots and lots of reading aloud. I implemented other things later but made sure to stretch preschool and kindergarten activities out so that none of our boys "officially" started first grade until they were six and a half, even though by that time they were usually doing some first-grade level work already in areas like handwriting and spelling. So, as you read through the curriculum choices below, be sure not to limit yourself to a final decision right away. Also, **make plans to start attending your state's annual homeschool convention or curriculum fair** no matter how young your oldest is, and glean all that you can from those who have gone before you. Take your time to research the top two or three that appeal to you, and you may even find yourself creating a plan that incorporates more than one source of materials sooner than you think you will.

     If you more closely fit under the **second profile** of families, however, you are usually much more pressed to make such decisions. This can cause issues because we tend to feel that if we choose one route, we are "missing out" on something else, constantly struggling against an **"opportunity cost"** mentality. Instead, **give yourself grace** and know that you *can* take time to gather your bearings and even put the academics on hold for a bit while you possibly need to reestablish some relationship basics with your child first. Since the decision to homeschool usually does not line up conveniently with whenever the next state homeschool convention or curriculum fair is being held, another option for these second

---

Note to Leaders and Mentors:

If your state has an annual convention and curriculum fair, it would be wise to encourage new moms to attend with a veteran mom. Events like these can be overwhelming, even for moms who have been homeschooling for years. Going with a friend can sometimes make all the difference!

Help your new moms to understand how to best plan to attend a state convention to gain the most out of the experience. Here are some points to get your discussion started:

— *Plan childcare in advance.*
— *Make a list in advance of those items that you wish to preview before purchasing.*
— *Set a budget in advance and stick to it.*
— *Bring cash for parking and plan meals in advance.*
— *You cannot attend every workshop so decide which ones you can purchase on CD or in a downloadable format. Inspirational or parenting discussions work great in this format while technical workshops and demonstrations are harder to follow on audio alone due to the use of visual aids.*
— *Bring materials needed to take workshop notes and start a binder that you can update with each year's notes and programs*
— *Bring a manageable roller bag or box to easily hold brochures and purchases.*
— *Wear comfortable clothes and always bring a sweater since the rooms tend to be cold!*

profile families is to network with other families who are currently homeschooling and ask to come to their home to see some of their materials. I know that I am a very visual person and if I just have the chance to have it in my hands, I can make quicker determinations about it than I can otherwise.

Note to Leaders and Mentors:

It is useful when looking at curriculum options to clarify for your moms the difference between a curriculum provider and a resource center. There are also hybrid organizations.

A curriculum provider writes, publishes, and sells at least some portion of the curriculum they represent and sell. All of the providers in the "Textbook Approach" section, for example, are considered curriculum providers. They usually sell only their own products and do so directly to the end user with no reseller in between.

A resource center, on the other hand, does not produce their own curriculum but sells what they consider to be "the best of the best" in all subject areas for all ages. Rainbow Resource Center mentioned later in the "Eclectic" section is an example of such an organization.

Still others are kind of a "hybrid". For example, Sonlight, who is discussed in the "Living Books Approach" section writes all their own curriculum and lesson plans for language arts, history, and science but they represent what they consider the "best of the best" for other topics, such as math or the arts. Even for the areas they write themselves, they are also using materials from other curriculum providers (i.e. Apologia) but just putting them together in a unique way.

Take encouragement that no matter where any family starts, whether it is from a first or second profile situation, **you *will* adjust your curriculum usage over time.** So, resist discouragement, thinking that whatever you pick now that you must stick with it forever. Out of the hundreds of families I have interacted with over the years, I know of no families, our own included, who have not made significant adjustments over time as experience is gained and the needs of the child changes. Sometimes the adjustments are minor, but sometimes it requires going with a completely different curriculum. The greatest concern is that most families do not want to feel like they are wasting money if they purchase one curriculum only to find that it does not suit their needs and they cannot even reuse it with another child. Since this is a possibility, then, be sure to look initially at curriculum providers who have a guarantee period where you can review it and send it back for a full refund within a certain number of days; thirty days is fine, but sixty to ninety days is better. We will touch on this and more details in a little bit when we discuss the "Four C's" of selecting curriculum.

Even *with* planning, however, no family will be able to avoid this issue completely. I am no exception when I say that I have certain books on my shelf that I wish I would not have purchased; think "Spanish graveyard"! However, that is part of the learning process, and it is sometimes from the mistakes we make that we experience our greatest growth opportunities.

One final note about assessing curriculum options is to **know how you best plan.** Make sure that you have a designated, quiet time, space, and resources to review your choices. If you work better with people, consider doing a curriculum planning retreat with girlfriends!

Curriculum by Approach

So, let us now look at some common curriculum choices as they relate to the homeschool approach options we discussed in chapter two. This is not intended to be an exhaustive list, and in each section I have provided space for you to add your own findings and those that your mentor may recommend. However, you will discover that **most of the proven providers in the homeschool community are listed here for your consideration**. Remember that no matter where you start, the longer you homeschool then the more eclectic you will become. That is just to be expected and you will know over time when and where to make those adjustments. So, do not worry about trying to identify those eventual adaptations now.

Also, **consider requesting a catalog from each of the major curriculum providers and resource centers** to be sent to you so that you can more easily compare their offerings. While their websites are helpful, sometimes having the physical catalog in hand is even more useful. As you build your curriculum plan, you will undoubtedly run across certain materials that are recommended from many sources while other tools may only be unique to one provider. Another benefit to requesting catalogs is that many providers do not just list product choices and reviews but also provide useful articles related to homeschooling as well as reviews on the products they offer that give insight into what kind of learner will benefit from one type of curriculum or program versus another. We will discuss learning styles in depth in chapter four.

As you work through this chapter, you will find that it is easy to get overwhelmed in a short period of time! This is again why I recommend parents work though the discussions and decisions outlined in chapter two before trying to tackle the question of curriculum. **A family who has narrowed down their "homeschool approach" to one or two options will have a much easier time digesting curriculum choices than one who has not considered their approach at all.** So, make sure that if you still have questions about your approach, take some extra time now to discuss those before moving on with the rest of this chapter.

What information do I still need to clarify to articulate our "approach" to homeschooling before I move on to selecting curriculum?

_____

_____

_____

_____

_____

_____

Textbook Approach Curriculum Choices

For families who are looking to make the switch to home education and just need to get up and going, identifying and sourcing curriculum quickly is an important priority. In many instances, for the sake of saved time and ease of implementation, these families will initially use an all-in-one, all-ages, all-subjects, traditional "Textbook Approach".

Three popular Christian publishers are **A Beka**, **Alpha Omega**, and **Bob Jones University Press**.[59] Each carry Christian-oriented textbook and workbook materials. These are all companies who publish homeschooling materials K-12 for all subjects and are not represented by private homeschooling families, as discussed above with the resource center examples. They typically have on-line assessment tools that you can utilize to understand where your child would place in their program and also offer on-line options.

Another traditional curriculum provider with a biblical worldview to consider is **Rod & Staff**.[60] As a Mennonite publisher, Scripture and situational ethics surrounding biblical principles are woven throughout their curriculum. In addition, since teens in the Mennonite community begin vocational work by about 11th grade, their programs only go through 10th grade. However, be aware that, since the material is accelerated, some students may find their "grade level" too challenging. For example, the 5th grade English text is considered advanced enough to be the place that a 9th grader would start in their program if they are just starting to homeschool and do not have a good grammatical foundation. They are best known for their reading, English, math, history, and science programs. Since they were originally designed for classroom use, however, parents need to be prepared to trim down the amount of busy work assigned throughout the lessons.

An interesting departure from the "big three" or Rod and Staff for a traditional option is **Easy Peasy**.[61] It too is a complete curriculum of core offerings from a biblical perspective and also offers extra subjects like art, physical education, and foreign language. Please note that the first link given below covers K – 8th grade while the second site is their high school offering. Generously provided as a FREE resource for homeschoolers by Lee Giles, this curriculum can mostly reside under the traditional category, though it does have a bit of unintended "Charlotte Mason" flavor to it as well. Parents should also be aware that since a great deal of the work is done on-line, learning can become more of a passive activity rather than an interactive one with parental involvement.

Those parents looking for traditional computer-based option that is like Easy Peasy, though not as comprehensive, can also consider **Time4Learning**.[62] Please note, however, that this a secular program.

---

[59] http://www.abeka.com/ ; http://www.aophomeschooling.com ; http://www.bjupress.com/
[60] https://www.milestonebooks.com/list/Rod_and_Staff_Curriculum/
[61] https://allinonehomeschool.com/ and https://allinonehighschool.com/
[62] https://www.time4learning.com

Here are some questions I have about these curriculum options and more thoughts regarding the research I want to do about it.

_____

_____

_____

_____

_____

_____

_____

_____

_____

_____

_____

_____

_____

_____

_____

_____

_____

_____

_____

_____

_____

_____

The Cultural Literacy Approach Curriculum Choices

Parents seeking resources to coincide with the cultural literacy approach popularized by Dr. E.D. Hirsch Jr. should check out his information about their "**Core Knowledge**" program.[63] There are no other curriculum providers who write curriculum for this approach.

Here are some questions I have about these curriculum options and more thoughts regarding the research I want to do about it.

_____

_____

_____

_____

_____

_____

_____

_____

_____

_____

_____

_____

_____

_____

_____

_____

_____

_____

_____

_____

_____

_____

_____

---

[63] http://www.coreknowledge.org/

Principle Approach Curriculum Choices

Like the "Cultural Literacy Approach", the "Principle Approach" does not have several providers who write curriculum for it. Instead and similar to the "Classical Approach", parents tend to focus on "note-booking" and creating individualized plans for each child rather than purchasing ready-made curriculum.

For families interested in this approach, the best way to research curriculum options is to begin with a visit to the website for **The Foundation for American Christian Education**.[64] For families who connect with this resource, they have a worthwhile DVD you can order called **Getting Started with the Principle Approach** as well as **Noah Plan Curriculum Guides** covering all ages (K-12) and subjects, including English, history and geography, math, science, reading, literature, and art.

Here are some questions I have about these curriculum options and more thoughts regarding the research I want to do about it.

_____

_____

_____

_____

_____

_____

_____

_____

_____

_____

_____

_____

_____

_____

_____

_____

_____

_____

_____

[64] http://www.principleapproach.org/

Classical Approach Curriculum Choices

While this approach does not have many complete program curriculum provider choices, there are growing number as well as several tools available that can aid parents in planning and delivering a successful classical program to their child. Both *Teaching the Trivium* and the third edition of *The Well-Trained Mind* mentioned in the previous chapter contain guidance for developing your program.[65] They offer several excellent resources, support communities, and articles that are essential in planning your curriculum. Parents can **use these tools to develop their child's classical program from preschool all the way through high school in every subject.** Various curriculum options per subject are reviewed, complete book lists are provided, and suggested schedules are presented.

The Bluedorns also have an online catalog at **TriviumPursuit.com** you can peruse as you seek to put together your classical curriculum that covers history, language arts, literature, art, logic, and ancient languages. They have written their book from a Christian perspective and offer recommended resources and curriculum on their site to complement it.

Similarly, if you choose to utilize Susan Wise Bauer's *The-Well Trained Mind*, you will find that she has her own publishing company called **Peace Hill Press**.[66] Through this brand, she publishes several helpful materials for parents who are putting together their own program, including the very popular ***Story of the World*** history curriculum, which is a four-year program that is best suited for grades one through four. This program is complete with activities, narration assignments, and map work as well as additional history and literature recommendations for each lesson. Peace Hill Press also has materials to teach writing, reading, and language arts. While *The Well-Trained Mind* and the related materials from Peace Hill Press are not written exclusively from a Christian perspective, they can easily complement the priorities of a Christian home. For example, the *Story of the World* series is not written from a Christian worldview but does include the historical significance of the Jewish Nation, Christianity, the Reformation, and so forth. Parents can emphasize and highlight additional points from their Christian faith with the program as they go along and pull in additional resources as necessary.

Parents can also decide to create their own program using the *Trivium Pursuit* or *The Well-Trained Mind* as their spine and yet also incorporate offerings from other organizations. For example, many families enjoy utilizing the ***Mystery of History*** by Linda Lacour Hobar.[67] It is an outstanding history program that is written from a Christian worldview and follows the classical four-year pattern. She does an excellent job of covering world and church history in a well-written, engaging text that is best suited for children in the fifth through eighth grades. However, the

---

[65] http://www.triviumpursuit.com/ ; http://www.welltrainedmind.com/
[66] http://www.peacehillpress.com/
[67] http://www.themysteryofhistory.info/

program does include projects, map work, and assignments that can be used in each of the levels of the Trivium (1st – 4th, 5th – 8th, and high school). Similarly, families can choose to use **Apologia's** popular Christian curriculum for science instead of following the approach outlined in *The Well-Trained Mind*.[68] Remember that you are in charge and can decide what your final program looks like!

For those families, however, who are looking for a more turnkey solution for classical education, there are some organizations out there that provide curriculum for all ages and stages of the Trivium. One option for a classical Christian program that has already been designed for you is to review the offerings from **Tapestry of Grace (TOG)**.[69] Curriculum is structured in a guided unit study format and is available for grades K-12. It cycles through history every four years with all of the family's children studying the same subjects at varying levels of difficulty. Detailed lesson plans and schedules are provided, and the program incorporates a biblical worldview. However, some parents have expressed that the program can be overwhelming so families investing in TOG will want to discern where to trim and adjust when appropriate.

Another Christian option for a classical curriculum is to check out the programs provided by **Veritas Press**.[70] Their offerings may be suitable for those looking for a more complete program that is classical in structure but provides parents with a one-stop-shop for making their curriculum purchases rather than having to pull it together on their own. However, some parents have difficulty with the academic rigors of the program and its strong Calvinistic perspective, particularly in the Omnibus series that teaches history, theology, and literature for the Jr. and Sr. High levels.

Trisms Curriculum by Linda Thornhill is an interesting classical curriculum choice because it combines critical thinking with a unit style approach, blending "literature, biographies, historical fiction, cultural studies, and (a variety) of reference materials."[71] However, it mostly focuses on the "Rhetoric Stage" (i.e. high school) and just a bit on the "Dialectic Stage" (i.e. 5th – 8th grade) while excluding "Grammar State" (i.e. 1st -4th grade) altogether.

A more recent option that has risen in popularity is **Classical Conversations** by Leigh Bortins.[72] What is unique about this program is that, in addition to serving as "classical homeschooling in a box", it largely relies on weekly, facilitated group meetings in your local area. These meetings are overseen by fellow homeschooling moms who have gone through a multi-day training process to become certified leaders. Meetings are divided into trivium equivalents called Foundations (1st –

[68] http://:www.apologia.com/
[69] http://www.tapestryofgrace.com/
[70] http://ww.veritaspress.com/
[71] http://www.trisms.com/
[72] http://www.classicalconversations.com/

4th), Essentials (5th – 8th), and Challenge (9th – 12th). There is an additional cost associated with these meetings, however, making it too pricey for many families to consider. Also, depending on how the groups are organized, it can be a strain on family schedules and logistics when one family has more than one child in a different trivium level and the parent is intended to accompany each child to their individualized session. In addition, anecdotal feedback reveals that a family's experience with the quality of the weekly classes can vary greatly from one group to another since the experience and the preparedness of the paid facilitator running the session is not necessarily consistent across the board.

Another relatively new option to consider for a classical program is **Memoria Press (MP)**.[73] While many homeschoolers associate MP with resources to teach Latin, Greek, and logic, they have developed packages from "Jr." Kindergarten 12th grade, helping parents to invest in a classical program without needing to pull everything together on their own. While MP has developed most of their own traditionally flavored material that they sell, they do currently use Rod & Staff for some areas, such as math. However, I suspect that they will continue to develop their own materials and may eventually replace any use of items from other publishers. MP is also unique because they have a growing number of on-line classes available through **MP's Online Academy** for homeschooling families to use, which may help take the intimidation out of teaching such courses as logic, history, government, writing, Latin, and more.[74]

One final resource worth exploring for the classical approach is the **Classical Christian Homeschooling** website.[75] Here you may read a detailed description about classical homeschooling, an overview on the trivium, detailed accounts of each stage, and many other classical homeschooling resources.

Here are some questions I have about these curriculum options and more thoughts regarding the research I want to do about it.

_____

_____

_____

_____

_____

_____

_____

---

[73] http://www.memoriapress.com/
[74] http://www.memoriapress.com/onlineschool
[75] http://www.classical-homeschooling.org/

Common Sense Approach Curriculum Choices

Curriculum for this approach simply gets down to the essentials of each subject and is less concerned about tying subjects together or worrying about keeping a certain order to science or history topics. As mentioned previously in chapter two, **Dr. Ruth Beechick's materials** reflect this approach and offer a sensible start for any home school.

For a publisher that echoes the heart of this approach, check out **Common Sense Press**.[76] It is an easy-to-use curriculum that teaches language arts in an integrated manner. Science, math, and Bible history are available too for a complete curriculum program.

For those who desire to have more "meat" as to how to construct their curriculum plan, purchasing *The Ultimate Guide to Homeschooling* by Debra Bell is a good idea. She **covers all aspects of homeschooling, including curriculum and high-tech options.** She incorporates many valuable Internet resources, reproducible forms, and great ideas for every homeschooler, regardless of their personal approach.

Another option is to check out Gayle Graham's *How to Homeschool: A Practical Approach*. It includes **general planning and scheduling advice** as well as recommendations on teaching each subject. This tool also provides several reproducible forms.

One **final resource** book that you may find to be of value with the "Common Sense Approach" is *The Home School Manual (7th ed.)* by Theodore Wade. It is a good overall resource that may be available at your local library to peruse. One of its good points is that it is really a compilation of articles on nearly every topic you can think of related to home education that were written by many different pioneers in the homeschooling community. However, just know that it has not been updated since 1997, so it does not cover the more modern considerations surrounding home education. As a result, the resource listing at the back will not be up-to-date

Here are some questions I have about these curriculum options and more thoughts regarding the research I want to do about it.

_____

_____

_____

_____

_____

_____

_____

[76] http://www.commonsensepress.com/

Living Books or Charlotte Mason Approach Curriculum Choices

A "Living Books Approach" Christian curriculum provider that covers every subject and every age group is **Sonlight**.[77] They depart from the traditional all-in-one providers described in the "Textbook Approach" section by structuring their curriculum around a "Living Books Approach" (i.e. fiction, nonfiction, biographies, etc.) for nearly all subjects. **This literature-rich approach incorporates heavily into their history, reading, and language arts programs.** They also provide everything you need for each grade in every subject, including all the materials you need for math and science experiments. It is a great alternative to a "Traditional Approach" that helps you build an excellent library of good books while giving you the security of following a structured program. This is a highly recommended organization for those who are looking for great materials and books but do not have the time to put the plan together or to decide what to buy or what to teach. They have even written their own lesson plans and schedules that you can use for teaching history, language arts, literature, science, etc. on either a four or five day-a-week school schedule. In addition, it works well for families who teach **multiple levels of ages** at the same time.

In addition to writing much of their own curriculum, **Sonlight also works like a resource center**. They are a family-run organization that incorporates what they have originated with products from other providers that they consider to be the "best of the best". For example, they have written their own language arts, history, and science curriculum but will give you a few handwriting books to choose from, telling you the pros and cons of each. The same goes for math, the arts, and so forth. Again, be sure to request the catalog as you will find it to be a very useful tool in developing your homeschooling plans.

There are, however, two primary cautions that new homeschoolers of faith should be aware of regarding Sonlight. First, be prepared for the fact that they do incorporate secular literature along with their Christian-flavored offerings. While it is meant to promote worldview understanding and prompt discussion, these selections may not be suitable or desirable for every family to use. Second, they also sell certain science-related materials that hold an "old-Earth" view of the world's creation. Again, parents should simply be aware of these points and decide for themselves whether these are "deal-breaking" issues or not. Therefore, as good as Sonlight is, it is not for everyone. So, requesting their catalog and then working through the section called "*27 Reasons NOT to use Sonlight*" would be helpful to clarify any questions or concerns that you may have.

Another curriculum provider that is worth your time in research is **My Father's World**.[78] They too take a biblical worldview and a strong international flavor in the construction of their multi-level curriculum like Sonlight does. However, they are somewhat of a blend of the "Charlotte

---

[77] http://www.sonlight.com/
[78] http://www.mfwbooks.com/

Mason" and "Classical" approaches, taking the teaching structure in a chronological, cyclical five-year cycle for children who are in second through eighth grade. The program has a strong emphasis on character development and is structured around what they call "easy-to-teach, hands-on, unit studies". They then have a separate four-year program for high school.

Another Christian curriculum provider that constructs its program around the "Charlotte Mason Approach" is **Heart of Dakota**.[79] Written over twelve volumes covering all grades, parents can teach multiple ages with one volume, stretching and adjusting the materials up or down as needed. The layout feels like a unit study method while also utilizing traditional and living books approaches. Choosing the correct initial placement of your child is very important, so if you go with this curriculum, make sure you understand that criteria before finalizing your decision.

If, however, you are more interested in building your own plan for a "Living Books Approach" by using the Charlotte Mason resources discussed in the previous chapter, you will want to align yourself with a reliable community of homeschoolers who also follow this approach. Karen Andreola's **CharlotteMason.com** or Catherine Levison's **A Charlotte Mason Education** are both great on-line resources to use as you begin your research.[80]

Another resource for building your own plan is to check out Christine Miller's *All Through the Ages: History Through Literature* book.[81] Even if you do not really follow a "Living Books Approach", this is a **great tool to supplement your history program** for students of all ages by incorporating historical fiction and other pieces of literature related to the period you are studying. Classical homeschoolers will also appreciate its chronological organization.

For **elementary and middle school science**, *Apologia's "Exploring Creation With…"* series is compatible with a "Living Books Approach", given the narrative nature of the lessons and the number and quality of hands-on activities and experiments. These one-year texts cover zoology, botany, astronomy, and the human body. There is also a text that covers physics and chemistry concepts, which I would recommend covering last since it is the most complicated.

One **final tool** that parents following these approaches may find useful is the book called *Teaching Children: A curriculum guide to what children need to know at each level through sixth grade* by Diane Lopez. This book serves as a scope and sequence that covers all subjects for children ages kindergarten through sixth grade. It emphasizes Charlotte Mason's "Living Books Approach", and the forward in the book is written by Susan Schaeffer Macaulay, who is the author of the previously mentioned book called *For the Children's Sake*.

---

[79] https://www.heartofdakota.com/
[80] http://www.charlottemason.com/ ; http://www.catherinelevison.com/
[81] http://www.nothingnewpress.com/

Here are some questions I have about these curriculum options and more thoughts regarding the research I want to do about it.

Lifestyle of Learning or Relaxed Approach Resources Curriculum Choices

Given the nature of this approach that can also be called an "Unschooling Approach", there are not many set resources out there that help families to implement it "out of a box", other than the books I previously listed in chapter two. However, one organization that I believe is worth mentioning here is **Hewitt Homeschooling Resources**.[82] Although they do not technically classify themselves as a "Lifestyle of Learning" or a "Relaxed" approach curriculum provider, they do pride themselves on offering programs that are complete and yet not "overly-structured" with an emphasis on developing a "lifelong, wholehearted learner". Hewitt offers programs for all ages and subjects as well as additional parental support resources for the Jr. and Sr. High levels. They also carry the *"Chronicles of………. A State History Notebook"* that can be customized for any state and is ideal for use anywhere from third to eighth grade.

Another resource that "unschoolers" may appreciate when seeking **inspiration and ideas for cultivating their child's freedom in learning** is *The Unschooling Handbook: How to Use the Whole World as Your Child's Classroom* by Mary Griffith. For families with teens, *The Teenage Liberation Handbook: How to Quit School and Get a Real Life Education* by Grace Llewellyn may be appealing, especially if their child may not be college-bound and will engage in the reading process of this book with you.

Here are some questions I have about these curriculum options and more thoughts regarding the research I want to do about it.

_____

_____

_____

_____

_____

_____

_____

_____

_____

_____

---

[82] http://www.hewitthomeschooling.com/

Eclectic Curriculum Choices

As I mentioned previously, most homeschoolers wind up eventually blending programs and curriculum from several sources. As you compare the options, there are a few additional considerations to keep in mind.

First, in addition to collecting information from specific providers, it is **wise to utilize third-party recommendation resources to gain the most objective perspective you can**. Resource centers and curriculum review books are great tools to obtain this type of feedback.

Most home schools over time develop an eclectic style of needing to pull together curriculum from a variety of resources.

Of all the **resource centers** out there for homeschoolers, the best ones are run by homeschooling families who have had actual experience with the product in their own home. A favorite source to gain useful and objective feedback is **Rainbow Resource Center**.[83] They have an extensive catalog that is bigger than a phone book covering just about every conceivable curriculum you could possibly want, except for proprietary providers that only sell directly to the end user. For most situations, I prefer to research and read their reviews online since it is more usable and current than flipping around in the printed catalog. However, when I am researching uncharted territory, the catalog can be more appealing to start with since they group offerings by topic and you may run across a new program that you have not even heard of before. One final benefit in working with them as compared to other resource centers is that they discount most all their products an average of 10-20% less than their competitors.

Make use of objective, third-party review resources when it comes to comparing "apples to apples" on curriculum you are considering.

Christian Book Distributors also has an extensive selection of homeschooling materials and offers them at discount prices.[84] It also includes many helpful reviews and product descriptions, and I have found that it carries certain items that are hard to source elsewhere.

More examples of general resource centers include **Covenant Home School Resource Center**, based in Arizona, or **Love to Learn**.[85] Other family-owned and operated resource centers who offer some of their products at a discount but who specialize in one area or another include the following.

---

[83] http://www.rainbowresource.com/

[84] http://www.christianbook.com/homeschool?event=AFF&p=1155849; Use this link to support TBH.

[85] https://www.chsrc.org/; http://www.lovetolearn.net/

➢ **American Homeschool Publishing** specializes in providing classical home education products with an emphasis on literature, biographies, and language arts as well as materials to assist in the study of modern and classical languages.[86]

➢ **Greenleaf Press** is an organization that is run by Rob & Cyndy Shearer and their family. They specialize in providing excellent resources and curriculum options for history.[87]

➢ **Tobin's Lab** is a resource center that is run by the Duby family. Tobin's Lab specializes in providing science resources that promote learning by discovery. They are an excellent resource for purchasing laboratory equipment, dissection kits, specimens, games and other specialized science items.[88]

Regarding **third-party curriculum review books and resources**, Cathy Duffy is the premier author of this type of tool. She has written *102 Top Picks for Homeschool Curriculum: Choosing the Right Curriculum and Approach for Your Child's Learning Style*.[89] It is an updated, excellent collection of comprehensive curriculum reviews for every subject and also includes a basic discussion about learning styles. Two dated, but still excellent resources by Cathy Duffy that you might find at the local library are her original *Christian Home Educators' Curriculum Manuals*. One is for Elementary and one focuses on Junior/Senior High curriculum. **Hunting for reliable on-line reviews are invaluable as well**. However, it can be difficult to separate out valid input from thoughtless comments. The *Well-Trained Mind* and *Sonlight forums* are quite useful as are *Homeschool Reviews* and *The Curriculum Choice*.[90] You can also

> **Note to Leaders and Mentors:**
>
> *Some libraries, like the Glendale Public Library system in Maricopa County, have "teacher's box" programs that homeschoolers can utilize for their families. A "teacher's account" can be tied to the family's regular account but operates as a separate account. It gives them the ability to check out a box full of books based on the typical maximum amount allowed that the librarian can pull either by subjects of interest or by a specific list that the homeschooler provides them in advance. Homeschoolers can get on a monthly rotation schedule that can save both time and money!*

---

[86] http://www.ahsp.com/
[87] http://www.greenleafpress.com/
[88] http://www.tobinslab.com/
[89] http://cathyduffyreviews.com/
[90] http://forums.welltrainedmind.com/ ; https://forums.sonlight.com/;
http://www.homeschoolreviews.com/default.aspx; http://www.thecurriculumchoice.com/

utilize any number of **homeschooling magazines** that often contain not only useful "how-to" articles but also reviews on various curriculum offerings. Some of the more popular titles include, *The Old Schoolhouse*, *The Teaching Home*, *Homeschooling Today*, and *Practical Homeschooling Magazine*.[91]

The second major point to consider when building your own curriculum plan, regardless of the age of your child and stage of your homeschooling season, is to **incorporate plenty of good books**. This is because reading is so important and foundational to all future learning and sometimes it can be difficult to weed out marginal books from the great ones, particularly in the younger ages where habits are nurtured and established. When we began our homeschooling journey, I had absolutely no experience in choosing good literature for our child. I needed to have a great deal of help in this area and, fortunately, there were and still are many wonderful resources available to help parents build their understanding of how to choose good books as they begin to build their home library. For, as you may be able to get many recommended books at the public library, some you will just want to source for yourself.

My typical **pecking order for sourcing books** that I wish our sons to access is to first try to find it at the **local library**. Also, if you plan a few weeks ahead, some hard-to-find titles may be obtained through your library's "inter-library loan" process. My second source is to go to a **homeschool resource center**, such as Christianbook.com or Rainbow Resource Center, as previously mentioned.[92] If neither the library nor a homeschool resource center has what I am seeking, then **Amazon.com** may have it, either new or gently used, through their "Amazon Marketplace" partners program. As a final resort, you may be able to find difficult-to-source items at a local teaching supply store, a used book sale, or a used curriculum sale in your local area. Arizona's **VNSA (Volunteer Nonprofit Service Association)** hosts one of the largest regional used book sales in the country every February and many families from around the state and even out-of-state will travel there to see what treasures they can find. [93] Used curriculum can also be sourced through local used curriculum sales or on-line at a variety of sites, including specialized social media groups or **HSLDA's Curriculum Market**.[94] If all of these options come up short, you can either borrow the book from a fellow homeschooler or simply purchase it from the publisher.

---

[91] http://www.thehomeschoolmagazine.com/; http://teachinghome.com/; http://www.homeschooltoday.com/; http://www.home-school.com/

[92] http://www.christianbook.com - You can visit my website at www.thebalancedhomeschooler.com and purchase most of the books that are referenced in this manual from Christianbook.com. Referral fees go to support the Evan C. Gary Memorial Scholarship, administered by the Grand Canyon University Scholarship Foundation. Use this specific link, add items within a four hour period, and complete your purchase within thirty days for it to "count": http://www.christianbook.com/homeschool?event=AFF&p=1155849

[93] http://www.vnsabooksale.org/

[94] http://market.hslda.org/auction/xcAuction.asp

But first, before you figure out the exact literature you are looking for, you would be wise to **invest in some of the wonderful booklist books** available for review. Most of these books spend time discussing the importance of reading to your child from various perspectives. They are all written from a Christian perspective, except for the *ReadAloud Handbook* and *How to Raise a Reader*, which are more secular. However, all of the resources do a good job in steering the parent to classic picture books and children's literature, which have stood the test of time and define the essence of good literature.

Every homeschooler would be wise to invest in a few good "booklist" books for assistance in choosing quality, age-appropriate literature for their child.

1. *The Book Tree: A Christian Reference for Children's Literature* by Elizabeth McCallum & Jane Scott; Literature & biography recommendations and extensive descriptions for each organized by age group written from a Christian perspective.

2. *Books That Build Character* by William Kirkpatick and Gregory and Suzanne M. Wolfe; Literature recommendations by age and type (i.e. picture books, fables, myths, etc.).

3. *Books Children Love* by Elizabeth Wilson; Organized by topic and can be very helpful for supplementing school subjects, such as science and history, with a Christian perspective.

4. *Books to Build On: A Grade by Grade Resource Guide for Parents and Teachers* by Dr. E.D. Hirsch; Descriptive bibliography by grade level and topic of recommended books to use for teaching with a "Cultural Literacy Approach".

5. *Great Books of the Christian Tradition* by Terry W. Glaspey; Literature recommendations organized by age and by historical era, which is very useful for a classically structured education. (i.e. Middle Ages, Ancient World, etc.)

6. *Honey for a Child's Heart* by Gladys Hunt; Classic literature recommendations guide organized by age group. She has also written *Honey for a Teen's Heart*.

7. *How to Raise a Reader* by Elaine McEwan; Literature recommendations and descriptions by age group from birth through the middle grades.

8. *A Landscape with Dragons: The Battle for Your Child's Mind* by Michael D. O'Brien; Literature recommendations (does not give detailed descriptions of each book) by picture books, easy readers, short chapter books, intermediate readers and even adult selections. It specifically addresses why the inclusion of fantasy literature is important to consider for a well-rounded education of our Christian children.

9. *The ReadAloud Handbook* by Jim Trelease; Literature recommendations and extensive descriptions organized by book type and age group.

10. *They are Never Too Young for Books: A Guide to Children's Books Ages 1 to 8* by Edythe M. McGovern & Helen D. Muller; Literature recommendations and descriptions for your young reader.

Write down any additional "booklist" books recommended to you that are not noted on the list above.

_____

_____

_____

_____

_____

_____

What other questions do you have about the curriculum options discussed so far and what additional research do you wish to do? What other questions do you have for your mentor at this point?

_____

_____

_____

_____

_____

_____

Revisiting the "Four C's" and the Forgotten "C"

Now let's return to the aforementioned **"Four C's"**. As you consider what selections are right for you and your child, we can more specifically spell out what you can look for in a good curriculum by using these guidelines. Then you will have an opportunity to organize your observations about the various curriculum choices you are pondering. The graphic organizer provided at the end of this chapter can be used to assess the probable success of an overall program, or it can be used on a subject-by-subject basis.

First, **consider whether you can deliver the material consistently**. You will undoubtedly come across several unique and intriguing options in your research. However, if you find a program to be too involved or overwhelming for what you know your temperament and schedule will allow, you should seriously consider moving on to something else. New homeschooling moms often become intimidated by what everyone else seems to be doing and loses sight of the fact that their journey is different than that of their friend who may have already been homeschooling for several years or has a different take on how she approaches teaching.

There are numerous books, essays, and blogs out there helping to identify a *child's* learning style but often mom's *teaching* style is overlooked. You know your limitations and strengths better than anyone and should not feel guilty if you cannot be the "Queen of Unit Studies" or do not wish to pursue an intensive survey of the "Great Books". Regardless of your child's learning style, the program you choose must first be in harmony with what you are comfortable and capable of delivering. This does not mean that you never try new or challenging methods or programs or that you ignore your child's learning style preferences, which we will discuss in further detail in chapter four. It just means that if you are not at ease in teaching the program consistently, the curriculum will sit on the shelf and be of use to no one and will ultimately be a waste of your resources.

"Consistency" is defined in Webster's as, **"a standing together, as the parts of a system, or of conduct; agreement or harmony of all parts of a complex thing among themselves, or of the same thing with itself at different times; congruity; uniformity"**.[95] So here are some prompting questions for discussions with your mentor about this concept of "Consistency".

1. Does it **match your teaching style**? Can you picture yourself working through the material with your child or do you find yourself overwhelmed with whether you are "doing it right"?

> ### Consistency
> The program you choose must first be in harmony with what you are comfortable and capable of delivering.

---

[95] http://webstersdictionary1828.com/Dictionary/consistency

2. Do you get excited about **the way it is structured** with clearly laid out course content or do you think you would spend too much time "rewriting" it and making up your own plans?

3. Does the curriculum offer **too much material or too little**? How much would I need to supplement it?

4. Is the **material consistent with itself** or do you find yourself wrestling to reconcile contradictory information or instructions?

Here are more thoughts about how to evaluate "Consistency"

_____

_____

_____

_____

_____

_____

_____

_____

_____

_____

_____

_____

_____

_____

_____

_____

_____

_____

_____

Second, **consider whether you can deliver the material constantly**. Remember that most curriculum programs, whether they are for history, math, science, and so forth, are designed to take a typical school year to complete, which is usually somewhere between thirty-six or even up to forty-two weeks. So, although you may be able to deliver it consistently because the structure of the program falls within your comfort zone, you must also ensure that the program presents the materials in an interesting and appropriate way. You must consider if your family would be best suited by materials that are more involved than others or if a simpler, less-cluttered style would be more productive.

Webster defines "constancy" as a "**fixedness or firmness of mind; persevering resolution; steady, unshaken determination; particularly applicable to firmness of mind under sufferings, to steadiness in attachments, and to perseverance in enterprise.**"[96] So here are some additional prompting questions for discussions with your mentor about the concept of "Constancy".

Constancy
You should be able to interact enthusiastically with the materials and persevere through all planning requirements for the entire school season.

1. Is the content presented in an **engaging and interesting manner** so you can persevere throughout the school year or will it be too boring, dry, fluffy, or disjointed for your taste?

2. What is your general **attitude towards the material**? Can you see yourself looking forward to helping your child progress to the next lesson using this material or would you dread opening the book each day?

3. For scalable curriculum, is the program **suitable for your child's age** or do you spend too much time adjusting the volume of work or difficulty of concepts up or down?

4. Will your schedule allow you to dedicate the **amount of planning and preparation required** to deliver the program successfully? Do you need something more turnkey?

Here are more thoughts about how to evaluate "Constancy"

_____

_____

_____

---

[96] http://webstersdictionary1828.com/Dictionary/constancy

Third, **think about how confident you are in the program's benefits, level of quality, and overall value.** The curriculum you choose should have a proven track record with blogs, reviews, and other feedback venues that describe the positive experiences of other families with that program. In addition, the company selling it should be able to clearly articulate the goals, design, and anticipated outcomes of the program to you. After reviewing it on-line, at a convention, or in a catalog, you should have a high level of assurance that the program will fulfill the educational priorities and homeschooling vision that you established early in the process. Companies with a high level of quality have accessible staff to help you with your decision-making process and a clearly defined guarantee or satisfaction policy.

Confidence Require your program to provide you a high-level of assurance in the program's benefits, level of quality, and overall value.

The program should also instill in you the confidence to know that the content of the program is sound and tested. You want it to be reliable and trust that it will not leave you guessing or left to wonder whether the content they provide you is correct or complete.

Regarding value, **NHERI** stated around ten years ago that homeschooling families spend an average of $450 per year, per child in purchasing curriculum. More recently, a NHERI study centered around $600 as the average per year, per child figure.[97] Of course this can vary up or down depending on your teaching priorities and family budget. However, one caution to note is that sometimes families are frightened off by single program price tags that cost several hundred dollars. Yet I can tell you, as a parent who has pulled together our own curriculum for many years and also invested in all-in-one programs, that **the $600 average is true whether you spend it all on one comprehensive program or you piece it together yourself from several sources.** Do also keep in mind that the investment per child tends to go down dramatically as you have more children to teach. This is because the upfront texts and non-consumable materials you purchased for your first child can used repeatedly for your subsequent children. Many families also will resell items via specialized Facebook groups designed for that purpose or other curriculum resale options in order to recoup some of their original investment.

Webster defines "confidence" as "**a trusting, or reliance; an assurance of mind or firm belief in the integrity, stability or veracity of another, or in the truth and reality of a fact**".[98] So here are some additional prompting questions for discussions with your mentor about the concept of "Confidence".

---

[97] http://www.hslda.org/docs/news/200908100.asp
[98] http://webstersdictionary1828.com/Dictionary/confidence

1. Is the curriculum you are considering a **good value** for what you expect your child to gain out of it? Do you find others heartily recommending it to you?

2. Does the provider offering this program **stand behind their product**, giving you the proper review period necessary to decide if it is right for you and your child?

3. Will the company you are sourcing it from **provide the extra support** you need throughout the year or are their resources limited?

4. How strong and active is the **user community** for this curriculum and can you easily connect with them via e-mail, website support, or blog postings as desired?

5. Will you be able to easily **assess your child's progress**? How will you know at the end of the year whether your child has achieved the learning objectives of the curriculum or if they have fallen short?

Here are more thoughts about how to evaluate "Confidence"

_____

_____

_____

_____

_____

_____

_____

_____

_____

_____

_____

_____

_____

_____

_____

_____

Lastly, **think about how comprehensive the program is.** Ideally, when you select curriculum programs, whether they are all-in-one or focused by subject, you should be able to clearly understand and outline what the learning and mastery goals are for your child before you implement it.

If you have invested in a **single, comprehensive program**, it should cover every subject of importance to you and provide not only the content for that subject but also the scheduling, grading, and review guidelines necessary to successfully deliver it. If it does not and you still find yourself needing to come up with a lot of other supplements or even need to create them yourself, then you should reevaluate how "comprehensive" the program really is.

On the other hand, **if you are pulling together a program yourself, be prepared to spend a great deal of time up front in research and planning activities.** Since I experienced this initially in our "Classical Approach" program we used up through about sixth grade, I would usually take large chunks of time in the summer to get the plans and materials together for the upcoming academic year. I reviewed our priorities for all the major subjects and developed the plans and booklists necessary to keep things running smoothly throughout the year.

Whether you use a program that is developed for you or by you, **your program should include a minimum of these subjects**: Bible study and character training materials, history, literature, science, math, and language arts. The language arts category generally includes spelling, grammar, writing, and reading activities, including phonics for young students. Other subjects to consider include appreciation and production training in music and art as well as foreign language, logic, health, and word study for middle to older students. Chapter four will provide even more considerations for you regarding subjects and development priorities that are important to your child's specific season of schooling.

Comprehensive
Regardless of the curriculum selected, your program should have clear evaluation standards and include a minimum of Bible study and character training materials, history, literature, science, math, and language arts. Consider important electives as well such as art, music, foreign language, and health.

Webster defines "comprehensive" as **"having the quality of comprising much, or including a great extent; extensive"**.[99] So here are some additional prompting questions for discussions with your mentor about the concept of "Comprehensive".

1. Will you **need to supplement the program** heavily with additional tools, resources, and books?

2. Are the **teacher "helps" with the program sufficient** in assisting you plan and get right to teaching or will you need to invest in additional upfront preparation?

3. Does your program **cover at least the minimum subject areas** of Bible study and character training materials, history, literature, science, math, and language arts? Can you easily add electives or other supplemental subjects, or do you need to go outside of the curriculum provider to locate or design those courses?

4. What about **mastery versus exposure**? Are you able to distinguish what skills and information you want your child to master in the program versus information that you just want your child to be exposed to or familiar with by the end of the course?

Here are more thoughts about how to evaluate "Comprehensive" qualities

_____

_____

_____

_____

_____

_____

_____

_____

_____

_____

_____

_____

_____

---

[99] http://webstersdictionary1828.com/Dictionary/comprehensive

Now it is time to take your research about the various curriculum options based on your homeschooling approach of choice and start narrowing down your selections. So, it is useful to balance the ones you are considering against these **"Four C's"** that we have discussed in detail.

On page 117, you will find a *Homeschool Planning and Curriculum Sheet.* It is designed to serve as a visual aid to help you summarize and plan out your next research steps. As you identify the curriculum that you are most interested in pursuing, highlight the potential curriculum choices you want to find out more about and make notes on this chart during your research process to help clarify how the program you are considering

Veteran and new homeschoolers alike can benefit from working with the "Four C's" as they shift from one stage of teaching to the next.

measures up to the "**Four C's**". Once you have done your initial research, you will begin to see a pattern emerge in ones that you feel address your needs and concerns and ones that do not measure up to what you need at this stage in your schooling. I have also provided a similar planning sheet (see page 119) for research that you may want to do by subject. **This second planning sheet is where your curriculum plan will start to take shape.**

Veteran homeschoolers are also encouraged to utilize this tool and process when making a shift to a new stage of homeschooling that is unfamiliar to them, such as transitioning from middle school to junior high programs or from junior high to senior high programs.

Before we close this chapter, I wanted to mention a relatively new "C" of consideration that I like to call **"The Forgotten C".** This "C" has to do with the issue of **copyright infringement**. With the vast accessibility of material available on-line in addition to well-intentioned homeschooling friends who may offer to provide us free material, copyright issues are becoming increasingly problematic.

In very basic terms that are of common occurrence in the homeschooling community, families should remember first that **consumable workbooks** you purchase should not be copied for additional children in your family. Also, if you purchase a **download, CD-Rom, or book that contains reproducible forms**, these materials may only be reproduced for the members of your own family. Additionally, **free e-books and materials available on the Internet** may be used directly by your family only. You would not have permission to distribute them yourself. Instead, point friends you know to the site directly and they can obtain what they need in a legal and direct manner. None of these situations allow you to copy and share materials outside of your own family or within your homeschool support group.

So, instead of running into such copyright issues, **check out free resource sites that are used for sourcing worry-free worksheets for this**

purpose. Check out Enchanted Learning, Donna Young's Printables and Resources, or Homeschooling Printables for free resources that will not pose copyright problems for you. Not Consumed also has free printable options for families.[100]

Still not sure about whether you may be crossing the copyright line? Take this **Copyright Quiz** to check your knowledge of the boundaries.[101] Another great resource for this topic may be found on **iHomeschoolNetwork.com**.[102] In a 2012 issue of *Practical Homeschooler*, read an article called "When Frugal is Illegal: How to Avoid the Copyright Trap" by Kim Kautzer. It is a great article about this topic that is worth your review as well.[103]

What are some current copyright concerns about materials I have been using or plan to use in our homeschooling curriculum plan?

_____

_____

_____

_____

_____

_____

_____

_____

_____

_____

_____

_____

_____

_____

_____

_____

_____

---

[100] http://www.enchantedlearning.com/Home.html; http://donnayoung.org/index.htm; http://www.homeschool.com/printables/; https://www.notconsumed.com/
[101] https://www.copyrightlaws.com/copyright-law-quiz/
[102] http://www.ihomeschoolnetwork.com/honor-copyright/
[103] http://www.home-school.com/Articles/frugal-illegal-homeschool-copyright-law.php

Homeschooling Curriculum Planning Sheet by Approach

Highlight Curriculum you are considering by "Approach"	*Can I deliver it CONSISTENTLY based on its structure?*	*Can I interact with it CONSTANTLY, maintaining a high level of interest?*	*Am I CONFIDENT in its quality, benefits, and value?*	*Is it COMPREHENSIVE enough to meet our needs?*
Textbook • A Beka • Alpha Omega • Bob Jones				
Cultural Literacy • Core Knowledge Program				
Principle • Noah Plan Curriculum Guides				
Classical • Trivium Pursuit • Well-Trained Mind • Mystery of History • Tapestry of Grace • Veritas Press				
Common Sense • Dr. Ruth Beechick • Debra Bell • Gayle Graham				
Living Books or Charlotte Mason • Sonlight • My Father's World • Andreola or Levison's Books • Diane Lopez				
Lifestyle of Learning/Relaxed • Hewitt				
Eclectic • Christianbook.com • Rainbow Resource • Cathy Duffy • Booklist Books • Library				

This page is left blank intentionally

Homeschooling Curriculum Planning Sheet by Subject

Highlight Curriculum you are considering by "Subject"	*Can I deliver it <ins>CONSISTENTLY</ins> based on its structure?*	*Can I interact with it <ins>CONSTANTLY</ins>, maintaining a high level of interest?*	*Am I <ins>CONFIDENT</ins> in its quality, benefits, and value?*	*Is it <ins>COMPREHENSIVE</ins> enough to meet our needs?*
Math				
Language Arts ▪ Phonics/Reading ▪ Spelling ▪ Grammar ▪ Logic				
Writing ▪ Handwriting ▪ Concepts				
Literature				
History				
Science				
Foreign Language				
Art & Music				

This page is left blank intentionally

More Chapter Notes...

Chapter 4

Nuts & Bolts: Styles, Seasons, Methods, Tools, & Records

"All this," David said, "I have in writing from the hand of the Lord upon me, and he gave me understanding in all the details of the plan." I Chronicles 28:19 (NIV)

Implementing the Plan

As homeschoolers, we too can seek "understanding" in the "details of the plan" that we are forming for our child's education. For, regardless of your homeschooling approach and related curriculum that you are going to use, there are certain **learning style issues, organizational teaching methods, essential tools, record keeping points, and other "seasonal" considerations that are somewhat universal for most homeschoolers.**

When King David was coming to the time of passing his reign onto his son Solomon, he went to great lengths to make certain that the supplies and tools were gathered together before his death to ensure that the temple would be made exactly to the Lord's specifications. David tells Solomon that the Lord gave him "understanding in all the details of the plan." So, think of the chapter divisions for Part I of this manual in the symbolic context of I Chronicles 28:19.

— Chapter one established **why** the temple was necessary
— Chapter two was the **plan** to build the temple.
— Chapter three was all about the **content** of the materials and supplies used to build the temple.
— And now, in chapter four, we will address **how** the temple is to be built

In our case, our "temple" is the child and we have already talked about why we teach them, what the plan is to teach them, and have determined the content we will use to teach them. So now it is time to discuss *how* to approach teaching them.

Understanding Learning Styles and Related Teaching Methods

As I briefly mentioned in the last chapter, understanding your child's learning style is a useful piece of knowledge to have when figuring out the best way to deliver the curriculum you have selected. Notice I am saying that **you will be better off basing most of your selection decision for curriculum on the criteria I previously mentioned and *then* consider your child's learning style to figure out delivery adjustments.** The reason I say this is because I have seen families over the years spend an excess of time finding and literally hundreds of dollars purchasing several different math curriculum or science programs for each child in their family in a never-ending quest to get just the right program to meet what they perceive to match their child's learning style. In the end, many of these families wind up wasting money on programs that do not get fully utilized and do not necessarily obtain the unique results they are looking for in the process. Mom gets burned out, and the children are often frustrated too.

Instead, it is my observation that families are better off choosing a solid curriculum that can be at least partially utilized again with more than one child. Then mom can make minor adjustments in the delivery of the material or the extra emphasis that one child may need versus another without purchasing multiple programs per subject. Remember that a program must *first* match mom's teaching style and comfort level before it is going to be utilized.

For example, if you purchase a solid math program that meets your personal "Four C's" we reviewed in the previous chapter, you may have one child who does great with it right "out-of-the-box" because they like a workbook approach and are very **visual**. Perhaps you also have another child who is more **auditory,** and they need additional assistance in understanding the material or problems. In this child's case, you may give them verbal assignments and have them orally explain the lesson back to you or have them respond verbally when you are reviewing math facts with them rather than having them do a written drill sheet. Still, another child may be more **kinesthetic** and need to "experience" the math. So, you help them understand material by drawing diagrams or pictures, role playing word problems, and also by using various math manipulatives and other physical objects to get the points across. Perhaps this same mom has a fourth child who is a **struggling learner** and is completely

AFTER you have mostly determined your curriculum, THEN look at ways to address your child's learning style needs in the methodology you employ.

overwhelmed. In this case, mom can greatly trim the number of problems each child works so that they can have success with five well-done problems rather than twenty-five incorrectly done problems. Breaking it down into bite-sized pieces will be the key to helping this child. In summary, this example described shows how mom can use the same math curriculum as the "spine" of what she does for her whole family but vary it as needed in *how* the materials are taught, depending on the strengths and weaknesses of each child's learning style.

So, let's take a look now at four commonly identified learning styles. While there are many assessment instruments available to dig deeper into this topic and countless ways to "label" them, you will find that most of these styles are easy to identify and have basic methods you can employ to make the most of your child's efforts to learn. Since I have not really been satisfied with how other authors have delineated the four styles, I came up with my own classification system that I observed in my own home! I like to refer to them as **the Moving Learner, the Structured Learner, the Analytical Learner, and the Community Learner**.

Another point to keep in mind as you consider these learner types is that most young children have at least some degree of the Moving Learner in them before fully developing traits of the other types of learners as they grow and mature. Furthermore, you will see that most children favor a primary learning style while also exhibiting a secondary preference that is important too. In addition, I will include a discussion about the **Struggling Learner**, since a child of any of the four following learning styles may struggle with making progress, either continuously or at one time or another throughout their school career.

Before reading the next section, write down your initial thoughts experiences about identifying or working with people or children of various learning styles.

_____

_____

_____

_____

_____

_____

_____

_____

_____

When you meet with your mentor, discuss any other thoughts they have in relationship to learning styles.

The Moving Learner

The Moving Learner (ML) likes to **live and learn "outside-of-the-box"**. They can conjure up unusual questions and hop down rabbit trails before you even have a chance to get through the introduction of the lesson. Their carefree nature tends to be more concerned with having freedom to act spontaneously, sometimes flitting from one topic to the next, rather than seeing each subject through to its completion before beginning the next one. ML's tend to be enthusiastic and engaged when they are interested in the subject at hand and are excellent observers. However, they can be very difficult to move along in the learning process when they are bored or feel restricted. On the other hand, ML's are also more flexible when curriculum changes are implemented and are more adaptable when unexpected schedule changes occur. Here are some other characteristics to keep in mind about ML's:

➤ **Goal Setting for ML's:** Giving the ML short-term, even daily goals and rewards to look forward to is helpful. Since planning is not an ML's strength, help them break down what they need to accomplish into smaller, digestible sections. This way, your ML can take in what is required for the day and does not need to worry about what the entire week may look like for them.

➤ **Schedules for ML's:** ML's do not tend to care for formal schedules. This does not mean that you do not have one but that you may not choose to involve them in the process of creating or maintaining it: at least not while they are younger. Instead, you can understand their schedule and just share with them the next thing that is going to happen as the day goes along. This is more of a progressive method of scheduling where you reveal it to them on an as-needed basis. By their middle years, perhaps as early as third grade, make a visual board or chart for your ML to physically update as the day goes by. You can make it out of poster board or on a three-panel display with cards and file folder pockets that they can move from an "assigned" section to a "completed" section each day.[104] Then it is a matter of you asking them to "check their cards" to see if they are done with the day's assignments rather than having them update a daily written schedule.

➤ **An ML's Day:** Try to incorporate physical activity whenever possible, especially for young boys. Requiring your ML, particularly when they are young, to sit at a desk lesson after lesson is not realistic for them and can be counterproductive. Allow your child to be in different locations in the house for different lessons. If helpful, encourage them to use a clip board and sit on the ground to work some lessons while having them stand at a counter or even go outside to work on others. Also, build in breaks for

---

[104] See chapter nine for more details on creating a schedule board. Detailed instructions for creating one are available on the private TBH Facebook site.

your ML throughout the day to keep their attention fresh on whatever subject you are teaching.

> **Subject Perspectives for ML's:** Creative subjects like art, story writing, and music are winners with ML's. However, by incorporating movement, physical crafts, and hands-on projects into subjects like history and science, they can also enjoy these. Language arts, math, and other seatwork subjects tend to be the most challenging for them. So be sure to include extra-curricular subjects, projects, and activities as an incentive to successfully complete the basic seatwork subjects. Tying school performance to areas of interest such as sports, dance, or league activities is also motivating to the ML. Lastly, if subjects like history and science tend to weigh heavily on your ML, consider involving them in a history or science fair that will encourage them to pull their learning accomplishments together into a visual presentation that will require various kinesthetic experiences as well as challenge their long-term focus to complete the project.

> **The Best Approach for ML's:** Variety in teaching methods work best for ML's. ML's are highly kinesthetic and need to "experience" the subjects they are learning. Moms with an ML will want to have a variety of delivery methods that she can rotate through for the various subjects. For example, when you want to drill your ML on grammar definitions, math facts, foreign language vocabulary, or scientific terms, you can have note cards or flash cards you can use as prompts scattered around the floor that they then pick up as they make their way towards you. You can make each card worth a piece of candy or a penny for an extra incentive. Other drill game ideas include "fishing" for the cards or passing a ball back and forth to try and "stump" each other on lesson points for a subject of struggle for them. History and literature can often be enhanced for the ML by role playing or working on related craft activities or projects to reinforce the lesson's points. Even having an ML do a simple coloring activity while you read to them can be useful since they tend to take in information while they are doing a repetitive task rather than just sitting and listening. Also, keep in mind that an ML benefits greatly from visual as well as auditory methods, so incorporate those too as needed.

Write down your observations and then later discuss more thoughts with your mentor about identifying and working successfully with a Moving Learner: _____

_____

_____

_____

The Structured Learner

The Structured Learner (SL) likes to **live and learn "inside-the-box"**. They love order, process, rules, and predictability, doing their best when expectations are clearly presented. While they like to understand the "big picture" of where they are heading for the year, they're not so much "big picture" people and tend to be more interested in what they need to accomplish on a daily basis. They are often perfectionists or "Type A's" and can be overly hard on themselves when the grade that they earned on a particular assignment does not measure up to what they want to receive. This perfectionist tendency can also manifest itself when they have difficulty making choices or decisions about something and they agonize over it because they either do not want to be "wrong" or they do not want to miss out on some option that they do not select. Anything from answering difficult school questions to trying to select something to eat off a menu at a restaurant can be torture for an SL, regardless of whether they have an insecure personality or not. Here are some other characteristics to keep in mind about SL's:

➤ **Goal Setting for SL's:** An SL likes to understand the plan and needs to know what is expected of them in a tangible way. Set both short and long-term goals for your SL that reward and reinforce to them that working efficiently and planning ahead are great perspectives to maintain throughout their life. However, be aware that SL's often focus on what is required at the detail level and may not venture past the minimum requirements since they tend to focus on just "getting it done". This is also why giving them monthly goals to achieve in relationship to their daily schedules can be more impactful than sharing a year's worth of expectations at a time.

➤ **Schedules for SL's** Daily schedules are important to SL's so the more you can involve them in helping to plan and run their day, the better. One useful method is to have a general schedule of lessons for the day and tasks for them to accomplish that you provide them. Then allow your SL to decide the order and timing of when they are completed so they have a sense of control and ownership. SL's generally like to be independent and get school going early, working through assignments until they are done.

➤ **An SL's Day:** SL's tend to like a primary location to conduct their school activities. Allow them to treat it like their study sanctuary and make sure that it is quiet and unencumbered from distractions. If your SL needs to do school in a public area of the home, consider investing in one of those "science fair", three-panel foam boards that you can put on a kitchen table to create their personal space. Also, since they are not so interested in exploring deeply into a subject as AL's do, if you want them to take their learning further in a subject, you will need to incorporate that expectation into your daily lesson requirements for that assignment or subject.

➢ **Subject Perspectives for SL's:** SL's are somewhat the opposite of ML's and tend to do well at the objective subjects of math and language arts. This is also true for history and science when the answers you are seeking are clear cut and non-subjective. Memory work and drill activities are easy for them. Even cause-and-effect relationships can be comfortable for the SL to discuss if they are straightforward and nonnegotiable. However, when answers start to move away from being black and white, they tend to become uncomfortable and may have a more difficult time in discussing or writing about opinion-based subjects, such as assessing and writing about literature or evaluating the necessity of certain historical events.

➢ **The Best Approach for SL's:** SL's tend to be mostly visual in how they take in information and enjoy writing in workbooks and filling out information neatly on drill sheets. However, their visual intake seems to be more tied to language than to diagrams and drawings. It is not that they do not benefit from these visual aids as well. Rather it seems that they benefit more from the written word or looking at written numbers and formulas to memorize, taking into their mind through their eyes. They are great readers and are usually very developed in reading comprehension but can sometimes seem unfocused if they are already thinking or worrying about getting the next subject done and off their plate. Utilizing a white board so that they can take notes and write out reference cards is a great way to help them internalize the lesson you are teaching them when they are older.

Write down your observations and then later discuss more thoughts with your mentor about identifying and working successfully with a Structured Learner:

_____

_____

_____

_____

_____

_____

_____

_____

_____

_____

The Analytical Learner

The Analytical Learner (AL) likes to **live and learn while "staring at the box"**. The AL is contemplative and can come across at times as spacey and be off in what we like to call in our home "Narnia" at a moment's notice. However, in reality, they are usually more intense than other learner types and tend to like to go deeper into the subjects they study. Even when you think they are somewhere else, they are usually in tune with what you are trying to teach them. Here are some other characteristics to keep in mind about AL's:

➤ **Goal Setting for AL's:** An AL can easily see the logic behind the subjects you are teaching them in the context of a year's worth of school. They are "big picture" thinkers. So, give your AL the overall understanding of what you are going to cover that year as well as long-term goals and rewards that reinforce to them that thoroughness and depth are valuable qualities to be appreciated. Be sure that your goals are clear to an AL and that you minimize or eliminate "busy work" from the plan, which they will resist and deem as unnecessary. Providing an AL monthly or bi-monthly goals can also be useful in keeping them on task.

➤ **Schedules for AL's** Schedules for an AL are better off defined in broad terms rather than based on lesson-by-lesson details. AL's often do well with weekly schedules, defining what needs to be completed by the end of the week rather than a daily set of expectations. Although AL's are fairly independent, they can tend to get down too deep into one subject and get off track. So, checking with them regularly on how they are progressing in their school priorities throughout the week will help keep them moving along as they develop their time management skills.

➤ **An AL's Day:** AL's like to work independently and tend to operate like "mad scientists". They can be in a room that is so cluttered with half-started projects, unfiled papers, in-progress books, and various toys that you cannot quite remember what the color of the carpet is that you are pretty sure is still underneath it all. Younger siblings can be wandering in and out with regular household noises going on consistently, and the AL does not seem to take anything in besides their current project of concern. This tendency can be great in helping to develop focus, but it can also lead to disorganization and problems with meeting the weekly deadlines.

➤ **Subject Perspectives for AL's:** AL's are typically fond of math and science and tend to like explaining more than discussing subjects like history and literature. AL's like to answer verbal questions with the famous phrase, "It depends…". Your AL will then proceed to articulate the various angles possible to address the question, depending on their current perspective. AL's are great at debate, solving logic problems, project planning, and technical details. However, an AL typically does not gravitate as much towards the subjective subjects and must be encouraged towards exposure to art, music, literature, and creative writing.

➢ **The _Best_ Approach for AL's:** AL's also tend to be mostly visual in how they take in information, like SL's. Yet, they seem to benefit more from diagrams and drawings than lists and written language like the SL appreciates. Give them plenty of notice when you have deadline-oriented tasks and try to find ways to have them "kill two birds with one stone" when completing assignments. For example, AL's really like being able to do a writing assignment for history and know that this work takes care of their writing *and* history requirements for the day. If their writing or English program requires them to write about some arbitrary topic, change it to be about something that they are presently studying in literature, history, or science so it is more interesting and so that they can efficiently address work requirements simultaneously in those subjects as well.

Write down your observations and then later discuss more thoughts with your mentor about identifying and working successfully with an Analytical Learner:

_____

_____

_____

_____

_____

_____

_____

_____

_____

_____

_____

_____

_____

_____

_____

_____

The Community Learner

The Community Learner (CL) likes to **live and learn while "talking to the box"**. They love an audience and learn best while engaging in dialogue with them and giving presentations to them. CL's can have difficulty focusing on the goal at hand when they are more concerned about the delivery or presentation of what they want to say more so that the content of what they are learning. However, CL's are interesting because they can really excel at any subject when motivated to do so. Motivated CL's tend to be the ones who make school seem effortless when the SL's and AL's around them are sweating it out. CL's often gain this motivation when subjects have a public aspect to it. CL's tend to be excellent all-around communicators and leaders. Here are some other characteristics to keep in mind about CL's:

➢ **Goal Setting for CL's:** A CL is usually not concerned with goal setting or plans. However, a CL can be motivated to meet short-term goals by sharing what the ultimate point of each subject is and how completing those subjects well will contribute to whatever is the most motivating to them. For example, if your CL is passionate about being involved in a drama club, help them to understand that certain levels of competency in the basic subjects you assign them are a pre-requisite for participating in the club.

➢ **Schedules for CL's** Schedules are optional to the CL, so it is usually wise to wait and present formal written schedules to them in their later years. By this point, involving them to help create it, especially if they know it will be shared in a public setting, will help build the ownership necessary for the life-long skill of organization. Show them what they need to accomplish on a daily basis and tie their successful completion of their assignments with their ability to participate in extra social experiences.

➢ **A CL's Day:** CL's love to interact with other humans but stuffed animals or Lego creations work almost as well when they are younger. Narration is a great tool with this child so that they are explaining what they learned in the lesson to Grandma, to their baby brother, or to the stuffed inhabitants of their room. Having them present lesson information even back to a video camera can be engaging for them as well so that dad can be involved in their progress throughout the week as well. You can even **Skype** or **Facetime** (i.e. video conference) with grandparents who are out-of-state so that they may listen to your CL first hand![105]

➢ **Subject Perspectives for CL's:** Like an ML, CL's enjoy the creative subjects, although they are not as hands-on as an ML tends to be. CL's do well in most any of the subjects when they either know that they will present their final product to others or discuss their answers face-to-face

---

[105] http://www.skype.com; https://support.apple.com/en-us/HT204380

with their mom. However, they can tend to struggle with subject basics, like math facts, grammar mechanics, and science definitions if they do not see the point in learning them. As with ML's, CL's generally do not enjoy workbook or drill activities. So, try to build in other kinds of activities and lessons in between subjects that require seatwork. Great motivators for a people-oriented CL to ensure that their schoolwork is progressing satisfactorily include field trips, social clubs, and community service activities. Remember that they are excellent communicators and if they know they are going to verbally present or read something they wrote, they will be more engaged in the learning process than they would be otherwise.

➤ **The Best Approach for CL's:** CL's tend to be mostly **auditory** in how they take in information since they absorb more when interacting with another person rather than just reading to themselves. When you are unavailable to give lesson content and instructions to your CL in person, consider making voice recordings of spelling lists, dictations assignments, vocabulary drills, and so forth to help your CL stay engaged in the learning process while freeing you up to teach another child. Recordings of unabridged literature, either ones that you purchase, borrow from the library, or create yourself are also great ways to keep the CL learning at a level higher than what they would naturally gravitate towards in reading to themselves. Another great method is to utilize role play. This can be an effective way for your CL to take in history, science, and even math word problem lessons that are otherwise confusing to them. Finally, as they mature, continue to help them see the connection to how their "non-public" school activities help to support their goals of the work they do that is eventually presented to or shared with others. For example, if your CL is musical they need to practice scales as a non-public drill with diligence so that the technique improvements they gain from it will be obvious in their performance pieces that are going to be shared in public.

Write down your observations and then later discuss more thoughts with your mentor about identifying and working successfully with a Community Learner:

_____

_____

_____

_____

_____

_____

_____

The Struggling Learner

Your child can exhibit tendencies in any one, or even a combination, of the four learner types discussed above and yet also exhibit signs that they are struggling. Unfortunately, many parents mistake the learning challenges of a struggling learner with the incorrect assumption that if they just switched to a new curriculum, everything would be better for the child. However, in most cases, such a knee-jerk reaction can serve to create more problems rather than to solve them. So, if you suspect that your child's difficulties go beyond any issues of obedience training or work ethic issues (see chapter five), it may be time to seek help and support outside of your home.

On the other hand, if your child has already been diagnosed or identified to have one or more learning challenges and you are presently working with the appropriate doctors, occupational therapists, speech therapists, and/or counselors, then you would benefit from educating yourself with these additional homeschooling resources that are designed specifically for families who need to plan for how best to home educate their struggling learner or special needs child. Here are some **useful resources for the struggling learner** to consider.

1. *Choosing and Using Curriculum: For Your Special Child and Learning in Spite of Labels: Practical Teaching Tips and a Christian Perspective* by Joyce Herzog; Practical Christian perspectives and suggestions for educating a child with learning disabilities.

2. Dianne Craft's Materials by Dianne Craft; Many families who have a struggling student have found Diane Craft's guidance and programs to be useful. As a nutritionist with a BA and master's degrees in special education, she has developed several pragmatic tools and programs that have helped many families who have children with autism, Asperger's, ADHD, and auditory processing issues; just to name a few. *The Biology of Behavior* and *Brain Integration Therapy* programs are particularly popular. However, as always, consult with your child's doctor before beginning any kind of supplement regimen or dramatic dietary changes.[106]

3. *Homeschooling Children with Special Needs* by Sharon Hensely; Good discussion and more practical insight for educating a child with learning disabilities.

4. *Simply Charlotte Mason with Special Needs Children* by Sonya Shafer; Useful, nine-point article about ways to apply Charlotte Mason methods with your special needs student.[107]

---

[106] http://www.diannecraft.org/
[107] http://simplycharlottemason.com/blog/charlotte-mason-homeschooling-with-special-needs-children/

In addition to the resources listed above, you may also find useful support by visiting the website for **NATHHAN (National Challenged Homeschoolers Associated Network).**[108] This organization seeks to "equip parents to raise their children with special needs or disabilities confidently." This is a membership group, and you may also contact them directly by e-mailing them at Nathanews@aol.com.

Also, **HSLDA** has an excellent resource for parents of struggling learners.[109] They not only have tools, articles, and resources on their website and employ qualified, full-time staff members who can talk directly with parents about the questions and concerns about their special needs or struggling learner. For additional information that is specific to your child's challenge, be sure to spend significant time pouring over their "Resources" section.[110]

If you have a struggling learner, network within your homeschool group and find out about other parents who have faced and managed similar issues.

_____

_____

_____

_____

_____

_____

_____

_____

_____

_____

_____

_____

_____

_____

_____

_____

_____

_____

---

[108] http://www.nathhan.com/
[109] http://www.hslda.org/strugglinglearner/
[110] http://www.hslda.org/strugglinglearner/sn_help.asp

Take Another Look...

On page 141, look at the summary provided for you regarding the four learner types. Use a highlighter and mark comments or characteristics that you think identify your child's primary learning style. Now make notations on other learner styles that may also apply to your child as their secondary learning style. You may use a separate sheet for each child, if you wish. Extra copies are available in the Appendices section at the end of this manual, or you can check TBH's private Facebook group for the printable version.

What other questions or observations do you have about any of the learning styles discussed?

_____

_____

_____

_____

_____

_____

_____

_____

_____

_____

_____

_____

_____

_____

_____

_____

_____

_____

_____

_____

What observations do you have about your child that helps to indicate their primary and secondary learning styles? Make note of the environment and circumstances that help or hinder their learning experiences.

What Learning Style Does My Child Exhibit?

Characteristics	Moving Learner "outside the box"	Structured Learner "inside the box"	Analytical Learner "staring at the box"	Community Learner "talking to the box"
Setting Goals	Give your ML the primary "digestible" sections that they will be expected to perform each day but not to the level of detail that you would give to your SL. Set short-term, even daily goals for them.	Keep goals tangible and clear. SL's like to understand the details but are not always as long-term in their thinking as you may assume. Instead, give your SL monthly goals.	Share yearly goals with your AL with the "big picture". Demonstrate how each subject ties to those goals. AL's like to know that each assignment they are doing is purposeful. Set Monthly or bi-monthly goals.	Usually not concerned with plans or goal-setting. So, help them understand the importance of meeting short-term goals by tying them to their social interests.
Schedules	Reveal on a need to know basis each day when younger. By middle years, give a physical chart that they can update daily.	SL's love to check things off so give a daily written schedule with flexibility on order and timing of completion.	Give a weekly schedule with flexibility but be sure to follow-up daily to check progress. Help your AL see how to manage their time wisely.	Do not give a formal schedule until later years. Do share what they need to do daily and tie it to their extra-curricular interests.
A Typical Day...	Incorporate physical teaching methods when needed. Include plenty of breaks and allow various "locations" for school.	Provide a single, quiet, undistracted setting. Be prepared to assign very specific tasks since "depth" may not be your SL's strength. Can tend to exhibit difficulties in making decisions.	Allow the "mad scientist" in your AL some freedom to be somewhat scattered in their space as long as progress in learning organizational skills and subject content are evident.	Give your CL the opportunity to present their work in front of an audience or one-on-one with different visitors regularly. Use video technology to share progress outside of your home.
Subject Perspectives	Appreciates creative subjects and the arts. Great at observing information. Utilize project forums like science or history fairs to increase interest in difficult subjects. Sports, etc. can be great motivators.	Likes subject with clear cut "answers" like grammar, math, and languages. Dislikes subjectivity and assessing material past the typical answers. Motivate with participation in local "bee" competitions.	Partial to math, logic, and science. Likes to explain more than discuss answers to other subjects from various angles. Allow your AL to become involved in a robotics or chess club as a great motivator.	Enjoys creative subjects but not so "hands-on" as an ML. Able to excel at most any subject. Social clubs, field trips, and community service activities are great motivators for the people-oriented CL.
Best Methods to Apply	▪ Kinesthetic and experiential learning activities ▪ Visual ▪ Auditory	▪ Visual – writing lessons on a white board to promote note taking and creating own reference cards ▪ Drill or memory work	▪ Visual – diagram or draw out lesson information for math, grammar, spelling, etc.	▪ Auditory - delivering lessons, record drill activities, audio books ▪ Role playing ▪ Connect non-public study habits to future public presentations
Overall Strengths	▪ Creativity ▪ Enthusiasm ▪ Flexibility ▪ Physical Ed. ▪ Social Skills ▪ Observation Skills	▪ Organization ▪ Time Mgmt. ▪ Self-control ▪ Efficiency & Details ▪ Independent Learning	▪ Focused & Logical ▪ Thoroughness ▪ Independent Learning ▪ Technical Subjects	▪ Excellent Communicators ▪ Creativity ▪ Confidence ▪ Social Skills ▪ Public Presentations
Potential Weaknesses	▪ Organization ▪ Long-term focus ▪ Planning ▪ Self-control ▪ Independent Learning	▪ Depth ▪ Flexibility ▪ Subjective or Opinion Subjects ▪ Social Skills	▪ Organization ▪ Creativity ▪ Time Mgmt. ▪ Efficiency & Details ▪ Literature & Writing ▪ Social Skills	▪ Focus ▪ Thoroughness ▪ Independent Learning
Child's Name				

Again, please remember that **your child will not necessarily fit neatly into only one of the four styles and that we are mostly all hybrids to some degree**. In most cases, you will be able to identify a primary and a secondary learning style in your child. You will see that they will have strong tendencies towards one style more than the others on a regular basis, but they will not be just exclusively one learner type. At times, you may find yourself employing methods across the board, which is to be expected. Remember that any discussion about learning styles is simply meant to help in your teaching approach and you should not feel like you need to only stick to one method of delivery over another. So, use your judgment and do not be too quick to label them into a box to the point that you ignore their other tendencies. Also recognize that children change and develop over time and you will have plenty of opportunities to help them develop their strengths while helping them learn how to address their weaknesses.

In our household, **we have representation in each of the four learning styles**. I am a text-book SL and enjoy working with subjects with well-defined boundaries more so than the subjective topics. Yet my secondary tendency is as an AL. I was an instrumental musician for many years, excelling in technical execution, and also have a gift for visual arrangement. As a technical thinker and "big picture guy", my husband is primarily an AL. Yet his secondary tendency is as an ML since he is very creative in solving problems and organizing hands-on projects. Our oldest son primarily exhibited signs of an AL, but his secondary style was as a CL as he loved being around engaging people in many of his learning experiences. Our middle son is mostly an SL but also exhibits ML tendencies in the way he physically engages with the world around him. Finally, as our socially adept "performer", our youngest son is mostly a CL but also exhibits ML tendencies of needing to fully experience each subject he is learning. Like most families, we represent quite the "buffet" of learning styles!

Write down any other thoughts you or your mentor about identifying or working your child's primary or secondary learning style. Write down any concerns you have about any possible learning challenges your child has or may have.

_____

_____

_____

_____

_____

_____

_____

_____

_____

Understanding and Teaching Specialty Topics to "Learning Seasons"

In addition to understanding the **"Four C's"** discussed in the previous chapter and the learning styles discussed above, another perspective that is useful to understand when contemplating your teaching methods and priorities is the concept of learning "seasons". **It is important for you as a homeschooling mom to understand that the longer you teach your children, the more variability you will experience in the "seasons" they pass through.** In addition to the typical maturity stages that children experience, there are certain generalities that can be made about each season that they are in which may further serve to guide you in the curriculum you select as well as the teaching methods that you employ.

Remember that **the following discussions are generalities and are not meant to be a rigid assignment of expectations and that each child is unique in their development.** Rather it is just meant to serve as a general guideline of concepts to keep in mind when working with each particular stage of your child's growth and development. Also, keep in mind that your opinion and those of your mentor will vary greatly on this subject, depending upon what homeschooling approach they may be using. For some, my observations and suggestions may be a bit too much too early while others may think the points I make are not aggressive enough. Keep in mind that we all have the freedom as homeschoolers to take or leave observations and advice that is given in this or any topic. However, the point of this section is to recognize that homeschool seasons *do* indeed exist and understanding some of the general characteristics about these seasons will help you in your teaching processes and decisions. I will also refer to these "seasons" during Part II of the manual. Finally, please note that I have included some **additional resource supplements** that you may compliment the curriculum you are using for your child in whatever season that are currently in today.

> **Note to Leaders and Mentors:**
>
> *Consider organizing events by "season" in your group. This is not to replace whole family activities. Rather it is so that parents who are in a similar place in their homeschooling can network easily with other parents who are facing the same challenges and concerns. Also look to host events or networking opportunities with moms in a later season with moms who are still in an earlier season so that they can encourage and inform them about what is coming.*

List the ages and corresponding "seasons" of your child(ren) as you read this section.

_____

_____

_____

_____

_____

_____

Little Ones: Instruct

For families in the "first profile" that we discussed back in chapter three, **the line between life and homeschooling for their little ones can and should be blurred.** Often in their anxiousness to "get going on the homeschooling thing", these families tend to put unnecessary pressure on themselves to become too formal too early. In most situations, however, the normal activities you engage your toddler in are more than enough at this point. Allowing them to help you in the kitchen, giving them age-appropriate chores, and reading to them several times a day are wonderful ways to build a positive learning environment and to help aid in the development of their focus skills. Learning biblical truths and obedience training at this age, as we will discuss more in chapter five, are the most important areas of focus. However, here are some tools that can help guide homeschoolers with toddlers in the two to three-year range. In other words, **this season is all about giving your little ones loving and consistent instruction.**

Focus for Little Ones: Instruct
1. *Basic Christian truths*
2. *Real-life experiences*
3. *Beginning chores*
4. *Read aloud to them multiple times a day*
5. *Focus skills*
6. *Obedience Training*

1. *Slow and Steady, Get Me Ready* by Joy Oberlander; This book can provide helpful guidance to new parents who would like some creative ideas to help engage your little one's learning and focus skills. The book uses many ordinary, around-the-house items in the suggested activities and covers a different activity per week for ages birth through five years.

2. *Beginning Reading at Home* by Elizabeth Peterson; This is a hands-on, simple kit that helps you to introduce the alphabet names, sounds, and basic blends to your young child. It is really a pre-phonics program that is great for children in the two-to-four-year age range. You can supplement it by helping the child make their own "ABC" binder with magazine pictures or drawings that represent the various sounds and blends.

3. *Beginning Math at Home* by Elizabeth Peterson; This is also a simple, hands-on kit that introduces young children to basic counting, size, shape, and comparison concepts. It includes a fun "Going to the Moon" game that you can use to reinforce any skill you are teaching and then reward them with coins or candy.

K-2ⁿᵈ Grade: Instill

Children in this "season" are in a **stage where they are getting their feet wet.** For our boys, we always took *two years* for kindergarten to make sure that they were truly ready for first grade, both physically and mentally. So, preschool is really more the two-to-three or even four-year-old range and kindergarten is in the four-to-six-year-old range. That way, they are not starting first grade until they are well into being six years old. They are still doing plenty of hands-on activities around the house with their mom in first and second grade, but they are also increasing their seatwork load a little bit each year. **This "season" is all about instilling information and learning processes in them bit by bit** rather than trying to draw connections across subjects or require them to flow independently from subject to subject.

For the **kindergartner**, continue to make sure to build in plenty of breaks as well as "life learning lessons" as you did when they were younger. Let them interact with the world around them in age appropriate ways that continue to peak their curiosity while challenging them a step beyond where they will naturally go. However, you may want to add a focus on three main seatwork tasks at this age. The first and most important is **phonics. Everything else in their school career hinges on having a good handle on their reading skills.** There are MANY good phonics programs out there to help your child systematically learn to understand letters and blends in their smallest parts and then work up from there. Some programs that have a lot of "bells and whistles" can be quite expensive but may work well for your child. However, other programs are very basic in their approach but can be just as effective. The key is to get them to enjoy the process and take time to instill the rules without rushing through it. This is another reason why we take two years to go through kindergarten, so we can spread the phonics lessons over two years rather than cramming them into one. The second seatwork task is **handwriting.** Again, there are various methods and programs to do this and you will want to read reviews about these different options for the curriculum providers mentioned in chapter three. Sonlight and the Rainbow Resource Center have good reviews on several options, and *The Well-Trained Mind* by Susan Wise Bauer has an excellent chapter about "*The Pre-School Years*" that is most useful to read for

Focus for K-2 Season: Instill

1. *Take every area noted above in your "Little Ones" plan and intensify each priority.*

2. *Add seatwork including phonics, handwriting, and math in Kindergarten.*

3. *Add science and history by first grade.*

advice on handwriting skills and other subjects for preschool and kindergarten aged children. The third seatwork area is **math**. Based on the curriculum you have chosen, look and see what they have for their kindergarten program and you will most likely find it to be sufficient. One other seatwork option that you can consider is to add a **spelling** program in the second of their two kindergarten years, which often will aid and complement the phonics lessons that your child is learning. Here are some recommended phonics resources that you can consider when building your kindergartner's program.

1. *Phonics Pathways* by Dolores Hiskes; This is an excellent and affordable primer that can be used with kindergartners and even as a good review aid for older children who may be struggling with some aspect of their reading or spelling assignments.

2. *Teach Your Child to Read in 100 Easy Lessons* by Siegfried Engelmann; Many parents have experienced success with teaching their child to read using this text. It is highly scripted and takes the parent step-by-step and word-for-word through each lesson on what to say and how to teach it.

3. *The Ordinary Parent's Guide to Teaching Reading* by Jesse Wise and Sara Buffington; This is also a very useable, highly scripted text. It is written by the author who also contributed to *The Well-Trained Mind*.

First grade is quite a transition for most children. The day for them will be much longer than they are used to, so try to pace them on their work so that they do not get too tired or frustrated. By the time they are done with kindergarten, they have completed or should have nearly completed their phonics program and are usually ready to add history and science to their plate. Use the tools of narration and dictation to have your first grader repeat back the lesson content of what they are learning in history and science since their writing skills are still quite new and they can learn much more in these areas than they can put onto paper at this point. Also, be sure to incorporate plenty of reading practice for them so that they are independently reading books that are just slightly below their reading level so they can feel accomplished at what they are doing, but you will continue to read to them books that are above their reading level so that their language and comprehension skills continue to advance. Keep using this method throughout their school career with you. For a specific resource that you can use during the child's first grade year along with your regular curriculum plan, use *Reading Pathways*, also by Dolores Hiskes. It is a good practice follow-up for children who have completed the *Phonics Pathways* book. However, it can be used as extra reading practice for a child who has finished any good phonics program and needs to continue applying phonics principles beyond the completed introductory program.

By **second grade**, your focus is to have them on a fairly similar schedule to their first-grade year, but **they will just be a bit more settled in their routine, and you will see their confidence increase.** They will understand the expectations more clearly by this time and will spend this year really solidifying their reading and writing skills. This is also a good time to expand their curriculum to include lessons in drawing so that they can complement their literature, science, and history lessons with appropriate drawings. In addition, start to introduce literary ideas by using a resource like *Deconstructing Penguins* by Lawrence and Nancy Goldstone. This book is especially suited for children in the 2nd through 5th grade and provides parents a resource to help children understand the structure of the books that they read and how to discuss literature. This is a good pre-cursor to *Teaching the Classics* by Adam Andrews, which is ideal for 6th grade and up.

What other thoughts or questions do you have about working with Little Ones or children the K-2 "season"? Discuss them with your mentor when you meet.

_____

_____

_____

_____

_____

_____

_____

_____

_____

_____

_____

_____

_____

_____

_____

_____

_____

_____

3rd Grade – 6th Grade: Integrate

According to Webster, the word "integrate" means "to form, coordinate, or blend into a functioning or unified whole." **That is exactly what the 3rd to 6th grade season is all about: integration.** During this time, children have established a handle on the basics of math and language arts. They understand the process that you use to teach history, science, and literature and can continue to build on these structures over the years of this season. They are ready to increase the volume of information they are learning as well as the related assignments to go with them. As they walk through this season, they are ready to start seeing relationships among various subjects and how to apply universal writing techniques that will appropriately express their ideas about a particular subject. By the end of it, they are ready to start climbing the next academic mountain towards junior high school as they learn how to combine their skills into a "functioning or unified whole".

Somewhere **during third grade, many children experience a spurt of growth in their maturity.** Up until that time, Mom is still doing quite a bit of the child's writing assignments for them in subjects like science and history. She has also been fairly hands-on in helping them through their assignments, like math and spelling, and has pretty much been at their side the whole time. Yet when your child hits this milestone of being able to work more of their assignments independently, do not make the mistake of pulling away too much. They still need your help and support in several areas, and you will want to continue to help them to challenge their skills to the next level as they work through these middle years. This is also usually a good year to begin incorporating a study of composers and artists, if you have not yet begun to do so.

Focus for 3/6 Season: Integrate

1. Firm grounding in Christian faith and principles
2. Increased independence in completing specific assignments
3. Add outlining skills by 4th or 5th grade
4. Teach typing, introduce logic, and cause/effect thinking by 5th grade
5. Exposure to all forms of writing and poetry
6. By the end of this season; clear understanding of all subject basics and skills including math, science, history, grammar, spelling rules, handwriting, literary techniques, and writing.

In fourth grade, they have gained independence in many areas, and you can seek to step up the number of lines you expect them to be able to write in a paragraph for history or science. This is also a great time to introduce the concept of outlining. If the child is still struggling in their handwriting, take time now to introduce therapies or exercises that will help them address their difficulty with this skill. Here are some specific resources that you can use to help prepare them for this fourth-grade year.

1. *Self-Instruction in Handwriting* by Zaner-Bloser; This is a good general reference and lesson tool for parents to have when trying to help a struggling student. You may also consider having your child use a specially designed "grip" that goes onto the pencil and requires them to grasp the pencil in a certain way so that they must hold it correctly.

2. *Beginning Outlining* or *Outlining* by Remedia Publications can provide easy exercises to help your student understand the concept of outlining. Though the concepts are very basic, working through some of these lessons can serve to provide a nervous student with the confidence they need to write solid topical outlines. Then you can work with your student afterwards to build the skill of writing full sentence outlines.

3. *Teaching Students to Read Nonfiction* by Alice Boynton and Wiley Blevins; This is designed for classroom use. However, if you have a child who needs assistance in understanding the difference in how reading and absorbing information from non-fiction books differ from the goals of reading literature, you will find it to be a handy reference.

4. *Writer's Express Series* by Patrick Sebranek, Dave Kemper, and Verne Meyer; These books serve as good ready references no matter what writing program you are using. The series covers essentially the same material but at varying levels of depth and difficulty. *Writer's Express* is a good reference for children who are fourth grade and younger.

Fifth grade is really a time when the bridge from just learning "what" crosses over to also learning "why". Their assignments for science and history now go beyond just the "what" of the content being learned and extend to cover cause and effect connections and relationships. Many parents at this age begin to include "critical thinking" curriculum in their child's school priorities as they make this transition from the "what" to the "why", but formal logic should really wait until seventh grade.

Typically, sometime between fourth and fifth grade is also a good time to help your child **learn to type**. Often, their progress in writing assignments by this age are hindered greatly if the child has to constantly rewrite an entire assignment to correct the content or grammar points that you wish to address. Remove that barrier by simply making sure that they learn to type properly so that they will be encouraged to see how quickly they can make corrections and enhancements. We call this effort to improve their paper beyond just making corrections "crafting" their work.

The other issue that can sometimes hinder writing assignments at this age is providing your child with too broad of an assignment. Asking them to write about Julius Caesar is too broad; asking them to write about why many Roman officials wanted to see Julius Caesar removed from leadership is a better, more concrete assignment. Here are some specific resources that you can use to help prepare them for this fifth-grade year.

1. *The Homeschooler's Book of Lists* by Sony Haskins; This is a great tool to have at this age when memory work and needing to quickly look up information about history, government, religion, and science topics intensify, just to name a few. It also contains book lists, writing helps, great people summaries, and listings of famous quotations and speeches. It is so extensive that I can hardly summarize its content for you! It also comes with a companion CD.

2. *Minder Benders* by The Critical Thinking Company; This company has resource from Pre-K through 12th grade. Children solve puzzles and use their logic skill to figure out missing information as they find the solution to each problem. Use them for fun and do not require them to do a certain number of puzzles.

3. *Typing Instructor for Kids* by Individual Software Inc.; This is a fun process for kids to learn typing skills while moving their way through "Typer Island". Parents can set the success parameters while kids learn the correct hand position and finger number assignments as they drill small sets of letters at a time.

4. *Writer's Express Series* by Patrick Sebranek, Dave Kemper, and Verne Meyer; These books serve as good ready references no matter what writing program you are using. The series covers essentially the same material but at varying levels of depth and difficulty. *Write Source 2000* is good for children in fifth to eighth grade.

Just as second grade was a "settling year" where your child is familiar with the routine and expectations and they are maturing in their application of what they know to do, so **sixth grade also is typified by being a year of solidifying new skills.** By now, your child has learned to type their assignments and is skilled at outlining and writing a "tight" paragraph or short essay. They have a thorough understanding of the scientific method and how to record observations and write up an experiment page. They can translate to paper two or three pages of complex dialogue dictations from literature they are reading with a minimal number of mistakes, demonstrating their understanding of basic grammar rules and their proper application.

Another area of accomplishment is that they have a **solid grasp of the basics of literary construction**, including devices used for prose and poetry. They can identify the major plot points, theme, setting, and characters of whatever literature they are studying and can complete any relating writing assignments about these points. They should possess a **good understanding of how to express learned math formulas** and show their work adequately so that they can easily explain the approach they took for each assigned problem and can often successfully troubleshoot where a problem went wrong, if it is incorrect. Keep in mind that by the end of this year, you want to be confident that all such skills are under control. If there are any major issues they are having, address those first before moving on to their seventh-grade program. In general, focus on mastery for language and math skills while intelligent exposure is the goal for the humanities.

Here are some specific resources and reference tools that you can use to help prepare you for this sixth-grade year.

1. *Teaching the Classics* by Adam Andrews; I cannot recommend this resource enough. It is a tool that any parent can benefit from, regardless of what curriculum they are using, to teach literature. Mr. Andrews uses the "Socratic Method" of asking questions to the student and provides an exhaustive reference in his materials to aid the parent. He takes a very simple approach to help parents understand how to converse with their children about literature and takes parents through several practice pieces of literary samples in understanding how to identify the points of plot, characterization, setting, and theme as well as the importance of the author's perspective and context in which the piece was written. It is taught using a workbook and about six hours of DVD instruction. Mature students are even encouraged to go through the process with their parents so that they learn the methods together. For more information, visit Mr. Andrews' site at the **Center for Literary Education**.[111]

2. **Institute for Excellence in Writing**; This organization has too many useful tools to highlight separately here. However, Andrew Pudewa's Teaching Writing: Structure & Style is a useful course for any homeschooling mom to utilize, even if they are using a different program for writing. Also, many of their writing courses are offered in literary or historical units that can serve to compliment your plans for the year on a variety of interesting subjects. I highly recommend their offerings and supplemental materials![112]

3. *Reading Strands: Understanding Fiction* by Dave Marks; This tool also uses the "Socratic Method" but is more of a reference tool than a

---

[111] http://www.centerforlit.com
[112] http://iew.com

teaching course. It is a useful resource to have and complements the *Teaching the Classics* course mentioned above.

4. *Writing Strands: Evaluating Writing* by Dave Marks; This book is a useful tool for parents to have who wish to see sample writing and teacher evaluations of those writings. It is written by the same author who wrote the entire *Writing Strands* series that you may run across in your curriculum research efforts.

5. *Figuratively Speaking* by The Learning Works; This book contains forty lessons that you can fit in and around your regular English, writing, and or literature lessons so that your child begins to familiarize themselves with common literary terms used in prose and poetry.

What other thoughts or questions do you have about working with children in the 3/6 Season? Discuss them with your mentor when you meet.

_____

_____

_____

_____

_____

_____

_____

_____

_____

_____

_____

_____

_____

_____

_____

_____

_____

_____

_____

Junior High, High School, and Beyond: Inspire and Influence

Unfortunately, these are the years that tend to intimidate homeschooling parents the most. Right when they have succeeded in teaching their child up through sixth grade and establishing good moral foundations, insecurities creep in and Mom begins to doubt her ability to "go all the way". Be encouraged, however, that there are many resources available to you to help move you into these junior and senior high years, and you can be successful! Now is the time when you will begin to really see the benefits of the work you have done with your child to lay the groundwork for their independence. Your children may *want* you more when they are younger, but they *need* you more now than ever!

Know that this is the season where you want to **inspire them** while you continue to **influence them**. You will seek to help them think beyond themselves and see how everything they have been learning so far fits together in the way that God designed the world to work. He governs man's affairs, expresses Himself through art, and uses all aspects of language to communicate His purpose. As they establish their independence, children in this season will see the coherence of these concepts and seek in various ways over these years to figure out their unique place in God's supreme system of life.

Now this may seem like a large grouping, having junior high and high school lumped together. However, the reality of most homeschooling homes is that many children in the junior high age are starting to complete coursework that can be counted towards high school. In addition, the junior high years are the ones you look to in order to assist your child's ultimate transition into high school. So, if there is a certain subject that they need to focus on fully developing before reaching high school, now is the time to do it.

In **junior high**, Mom should perform **a "mid-point check-up"**. Take the seventh and eighth grade years not only to add new skills to their growing list of abilities and accomplishments, but also to coach the child in all-around confidence and development. This is often a good time to take a step back from it all to assess what has or has not worked for them up to this point. Revisit the information discussed about learning styles and ask for their input in understanding the teaching methods that work best for them. Make note of any maturity changes that may have taken place in their primary and secondary styles. Also, look to add some of your final new subject and skill areas by junior high, including calculator use, logic, and word study skills. Also, consider adding foreign language if you have not done so already. Remember that **by now they have all of the basic tools they need to be academically successful** and that these years are mostly about providing them challenging opportunities to practice and present their work and

> *Your children may __want__ you more when they are younger, but they __need__ you more now than ever!*

ideas. In particular, teaching writing can often be difficult for parents of teenagers. So, consider these additional resources that will **carry your teen through high school**.

1. Institute for Excellence in Writing; Just like I mentioned in the previous "season" section, this organization has too many useful tools to highlight separately here. However, Andrew Pudewa's *Teaching Writing: Structure & Style* is a useful course for any homeschooling mom to utilize, even if they are using a different program for writing. *The Elegant Essay* is also worth completing in junior high as an overall preparation for high school. Also, many of their writing courses are offered in literary or historical units that can serve to compliment your plans for the year on a variety of interesting subjects. I highly recommend their offerings and supplemental materials![113]

2. *Jensen's Format Writing* by Frode Jensen; This is a good, no-nonsense resource for junior and senior high school. It is written in a very dry style but has all of the basics in one resource and covers every imaginable writing topic.

3. *Writer's Express Series* by Patrick Sebranek, Dave Kemper, and Verne Meyer; These books serve as good ready references no matter what writing program you are using. The series covers essentially the same material but at varying levels of depth and difficulty. *Writer's Inc.* is good for high school and mature junior high students.

4. *Writing a Research Paper* by Edward J. Shewan; Published by Christian Liberty Press, this little guide is surprisingly packed with detailed guidance for your teen on all of the elements needed to write a successful research paper. Another reference you might consider for this purpose is *How to Write a Great Research Paper* by Beverly Ann Chin, Ph.D.

This is also a critical time to intensify your work with your child regarding any **discipleship milestones** you are working towards with them or any issues you need to address regarding character development issues that are impacting their ability to perform in their academics at the appropriate levels. Refer to chapter five for more information and discussion about this topic for this season.

In addition, really settle on what expectations you have of them regarding their **time management and organizational skills.** Some learner types will have an easier time with addressing these issues than others, but the fact is that some level of independence needs to be established at this point to fix a firm foundation for how high school expectations are going to be managed.

---

[113] http://iew.com

The final point to recognize in your preteen is that by twelve or so years of age, **their "worldview" has been established.**[114] The ways they view authority, their relationships with their parents, others, and with Jesus are all pretty much set by this time. You will also see that their broad attitudes towards systems outside of the home, such as societal issues, the political process, and other faiths are quickly forming. For more information about training your child in apologetics and helping them firmly establish their biblical "worldview", see chapter five. You can also look at the following formal training options that will aid you, helping them incorporate Christian principles into the skills and attitudes that have now and are still developing.

1. *Worldview Detective* by Adam Andrews of the Center for Literary Education builds on his original *Teaching the Classics* program previously mentioned. This 2-hour DVD teaching program "goes beyond the basic question of 'What does the author say?' and tackles the crucial follow-up question: 'Is the author telling the truth?'"[115]

2. *Answers Academy Curriculum* by **Answers in Genesis (AIG)**; If you have not familiarized yourself with AIG in your child's earlier seasons when looking for supplemental information for creation science, you need to do so now! They have a vast library of articles and information that are targeted to every season of homeschooling but are particularly geared for the junior high school or high school ages. This particular curriculum, the *Answers Academy*, is described as a "one-of-a-kind study series will equip you to understand

Focus for Junior High Season: Inspire and Influence

1. Do a "mid-point academic check-up".
2. Solidify their spiritual beliefs, character qualities and organizational skills.
3. Have student articulate their "worldview"
4. Recognize that they "are who they are going to be" and help them to identify and pursue their "passion".

---

[114] http://www.drjamesdobson.org/popupplayer?broadcastId=9c03ad4a-fd07-4cdc-aab5-e9defde728ae
[115] https://www.centerforlit.com/worldview-detective/?rq=worldview%20supplement

the world through "biblical glasses", and to answer the questions our culture is asking about the authority and accuracy of the Bible." It is organized into thirteen separate lessons covering Christian apologetics and other topics essential to understanding key pillars to the creation science perspective. This is a particularly great tool for dads to facilitate as an evening time or even summer study.[116]

3. *Starting Points* by David Quine of **Cornerstone Curriculum**; This is designed to be used as a one-year worldview primer covering theology, literature, and American History. It is divided into four parts: Building a Biblical World View, Examining Literature from the Biblical World View, Speaking the Biblical World View into the Culture, and Applying the Biblical World View to a Nation. This course is also useful for students who intend to use this author's three-year *Worldviews of the Western World* in high school. See the next section for more information about this program.[117]

> **Note to Leaders and Mentors:**
>
> *This is the when encouraging teens to learn how to speak in public becomes a critical issue for many families. Consider organizing an informal class on the basic skills of giving a presentation, providing your teens with an opportunity to practice in a safe environment with other homeschooling families.*
>
> *For a more formal approach, check out Toastmasters' Youth Leadership Program at www.toastmasters.org and find out how to start or join a group in your area.*

In addition, children at this stage have demonstrated to you over the previous years what interests them most so that you should be able to start making some general observations as to **how God is purposing them for their future**. The years ahead of them will serve to build experiences and maturity in all areas of life, but their basic views and interests are fairly established at this point. Now is the time to nurture theses interests into maturity!

Though it may seem a far off now, one other useful detail to consider during this season is your child's preparation efforts towards the mainstream college entrance exams. So first check out the basic requirements at the **College Board** as **PSAT, SAT, and ACT test preparation resources** are essential during this time.[118] Although many preparation websites exist that

---

[116] http://www.answersingenesis.org/

[117] http://www.cornerstonecurriculum.com/

[118] http://www.collegeboard.com/testing/; Differences between the ACT and SAT instruments can be confusing. Depending on your child's goals, however, it is good to understand their different points of emphasis. In general, colleges prefer the SAT when testing reasoning and verbal abilities. It has a greater emphasis on vocabulary and covers critical reading, math, and writing; recycling through the concepts within each of the ten sections of this 140-question exam. It takes 3 hrs. and 45 min. to complete and requires written answers for some of the math and, of course, the essay. It does not include science. The

are useful, some of the common sample test and preparation materials include *Kaplan's* SAT, ACT, and PSAT materials, the *Princeton Review SAT and PSAT* practice tests, the *New SAT* series, and *Walch Publishing's Daily Warm-Ups SAT Prep* books for math, reading, and writing.[119] These basic materials and more are available at resource centers like **Christianbook.com** and **Rainbow Resource Center**. Online or video-based resources for taking college entrance exams include **Princeton Review, College Prep Genius, Khan Academy,** or **OnToCollege with John Baylor**.[120] As mentioned in chapter one of this manual under "What about testing?", **James Stobaugh's newly designed *SAT Prep for the Thoughtful Christian* is another good resource**, and he often travels throughout the country delivering in-person seminars.[121] Even so, before making a final decision on which test to pursue or whether to do both, verify with the universities or colleges you are considering for your child to see if they only accept ACT or SAT scores or if they have a preference that would impact your plan.

Also remember that, even though students are not required to take it and it does not include an essay, certain scholarship opportunities are tied to the PSAT test if your child qualifies for the **National Merit Scholarship (i.e. NMSQT)**.[122] Though students may take the PSAT at any time, only results collected during the fall of their junior year count towards this opportunity. Even if your student is not a finalist or a winner of the scholarship, receiving a commendation level or advancing to the semi-finalist level is a great accomplishment to mention on a college entrance application. Even more, taking the PSAT is a good practice run for most anxious students and parents alike, which is why thinking about these points early helps.

In recent years the College Board has developed a **PSAT 8/9** and **PSAT 10**. While most parents do not engage in these tests, those who are motivated to introduce their child early to the format and skill of taking this standardized test may wish to consider it since they are intentionally designed for younger high school students. Why? Think about this. Many homeschooling students wind up taking the PSAT at least twice for the sake of practice and exposure to a group test taking environment. Yet that may not be the best approach since students are quick to realize that some of the concepts required to succeed on the PSAT, particularly for the math section, may not yet have been covered during their regular studies until they complete at least their sophomore year. As the test is only administered in

---

ACT, on the other hand, is a more of a straightforward achievement test. It covers more advanced math concepts and has a greater emphasis on punctuation; although grammar is important on both tests. It takes 3 hrs. and 25 min. to complete. It does include science, English, math, and reading, covering them as separate sections at a consistent level of difficulty across 215 multiple choice questions with an optional essay. See this link for more details: http://www.princetonreview.com/sat-act.aspx.

[119] http://www.mysatreview.com/

[120] http://www.princetonreview.com/; http://www.collegeprepgenius.com/; https://www.khanacademy.org/sat; http://www.ontocollege.com/families/

[121] https://www.forsuchatimeasthis.com/seminars.php

[122] http://www.nationalmerit.org/s/1758/start.aspx?gid=2&pgid=61

the October timeframe, a sophomore who has barely started their second year of high school may experience frustration in trying to navigate unlearned concepts, unless they do a great deal of preparation ahead of time.

While **local testing centers** may cater to serving the homeschooling community, families usually need to coordinate their student's registration to take PSAT tests through the local school system.[123] Furthermore, since the 8/9 and 10 version of the PSAT are relatively new, it is often difficult to find a school that even offers those, which may only leave you with the regular PSAT option. So, make sure that you research your options thoroughly and understand the various requirements (i.e. registration deadlines, preparation needs, approved calculators, identification requirements, etc.) prior to finalizing your decision.

Before leaving the subject of college entrance exams, there is one more option that needs mentioning called the **Classic Learning Test (CLT)**.[124] Spurred from growing concern of the Common Core's influence on standardized testing and other politically correct verbiage issues in the SAT and ACT, **Classic Learning Initiatives** developed an alternative college entrance exam.[125] It is gaining momentum as many colleges are now beginning to accept it in lieu of the traditional options of SAT or ACT. Even more, it is interesting to note the growing number of institutions that do not even require a standardized entrance exam at all as research continues to suggest that it is the least important indicator of potential student success that exists when compared to grades, community involvement, leadership experience, etc.[126] So, if you wish to pursue such testing, look at HSLDA's assessment of these three instruments for a complete overview before you decide which test or combination of tests is best for your child.[127]

What additional research do I need to perform in order to know what college preparation tasks are important for my child? Which test, or combination of tests, will they take and what study resources will be needed to ensure success?

_____

_____

_____

_____

_____

_____

[123] http://www.chsrc.org/psat
[124] https://www.cltexam.com/
[125] http://classiclearninginitiatives.com/
[126] http://www.fairtest.org/university/optional
[127] https://www.hslda.org/highschool/Newsletters/2016/December.asp

For most of the families that I have known over time and in our own experience, homeschooling the **high school** years is not the impossibly scary experience that most parents believe it to be. While there are definitely tough transitional issues you will face if your child has been in public, private, or charter schools all through eighth grade and you are just now bringing them home to educate them, most homeschooling families find the level of independence and cooperation their teenager exhibits at this stage to be surprisingly high. Will your high school student never give you a hard time or push back against the authority that you still have over them? Of course not! However, if you are careful at this point to **recognize the maturity gains they have made, build on those strengths, and transition successfully from being their coach more than their teacher**, you *can* effectively navigate this final season of homeschooling with them not only in respect to their academics, but, more importantly, in your relationship with them.

The following are additional curriculum and resource considerations for your teenager as they take their final steps in preparing for adulthood.

1. *Thinking Like a Christian* by David A. Noebel; Designed as a 14-week study for homeschoolers, this course is derived from the *Understanding the Times* material but is structured in a less intensive, more affordable format. The follow-up course to this is David Noebel's *Countering Culture: Arming Yourself to Confront Non-Biblical Worldviews*.

Focus for High School Season: Inspire and Influence

1. Ensure solid apologetics training is completed.
2. Transition your role from "teacher" to "coach".
3. Your teen is totally responsible for managing their school schedule and meeting deadlines.
4. Focus resources on extra-curricular activities that relate to their "passion" while supporting their academics.
5. Decide if your child is college-bound and prepare accordingly.
6. Train in life skills.

2. *Understanding the Times* by David A. Noebel; This is an excellent apologetics program for high school students in their junior or senior year. It looks at each of the five main worldviews, including Secular Humanism, Marxism/Leninism, Cosmic Humanism, Islam, and Biblical Christianity. The student not only learns how to defend their faith but gains a solid foundation in understanding how each of these faith systems compares with one another other across ten different major areas. Excellent for college-bound students and highly recommended that parents go through the program with their teen!

3. *Worldviews of the Western World* by David Quine of **Cornerstone Curriculum**; This is a three-year, comprehensive curriculum that includes seven areas of integrated study; philosophy/theology, literature, art, music, government, economics, and science history. By the time the child has progressed through the program, they will have earned 18 credit hours. So, families choosing this program will be basing most of their child's high school work on going through it.[128]

This is also the time to trim out excessive demands on your child's schedule and help them to really focus on one or two "extra-curricular" interests that relate to their "passion" and that they can spend time building "depth". For example, if you have a child who is inclined towards political issues and public service, make sure that you work to align them with organizations like **Generation Joshua, TeenPact,** or the **YMCA Youth in Government** programs.[129] You can also check out **Patrick Henry College** a private Christian institution known for its emphasis on training students for law and public office professions, for its programs that support high school.[130] They have teen leadership camps, writing mentors, and on-line courses, such as HSLDA's *Constitutional Law*, that you may want to explore for your child. If your teen wants to enter the medical field, check with your local universities for internship or high school workshop opportunities that encourage children to explore medical career options.[131] If you have a child who thinks they want to be a pilot or is interested in computer or aerospace engineering, check out exploratory programs and camps offered from a specialized institution like

---

[128] http://www.cornerstonecurriculum.com/Curriculum/wvww/wvww.htm

[129] http://www.generationjoshua.org/; This is a Christian, civic responsibility club with chapters throughout the country that is under the organizational leadership of HSLDA.; http://www.teenpact.com/; Also a Christian civic responsibility organization, but it is centered on annual workshops and training camps; http://www.ymca.net/youthandgovernment/; This program is a hands-on experience for students to become more connected with their local state government structure and processes.

[130] http://www.phc.edu/

[131] For example, Midwestern University in Glendale, AZ offers summer medical programs and volunteer opportunities for high school students on a regular basis. See this link for more information. https://www.midwestern.edu/. Grand Canyon University (https://www.gcu.edu/) has options as well for STEM, Cybersecurity, and exploratory camps via their Summer Institute programs.

Embry-Riddle Aeronautical University.[132] Another option for this child would be to participate and compete in a **FIRST** or **VEX** robotics competition program.[133] Are they interested in going into ministry work? Work with your church to have them participate in short-term mission trips or even possibly intern at your church's office or under the care of a pastoral leader.

I could go on and on with examples, but you get the idea! **Take their passion and then research what exploratory options to build on their strengths exist in your community and around the country.** What other activities and experiences, beyond their day-to-day academics, can help to nurture and sharpen their passion and natural interests? It is also a good idea to introduce your child to professionals who already work in their potential field of interest, so they can get first hand feedback or even shadow them to learn about the realities that go along with that particular type of work. **Remember that the rule of thumb to master any kind of life skill or job is ten years or ten-thousand hours of focused practice and progression.** So, allow your motivated teen to begin working towards their life's future passion sooner rather than later! They may even be able to start collecting valuable **letters of recommendation** from established leaders in the area of study or work that interests them.

Within this season, it is also essential that parents ensure their teens obtain all of the **life skills** needed to not just survive but to thrive. Students who fail in college usually do so not so much due to poor academics as to insufficient self and time management skills. Can they get to class on time, eat properly, communicate appropriately, manage their clothing, and take care of other living logistics well? If the answer is "no" or "I don't know", then plan to address such areas before they complete high school. This includes ensuring that they can drive and perform basic maintenance on a vehicle, including oil and tire changes.[134]

> *Note to Leaders and Mentors:*
>
> Sometimes families desire leadership opportunities beyond the idea of scouting programs, and there are so many to specialized options choose from! Even the **Home School Foundation** has a **Youth Ambassador** option for teens. The following is a listing of just a few established leadership program opportunities to consider for your child.
> - *4-H Club-business, agriculture, citizenship, etc. (ages 5 to 21 years)*
> - *Civil Air Patrol – pilots, flight, or the air force (min. age is 12)*
> - *JROTC-military (high school program in connection with local public school)*
> - *Police Explorers- law enforcement (min. age is 14)*
> - *Naval Sea Cadets –naval skills (13-17 yrs.; min. age is 11 for the junior group)*
> - *Young Marines-military; law enforcement (min. age is 8)*

---

[132]http://www.erau.edu/; http://summercamps.erau.edu/camps/index.html#prescott

[133] http://www.usfirst.org/; https://www.vexrobotics.com/

[134] https://drivingmba.com/ (fee based service example); Search HSLDA for parent-led options at this link: https://www.hslda.org/highschool/academics.asp#driversed or http://www.usdrivertraining.com/

For **further information** about preparing yourself and your child to move through this season of homeschooling during their junior high as well as high school years, consider the following resources for inspiration and ideas.

1. *The Balanced High Schooler: Getting Parents and Homeschooled Teens "On the Grid" for College and Beyond* by Carol Gary; Time for a shameless plug of my newest title! I am so excited about this mentoring tool for parents and teens that takes your relationship with them on a forty-day journey, exploring preferences, spiritual development, course planning, life skills, goal setting, college planning, vision casting, and so much more! Each "day" is an easily digestible read that starts with a scripture, covers a single topic, and finishes with a writing task, a discussion guide, and a prayer point.[135]

2. *The High School Handbook* by Mary Schofield; Although limited in its distribution to purchase it, this is a useful tool to address all issues relating to homeschooling a high school student including record keeping and getting into college.

3. *Homeschooling High School: Planning Ahead for College Admission* by Jeanne G. Dennis; Very practical and comprehensive guide that covers everything you need to know for homeschooling through high school. Forward is written by Michael Farris, co-founder of **HSLDA** and **Patrick Henry College**.

4. *Homeschooling the Teen Years: Your Complete Guide to Successfully Homeschooling the 13 to 18-Year-Old* by Cafi Cohen and Janie Hellver; This comprehensive text helps families to prepare for the high school years by providing loads of resource information on what they need to know and when as well as helping parents to assist their child in making the final transition out of school. This text is broad enough in its coverage of topics to be particularly useful to the family who has perhaps not homeschooled prior to the teen years and needs extra support on the basics.

5. *Homeschoolers' College Admission Handbook: Preparing your 12 to 18-Year-Old for a Smooth Transition* by Cafi Cohen; This book covers everything you would expect from calculating credits to preparing transcripts. It also has useful information about issues that a student faces when entering college, such as financial aid and interview processes.

---

[135] Read more about this title on Carol's home page (http://www.thebalancedhomeschooler.com/), including access to a full table of contents. The paperback or Kindle format can be ordered directly from Amazon.com. To obtain the searchable, clickable PDF version, order directly from my site. Send your proof of purchase to Carol (orders@thebalancedhomeschooler.com) to obtain the printable PDF version of the "Grid" document used throughout the discussions.

6. **HSLDA**; Homeschool Legal Defense Association has many resources available to encourage you to "stay the course" through high school.

7. Let's Homeschool High School is a website that provides a great deal of information and resources to families navigating the high school years and even post-graduation considerations.[136]

8. *Reaping the Harvest* by Diana Waring; This book is a MUST READ for any parent of children in the junior and senior high season. Though there are no "nuts and bolts" here, it is very inspiring and heartfelt. It is a follow-up to her earlier book called *Beyond Survival*.

9. *Senior High: A Home-Designed Form+U+la* by Barbara Shelton; This is an encouraging text that covers eight sections: Out of Fear and Into Freedom, Requirements, College, Promotion, and Graduation, Record-keeping System, Potpourri of Curriculum Supplements, Grading Guidelines and Portfolios, Personalizing All This Stuff, Lifestyle of Learning Applications, and a Resource Section.

10. *Teaching Highschool at Home* by Dr. Jay Wilde; This author of the wildly popular, Christian Apologia Science Curriculum has produced an encouraging and informative audio CD that you can use to jumpstart your high school planning thoughts.[137]

11. *The Ultimate Guide to Homeschool Teens* by Debra Bell; Once again, as with *The Ultimate Guide to Homeschooling*, Debra Bell provides an immensely comprehensive and practical tool with this one focusing on the high school years. I recommend that moms start reading this tool when their child is starting 7th grade since there is a significant section at the beginning devoted to points of consideration for your junior high school student prior to starting high school coursework.

What questions do you have about navigating the junior high or senior high school season? How will you nurture their "passion"?

_____

_____

_____

_____

_____

_____

---

[136] http://letshomeschoolhighschool.com/
[137] http://www.apologia.com/

This is where we discuss the **"and Beyond"** part of this section. Now your child has nearly or even officially completed their homeschooling season with you but is most likely still in your home: perhaps still deciding what path God will lead them towards. Allow them to take the time they need after high school with your guidance to follow the Lord's leading and help them make this final transition into adulthood. You are now transitioning away from your role as their coach to beginning a life-long friendship with them.

Remember that not all young adults will or should attend a traditional college or university. Some of them will be well suited for a path at a **technical college** or may enter a **specialized apprenticeship or vocational training**. Still others may choose to **transition directly into the work force or their family's business**.

On the other end of the spectrum, some young adults will take the steps that are necessary to enter a branch of the **military** or even prepare themselves to go into **full-time missionary work**. Remember that where your child's passion and gifting lies is where they will be able to accomplish the most for God's Kingdom and where they will experience the greatest degree of personal satisfaction. For further guidance on helping your child in making these decisions and choosing a direction, I highly recommend the *Career Direct Guidance System* software tool that is published and sold by **Crown Financial Ministries**.[138]

However, since a majority (over 70%)of children will seek a path that necessitates a college education, you will want to fully explore these options, preferably while they're still in high school.[139] That way, you can take advantage of any scholarship or grant opportunities that need to be applied for early.[140] Options for your child to attend **college** are not what they used to be. When most of us were in the season of graduating from high school and possibly moving on to college, you either started out at a **community college**, attended one of the state universities, or your family may have been financially able, perhaps with some type of scholarship assistance, to help

> *Remember that where your child's passion and gifting lie is where they will be able to accomplish the most for God's Kingdom and where they will experience the greatest degree of personal satisfaction.*

---

[138] https://www.crown.org/career/
[139] http://www.amazon.com/Will-College-Pay-Off-Important/dp/1610395263
[140] There are many websites like http://www.scholarships.com/ that can aid you in your search for scholarship information. However, your best source of information still rests with the institution of choice that your child would like to attend. Find out what they offer and figure it out early!

you to look at options that were available at an **out-of-state public or private university**. Of course, these are still viable options for many families today. So, parents who are looking for their child to attend a specific college or university should spend time understanding that specific college's admissions process. Request a course catalog and understand all of the entrance requirements: essays, special exams, expected standardized testing, etc. It is also essential for families to understand the financial obligations of that school as well as aid and scholarship options that are available, as mentioned previously.

Despite skyrocketing costs for higher education, there are some institutions that are getting creative with containing those costs or helping students to pay for their education beyond typical grant or scholarship opportunities. For example, **Pensacola Christian College** in Northwest Florida has recently been aggressively marketing a $7,500 yearly tuition, room and board program to attract students to their campus as well as a get "one year free" program for four-year students.[141] It will be interesting to observe in the coming years how competition and a desire to entice student attendance at their university, especially homeschoolers, will prompt even more compelling offers and arrangements. Private Christian institutions like **Grand Canyon University** in Arizona also provide generous scholarship programs for homeschooled students who excel in various areas (i.e. academically, athletically, musically, etc.) or choose to enter a specific field that the school is especially interested in promoting, such as engineering as an example.[142] Still other universities may take an even more creative stand in trying to contain costs for prospective students who demonstrate a pronounced need for financial assistance by offering a work-for-tuition campus program, such as **College of the Ozarks** (i.e. "Hard Work U") where students who are capable but have little financial means can graduate debt-free![143] The bottom line, then, is that there are so many more choices that exist today that you will want to consider even beyond attending a competitively priced "brick and mortar" university.[144]

The first and most obvious trend in alternative college credit and degree programs is that so many of them are available on-line now. No longer must families physically send their child to an out-of-state university to receive a degree from their institution of choice. Some of these degree options are offered by on-line only schools or are offered as an option through a traditional college or university setting. Through on-line, remote, and correspondence tools and curriculum, students can still live at home while earning a college degree on very flexible schedules and at a much lower cost than traditional arrangements for higher education. Nontraditional distance

---

[141] http://www.pcci.edu/
[142] http://www.gcu.edu/
[143] http://www.cofo.edu/
[144] *The Fiske Guide to Colleges* by Edward B. Fiske or *Barron's Profile of American Colleges* are texts that are published annually and help provide the basic information about a plethora of institutional options.

methods and options can be discovered by checking out *Bears Guide to Earning Degrees by Distance Learning* by Mariah Bears.

Second, because students have more options today to take college courses in high school that will give them **dual credit for college and high school**, many are entering college with several credits already earned. Such credits are also usually available at a fraction of their normal price. For example, at Grand Canyon University, the nation's leading distance learning institution for undergraduate and graduate degrees, homeschoolers via their **ALPHA (Alliance Program for Home School Achievement) program** can take required courses as early as their sophomore year of high school at about one-fourth of their original cost.[145]

In addition, students can take **AP (Advanced Placement) exams** and generally net about six hours of college credit, if they have been doing honors-level work. AP is considered the "gold standard" and is administered by the College Board. Parents cannot just label any course as an AP course since it must be recognized by the College Board as such. So, if you are interested in having your child take an AP course, it is best to align with an approved organization that serves homeschoolers and can offer you that option.[146]

Students can also take **CLEP** (College-Level Examination Program) exams to count towards college credit requirements.[147] Choices like these means lower costs and less time spent in their college or university of choice. Some organizations like **Unbound** or **Lumerit Scholar Unbound (formerly CollegePlus)** even specialize in helping these students accelerate their college plans.[148] They do this by working through a **coaching program that prepares them to choose a degree program and how to study for CLEP/DANTES tests,** which then can count towards college credit towards the various topics studied.[149] Then the student spends one to two years taking the CLEP/DANTES tests followed by three to six months of additional on-line or on-site courses offered at a designated college, after which they earn their degree. Coaching programs like this can appeal to a student's desire to just get it done while at the same time earning a degree for a fraction of the cost of a typical program and avoiding the social issues that go along with attending a traditional college. From beginning to end, this program costs typically costs under $17,000 total for a degree under their standard program, which is a dramatic difference compared to the average four-year public institution costing over $96,000 or a whopping $191,000 for a private institution.[150] Do be aware, however, that some universities limit the number of college credits a freshman can earn before they lose their

---

[145] https://www.gcu.edu/academics/educational-alliances/alliances.php
[146] https://academy.hslda.org/courses/ or https://www.forsuchatimeasthis.com/ap.php
[147] http://www.collegeboard.com/testing/
[148] https://getunbound.org/; https://getunbound.org/hscom/about-collegeplus
[149] DANTES stands for Defense Activity for Non-Traditional Education Support. It is mostly designed to support returning military personnel and prepares students for DSST (Dantes Subject Standardized Tests). See http://www.dantes.doded.mil/index.html#sthash.8NbkweG3.dpbs for more information.
[150] http://www.collegedata.com/cs/content/content_payarticle_tmpl.jhtml?articleId=10064

freshman status, which may impact scholarship eligibility. So, know the limit beforehand.

If you are **questioning the appropriateness of the traditional college** route for your child, consider reading *"Is College Worth It?"* by William Bennett. This book covers a pragmatic look at whether your student should consider entering the job market directly after high school. Whether your child is college-bound or has other plans in mind, this is the time to help them make that final transition into adulthood, ensuring that they follow their passion while staying true to God's calling in their life.

For **further information** about the college admissions process, your best approach is to directly connect with the admissions counselors for the institutions under consideration for your child. Requirements will often vary greatly on what each college or university requires. So, building those bridges often and early is a great strategy to employ. In addition, you may also wish to look at these other research resources for the college-bound student.

1. *And What About College? How Homeschooling Leads to Admissions to the Best Colleges and Universities* or *Homeschoolers' College Admissions Handbook*, both by Cafi Cohen. The first chronicles a homeschooling mom's journey in navigating college admissions for her two children. Since this was updated in 2000, the detailed advice of navigating college admissions will be outdated. However, the theme of tenacity Cafi describes in her experience can still be useful to modern-day moms, especially if you appreciate a "lifestyle of learning" vibe to the guidance you receive. She does also spend a good deal of time covering college alternatives.

2. *The Balanced High Schooler: Getting Parents and Homeschooled Teens "On the Grid" for College and Beyond* by Carol Gary; Though this mentoring journey covering forty pointed topical exercises is a powerful experience for any homeschooled teen and their parents, it is particularly suited for the college-bound student. In addition to the points mentioned about it in the previous section, it engages teens to work with their parents in the detailed planning, documentation, and research requirements for college.[151]

3. *The Guidance Manual for the Christian Home School: A Parent's Guide for Preparing Home School Students for College or Career* by David Callihan and Laurie Callihan. Again, though some of the

---

[151] Read more about this title on Carol's home page (http://www.thebalancedhomeschooler.com/), including access to a full table of contents. The paperback or Kindle format can be ordered directly from Amazon.com. To obtain the searchable, clickable PDF version, order directly from my site. Send your proof of purchase to Carol (orders@thebalancedhomeschooler.com) to obtain the printable PDF version of the "Grid" document used throughout the discussions.

material found here is dated, there are still good nuggets of wisdom to be found in this handbook.

4. *The HomeScholar Guide to College Admissions and Scholarships: Homeschool Secrets to Getting Ready, Getting In, and Getting Paid* by Lee Binz, founder of the **HomeScholar**.[152] Lee's materials are currently considered the most practical and relevant resource options for helping homeschooling parents navigate the college admissions process. She is also the author of several recordkeeping reference books including *Comprehensive Homeschool Records* and *Setting the Record Straight* as well as a myriad of other books that focus on high school and college preparation topics.

What other thoughts or questions do you I have about helping my child with this final transition into adulthood? Discuss more ideas with your mentor when you meet.

_____

_____

_____

_____

_____

_____

_____

_____

_____

_____

_____

_____

_____

_____

_____

_____

_____

_____

_____

---

[152] https://www.homehighschoolhelp.com/

Organizational Teaching Methods: Note-booking, Unit Studies, Lapbooks and Learning Centers

Another point to consider when establishing your home school is that you will sometimes run across a particular organizational method to teaching that you can feel free to incorporate into any homeschool approach or related curriculum that you choose. **Options beyond basic note-booking** are the concepts of unit studies, lapbooks, and learning centers.[153]

Unit studies are an approach to education that ties several subjects together around one topic. For example, the Civil War, the Renaissance, great inventors, or ancient Egypt are all potential good topics for a unit study. It is a very hands-on approach as students incorporate crafts, projects, dramas, writing assignments, literature, history, biographies, art, music, cooking, and other elements that relate to the topic of study. Often, unit studies are great to utilize in a co-op setting with other families. Math and science are usually handled separately, outside of the unit study structure.

Lapbooks are graphic organizers made from a simple system of file folders, paper "windows", and mini-books that pull all information studied about a specific topic into one physical place. Parents often must see many examples of completed lapbooks to comprehend how they work, but many major cities have workshops available where families can practice putting them together under the guidance of a seasoned parent or consultant. We used this methodology with science when our oldest was in kindergarten and the early grades. They are fun and very "hands on" but can be quite time consuming to implement. They can be as simple or elaborate as you choose and can also help organize information to be presented at a homeschool support group history, art, or science fair. For more information on using lapbooks, you may reference the books at the end of this section or check out **Lampstand Press**, the publisher of Tapestry of Grace mentioned earlier in chapter three.[154] They have templates and lap book kits that can be useful to parents who are interested in this tool. Another company that provides lapbook tools but with a focus on history is **Homeschooling in the Woods**.[155]

One final curriculum aid worth mentioning is the concept of **learning centers** in the home. This is a particularly good strategy for homes with young children since hands-on activities are very much a part of each day's experiences. The basic concept is that you have different areas in your home that are set up to promote a certain kind of activity. The child can then "float" from one area to another freely and have everything they need there to accomplish a learning task. For example, you would have a reading center that is set up with lots of good books and comfortable seating in an undistracted area. Your math center would be stocked with materials and manipulatives necessary to learn the arithmetic lesson for the day. Another part of your house can be set up with art and craft supplies, either just for general activities or related to a

---

[153] Note-booking is simply the practice of organizing your student's work into binders. Parents may choose to have one binder per subject or just create one large representative binder across subjects annually.
[154] http://www.lampstandbookshelf.com/
[155] http://homeschoolinthewoods.com/index.html

lesson you are teaching. Still another area may have interested activities and resources for performing science experiments. Another example could be a music area and still another area could be a place for putting on performances or giving presentations about the lessons they are learning.

Related to this idea of learning centers is that you will want to **physically figure out where school takes place in your home**. While it is true that school happens all over the place, you will generally have a **designated spot for your child to do independent, quiet work and another area for gathering as a group** or teaching them. Make sure everything, including books and supplies, is handy and, ideally, you will have a place available that you do not have to clean up all of the time. We used to do school at the kitchen table, which works well for many families, particularly when they are young. However, as they mature, being in a public setting all of the time does not work well and it becomes a hassle to have to put everything away so that you can have dinner or have guests over to your home. At the same time, be careful of falling into the trap that a fair amount of homeschoolers experience in the beginning. Avoid setting up a school inside your home that looks and feels like a public schoolroom. Let your home be your home and your teaching space be your teaching space, if you can. We used a loft in our previous home that worked great as well as our current public pass-through room that is near our boys' bedrooms. Both are examples of common areas that can hold shared desks, bookshelves, a storage closet, and a possibly a couch nearby. When they were younger, I could also coach them on their music practice while still being near the other boy to answer questions, etc. for school. Children can also use their rooms for independent work, if they have shown the maturity and focus to be able to do so. That leaves the remaining areas free to just be a home so that school work, projects, etc. are (for the most part) not strewn everywhere about the house.

Let your home be your home and your teaching space be your teaching space, if you can.

For additional information about these methods, I recommend you use these books.

1. *Big Book of Books and Big Book of Projects* by Dinah Zike; These are the original books that introduced families to the concept of using lapbooks. They are practical and provide many useful templates for families who want to get going on their projects.

2. *Five in a Row Curriculum* by the Lambert family; Provides unit-study style curriculum that uses literature as its spine. Suitable for young children up to the age of twelve.[156]

---

[156] http://fiveinarow.com/

3. *Geography Matters* Products by GeoMatters; Many families enjoy using their various products, such as their "*Trail Guide*" books as a spine for planning their unit studies. They also offer several lapbooking resources to help organize or compliment your student's projects.[157]

4. *How to Create Your Own Unit Study* by Valerie Bendt; Explains ways to create your own unit study and even gives starting information for several subjects.

5. If you are interested in unit studies, **KONOS** is considered the "granddaddy" of unit study curriculum if creating your own seems too overwhelming.[158]

6. *How to Set Up Learning Centers in Your Home* by Mary Hood; Mary writes from a "Lifestyle of Learning Approach", but her concepts can be adapted to just about any setting or homeschooling perspective. This method is particularly useful for households with younger children.

7. *Trisms Curriculum* by Linda Thornhill; This curriculum combines critical thinking with a unit style approach by blending "literature, biographies, historical fiction, cultural studies, and most varieties of reference materials." It is also considered a classical curriculum, yet it only focuses on the Dialectic and Rhetoric Stages, excluding the Grammar Stage (i.e. 1st -4th grade) altogether.[159]

8. *The Ultimate Lapbook Handbook* by Tami Duby; This is an updated resource that takes the lapbook concept and explains it and several related options in greater detail.

9. *The Weaver Curriculum* by AOP; This is unit-study curriculum published by Alpha Omega Publications. Marketed as a biblically integrated, family-friendly, hands-on curriculum, families who wish to teach multiple ages and wish to have a program take them from kindergarten through high school, this program is worth a look!

What other ideas or questions do you have about different methods or organizational tools you can use to creatively teach your child? _____

_____

_____

_____

[157] http://www.home-school-curriculum.com/
[158] http://www.konos.com/
[159] http://www.trisms.com/

"Laminators, Printers, and Timers; Oh My!"

Every homeschooling mom needs to make sure that she is equipped with a certain laundry list of basic tools, like crayons, paper, pens, pencils, glue sticks, etc. So be sure to put together your **basic supply and science experiment lists** every year so that you are not derailed when you cannot locate these essential items. However, here are some other standard and not-so-standard items listed in no particular order that you may want to also incorporate into your resource list to be used throughout the years at various times and seasons.

1. **Webster's 1828 American Dictionary of the English Language**: Did you ever think about how God spoke our entire universe into existence? **Language is one of the most powerful creations of all.** Unfortunately, the more "modern" our references become, the more we slip unknowingly into educational patterns that mirror humanistic thoughts rather than God's. Take the word "education" for example. If you looked up this word over a span of 180 years using Webster's, you would find evidence of definition disintegration such as this:

   EDUCA'TION, n. [L. educatio.] The bringing up, as of a child, instruction; formation of manners. Education comprehends all that series of instruction and discipline which is intended to enlighten the understanding, correct the temper, and form the manners and habits of youth, and fit them for usefulness in their future stations. To give children a good education in manners, arts and science, is important; to give them a religious education is indispensable; and an immense responsibility rests on parents and guardians who neglect these duties.[160]

   (noun) Education
   The act or process of educating; the result of educating, as determined by the knowledge skill, or discipline of character, acquired; also, the act or process of training by a prescribed or customary course of study or discipline; as, an education for the bar or the pulpit; he has finished his education.[161]

   Main Entry: ed·u·ca·tion; Pronunciation: \ˌe-jə-ˈkā-shən\; Function: noun; Date: 1531; 1 a : the action or process of educating or of being educated; also : a stage of such a process b : the knowledge and development resulting from an educational process <a person of little education> 2 : the field of study that deals mainly with methods of teaching and learning in schools.[162]

   Do you notice the dramatic shift of education being defined in comprehensive terms to one that is limited to acquiring knowledge?

---

[160] http://webstersdictionary1828.com/Dictionary/education; Webster's 1828 Dictionary
[161] http://www.definitions.net/definition/Education; Webster's 1913 Dictionary
[162] http://www.merriam-webster.com/dictionary/education; Modern Merriam-Webster's Dictionary

Do you see how education has changed from being the "parent's" responsibility to that of the "school's"? Nowhere is "religious education" or "discipline of character" to be found any longer. Do you see the correlation between the development of the modern school system in the late 1800's to the shift in how the definition reads? **Words are indeed powerful, so be sure to equip your child to know how to source the best definitions to glorify God and reflect truth.** Any version, then, of *Webster's Dictionary* that is past 1828 has a certain amount of "political correctness" incorporated that needs to be addressed. You may purchase the dictionary or at least reference the on-line site as needed. There will, however, be some modern terms that just will not show up in the 1828 version, so having a trustworthy online version or other reference to fill in those gaps is useful too. Do also keep these issues in mind when having your child use other reference and encyclopedia sources.

2. **Computer with a Color Printer/Copy/Scanner Machine:** In these modern times, homeschoolers need to make an investment in a reliable computer as well as a color printer/copy/scanner machine. Not only will a computer help your child in the **research process** for school assignments, but it is very difficult to investigate the homeschooling options available to you in terms of tools and curriculum if you do not have regular and reliable access to a computer. Be sure, however, to invest in a reputable solution for your security needs so that your child does not accidentally venture into inappropriate websites or encounter other undesirable technology intrusions, such as SPAM e-mails or unwanted pop-ups.[163] One other thing that you will find over time is that there are some very good websites for **printable worksheet and forms** that you can start putting in your "favorites" for times when you need a specific form.[164] Your printer also **should have copy and scanning capabilities** so that you can place full books on the flat bed platen to make copies as needed and scan items into your system, such as hard copy photos, hand-drawings, certificates, programs, and the like for either sharing or record keeping purposes.

3. **Digital Camera:** Though you most likely already own one or at least have a smartphone, you may not have thought about your digital camera playing an important role in your home school. Digital cameras are great for taking photos of field trip experiences, projects, and science experiments that you wish to document or share with other family members. **Make sure it can also take video clips** so

---

[163] For suggestions on specific media protection tools visit Focus on the Family at http://www.focusonthefamily.com/parenting/family-safety.
[164] Examples of two reputable sites that provide good information for homeschoolers include www.enchantedlearning.com for school-oriented worksheets and www.donnayoung.org for planning worksheets.

that you can share video files with loved ones who are out-of-state. Recitals, presentations, and just your child reading a paper they wrote are even great ways to stay connected with other people in your life that can cheer your child on over the years. You can also use the video function to record some of their music practices if you are helping them work out a difficult passage, and they are having trouble hearing or seeing what you are talking about. It can also be a great aid to use when helping your child learn to give a presentation since they can watch themselves, making adjustments and corrections as you review the clip together.

4. **All-Purpose Laminator:** Owning a laminator to be an indispensable tool. The **Xyron** brand has interchangeable cartridges that allow you to make magnets, permanent stickers, repositionable stickers, and laminated cards.[165] This is especially **useful in working with young children where hands-on activities are so prevalent**.

5. **Digital Timer**: Using a digital timer has been a **great, objective tool** for me over the years. When you give your child a ten-minute break, you do not want to get distracted and realize that ten minutes has slipped into twenty. Instead, set the timer so they can hear it all throughout the house when it beeps. You can also utilize it for timed drill activities, especially if you have a competitive "Structured Learner" in the house!

6. **Recording Device**: It is useful to have a recording device like a basic tape recorder, MP3 player, or cell phone that has the capability to take voice notes. Younger students can recite poetry or other memory work into the machine and then play it back to hear themselves speak, working on their dictation, projections, and pronunciations of words. For older children, make recordings of spelling lists or dictation assignments that they can use to complete their assignments while you work with a younger child.

7. **Personal Tape and/or CD player**: Okay, so I am "dating" myself here, and we do use a good deal of digital media. However, since we still have literature recordings, Bible resources, and music on physical media, I have personal tape players available that we have used over the years either for leisure or to help with multitasking. I also have a personal CD player that they can use for any CD discs. In addition, they are great to bring in your car while traveling around town, particularly when digital media is not easily accessible. Plus, for young ones, it enables media use without the stress of them accessing other areas of a smartphone, etc. that are either a distraction or are inappropriate. Here are some specific ideas for their use.

---

[165] http://www.xyron.com/

➢ **Record stories on tape or digital media** that you want your child to listen to or borrow audio media from the library. When our oldest son was quite young, I recorded all the *Magic School Bus* stories on about a dozen different tapes while reading to him over a period of a few months. Since then, our other two boys have been able to utilize those same tapes along with the books during quiet time or in the car. So whatever books you want your children to review repeatedly, consider recording them yourself or trying to find it at your local library. **Blackstone Audio Books** are a particularly good publishing company of high-quality, unabridged, children's literature.[166] Another more recent option for audio books is **Audible** from Amazon.[167]

➢ When studying **classical or other types of music**, have your child listen to the recordings when they are drawing, coloring, or doing some other kind of low concentration activity. You can often find the recordings you want at the library rather than purchasing them and can even download them for a few weeks from digital libraries. A good investment for young children is the **Classical Kids** series including *Beethoven Lives Upstairs, Vivaldi's Ring of Mystery, Hallelujah Handel, Mozart's Magic Mystery, Mozart's Magnificent Voyage, Tchaikovsky Comes to America,* and *The Song of the Unicorn*.[168]

➢ Another great investment with an emphasis on creation science and history as well as apologetics is the **Jonathan Park** audio library.[169] The CD series has eleven volumes with four stories each. It follows the adventures of the Park and Brennan families as they learn different truths about God's Word, particularly as it relates to creation science. They are well written and enjoyable for the whole family. There are also special productions of *Jonathan Park Goes to the Zoo* and *Jonathan Park Goes to the Aquarium.*

➢ **Audio Memory** is another source for audio educational materials you may want to check out. They produce the popular *Geography Songs* and *States and Capitols Songs* as well as other memory aids that you can use to supplement your teaching priorities.[170]

---

[166] http://www.blackstoneaudio.com/
[167] http://www.audible.com/
[168] http://www.classicalkidsnfp.org/
[169] http://www.jonathanpark.com/
[170] http://www.audiomemory.com/

8. **Postal Scale:** In math, you will often need to help the child understand the **difference between pounds and ounces as well as kilograms and grams**. Although you can purchase special scales for each purpose, a digital postal scale is not only great to help teach these variations but is also a useful tool to have around the house for determining postage for odd items.

9. **Flashmaster:** There are MANY tools and manipulatives out there that are useful for helping families **drill math facts** with their kids and I have used quite a few of them over the years with mostly moderate success. However, a good investment for this type of tool that does not rely on distracting smartphone technology is the **Flashmaster**.[171] It is a handheld "mini-computer" that drills addition, multiplication, subtraction, and division. I could set it one way for my youngest but then make it more challenging for the older boys as well. The system keeps track of what problems the child misses and puts them in a "missed problem" category that you can review later to see where they are struggling and then you can just drill those. It keeps track of up to nine different iterations of drills so that if you cannot work with your child at that time, you can later evaluate how they scored. Then when you have assessed their progress, you can reset it for the next child. It is a bit expensive at just about $50, but we found it was well worth the price.

10. **Selection of small candies, cash, stickers, and tokens:** Some homeschoolers frown on the idea of rewarding children for their schooling, but I am in hearty support of it. We have always felt that when there is an extra "above and beyond" achievement that using something small, like a favorite treat, coins, or tokens they collect and "redeem" for something later works well. My husband and I also feel that **rewards reflect how the world works**; those who go above and beyond often receive "extras" in life. Here are some examples of this tool in action within our home.

   ➢ Have a jar of **Hershey's Chocolate Kisses** or a dispenser for candies like **Skittles** or **Gimbal's Gourmet Jelly Beans** readily available. You can also keep a supply of sugarless gum on hand. When they were younger and I was trying to reinforce a good habit like making their beds, grooming themselves, or helping to get the kitchen and breakfast duties going, they would receive a chocolate candy in their cereal bowl. When they did not meet these objectives cheerfully, then they did not get one. I did not make a big production of it but simply gave them to the one or ones who stepped up to all of those expectations and the

---

[171] https://www.flashmaster.com/

one or ones who did not quite get their act together that morning knew that there is always another opportunity tomorrow. When they are in braces or you do not want them to have candy, substitute with a quarter instead. It does not matter what small items you use as long you are consistent, and it is a meaningful gesture to your child.

➢ When one of your children **gets all their spelling words** right on a test, give them a sticker or a candy. If all your children get 100% on their weekly spelling tests or some other big test or quiz, which is probably an infrequent occurrence, celebrate with them by giving them each a $1 or some other special treat!

➢ These little rewards are **great for memory work**. If I have a son who is learning the parts of speech, or lists of various verbs, I may give him a different value coin for each one he gets correct on a verbal review, depending on the difficulty of the question.

➢ For **drills like foreign language vocabulary lists or musical theory symbol review**, I would reward the child with a penny for each correct answer. Then they tell me what coin combination they should receive in return if they "cash" all of those pennies in with me.

➢ **Tokens or tickets can be used when you want the child to work towards a longer-term goal**. For example, you can reward your child when you see them doing an act of kindness towards their sibling or when they have accomplished a school task that was particularly challenging with a good attitude. If your child is studying a musical instrument, you can reward them with a token or a ticket for each practice session that is done thoroughly and cheerfully. Then at the end of the month, have the child collect their tokens or tickets and "redeem" them for something special. Perhaps you have a grab bag of toys from the dollar store that they can select from, or maybe you will take them on a special outing for ice cream or some other destination, like the zoo or local park.

11. **Blank Composition Books:** Do you remember those black and white composition books from grammar school? I like to purchase a few at the beginning of each school year when they are very inexpensive and then have them on hand for various purposes.

➢ For young children who are not really doing a formal science curriculum, you can use them as a kind of **scrapbook** where you have the child tell you some animal or plant they want to know about and then you have them put drawings or writings in there about that subject. You can also include photos of them learning about whatever the subject is and then they will have fun sharing it with other people when they come to visit.

➢ They make great "**nature journals**" when your children are collecting flower, seed, or leaf specimens. Then you can simply use clear packing tape to secure each treasure into the binder. They can then label whatever it is that they are learning about.

➢ For older children, they are a good way to **keep observations** that the child needs to track for their science experiments so that all of the notes are in one place when they go to write up their information for their assignments.

➢ Another great use for older children is for **notetaking when they are reading a longer book.** That way, if you are going to have a discussion with them about the book or require them to write a book report or literary analysis, they can simply go back to their chapter notes to jog their memory about some point or another.

12. **Ream of Cardstock Paper:** Instead of regular computer paper or investing in specialty paper, I like to have a package of 8 ½ by 11, white cardstock available for use when the boys draw and for documenting science or history projects.

➢ **Cardstock is easier to work with for drawing assignments.** Often, they are erasing repeatedly when drawing, and regular paper tends to wrinkle, smudge, and tear easily. Also, if you do not use page protectors, cardstock holds up well in a binder.

➢ Cardstock paper can also be **useful when you are either collecting photos together or a project that you want to document in their school binders.** You can either take photos and cut and paste them right onto the cardstock or you can print photos related to some history project or science experiment right onto the paper.

➢ Another use of card stock is when you need to have a **stiff backing for flash cards or paper dolls** that you want to make and then laminate. They also hold up better than just laminating items copied onto regular paper.

13. **Tracing Paper**: Even as your child learns to draw, having tracing paper on hand is also a useful tool. Children will often **love to see how they can bring a picture in their favorite book to life** if they can use a tool like tracing paper. Then you can point out the similarities of the strokes and techniques that they use in their drawing lessons to instill confidence and enthusiasm that "they can do it too!" For other products that may be useful for drawing or crafting purposes, check out **Miller Pads and Paper**.[172]

14. **Clear Plastic Page Protectors:** For the younger and middle ages, buy a large box of plastic page protectors that we can use for their history and science notebooks. You will find that most school writing paper that you will use when they are young is the brown, thin, lined paper that is prone to tear right out of the binders over time. So, I used page protectors in their three-ring binders to put a written assignment with its corresponding coloring sheet, project page, or map on the back side of the "window". That way, as the child flips through their notebook, it really presents like a book with information and drawings on both sides of the page protector throughout the book rather than just being one-sided. The same is true for their science books where you can put their experiment write-up on one side of the "window" and the corresponding drawing or even photo page of the child conducting the experiment on the back side.

15. **Dry Erase Board:** Although I admit I owned a small chalk board that our boys used to play with, long gone are the days of chalk and blackboards! Instead, make sure to have various sizes of dry erase boards in your home for relating and reinforcing learning concepts quickly and effectively. Small, portable ones are good for illustrating quick concepts to your child in their room, outside, or when you are out of the home. If you have the wall space, finding room for a 4x8 board is ideal for working a series of problems or having multiple lessons on the board at a time for your various ages of children. Although you could purchase a nice board at any office supply store for around $100, the best and least expensive option I have found is at your local home improvement store. For under $15, you can purchase a 4x8 sheet of solid white tile board, also known as **Melamime tile wall panel**. If this is too large, have an associate at the store cut it to your specifications. You can also purchase the accessory trim necessary to make it have a finished look on your wall. "Nail glue" works the best to attach it, but realize that once it is up there, it is there to stay! In our previous home, we purchased two of the 4x8 boards since we had nine-foot ceilings and arranged them with one on top of the other for a total size of 8 x 16! This allows your younger ones to use the lower half of the board easily for fun or to work on something you have

---

[172] http://www.millerpadsandpaper.com/

assigned them while teaching concepts to your older child on the space above that will not be accidentally disturbed or erased prematurely. It is also nice to just be on the floor sometimes with your older child and have the board accessible there too. The one drawback to this material is that it can lose luster over time and require more powerful cleaners the longer you have it. Once a month, I used a type of graffiti cleaner on it to get stubborn marks off and start fresh again. Another option that is less labor intensive to install and maintain is the removable **Opti-Rite** dry erase rolls that come in various sizes.[173] These are great because they are easy to install, come in white or clear, and do not ruin your wall if you need to take it down or move it. One final idea is to use a **metal or foil pan**, as you may find at an auto supply or hardware store. These essentially behave as a white board but are also metallic when magnetic learning tools are needed.

16. **Shade Screens and Wall Maps:** At one of the many conventions I have attended, I hopefully approached a representative from **Geography Matters** looking for some insight.[174] I had three large wall maps that needed displaying in a central spot, but I did not really have the wall space for them. I had been using **shade screens to display our maps** since we do have large windows and found that to be the only solution that worked for us. But sometimes the shades would be a bit stubborn to put up when we were done, so I looked for something that was specifically designed for displaying maps rather than just using clear packing tape to attach them to our shade screens. When I explained my question, he sheepishly admitted that there really is not another standard way of having them displayed but not in view all of the time. You can take them out only when you need them, tack them on a large wall so they are out all the time, or use shade screens; that was it. So perhaps someday there will be a better way to do it. But, in the meantime, shade screens work for us. The main consideration when purchasing a shade screen for this purpose is that you do not want it to be an overly thick one since that makes it more difficult for the screen to roll up when you are done referencing the map. If you ever think of something better, be sure to share it with your group and then let me know too!

17. **3x5 Card Binders/Book Rings:** No matter what approach or curriculum you use, there is always usually a need to utilize a method of binding related study cards together. Whether your child makes **fact cards for Bible, science, history, math, grammar, foreign**

---

[173] http://opti-rite.com/ - Can also be purchased through Amazon.com or other distributors. Contact them directly to receive a sample to try before you purchase one. Be aware that you will feel the texture of your wall through this product.
[174] http://www.geomatters.com/

language, or spelling, there comes a time where the volume of cards grows to the point of needing a uniform way of storing and using them. Binders of a 3x5 size are quite useful for organizing collections of index cards. However, purchasing a small container of book rings can also serve this purpose at a much lower cost.

18. **11x17 3-Ring Binder Timeline Book**: Somewhere around fourth grade, history curriculums begin to emphasize the importance of your child assembling their own timeline. Most programs require families to find a minimum of eight to twelve feet, preferably longer, of blank wall space to roll out some butcher paper and start gluing time-line figures onto them as they go along in their study. However, while this is a great supplement to what your child is learning, many of us do not have that kind of wall space available for such an activity. In addition, if we put it low enough for our child to work with it, younger siblings may unknowingly tear at or damage it in some other way. Instead, I have found that purchasing an 11x17 binder, which can be ordered at any office supply store, and filling it with blank, white 11x17 card stock paper works best. **Your child still gets the flow of history and is able to work through the book just like a regular timeline but then can use it when they need it or want to show it to someone and then put it away when it is not being used.** Although the initial binder cost is somewhere around $30, you can use it to cover ancient history all the way through modern times so the costs are spread over several years. In addition, you can purchase a ream of 11x17 colored construction (or regular) paper that can be cut into one-inch strips. These colored strips are then glued down the middle of your timeline pages so that you can write dates on them or designate a different middle color strip for each major period in history. The other thing that is useful to do is, when you have an event like the Hundred Years' War (which incidentally lasted over 100 years), you can have your child draw an arrow out from the timeline figure to the approximate date where the war ended, showing the span of time of the event in relationship to other things that were happening. Children can also glue other items or draw pictures in their book to enhance any figures that you already have down. One other point to make about timeline books is that to really get the effects of time passing, it should be done to scale. What I mean is that some curriculum providers offer pre-printed timeline books that, while they are nice-looking and easy to use, will just collapse a period of years since not much is going on there historically and then spreads them out in the later years when there is a lot going on in history. This means that one page in the book might equal 100 or even 1000 years while later time pages only equal 25 or 50 years since it was more historically active. However, doing this defeats the point of a timeline. **Keep your book to scale and it will prove to be a useful tool**. I have every page represent 50 years

so that when the book is open flat, the child is viewing 100 years of history. You will have a lot of pages that are sparse or even blank during the ancient times but resist the temptation to take the pages out! Instead, have your child paste in dinosaurs or people working simple farms. Show when the span of the Ice Age took place over many centuries and draw life lines that show how long Adam lived and so forth, showing overlap in who knew each other and lived at the same time during the period in history where people had long life spans. Get creative and have your child think of unusual pictures or drawings to include. Then, by the end of their study, the project does not get thrown away every year or rolled up and forgotten about. Instead, they will have a wonderful project to share with others and a great reference tool for them to use in years to come.[175]

Work with your mentor for additional ideas about other essential tools to add to your "must have" list!

_____

_____

_____

_____

_____

_____

_____

_____

_____

_____

_____

_____

_____

_____

---

[175] See the "Files" section of our private Facebook group for detailed instructions on making an 11x17 history timelines book; https://www.facebook.com/groups/thebalancedhomeschooler/files/

Keeping Records for Your Child

Understanding what to keep or not to keep in your home school can be a daunting task. Some families look at their child's schoolwork a bit like they view their tax files; keep everything in case we are audited! Other families hardly keep anything but the very best of the best and throw all of the daily work away at the end of the year. Most families, however, fall somewhere in the middle of these two extremes. The first thing to understand when dealing with recordkeeping is to know what state law requires. After that, families have the freedom to decide what level of records and work they wish to keep for each child.

In Arizona, state law does not require families to produce yearly proof of progress so that does not factor into your decision in this case. However, since laws are always subject to change, having a good management system in place now could save unnecessary heartburn later. For an understanding of what other states require, visit **HSLDA** for specific state statutes and guidelines.[176] After state requirements are met, **each family needs to decide the level of detail they wish to keep from year to year of their child's progress, increasing as the child gets older.**

Building a Portfolio

Usually, a summary of their best work kept in a **portfolio** from year-to-year with related "proof" of schooling is adequate. If you are wondering about what the contents of a portfolio might be, here are some suggestions to keep in mind as you build one with your child. You can either have multiple notebooks per year per subject, or you can just prepare one notebook as a summary for each year's learning and achievements with sections divided for each subject. Another option is for you to have one binder that has a division for each child per year that covers the information. Page 189 has a **"Portfolio Contents Checklist"** that you can review annually as you make sure to include all of the important elements in your child's portfolio. These include, but are not limited to, grade/progress summaries, title page/table of contents Information, major tests/exams, written reports/outlines, formal booklists, special projects or science experiences with photos, field trip and special event documents, competition or contest documents, standardized testing summaries, and a copy of your child's affidavit. These are usually all you need to consider doing in their younger years through eighth grade, but you may also list other ideas in the space provided. I have also included a sample copy of a detailed **"Monthly Reading List"** on page 190. Blank copies for both forms are available in Appendix B.

Other tools that may interest you in **organizing your child's portfolio** include the digital *Homeschool Portfolio Pack* by Kim Sorgius of NotConsumed also available on Amazon.[177]

---

[176] http://www.hslda.org/laws/default.asp
[177] http://courses.notconsumed.com/product/homeschool-portfolio-printable-pack/; https://www.amazon.com/Homeschool-Portfolio-Everything-need-record/dp/1517052912/ref=sr_1_8?s=books&ie=UTF8&qid=1509303149&sr=1-8

What other documents do you think are essential to include in your child's portfolio?

_____

_____

_____

_____

_____

_____

_____

_____

_____

_____

_____

_____

_____

_____

_____

_____

_____

_____

_____

_____

_____

_____

_____

Note to Leaders and Mentors:

Some parents will tend to stress out over what grade they should assign to their child for a particular subject. Some subjects are easy to assess, like math, grammar, or spelling, while others are more subjective, like history, science, or literature.

In our house, we only assign one of three grades; either A, B, or C. At times, I have also used a + or – notation (i.e. weighted system) when needed to get the point across for how close or far they are from one grade to another. Here is a summary of our grading system:

- *A = Excellent (Proficient in ALL major subject areas)*
- *B = Very Good (Proficient in all but ONE major area)*
- *C = Needs Improvement (Needs improvement in MORE than ONE major area)*

If the child is more of a "D" or "F" in their performance, then it is probably a teaching problem or a discipline issue more than a learning deficiency.

There is no one right way to grade or best verbiage scale to use. As long as you are clear on how to assess their work and how to communicate it to your husband and child, then you have done your job!

Portfolio Contents Checklist

Portfolio Contents for _____ *(child's name)*	Notes Section/ Check When Completed
Include any **grade/progress summaries** that you have written for your child. For each of our boys, I prepare a tri-fold report that has the look and feel of a "grade card". It summarizes each of the subjects they completed that year with what grade I assigned to it along with a note on each one for any "areas for development". It makes a great discussion tool to utilize with your husband as well as your child when encouraging them about what they did well that year while looking towards what will be the focus of the development or improvement for the next year.	
Include photo copies of the **title** and **Table of Contents pages** from each text used to serve as a kind of syllabus for what was covered that year and what materials were used. Check subjects off when you are done: History Science English Math Logic Foreign Language Spelling Handwriting Writing Other:_____	
Keep at least copies of the child's **major tests and exams** for all subjects to show progress and achievement in each area.	
Keep at least copies of all of your child's **completed written reports and outlines** that you know took a certain amount of effort to do and is representative of the child's abilities.	
Include **special history and science projects or experiments** that your child completed. **Include photos** of related events or large projects that you will not keep for the long term. After all, most homes do not need to have three different models of the solar system or will not keep Viking ship or adobe home replicas forever!	
Include any **formal booklists of literature** that they read that year that you wish to track for your child.	
Include a section for keeping information about **field trips or other special events** that your child experienced. Event programs or brochures as well as earned certificates or other awards would be included here. Other examples include photos and related materials from concerts or presentations that the child participates in or gives.	
Keep copies of any work that your child submitted for writing, poetry, etc. **contests** or documentation about any **competitions** they competed in.	
Include result copies of any **standardized tests** that they completed for that year.	
Keep a copy of their **affidavit** or other paperwork needed to show that you had legally designated them to homeschool that during that year.	

Monthly Reading List

Reading List For: Evan C. Gary   *Month: September 2006*

Subject: Literature   *Grade: Third Grade*

Title	Code(s)	Author	Date Completed
The Pilgrim's Progress	R/A	John Bunyan	In Progress
WEEK 1: The Ghost in the Tokaido Inn	I/R	Dorothy and Thomas Hoobler	09/08/06
The Inch-High Samurai [Own]	I/R	Shiro Kasamatsu	09/08/06
Night of the Ninjas	I/R	Mary Pope Osborne	09/08/06
The Samurai's Tale	R/A	Erik Haugaard	09/08/06
The Samurai's Daughter	R/A	Robert San Souci	09/08/06
WEEK 2: An Early American Christmas	I/R	Tomie dePaola	09/15/06
Finding Providence: The Story of Roger Williams	I/R	Avi	09/15/06
The Journal of Jasper Jonathan Pierce	R/A	Ann Rinaldi	
On The Mayflower: Voyage of the Ship's Apprentice & a Passenger Girl		Kate Waters	09/15/06
The Pilgrims of Plimouth	I/R	Marcia Sewall	09/15/06
Sarah Morton's Day	I/R	Kate Waters	09/15/06
Thanksgiving on Thursday	I/R	Mary Pope Osborne	09/15/06
Three Young Pilgrims	I/R	Cheryl Harness	09/15/06
The House on Stink Alley: A Story About Pilgrims in Holland	I/R	F.N. Monjo	
WEEK 3: Amistad Rising	I/R	Veronica Chambers	09/22/06
Nzingha, Warrior Queen of Matamba	I/R	Kim Siegelson	
To Be a Drum	I/R	Evelyn Coleman	09/22/06
The Village That Vanished	I/R	Ann Grifalconi	09/22/06
WEEK 4: A Treasury of Turkish Folktales for Children	R/A	Barbara Walker	09/29/06
Little Mouse and Elephant	I/R	Jane Yolen	09/29/06

R/A = Read-Aloud   Ref. = Reference Only   FML = Folktales/Myths/Legends
I/R = Independent Reading   Int. = Internet Resource   HF = Historical Fiction
P = Poetry Selection   A = Audio Selection   B = Biography

Calculating Credits

For your high school student, you will also want to understand how to **calculate credits as well as how to prepare a transcript**. Even if you do not think your child is college-bound, you will want to do the appropriate recordkeeping now in case they change their mind later or if they need to produce it for future employment, a trade school, or the military. Calculating credits does not have to be difficult, so let us now look at the basic steps.

1. **Define a credit**: First, recognize that generally one year of work is equal to one credit and a half year of work (i.e. a semester) is equal to one half of a credit.

2. **Define the school year**: In most cases, moms can assume that they are working on a 36-week schedule, although it can certainly be longer depending on your curriculum. However, a typical school year would generally not be shorter than 36 weeks.

3. **Associate instructional hours to a credit hour**: If a typical year is 36 weeks in a "brick and mortar" school, then you can reason that the number of minutes spent on a particular subject is 9,000 minutes (i.e. 5 days a week X 36 weeks X 50-minute daily class periods). However, since most schools do not have a solid 50 minutes of instruction every day for five days a week and it is probably closer to only 30 minutes per day of actual instruction time, you can estimate one credit to be assignable for a course completed that falls between a minimum of 90 instructional hours (i.e. 5 days a week X 36 weeks X 30-minute daily instruction time) and 150 hours for the year. The average standard is typically 120 hours for time spent per subject. Families can also schedule their plans on a four-day school week if they plan on going for a longer period of weeks during the year. For example, a family on a 42-week school schedule will be at 140 hours per subject for a credit hour when you do the calculations (i.e. 4 days a week X 42 weeks X 50-minute daily class periods).

4. **Keep a Log for Self-Designed Classes**: For classes like physical education, auto mechanics, or home economics that do not have as rigid of a delivery program as the typical subjects, be sure to have your child log time spent doing activities related to that subject. These are elective classes, internships, or practicum experiences where you assess whether they completed the tasks and objectives set forth or not. The amount of time spent doing the course will determine whether they receive one half or one full credit. Also, note that one semester of college courses taken in high school generally receive one full credit for high school.

5. **Understand the Credits Your Child Needs to Graduate**:
   Although most homeschoolers are not bound to follow the mix of **credits specified by the state**, it is a good guideline since most colleges that your child applies for will expect to see at least this basic mix of subjects. The easier you make it for the admissions department at the college your child is going to attend to interpret the credits and related transcript you have developed, the better off your child will be. Other states are different, so research your specific state's requirements to use it as a planning guide. However, let us look at Arizona's current requirements as an example, which requires twenty-two credits over four years.

English	4 credits
Mathematics [1]	4 credits
Science [2]	3 credits
Social Studies [3]	3 credits
CTE/Fine Art [4]	1 credit
Electives	7 credits
Total	**22 credits**

(1) Mathematics courses shall consist of Algebra I, Geometry, Algebra II (or its equivalent) and an additional course with significant mathematics content as determined by district governing boards or charter schools.

(2) Science courses shall prepare students for the high school AIMS test (life science). A.R.S. § 15-203 prohibits the SBE from adopting changes to these requirements

(3) Social Studies "shall consist of one credit of American History, one credit of World History/Geography, one-half credit of government and one-half credit of economics.

(4) CTE stands for Career Tech. Education[178]

So, as you track your child's credits, taking time to understand the state's requirements is a good place to start. However, do not just stop there. **Look at the local state college or other potential universities where your child might attend and understand what their expectations are in advance.** You are much better off at the beginning of your child's high school season to know if they require a more intensive level of math or foreign language that your child might not otherwise pursue.

[178] http://www.azed.gov/hsgraduation/

Calculating GPA (Grade Point Average)

Before you can calculate GPA, you need to determine how you will assign grades to your child. Assigning grades is typically an informal process when they are quite young, as discussed in the beginning of this section. However, as your child ages, they need to have an that grades are often assigned in a more objective manner in the junior high and high school years. Subjects like math, spelling, and grammar are typically easy to grade in relationship to point values that are assigned to whatever the child is expected to do. **In a simple system, assignment categories are not weighted, and you simply log how many points were possible versus earned for each major component for every subject taught.**

For example, in a science course, you may have study notes, labs, and tests that your child completes on a regular basis. Using an example of a course that takes sixteen lessons and approximately thirty-two weeks to complete, your tracking system for a **standard grading scale** can be managed by a simple spreadsheet and might look something like this.

	Study Guides & Notes	Labs	Tests	Extra Credit	TOTALS	GRADE
Science - Actual Points Poss.	160	1600	1600		3360	**90.06%**
Science - Actual Points Earned	160	1312	1504	50	3026	**A-**

In this example, the child earned 10 points a lesson for completed study guides (i.e. 160 points), 50 points for each lab completed (2 per week at 50 points each equals 1600) and then 100 points on each test that was taken (i.e. 1600 points for 16 tests). Also, by allowing them to do an extra credit assignment, this student was able to bring their overall grade up and squeak out an A-. This assumes the use of a typical grading scale of 90+ for an A, 80-89.99 for a B, 70-79.99 for a C, and so forth.

Now take this same student and consider applying a **weighted grading scale** for them. Those same points earned might look like this.

	15% Study Guides & Notes	25% Labs	50% Tests	Extra Credit	TOTALS	GRADE
Science - Actual Points Possible	24	400	800		1224	**90.20%**
Science - Actual Points Earned	24	328	752		1104	**A-**
Science - Actual Points Poss.	160	1600	1600			
Science - Actual Points Earned	160	1312	1504			

Notice that the actual and possible points are the same as before but now each subject category has a weight associated with it, allowing you to adjust as needed. Also notice that this same student did *not* need to complete the extra credit assignment to earn an A- since the weight for the tests "counted" more than the weight for the labs. **Either system is fine, so it is just a matter of personal preference.**

When calculating GPA, there are multiple grading scales to consider. So, make sure you understand the scale that should be used in associating each grade with its corresponding GPA points. In my first example, I will show you a **standard 4.0 scale GPA approach**, making sure only to include course performance in the GPA where a letter grade is earned. If your child has any "pass/no pass" classes, those would not be included in the GPA credits even though they do count towards their overall credits earned.

Typical GPA Scale	
A	4 points
B	3 points
C	2 points
D	1 point
F	0 points

A typical GPA scale would associate an A with 4 points, a B with 3 points, a C with 2 points, a D with 1 point and an F would earn no GPA points. To calculate a GPA, simply take the letter grade earned for each course and add up their associated points. You then divide that point score by the number of credit hours that relate to those points to calculate your child's GPA. Typically, you will want to track it for each year of high school as well as the final cumulative GPA, making those notations on the transcript. There is also a way to note GPA by subject, as we will cover later.

Course Description	Grade Earned	Credit
Algebra I	A	1
English I	B	1
World History & Geog. I	A-	1
Biology w/ Lab	B+	1
Fine Art: Piano Studies	A	1
PE & Health	A	1
Spanish - Year 1	B+	1
Latin - Year 1	A	1

Here is an example to consider. Say you have a student who took a full load of classes during their freshmen year that looked like this table to the left.

In the example given using the "Typical GPA Scale", this student earned a total of 29 "points" for the grades that they received, and they earned eight credit hours. When you divide 29 by 8 credits, you come up with 3.625, which rounds to a GPA of 3.63.

If your child is taking **AP or honors classes**, however, the standard way to handle that is to give each grade one point more than the standard scale shows.[179] This usually only applies to A, B, or C grades that are earned, as indicated in the table to the right. Remember that AP classes must be sanctioned by the College Board to count as such whereas honors courses can be self-designed but must have college-level rigor to substantiate the difference

Honors GPA Scale	
A	5 points
B	4 points
C	3 points
D	1 point
F	0 points

---

[179] For more information on designing AP (Advanced Placement) equivalent courses or preparing your student to test out on an AP class, see this link: https://apstudent.collegeboard.org/home?navid=gh-aps

from a typical course. College-level courses also use this scale. Also, note that college-level courses earn more credit since a one-semester college course usually equates to a full credit for high school.

However, if you want to add a variation to how a **+ or – grade** is treated, you may consider a different scale such as the one noted here on the right. These point assignments are standard for this type of expanded system that we call a "Weighted GPA Scale".

You may also round them to the nearest tenth of a point instead of using them as shown. Using our previous student example again now with the weighted GPA scale shown to the right with the + and – grades, this same student under this system would have a higher GPA of 3.67 (i.e. 29.33 divided by 8).

Weighted GPA Scale	
A+	4.33 points
A	4.00 points
A-	3.67 points
B+	3.33 points
B	3.00 points
B-	2.67 points
C+	2.33 points
C	2.00 point
C-	1.67 points
D+	1.33 points
D	1.00 points
D-	0.67 points
F	0 points

One final point about calculating a GPA is regarding classes that are only worth half a credit (i.e. only **one semester** long). For such classes, simply take the GPA scale you are using and divide the grade points in half. For example, on a standard GPA scale, an "A" earned for a one-half credit course is worth two instead of four GPA points; a "B" earned for a one-half credit course is worth 1.5 GPA points and so forth.

Creating Transcript Content

Once you get a feel for calculating credits, then you can start constructing the basics of your transcript. Rather than waiting until the end of your child's senior year of high school, take some time once or twice each year to update and assess how the transcript is shaping up. **Transcripts are usually either organized chronologically by grade level or they can be organized by subject.** Although the grade-by-grade structure is the more common approach, sometimes it makes sense just to summarize it by subject, as we will explore in the next section.

While the university will need to have the actual records sent to them from the testing service, you may also want to consider including your child's standardized test scores for the **SAT** or **ACT** exams. Since your child can take these tests multiple times, you may choose the score set that reflects their best result. While some institutions will accept what are called "super scores" (i.e. the best separate math and verbal results achieved) most still require the single best overall effort to be reported. PSAT results are not collected in the college admissions process, though if they receive commendation, you will want to include that. You may also wish to create summary comments about any notable extracurricular activities that they participated in during high school, such as homeschool honor societies or internship programs. This is also a good place to note courses that were taken at or through an outside organization, which is common for music, drama, speech and debate, and foreign language. You may also explain dual enrollment, AP, co-op, etc. classes here.

For parents desiring **more information** or support, check out the following tools as you plan your recordkeeping approach for your child in the older grades.

1. Use a personal software tool like **Homeschool Minder** or **Microsoft Excel** to track booklists and grades.[180]

2. *The Balanced High Schooler: Getting Parents and Homeschooled Teens "On the Grid" for College and Beyond* by Carol Gary. I will mention my book here as well as it covers a comprehensive overview of transcript on "Day 36". However, *The Balanced Homeschooler* manual you are currently reading gives you all the calculation details you need to succeed. Current TBH moms also have access to my fully customizable **TBH High School Transcript Template** (MS Excel) that calculates GPA, points, and course credits automatically.

3. Homeschool Today provides **Transcript Creator**. However, as a free service, keep in mind that none of the information you enter will be saved. So, this is only recommended if you have tracked your information separately and then plan on creating your student's transcript in one sitting.[181]

4. For moms looking for more extensive guidance in creating transcripts and all of the topics related to it, consider **Transcript Boot Camp** by Inge Cannon, **Transcripts made Easy** by Janice Campbell. [182]

5. Moms may also wish to consider using the paid **Teascript** service to work on the document overtime and ensure that your updates are saved along the way.[183]

6. **HSLDA's high school consultants** also offer support to families regarding how to calculate credit hours and prepare a transcript. They will even perform a full transcript review right down to the checking your calculations if you are a an HSLDA member.[184]

---

[180] http://www.homeschoolminder.com/

[181]
http://www.howtohomeschooltoday.com/freebies/homeschool_forms/record_keeping_forms/transcript_creator/

[182] http://www.homeschooltranscripts.com/; http://www.homeschooltranscripts.com/

[183] https://www.teascript.com/

[184] https://www.hslda.org/highschool/docs/EvaluatingCredits.asp

What questions or concerns do you have about keeping records, calculating grades, or creating your student's high school transcript?

Grade-Level vs. Subject-Level Transcript Formats

Again, as your child navigates the high school years, it is **best to track progress as you go** on their transcripts rather than waiting until their junior or senior year to piece together the past. It also enables you to adjust earlier in their high school coursework plan if you are tracking as you go rather than realizing halfway through their junior year that some vital piece is missing.

Pages 202-205 contain samples of how you can choose to format the transcript: **grade-level or subject-level**. The grade-level one is what we associate to a traditional transcript where each year details the courses completed, credits assigned, and grades earned. However, the subject-level one simply organizes information by subject regardless of when the courses were completed. If the university specifies they want the grade-level one, then use it. However, as colleges have become increasingly friendly to homeschoolers during the admissions process, you may want to use a subject-level one if format is not of issue to them. I personally prefer this one since you do not need to specify when the course was completed as some high school courses were completed prior to 9th grade. For example, our two youngest sons both earned two years of high school Spanish credit from Home School Spanish Academy when they were younger (i.e. two years completed by 7th grade and 9th grade, respectively). Also, we always have Algebra 1 completed by the end of 8th grade. So, both of these are situations where they have done the work to earn the credit, but they were not done within the last four years of school, Thus, the subject-level format works better for us. A final reason to favor the subject-level one is that it emphasizes subject strengths that relate to the degree program they wish to enter. For example, an engineering student can more easily highlight their 4.0 in math and science using a subject-level transcript even if they earned "B's" in English.

Current moms in our program have access to customizable templates for both of the following formats so that all they need to do is customize course descriptions, plug in personal information, assign the grade earned and credit earned, and the GPA and cumulative data automatically calculates according to the math discussed earlier in this chapter under the sections called "Calculating Credits" and "Calculating GPA". Just for fun, I gave our sample child "Joe Student" all A's on the first set of samples and then lowered them on the second set so you could see the calculation changes at work. You will also notice that the samples include a space for the parents to sign and date the transcript. Some parents even have it taken to a notary, although that is not necessary in most situations. The "Comments" box is where you can note information about any classes that were conducted by other organizations, awards earned, competitions won, volunteer work, and other extracurricular activities. Make the notes concise as it will act like a mini-resume. While some institutions accept resumes, most prefer not to hassle with them.

What thoughts do you have about grade-level vs. subject-level formats for your child's transcript? Do you wish to create your own transcript or use a prescribed template or service to create it?

_____

_____

_____

_____

_____

_____

_____

_____

_____

_____

_____

_____

_____

_____

_____

_____

_____

_____

_____

_____

_____

_____

_____

_____

_____

One final point regarding documentation is the **diploma**. While it may not seem necessary, it is a good idea to issue one. It can be one that you create or that you order through a company, such as your state support organization or HSLDA. [185] More than just for show, a diploma states that the student has completed requirements for high school whereas a transcript communicates what specifically was done to meet that requirement.

Finally, have a discussion with your teen on whether they wish to participate in a **graduation ceremony** or not. While some students and their families find the experience important, others do not. So, talk to your teen in the last couple of years of their high school program about their celebration and ceremony options. Often local groups or the state support organization will offer one for a fee.

Does your teen wish to have a graduation ceremony experience? Do they want it in a group setting with other homeschoolers or do they just want a private event? How will you create and maintain your child's transcript? Record your thoughts, details, and arrangement plans here.

_____

_____

_____

_____

_____

_____

_____

_____

_____

_____

_____

_____

_____

_____

_____

[185] https://store.hslda.org/graduation-essentials-c19.aspx

Homeschool High School Coursework Transcript - Grade Level Format

Student Name: Joe Student

Student's Parents: Richard and Jane Student

Birthdate: 10/10/1999

Social Security #: 123-45-6789

Address: 123 Main Street

Anytown, State USA

Phone #: 555-555-5555

Grading Scale

90+	A	4 points
80-89.9	B	3 points
70-79.9	C	2 points
60-69.9	D	1 point
Below 60	F	0 points

Cumulative Summary

Graduation Date:	5/20/2020
Cum. Credits:	32.00
GPA Credits:	32.00
GPA Points:	123.0
Cum. GPA:	3.84

Testing

	PSAT	Semifinalist for NMSQT
		Total Score	Percentile
SAT	1320	90
ACT	28	90

Year 1 - Ninth Grade

Year	Course Description	Grade	Credit	Points
2016/2017	Algebra I	A	1.0	4
2016/2017	English Literature & Composition I	B	1.0	3
2016/2017	Biology w/ Lab	A	1.0	4
2016/2017	Ancient History	B	1.0	3
2016/2017	Old Testament	A	1.0	4
2016/2017	Spanish - Level I	A	1.0	4
2016/2017	Music Performance & Theory - I	A	1.0	4
2016/2017	Musical Theater & Drama - I	A	1.0	4
Fall 2016	Intro to Logic	B	0.5	1.5
	Year 1 Credits; Points		8.5	31.5
	Cum. Credits		8.5	
	Year I GPA		3.71	
	Cum. GPA		3.71	

Year 2 - Tenth Grade

Year	Course Description	Grade	Credit	Points
2017/2018	Geometry	A	1.0	4
2017/2018	English Literature & Composition II	B	1.0	3
2017/2018	Chemistry w/ Lab	A	1.0	4
2017/2018	World History & Geography	A	1.0	4
2017/2018	New Testament & Church History	A	1.0	4
2017/2018	Spanish Level II	A	1.0	4
2017/2018	Music Performance & Theory - II	A	1.0	4
2017/2018	Musical Theater & Drama - II	A	1.0	4
2017/2018	Health and Physical Education	A	1.0	4
	Year 2 Credits; Points		9.0	35.0
	Cum. Credits; Cum. Points		17.5	66.5
	Year 2 GPA		3.89	
	Cum. GPA		3.80	

Year 3 - Eleventh Grade

Year	Course Description	Grade	Credit	Points
2018/2019	Algebra II	A	1.0	4
2018/2019	English Literature & Composition III	B	1.0	3
2018/2019	Physics w/ Lab	A	1.0	4
2018/2019	American History	A	1.0	4
Fall 2018	Speech	B	0.5	1.5
Spring 2019	Driver's Education	A	0.5	2
2018/2019	Music Performance & Theory - III	A	1.0	4
2018/2019	Musical Theater & Drama - III	A	1.0	4
Fall 2018	Art Appreciation	A	0.5	2
	Year 3 Credits; Points		7.5	28.5
	Cum. Credits; Cum. Points		25.0	95.0
	Year 3 GPA		3.80	
	Cum. GPA		3.80	

Year 4 - Twelfth Grade

Year	Course Description	Grade	Credit	Points
2019/2020	Pre-Calculus	A	1.0	4
2019/2020	English Literature & Composition IV	A	1.0	4
2019/2020	Computer Science Fundementals	A	1.0	4
Fall 2019	U.S. Government & Politics	A	0.5	2
Spring 2020	Intro to Economics	A	0.5	2
2019/2020	Music Performance & Theory - IV	A	1.0	4
2019/2020	Musical Theater & Drama - IV	A	1.0	4
Fall 2019	Art Appreciation	A	0.5	2
Spring 2020	Personal Finance	A	0.5	2
	Year 4 Credits; Points		7.0	28.0
	Cum. Credits; Cum. Points		32.0	123.0
	Year 4 GPA		4.00	
	Cum. GPA		3.84	

Our signatures attest that Joe Student has successfully completed the courses recorded above and that this document serves as his official high school transcript.

Richard Student (Father/Administrator) - Date   Jane Student (Mother/Teacher) - Date

Comments:

Homeschool High School Coursework Transcript - Grade Level Format

Student Name: Joe Student

Student's Parents: Richard and Jane Student

Birthdate: 10/10/1999

Social Security #: 123-45-6789

Address: 123 Main Street

Anytown, State USA

Phone #: 555-555-5555

Grading Scale

90+	A	4 points
80-89.9	B	3 points
70-79.9	C	2 points
60-69.9	D	1 point
Below 60	F	0 points

Cumulative Summary

Graduation Date:	5/20/2020
Cum. Credits:	32.00
GPA Credits:	32.00
GPA Points:	128.0
Cum. GPA:	4.00

Testing

PSAT	Semifinalist for NMSQT	
	Total Score	Percentile
SAT	1450	98
ACT	30	95

Year 1 - Ninth Grade

Year	Course Description	Grade	Credit	Points
2016/2017	Algebra I	A	1.0	4
2016/2017	English Literature & Composition I	A	1.0	4
2016/2017	Biology w/ Lab	A	1.0	4
2016/2017	Ancient History	A	1.0	4
2016/2017	Old Testament	A	1.0	4
2016/2017	Spanish - Level I	A	1.0	4
2016/2017	Music Performance & Theory - I	A	1.0	4
2016/2017	Musical Theater & Drama - I	A	1.0	4
Fall 2016	Intro to Logic	A	0.5	2
	Year 1 Credits; Points		**8.5**	**34.0**
	Cum. Credits		**8.5**	
	Year I GPA		**4.00**	
	Cum. GPA		**4.00**	

Year 2 - Tenth Grade

Year	Course Description	Grade	Credit	Points
2017/2018	Geometry	A	1.0	4
2017/2018	English Literature & Composition II	A	1.0	4
2017/2018	Chemistry w/ Lab	A	1.0	4
2017/2018	World History & Geography	A	1.0	4
2017/2018	New Testament & Church History	A	1.0	4
2017/2018	Spanish Level II	A	1.0	4
2017/2018	Music Performance & Theory - II	A	1.0	4
2017/2018	Musical Theater & Drama - II	A	1.0	4
2017/2018	Health and Physical Education	A	1.0	4
	Year 2 Credits; Points		**9.0**	**36.0**
	Cum. Credits; Cum. Points		**17.5**	**70.0**
	Year 2 GPA		**4.00**	
	Cum. GPA		**4.00**	

Year 3 - Eleventh Grade

Year	Course Description	Grade	Credit	Points
2018/2019	Algebra II	A	1.0	4
2018/2019	English Literature & Composition III	A	1.0	4
2018/2019	Physics w/ Lab	A	1.0	4
2018/2019	American History	A	1.0	4
Fall 2018	Speech	A	0.5	2
Spring 2019	Driver's Education	A	0.5	2
2018/2019	Music Performance & Theory - III	A	1.0	4
2018/2019	Musical Theater & Drama - III	A	1.0	4
Fall 2018	Art Appreciation	A	0.5	2
	Year 3 Credits; Points		**7.5**	**30.0**
	Cum. Credits; Cum. Points		**25.0**	**100.0**
	Year 3 GPA		**4.00**	
	Cum. GPA		**4.00**	

Year 4 - Twelfth Grade

Year	Course Description	Grade	Credit	Points
2019/2020	Pre-Calculus	A	1.0	4
2019/2020	English Literature & Composition IV	A	1.0	4
2019/2020	Computer Science Fundementals	A	1.0	4
Fall 2019	U.S. Government & Politics	A	0.5	2
Spring 2020	Intro to Economics	A	0.5	2
2019/2020	Music Performance & Theory - IV	A	1.0	4
2019/2020	Musical Theater & Drama - IV	A	1.0	4
Fall 2019	Art Appreciation	A	0.5	2
Spring 2020	Personal Finance	A	0.5	2
	Year 4 Credits; Points		**7.0**	**28.0**
	Cum. Credits; Cum. Points		**32.0**	**128.0**
	Year 4 GPA		**4.00**	
	Cum. GPA		**4.00**	

Our signatures attest that Joe Student has successfully completed the courses recorded above and that this document serves as his official high school transcript.

Richard Student (Father/Administrator) - Date   Jane Student (Mother/Teacher) - Date

Comments:

Homeschool High School Coursework Transcript - Subject Level Format

Student Name: Joe Student
Student's Parents: Richard and Jane Student
Birthdate: 10/10/1999
Social Security #: 123-45-6789
Address: 123 Main Street
Anytown, State USA
Phone #: 555-555-5555

Cumulative Summary	
Graduation Date:	5/20/2020
Cum. Credits:	32.00
GPA Credits:	32.00
GPA Points:	128.00
Cum. GPA:	4.00

Comments:

Unweighted Grading Scale & Points		
90+	A	4
80-89.9	B	3
70-79.9	C	2
60-69.9	D	1
Below 60	F	0

Testing		
PSAT	Semi-Finalist for NMSQT	
	Total Score	Percentile
SAT	1450	98
ACT	30	95

Subject Overview					
Subject	Total Subject Credits	Course Titles	Grade Earned	Points Earned	GPA by Subject
Math	1.0	Algebra I	A	4	4.00
	1.0	Geometry	A	4	
	1.0	Algebra II	A	4	
	1.0	Pre-Calculus	A	4	
English & Literature	1.0	English Literature & Composition I	A	4	4.00
	1.0	English Literature & Composition II	A	4	
	1.0	English Literature & Composition III	A	4	
	1.0	English Literature & Composition IV	A	4	
History & Government	1.0	Ancient History	A	4	4.00
	1.0	World History & Geography	A	4	
	1.0	American History	A	4	
	0.5	U.S. Government & Politics	A	2	
	0.5	Intro to Economics	A	2	
Science	1.0	Biology w/ Lab	A	4	4.00
	1.0	Chemistry w/ Lab	A	4	
	1.0	Physics w/ Lab	A	4	
Bible	1.0	Old Testament	A	4	4.00
	1.0	New Testament & Church History	A	4	
Foreign Language	1.0	Spanish - Level I	A	4	4.00
	1.0	Spanish - Level II	A	4	
Fine Arts	1.0	Music Performance & Theory - I	A	4	4.00
	1.0	Music Performance & Theory - II	A	4	
	1.0	Music Performance & Theory - III	A	4	
	1.0	Music Performance & Theory - IV	A	4	
	1.0	Musical Theater & Drama - I	A	4	
	1.0	Musical Theater & Drama - II	A	4	
	1.0	Musical Theater & Drama - III	A	4	
	1.0	Musical Theater & Drama - IV	A	4	
	1.0	Art Appreciation	A	4	
Other Electives	0.5	Introduction to Logic	A	2	4.00
	1.0	Physical Education & Health	A	4	
	1.0	Computer Science Fundamentals	A	4	
	0.5	Speech	A	2	
	0.5	Driver's Education	A	2	
	0.5	Personal Finance	A	2	
Total Credits	**32.0**	**Total GPA Credits**	**32.0**	**128.0**	
		Cum. GPA	**4.00**		

Our signatures attest that <u>Joe Student</u> *has successfully completed the courses recorded above and that this document serves as his official high school transcript.*

_____   _____
Richard Student (Father/Administrator) - Date   Jane Student (Mother/Teacher) - Date

Homeschool High School Coursework Transcript - Subject Level Format

Student Name: Joe Student
Student's Parents: Richard and Jane Student
Birthdate: 10/10/1999
Social Security #: 123-45-6789
Address: 123 Main Street
Anytown, State USA
Phone #: 555-555-5555

Cumulative Summary	
Graduation Date:	5/20/2020
Cum. Credits:	32.00
GPA Credits:	32.00
GPA Points:	123.00
Cum. GPA:	3.84

Comments:

Unweighted Grading Scale & Points		
90+	A	4
80-89.9	B	3
70-79.9	C	2
60-69.9	D	1
Below 60	F	0
Testing		
PSAT	Semi-Finalist for NMSQT	
	Total Score	Percentile
SAT	1320	90
ACT	28	90

Subject Overview					
Subject	Total Subject Credits	Course Titles	Grade Earned	Points Earned	GPA by Subject
Math	1.0	Algebra I	A	4	4.00
	1.0	Geometry	A	4	
	1.0	Algebra II	A	4	
	1.0	Pre-Calculus	A	4	
English & Literature	1.0	English Literature & Composition I	B	3	3.25
	1.0	English Literature & Composition II	B	3	
	1.0	English Literature & Composition III	B	3	
	1.0	English Literature & Composition IV	A	4	
History & Government	1.0	Ancient History	B	3	3.75
	1.0	World History & Geography	A	4	
	1.0	American History	A	4	
	0.5	U.S. Government & Politics	A	2	
	0.5	Intro to Economics	A	2	
Science	1.0	Biology w/ Lab	A	4	4.00
	1.0	Chemistry w/ Lab	A	4	
	1.0	Physics w/ Lab	A	4	
Bible	1.0	Old Testament	A	4	4.00
	1.0	New Testament & Church History	A	4	
Foreign Language	1.0	Spanish - Level I	A	4	4.00
	1.0	Spanish - Level II	A	4	
Fine Arts	1.0	Music Performance & Theory - I	A	4	4.00
	1.0	Music Performance & Theory - II	A	4	
	1.0	Music Performance & Theory - III	A	4	
	1.0	Music Performance & Theory - IV	A	4	
	1.0	Musical Theater & Drama - I	A	4	
	1.0	Musical Theater & Drama - II	A	4	
	1.0	Musical Theater & Drama - III	A	4	
	1.0	Musical Theater & Drama - IV	A	4	
	1.0	Art Appreciation	A	4	
Other Electives	0.5	Introduction to Logic	B	1.5	3.75
	1.0	Physical Education & Health	A	4	
	1.0	Computer Science Fundamentals	A	4	
	0.5	Speech	B	1.5	
	0.5	Driver's Education	A	2	
	0.5	Personal Finance	A	2	
Total Credits	**32.0**	**Total GPA Credits**	**32.0**	**123.0**	
		Cum. GPA	**3.84**		

Our signatures attest that Joe Student has successfully completed the courses recorded above and that this document serves as his official high school transcript.

_____   _____
Richard Student (Father/Administrator) - Date   Jane Student (Mother/Teacher) - Date

More Chapter Notes...

Homeschool Plans Summary Sheet (Chapters 1 – 4)

Family Vision Statement: _____

_____

_____

_____

_____

Why do I want to homeschool? _____

_____

_____

_____

Will I have my child participate in standardized testing? If so, which one?

_____

_____

_____

Will I participate in a co-op or outsource part of my child's education? If so, who will I network with? _____

_____

_____

_____

What other concerns about socialization do I still have? _____

_____

_____

What will my approach to home education be? _____

_____

_____

What curriculum will I use to adequately address the "Four C's"?

Bible: _____

Math: _____

History: _____

Science: _____

Literature: _____

English: _____

Spelling: _____

Handwriting: _____

Foreign Language: _____

Art: _____

Music: _____

_____

_____

I have these types of learner in my home: ML, SL, AL, or CL

_____

_____

_____

_____

I am homeschooling these seasons right now: Little ones, K-2, 3-6 G. or Jr./Sr. High

_____

_____

I will use the following tools and methods to teach, keep records and grades:

_____

_____

_____

This page is left blank intentionally

Chapter 5

Spiritual Discipleship

*Your word is a lamp to my feet and a light
for my path. (Psalm 119:105)*

*Train a child in the way he should go, and when he is old he
will not turn from it. Proverbs 22:6 (NIV)*

Ground Yourself in the Word

When thinking about the spiritual discipleship of your child, few scriptures can more easily lay out the plan for you than the ones noted above. First, we must recognize that our handbook is God's Word and that we must consistently reference it as we navigate the various seasons of parenting challenges over the years. Sometimes my husband and I would joke with each other saying, "Why didn't this kid come with a set of instructions?" But the fact is, they did! He did not need to send an individual manual for each child that He brings into this world because He already did so in His Word. While you will never run across a specific set of instructions in the Bible on how to "potty train" or whether to allow your teenager to have their own cell phone, **He does give us all the *principles* we need** to be successful in facing each of these unique parenting experiences and decisions.

Second, we must remain confident. Even though it is not an easy process by any means, **if we stay the course and do not give up, God *will* take the foundation that you have laid and build upon it throughout your child's life: regardless of the path that your child takes.** As I mentioned in chapter one, we are not responsible for the harvest of our child's spiritual walk. Although you may indeed be part of the harvesting process, **parents are instead responsible for tilling the soil, sowing the seeds, and caring for the seedlings until they are out of your home and have been transplanted into God's world for service.** Know that God is more than able to produce fruit in your child, even if you do not see it as quickly or assuredly as you would like. So just stay the course and leave the rest to Him. Once a firm foundation is established, it will not be easily shaken or abandoned.

Therefore, as parents, you and your husband have been entrusted to provide the care, discipleship, and education that your child needs so that God can accomplish the fullness He desires to see in your child's life. **Biblical parenting becomes a natural outpouring of loving but firm decisions you make for and with your child when you have a solid spiritual foundation established in your own life.** In each "season" your child passes through, relate the "spiritual organizational chart" of your family to your child, beginning with their role and God's expectations of them. They then should understand that they are accountable to Dad and Mom who are, in turn, accountable to God as the ultimate ruler of their lives. It takes the guesswork and pressure off of parents who may otherwise feel like they constantly need to explain and justify everything they decide and do on a daily basis. Instead, spend your time relating your thought processes and decisions to God's Word so that your child not only understands why you operate the way you do but can also internalize the process that you are modeling to them for future reference. Parenting, then, becomes a matter of consistently reminding the child that the requirements you have of them are directly tied to God's expectations of how Dad and Mom are to raise them. Remember that you are agents of the Lord and, as His representatives, you and your husband will be much more successful in building strong relationships with your child and parenting them with confidence if you realize that it is all about His plan and not about yours. **However, before you can seek to ground your child in God's Word, *you* must be grounded in it first.** This is true for yourself as an individual as well as in your relationship with your husband.

Regarding your relationship with yourself, recognize that **most wives, especially those who focus on fulltime homemaking and mothering responsibilities, hit a wall at some point** in their spiritual growth while the children are still young. Early on, while still pregnant with the first child, we read all the right books and make careful efforts to take care of ourselves. Our homes are relatively organized and attractive, and we still have some time to pursue friendships and certain outside interests. We are generally pleasant to be around and can typically be described as nice, sweet, kind, and thoughtful. Yep! We all pretty much have it together as all-around wonderful ladies, wives, and young mothers, and then something happens.

One day, **you half-heartedly look at yourself in the mirror and you think, is that really me?** You start to wonder what happened to "what's her name" and "so and so" and why you do not hear from them anymore. You become so tied to just surviving your routine that you find you are not entirely sure what your goals are with your child or whether you can really stick with this homeschooling thing or not. You find yourself to be grumpy more days than not and keeping difficult emotions and even sometimes resentments in check becomes more and more challenging.

But there is good news! If this is where you are at right now or you have been there recently, you are right where God wants you to be! I believe that God allows these difficult seasons, no matter how long or short lived, to challenge and stretch us to be more like Jesus each day. Know that **difficulties always precede growth opportunities**; so be encouraged that the Lord is just around the corner, waiting for you to come to Him! I am reminded of Paul's words when he shares with us the following words.

> *"Three times I pleaded with the Lord to take it away from me. But he said to me, "My grace is sufficient for you, for my power is made perfect in weakness." Therefore I will boast all the more gladly about my weaknesses, so that Christ's power may rest on me. That is why, for Christ's sake, I delight in weaknesses, in insults, in hardships, in persecutions, in difficulties. For when I am weak, then I am strong."*
> II Corinthians 12:8-10 (NIV)

We need to allow Jesus to <u>be</u> our life rather than just <u>being in</u> our life.

It is speculated that Paul had a problem with his eyesight that was never resolved throughout his lifetime that was perhaps associated with the episode of blindness he experienced when he encountered Jesus on the road to Damascus[186]. Others speculate it was a spiritual burden. Whatever the issue or ailment was, in a sense Paul wanted to "get back to normal". But God said, "No"—not because He delights in Paul's suffering but because it is only through Paul's total dependence on God that the fullness of what Christ can and does do for us shines through. In the same way, we Christian mothers need to not be so consumed with God "taking away" this annoyance or making that challenge easier. Instead, in the similar manner of Paul, we too need to stop struggling to "get back to normal". Rather, **we need to focus our energies on the fact that God is creating in us a "new normal" and that "new normal" requires Him, not us, to be in the driver's seat**. When we were less taxed by the daily demands of life, we were doing okay and satisfied with allowing Jesus to *be in* our life, but we may not have really and totally depended on Jesus to *be* our life.

So, what is a mom to do? Regardless of where we are on a spectrum in our spiritual walk, **continued growth is always an option**. None of us ever really "arrives". However, we *can* strive to have joy in the process of God's development of us while at the same time serving and nurturing other moms along the way. That's what being in a "Titus 2" relationship is all about as both the mentor and the mentored are blessed. Even the most grounded mom can

---

[186] Read the book of Acts, chapter nine for a full account of Paul's (i.e. Saul's) conversion story.

become stagnant when she isolates herself from others and shifts from growth and improvement to stagnation and survival.

Therefore, take a moment to **think about where *you* are on the spiritual growth spectrum** and journal a few ideas about where you think God wants you to journey next. If the middle bar is "average", where would you mark your line? Now draw your own arrow in the direction that you are heading. Did you draw it pointing left? You may be experiencing a spiritual drought, confusion, or even depression. If you drew it pointing right, then you may be in a season of growth or rebuilding. Just remember that this is a snapshot in time and not a permanent definition!

I have also included a few ideas of materials that you can use, either independently or with a friend, to continue down the path that God intends for you to walk. I have arranged them in what I believe to be the **least to the most intensive study experiences**.

1. *Becoming the Woman God Wants Me to Be: A 90-Day Guide to Living the Proverbs 31 Life* by Donna Portow; You *knew* there would be a reference to the seemingly perfect "Proverbs 31" woman sooner or later! Donna's book is full of practical advice and direction in every aspect of life and makes us see that the Proverbs 31 woman is not so elusive after all! It is very comprehensive and highly recommended!

2. *Experiencing God: Knowing and Doing the Will of God* by Henry T. Blackaby and Claude V. King; As I have learned to appreciate many studies and spiritual growth books over the years, I have yet to find one to take the place of *Experiencing God*. Whether you go through it on your own or in a group setting, it is one of the few studies out there that you cannot "fluff" your way through. If you work through this material, prepare to be spiritually exposed and stretched!

3. *Grace Walk: What You've Always Wanted in the Christian Life* by Steve McVey. I will mention this resource again in chapter eight. However, it is worth mentioning here too if you feel you are in a place in your life of just "doing out of obligation" or trying to "do enough for God" but feeling very unfulfilled.

4. Any studies by Beth Moore are excellent and vary in their depth of material covered and is particularly great for those moms who like to dig deep into individual chapters of the Bible.[187] However, one of her newer titles can be particularly encouraging to the discouraged wife

---

[187] http://www.lproof.org/

and mom who has difficulty being "in the world but not of it". It is called *So Long Insecurity; You've Been a Bad Friend to Us*.

Honestly journal what thoughts are concerns you have about your own personal, spiritual status and current path. What do you think God is trying to say to you? What messages from Him have you been ignoring?

_____

_____

_____

_____

_____

_____

_____

_____

_____

_____

_____

_____

_____

What other approaches or resources does your mentor suggest to address your concerns about your spiritual growth?

_____

_____

_____

_____

_____

_____

_____

_____

_____

_____

_____

_____

_____

Ground Your Marriage in the Word: Five Principles

Regarding your relationship with your spouse, there are many areas to examine when looking to enhance your connection with one another as well as in your mutual job of parenting. No matter how difficult it may seem some days, make your marriage and the issues you need to address a priority. After all, **your marriage started out with just the two of you and one day it will just be the two of you again.**

Now the opportunities to improve all of our marriages are endless and the scope of this manual is not to address them all. However, if there is one point that would be useful to make above all others, it is this one. **Guard your heart against any desire you maintain to set yourself up as the head of the household.** This caution applies to the pragmatic issues of life as well as ones regarding the discipline and spiritual mentorship of your child. I know that some of you are cringing at this point, but please hang with me as I have struggled personally with this and know what a shock hearing the words can be! Scripture warns us right in the beginning that when mankind sinned, leading to the Fall, God pronounced three curses: one to the serpent, one to womankind, and one to mankind. Looking closely at the curse placed on Eve and future women in Genesis, we see that God states the following.

"I will greatly increase your pains in childbearing; with pain you will give birth to children. Your desire will be for your husband, and he will rule over you." Genesis 3:16 (NIV)

Of course, most all of us know that the first part of this curse is true, but often we ignore the rest of what God is saying to us here. So, probably the most understandable article I have read recently on this topic can be found in an **Answers in Genesis** article entitled, *"Genesis, Wifely Submission, and Modern Wives".*[188] In it, Dr. Georgia Purdom makes the statement, after walking through a number of supporting scriptures about the usage application for the word "desire", that this verse is essentially saying...

"Eve will want to rule over Adam ("your desire shall be for your husband") as a part of the curse. So, if the curse is that Eve would want to rule or lead Adam, then that must not have been Eve's role before the Fall, and she was originally created to be a helper not a leader. Otherwise, it's not much of a curse."

In other words, God originally designed the husband to exercise responsible headship over his wife and, as Godly wives, our role is to seek to be the helpmeet that God created us from the very beginning to be. To do this, then, we must stop competing with our husbands for the job title of "family leader" and start supporting God's plan for how the family is best designed to operate.

---

[188] http://www.answersingenesis.org/articles/2009/11/24/genesis-wifely-submission-modern-wives

Now, I realize that some of you do not see your husband as even *wanting* to take on a headship role when it comes to disciplining or discipling your child. Our husbands are working harder than ever, trying to earn a living so that we can stay at home with our children and educate them ourselves. So, the thought of him having the energy or the inclination to carve out the necessary time and mental investment needed to truly lead the family seems, at best, a remote possibility. However, rather than trying to "help" our husbands by unwittingly taking over these headship responsibilities, we must **examine our own hearts and priorities to see what we can do to support *his* fulfillment of his God-given role.** So, as Christian wives, we must then seek to understand some basic principles of what the Lord expects of us in our role and translate them into practical action.

Five Principles of Focus for Your Marriage

1. *Forgiveness*
2. *Constancy*
3. *Compassion*
4. *Unity*
5. *Intimacy*

Although this section about marriage is not an exhaustive discussion of this concept, I have personally observed five essential or key principles to embrace that will focus your perspective in the right direction. As you move along in your contemplation of these ideas, then, you can and should **come up with additional principles that God is laying on your heart to embrace.**

If you are **married to a non-believer**, work through this section with the understanding that even though your husband does not view Jesus as their personal Lord and Savior, you can still be a Godly, Christian wife to him. Remember that you are still accountable to the Lord for how you work out your Christian faith and that these principles still apply even if you and your husband are not equally yoked. Also, be encouraged to remember these words from the Apostle Peter.

> ➢ **Scripture to ponder**: *"Wives, in the same way be submissive to your husbands so that, if any of them do not believe the word, they may be won over without words by the behavior of their wives, when they see the purity and reverence of your lives. Your beauty should not come from outward adornment, such as braided hair and the wearing of gold jewelry and fine clothes. Instead, it should be that of your inner self, the unfading beauty of a gentle and quiet spirit, which is of great worth in God's sight. For this is the way the holy women of the past who put their hope in God used to make themselves beautiful. They were submissive to their own husbands, like Sarah, who obeyed Abraham and called him her master. You are her daughters if you do what is right and do not give way to fear." 1 Peter 3:1-7 (NIV)*

For **those moms who may be single**, you may be tempted to skip this section. However, I encourage you to still work through the information since these concepts can be useful to you in other relationships in your life and they are principles that you will want to teach your children about some day when it comes time for them to seek out their future spouse. Also, remember that **in absence of an earthly husband, God promises to be a "father to the fatherless" and a "defender of widows".** He will not leave you in your time of distress and can still grow you in these principles for the benefit of your child and yourself.

1. **Forgiveness**: This is probably one of the most difficult human tasks that God ever equipped us to exercise, which is why I placed it first on the list! It is also a necessary experience to work through in order to address the other principles of marriage I have listed below. Forgiveness is one of those things that we can ignore or "fake" for a while, but we cannot run away from *really* forgiving forever. Eventually, any resentment or anger you have towards your husband, whatever the reasons, will only serve to drive a wedge between you both and transform you personally into a bitter, angry wife and mother. So now it is time to become very real with yourself. **If you are having difficulty with forgiveness in your marriage, ask God to help you see with His eyes so that you can peel back the layers of the anger onion to figure it out.** It is uncommon that deep-seated issues are the result of a single incident, but rather they are born from a series of difficult events that have been experienced over a long period of time: sometimes years. However, it is also important to admit that rarely are issues one-sided and even the best of Christian wives can shut down their husbands from engaging in effective communications when criticism and disappointment are the constant theme of every conversation. No matter how justified you think you are in your frustration with your husband, remember that with every exasperated roll of your eyes or each indignant expiration of your breath during these situations, your husband's perception is that you do not respect him, nor do you believe in him as the leader of your household. Since these kinds of perceptions cannot be tolerated by most husbands for any length of time, one of several things may happen; your husband may lob back criticisms at you, shut down emotionally, or even become physically absent from the household. As if these challenges are not tough enough, it is also important to realize that you are setting a negative example for your child on how Christian married couples resolve issues. The bottom line, then, is to make sure to *really* extend forgiveness to your husband, even when you do not feel like it. Let go of the negativity that is poisoning your thought processes and relationship with him by separating out the facts of the situation from the emotions of it. Only then will you find untold freedom in extending to your husband what God has already freely given to you.

➤ **Scripture to ponder:** *Bear with each other and forgive whatever grievances you may have against one another. Forgive as the Lord forgave you. Colossians 3:13 (NIV)*

➤ **Scripture to ponder**:
For as high as the heavens are above the earth,
*   so great is his love for those who fear him;*
as far as the east is from the west,
*   so far has he removed our transgressions from us.*
Psalm 103:11-12 (NIV)

Take some time to note areas in your marriage where you need to extend forgiveness OR ask for it yourself.

_____

_____

_____

_____

_____

_____

_____

For an even more powerful experience, take a separate sheet of paper, list out your sins that are bothering you, repent, pray for forgiveness by reading Psalm 103:11-12, and then shred the paper! God has forgiven you, so YOU need to forgive yourself.[189]

_____

_____

_____

_____

_____

_____

_____

_____

---

[189] Are you still having troubling forgiving yourself or others? Read I John 1:9 too!

2. **Constancy**: Have you ever heard the concept of "behaving your way through it"? I am not speaking of false behavior. Rather I am referring to the concept of valuing commitment over the pull of daily emotions. We wake up some days and do not "feel" like being a wife, or "feel" like doing school with the kids, or even "feel" like getting out of bed some days! But as the devoted wives and mothers we want to be, we persevere through these idle thoughts and uphold the commitment to fulfill these daily roles above our unreliable feelings of the moment. Drive your decisions by the unchanging and trustworthy *fact* of God's love for you and plan for your life rather than allowing your feelings to rule, which are changing and unreliable. In fact, I would like to suggest taking this idea of constancy one step further and even be so bold as to say that **constancy be a synonym for sacrificial love**, also known as "agape" love. God did not *want* the Israelites to disobey him and violate His laws repeatedly from generation to generation, and yet He continued to love them with constancy. God did not *enjoy* having his Son die on the cross for us, yet He allowed it because His loving constancy for us is more than we can ever understand. And God did not *take pleasure* in nearly every one of the early disciples suffering a martyr's death, but he allowed it so that the power of their faithful testimony would be heard around the world and for generations to come. **So, if God can display constancy towards mankind in ways that we can barely conceive of, why is it so difficult for us give it to the one person in life that we have promised to love above all others and under all circumstances?** Constancy is what separates the new from the mature believer because it requires the manifestation of the fruit of the Spirit, regardless of whether life has brought you blessings or hardships. It is the difference of displaying the steadfastness of Job when he was tested in every conceivable way versus the fickleness of Sarah when God's timing did not meet her own plans and expectations.[190] Without constancy, there is no love, which is a good principle to serve as a follow-up to forgiveness.

➢ **Scripture to ponder**: *Love does not delight in evil but rejoices with the truth. It always protects, always trusts, always hopes, always perseveres. Love never fails. I Corinthians 13:6-8a (NIV)*

➢ **Scripture to ponder**: *But the fruit of the Spirit is love, joy, peace, patience, kindness, goodness, faithfulness, gentleness and self-control. Galatians 5:22-23a (NIV)*

➢ **Scripture to ponder**: *For I am convinced that neither death nor life, neither angels nor demons, neither the present nor the future, nor*

---

[190] Read the account of Job's constancy in the book of Job. Contrast that with Sarah's decision in Genesis 16 to place God on her timetable when she had still not borne Abraham's promised heir and decided to take matters into her own hands.

any powers, neither height nor depth, nor anything else in all creation, will be able to separate us from the love of God that is in Christ Jesus our Lord. Romans 8:38-39 (NIV)

Take some time to note areas in your marriage where you need to improve your constancy. Does your outward behavior or words to your husband reflect the love that you have for him?

_____

_____

_____

_____

_____

_____

_____

_____

_____

_____

_____

_____

_____

_____

_____

_____

_____

_____

_____

_____

_____

3. **Compassion**: Ask yourself, "What can I do to help my husband succeed in his goals?" It could be as simple as making sure he has lunches prepared for the day or week so that he can just grab them and go. It could involve making sure to send him a quick, gentle reminder of a special appointment that needs to be kept later or helping to ensure that he follows through on important doctor appointments. Some of you may be thinking, "I am not his mother. Can't he be responsible to do these things himself?" And, of course, that is true. You are not his mother. But you are his wife, and as his helpmeet, **you have an opportunity to express your love and concern for him as well as to help ensure that your family's experiences as a whole for the week are as smooth, positive, and fruitful as possible**. So, the best way to seek out how you can show more compassion to your husband is to review your regular interactions with him and ask yourself, "Where do the tension points in our life seem to be, and how can I behave to help ease and address those areas while remaining Godly in my attitude and creating a positive witness for my child?" Think, "What can I do to empathize with my husband's present circumstances and extend the help and grace to him that he needs to be successful in his responsibilities?" Consider, "Regardless of what some of my husband's shortcomings may be, what can *I* do that will honor both him and the Lord?" You also may be surprised how your husband will notice your efforts and reciprocate to also help you meet *your* goals!

➢ **Scripture to ponder**: *The Lord God said, "It is not good for the man to be alone. I will make a helper suitable for him." Genesis 2:18 (NIV)*

Take some time to note areas in your marriage where you need to improve your compassion. As far as it depends on me, what can I do to ease the "tension points" in our marriage? How can I be the helpmeet that God designed me to be?

_____

_____

_____

_____

_____

_____

_____

_____

4. <u>**Unity**</u>: The first priority you have in applying this concept of unity is to make sure that you and your husband are on the same page. Of course, as we will discuss later, this is true for the way that you parent so that your decisions are consistent for your child, regardless of which one of you is interacting with them. But it is also true for how you define and view your marriage. Even before my husband and I were married, we made a decision that divorce was *not* going to be an option. It was never going to be something that would be casually thrown around during disagreements, nor would it be an idea that we would secretly harbor as an escape route if circumstances become too difficult. Instead, we crossed if off our vocabulary list, establishing the fourth principle we will discuss called unity. Unity not only applies to the concept of making a life-long commitment to one another but also to the way that we daily interact with our husbands. However, to have unity in our communications and perspectives on all of life's major issues, **we must first possess a submissive heart, respecting our husband's position as the leader of our family while understanding our own essential role.** Wives today, even Christian wives, dislike the "s" word. It kind of goes back to that issue we discussed earlier in this chapter: that part of the "curse" we women live with is the constant "desire" for our husband's position. However, if we look at our marriage through God's eyes, we will see that submission is simply a necessary attitude we need to display so we can fulfill our God-given responsibilities to the best of our ability while at the same time modeling Christ's bridegroom relationship to His church, the bride. Yes, husbands have an essential responsibility to sacrificially *love* their wives as Christ loves the church, but wives are called to *respect* their husbands and honor their role as the head of our households.

➤ <u>**Scripture to ponder**</u>: *Wives, submit to your husbands as to the Lord. For the husband is the head of the wife as Christ is the head of the church, his body, of which he is the Savior. Now as the church submits to Christ, so also wives should submit to their husbands in everything. Husbands, love your wives, just as Christ loved the church and gave himself up for her to make her holy, cleansing her by the washing with water through the word, and to present her to himself as a radiant church, without stain or wrinkle or any other blemish, but holy and blameless. In this same way, husbands ought to love their wives as their own bodies. He who loves his wife loves himself. After all, no one ever hated his own body, but he feeds and cares for it, just as Christ does the church— for we are members of his body. "For this reason a man will leave his father and mother and be united to his wife, and the two will become one flesh." This is a profound mystery—but I am talking about Christ and the church. However, each one of you also must* *love his wife as he loves himself, and the wife must respect her husband. Ephesians 5:22-33 (NIV)*

Take some time to note areas in your marriage where you need to improve your unity. Do you communicate appropriately in front of your children? Do you resolve disagreements with respectful discussion?

_____

_____

_____

_____

_____

_____

_____

_____

_____

_____

_____

_____

_____

_____

_____

_____

_____

_____

_____

_____

_____

_____

5. **Intimacy**: If you have ever read the Song of Solomon, you know that God has much to communicate to us about the value that He places on the intimate connection that exists within between a husband and his wife! But even beyond this private look at the marriage relationship, we find that right from the beginning, God created the institution of marriage to establish the oneness that He intended for every one of us to have with our husbands. These thoughts include our sexual relationship with our husbands, but it does not just stop there. Intimacy also requires trust to exist between a husband and a wife so that each partner honors and respects each other's needs, opinions, desires, and goals. Creating intimacy is a full-time occupation as you look for ways to regularly remind your husband that you cherish him above all others and that you have faith in his leadership of the home. When you have this bond with him, you will find that all of the other areas of your life, although challenging and sometimes stressful, will be much more easily managed. When you want to offer your opinions and feedback to him on some subject and you have intimacy, he is much more receptive to discuss serious and even difficult topics when trust and honor are a part of your everyday dealings with him. When crisis comes and you have intimacy, he will know exactly what to do and how to support you in a way that will best serve you and your family. When major development milestones in your family occur and you have intimacy, you will both be in tune with each other's perspectives on how best to enjoy and celebrate those moments. You will notice that I have placed this principle last and there is a reason for it; **for all the other four principles need to be addressed before true intimacy can occur.** If you have not forgiven each other for some offense, intimacy cannot exist. If you do not exhibit constancy in your internal thoughts and external interactions with your husband, intimacy cannot exist. If you do not extend the necessary compassion in your marriage to put him first, intimacy cannot exist. Finally, if you do not make efforts to be unified in your marriage commitments and parenting decisions, intimacy cannot exist. On the other hand, if you have both made efforts in love to address the first four principles, then the trust necessary to have true intimacy will be firmly established.

➢ **Scripture to ponder**:

The man said,
"This is now bone of my bones
and flesh of my flesh;
she shall be called 'woman,'
for she was taken out of man."

For this reason a man will leave his father and mother and be united to his wife, and they will become one flesh. The man and his wife were both naked, and they felt no shame. Genesis 2:23-25 (NIV)

➤ **Scripture to ponder**: *Proverbs 5:15-19 (NIV) states:*

Drink water from your own cistern,
*   running water from your own well.*

Should your springs overflow in the streets,
*   your streams of water in the public squares?*

Let them be yours alone,
*   never to be shared with strangers.*

May your fountain be blessed,
*   and may you rejoice in the wife of your youth.*

A loving doe, a graceful deer—
*   may her breasts satisfy you always,*
*   may you ever be captivated by her love.*

Take some time to note areas in your marriage where you need to improve your intimacy. Remember that the other four principles need to be addressed before true intimacy can occur.

_____

_____

_____

_____

_____

_____

_____

_____

_____

_____

_____

_____

Scripture tells us that in the end **only two things will remain: God's Word and those who have accepted Jesus Christ as their Savior.**[191] As women who base our daily purpose upon God's plan, be sure to continually feed your heart and mind with biblical teachings that will promote success in the five principals previously covered. Free yourself from contradictions and give up habits, magazines, media, and even friendships that urge you to operate in a way that is contrary to these concepts.

If you are interested in developing your spiritual walk further as a Christian wife, **summarize your thoughts on the following page and then consider taking yourself through one of these teaching books or programs**.

1. *The Excellent Wife* by Martha Peace; This is one of the most thorough and systematic studies I have ever been through on the topic of being a Godly wife. It starts first with foundational truths and then moves to defining roles and commitments as well as dealing with the topics of submission, communication, and conflict resolution. It concludes by dealing with the difficult issues of anger, fear, loneliness, and sorrow. Be sure to purchase the accompanying study guide for a complete experience.

2. *The Five Love Languages: The Secret to Love that Lasts* by Gary Chapman; Taking couples through a discussion about the fact that we all have love languages that we "speak" in and want others to "speak" to us, Gary Chapman does a service to the Christian Community by given us a common language of communication about an otherwise difficult topic. He defines and discusses the love languages of physical touch, words of affirmation, receiving gifts, acts of service, and quality time.[192]

3. *Intimate Issues* by Linda Dillow and Lorraine Pintus; Whether or not you think you have questions about your sexual relationship with your husband, Christian wives would be wise to work through this book as a Godly way to either address or reaffirm their thoughts about this topic and what God's perspective is about it.[193]

4. *Love Dare* by Stephen and Alex Kindrick. The movie *Fireproof* popularized this forty-day challenge that helps couples to behave their way through a love challenge each day to restore a broken relationship or strengthen a healthy one. There is a companion

---

[191] Luke 21:32-33, I Thessalonians 4:17, and John 14:1-3
[192] http://www.5lovelanguages.com/
[193] http://www.intimateissues.com/; The authors conduct weekend conferences for women.

book called The *Love Dare for Parents* that helps transfer these concepts to teens.[194]

5. *The Power of a Praying Wife* and *The Power of a Praying Husband* by Stormie OMartian. For wives, she guides us to pray through 30 different areas of our husbands' lives including such topics as his work, finances, sexuality, affection, temptations, and fears. The counterpart book covers some different but many similar areas in also guiding husbands to pray for their wives. She also wrote *The Power of Prayer to Change Your Marriage Book of Prayers.*[195]

6. See **Focus on the Family** for other Christian marriage support resources and workshops as well as counseling information.[196]

Work through certain resources noted above with your husband, as appropriate, and take time with him to fill out the ***Marriage Enrichment Summary Sheet*** on the following page. Make time to intentionally and regularly discuss these points with your spouse either at a set time when your children are in bed or during a date night when you will not be interrupted.

What additional concerns do you have about strengthening your marriage and addressing the principles discussed in this chapter?

_____

_____

_____

_____

_____

_____

_____

_____

_____

_____

_____

_____

---

[194] http://lovedarestories.com/
[195] http://www.stormieomartian.com/
[196] http://www.focusonthefamily.com/marriage.aspx

Marriage Enrichment Summary Sheet

Marriage Principle	Positive Observations	Areas that Need Improvement	Steps We Will Take
Forgiveness			
Constancy			
Compassion			
Unity			
Intimacy			
Other:			

This page is left blank intentionally

Teaching Spiritual, Character, and Behavioral Truths to Your Child

Early in this chapter, I referred to a **"spiritual organizational chart"** that you can use to communicate with your child their place in the family and how that relates to your role as their parents. It is important that throughout each "season" of parenting that children have a continually expanding idea of how God designed their relational world around them and how He intended them to interact with it.

I grew up in a Christian home and was baptized by the age of nine. We attended church faithfully every week, prayed at mealtimes, and were expected to live by biblical principals in our day-to-day lives. I even remember receiving a dollar on occasion when I accomplished memory work like the Lord's Prayer or the books of the Bible. My excellent father was a Godly man who continually strove throughout his life to understand God's Word and how to apply it. However, if there was one area that he struggled with, it was the **concept of legalism**. While my father was very "by the Good Book" when it came to training my brother and me, there was often an absence of grace and sometimes a rationing of outward signs of love towards his children and even our mother.

It is interesting to note that towards the end of his seventy-one years on this earth, he became quite **reflective** and shared with me on more than one occasion how he wished he had done things differently with us. He observed that, as one who was born during the Depression and grew up during World War II, it had been instilled in him that providing financially was the most important job he had and that "the father earned the living and supported the family while the nurturing was left to the mother". He wished he had been more involved in the nurturing part of our childhood but never felt equipped to do it. Wow.

His humble observations in these moments were little nuggets of wisdom that I have since sought to address in my own family over the years as my husband and I have worked consistently to establish and deliver our parenting approach. I realized that I too tended to be legalistic and lack mercy. So, as I have thought about these concepts further, it occurred to me that the biggest single concept from my childhood experience that brought about these issues was that my father had not taken the essential steps necessary to make the connection for us at an early age that we were ultimately **not only accountable to God for our *outward behavior* but that we were to pursue a *relationship* with Him through His Son.** As children, my brother and I completely understood the fact that we accepted Jesus as our Savior and the significance of the work that He did for us all on the cross. However, we did not understand that our daily goal should have been to pursue a relationship with Jesus. Instead, we were focused on outward compliance more so than inward development. As a result, we saw that we ultimately needed to please our parents, particularly our father, more so than God Himself. From a simplified perspective, our spiritual accountability organizational chart stopped with our parents as the following diagram shows.

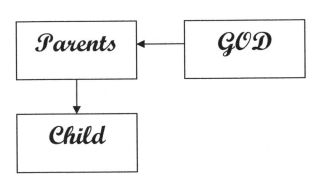

While we knew God *influenced* our parents, the buck ultimately stopped with our parents rather than God. I also realized that this organizational chart never really expanded much over time. Even as young adults, we perceived that responsibilities and relationships never really went beyond our own four walls.

Therefore, in the following sections, you will notice that I have designed an **ever-expanding organizational chart** that you can use as a guideline to continue to train your child in age appropriate ways that will **ultimately lead to the development of their *own* relationship with the Lord.** By the time they leave your home, you want them to have ownership of their relationship with Jesus and a firm grounding in God's Word. These critical elements must be established so they can go on to lead the influential and fruitful life that God intended them to have within the context of their community. No longer are they Christians because Dad and Mom are Christians. They are Christians because they own that identity themselves. It is like what David and Shirley Quine of Cornerstone Curriculum have said when they **liken raising children to writing a letter.** We write on their hearts, edit their choices, shape their style, and craft their purpose. Yet, one day, we must mail them out into the world to fulfill God's calling on their life.

So, to achieve that goal, make sure that you and your husband exercise parental unity and plan in advance how you make decisions for and with your child, how you discipline them, how you incent them, and how you introduce them to the complex world that they live in. Interestingly enough, **a vast majority of conversations that I have had with parents over the years about what they believe to be homeschooling concerns are really parenting or spiritual discipleship problems.** Perhaps the problem is not that Timmy will not do his schoolwork carefully; it is that there is a heart training issue of slothfulness that needs to be dealt with so that he exercises diligence. Maybe the problem is not that Suzy will not pay attention to her lessons and instructions; it is that there is stubbornness and pride in her heart that needs to be corrected so that she becomes teachable. And perhaps it is not that the work Megan has been asked to do is too hard for her; it is that there is a resistant heart of disobedience that needs to be cleaned out and redirected so that she understands the difference between when you give her requirements versus when you give her suggestions.

So, **regardless of what season you are in, take time to read through each of the following sections** since the observations and suggestions provided are somewhat cumulative. If you find yourself struggling in one area or another as your child gets older, perhaps going back to a foundational suggestion located in a section for children in a younger season may prove helpful to you.

Little Ones

When our children are quite young, Dad and Mom are their whole world. Others may be floating in and out of the home, but **their parents are "it" as far as they are concerned.** Part of this comes from the fact that they understand right away that parents are the ones who provide them what they need. They come to them for love, help, comfort, protection, security, and all of life's basic needs.

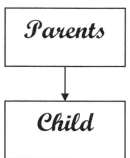

Although you should speak to them often about Christian faith ideas in age appropriate ways, their concept of God and Jesus is quite limited. Emphasizing that God is Jesus' Father and that Jesus is our friend are the primary areas of focus at this age. Reading Bible stories are an essential part of establishing a faith-training routine with them. However, recognize that these will just mostly be understood as "stories", like other character books you read to them, until they are older. So, **at this stage, parents are the ultimate authority and influence**, and the child does not yet understand the accountability relationship between God and their parents. Here are training steps that parents can take at this season in their child's development.

Spiritual Truths in Action

This age is more about training *you* in your interactions with your child than about any volume of information that they will absorb from your formal reading or teaching time. It is also about building routine and consistency in the spiritual truths that you teach to them so that they always know God's priorities have been a part of what your family identity is from day one.

➤ **Scripture to ponder**: *And whoever welcomes a little child like this in my name welcomes me. But if anyone causes one of these little ones who believe in me to sin, it would be better for him to have a large millstone hung around his neck and to be drowned in the depths of the sea. Matthew 18:5-6 (NIV)*

1. **Read plenty of Bible stories**. At this age, I regularly ensured that for every time we sat down to read storybooks that we would end with at least one Bible story. Your local Christian bookstore is a great source to find ones that you like from board books to early readers.

2. **Engage in respectful conversation** with them that show Dad and Mom care about what God thinks. Even when they are too little to understand what you are saying, establish the habit now so that when they are old enough to start comprehending, it is

just part of your natural interactions with them. Treating them considerately and speaking in a normal, thoughtful voice sets the groundwork for healthy parent-child relationships. Always remember that you are *not* raising children; you are raising men and women.

3. **Take them consistently to their church program**. Some homeschooling families tend to isolate themselves away from church membership or even attendance, believing that family worship experiences are enough. However, I encourage you to reconsider so you can establish early on the routine of regularly fellowshipping with other believers. You want the expectation of going to church to be heavily tied to your family's identity. Notice I am saying the *expectation* of going to church is tied to your family's identity, not the specific church's identity that you attend. As families move or make different choices in where they attend church, the expectation of associating with the local church should remain consistent even when the church attended changes. As it says in Hebrews 10:25, *"Let us not give up meeting together, as some are in the habit of doing, but let us encourage one another—and all the more as you see the Day approaching."*

Character Truths in Action

Model, model, model; this is the way that your little one is going to absorb what is important in your home. A three-year old can see what is important to Mom if he noticed that she screams and yells at the older brother for breaking a fragile object but then later that same day does not make sure that older brother treats three-year old brother kindly. The message becomes, "objects are more important than people." Whether we realize it or not, this kind of "messaging" takes place all of the time based on what we say and do just as much as what we do not say and do. So, work at this young season to make your message clear, Godly, and consistent.

> *Model, model, model; this is the way that your little one is going to absorb what is important in your home.*

➤ **Scripture to ponder**: *But the fruit of the Spirit is love, joy, peace, patience, kindness, goodness, faithfulness, gentleness and self-control. Against such things there is no law. Those who belong to Christ Jesus have crucified the sinful nature with its passions and desires. Since we live by the Spirit, let us keep in step with the*

Spirit. Let us not become conceited, provoking and envying each other. Galatians 5:22-24 (NIV)

1. **Start building relationships now with like-minded parents.** Typically, the early relationships you have with other parents of young children are the ones that will carry you through at least the years of their early development, so spend time making this a priority. If the parents are of like-mind, then usually their children will make good playmates and mutual role models for your child as you teach them important character qualities by "doing life" together and with others.

2. From your experiences and/or in relationship to the parenting class options mentioned in the next section, **decide now what are going to be the key characteristics of your parenting priorities.** This is where that concept of unity comes into play for your role as parents. To get started, use the fruit of the Spirit from Galatians we discussed earlier and decide, "How am I going to apply each of these elements to my parenting decisions with my child? How will we help our child to exhibit this fruit?" Then add other elements as you go along. Take some time to work through this list with your husband and also look for suggestions from your mentor. Be specific about how you will express these ideas to your child in tangible ways but be careful about creating a "rules-oriented" relationship with your child rather than one based on principles. I have a sign that we obtained many years ago from the San Diego Zoo that says:

> "PLEASE DO NOT
> TREAD, MOSEY, HOP,
> TRAMPLE, STEP,
> PLOD, TIPTOE, TROT,
> TRAIPSE, MEANDER,
> CREEP, PRANCE,
> AMBLE, JOG,
> TRUDGE, MARCH,
> STOMP, TODDLE, JUMP,
> STUMBLE, TROD, SPRINT,
> OR WALK
> ON THE PLANTS."

This is just what we communicate as parents sometimes. We become so focused on the "don'ts" and completely ignore the overall spirit of what we want them to move towards. Rather than rattling off that entire list above, the sign could have simply stated, "STAY ON THE PATH". So that is what we need to do too. Keep your priorities somewhat broad as well and add other thoughts as you go along in your parenting journey to help your child **"STAY ON THE PATH"**. In other words, communicate to your child what they need to more towards and not only what they should avoid. Put these thoughts on a small reminder card that you can keep with you throughout the day or as you travel in your car. A great character-building book to use during this season with preschoolers is *Creative Family Times: Practical Activities for Building Character in Your Preschooler* by Allen and Connie Hadidian and Will and Lindy Wilson. Use the **"Parenting Priorities for Our Children"** worksheet on page 238 for additional assistance with this concept.

3. Talk with your husband now about **faith-building holiday traditions** you want to establish in your home. Children enjoy the anticipation of holidays and building memories during major milestones. However, times of celebration can be stressful events. So make the necessary plans in advance to ensure that the joy you create during these times are meaningful and pleasant for everyone. Set expectations with your extended family about what your plans are so that you always have some time during the holidays that are just for you, your husband, and your child. Here are some general resources that can help you with these discussions:

    ➢ *Let's Make a Memory* by Gloria Gaither and Shirley Dobson; This is filled with a number of practical ideas for creating "traditions and togetherness" with each other.

    ➢ *Celebrating the Christian Year; Building Family Traditions Around All the Major Christian Holidays* by Martha Zimmerman; This is an excellent resource that steps you through an entire calendar year with thoughts and information on celebrating all of the major and not-so major holidays available to us.

    ➢ *A Family Guide to the Biblical Holidays With Activities for All Ages* by Robin Carlata and Linda Pierce; This 583-page manual is massive! For Christian families who wish to understand more about the Jewish holidays and how to incorporate certain experiences into their home based on these long-standing traditions, this is an indispensable resource.

I have also included in the Appendices section (Appendix D) some **suggestions that you may want to incorporate into your family's traditions** that we have found to be meaningful in our home. There, you will find useful ideas and "food for thought" on how to plan special moments and traditions into your family's celebration for birthdays, your wedding anniversary, Valentine's Day, Easter, Memorial Day, Mother's and Father's Days, Fourth of July, Thanksgiving, Christmas, and New Year's Eve. I have also included a planner sheet for you so that you can start recording some of your own ideas for these special occasions as well as a separate section addressing the controversial holiday of Halloween.

Set expectations with your extended family about what your plans are so that you always have some time during the holidays that are just for you, your husband, and your child.

So before advancing to the next part of this chapter, take some time now to go over the next two worksheets that will help you to establish some daily, tangible parenting priorities and to record some thoughts about family traditions that you want to establish now as each holiday comes and goes. Then discuss these planning activities with your mentors for more input.

Other notes thus far for the Little Ones "season":

_____

_____

_____

_____

_____

_____

_____

_____

_____

_____

Parenting Priorities for Our Children

I want to instill…	We will do this through these daily interactions and methods.	
Love		
Joy		
Peace		
Patience		
Kindness		
Goodness		
Faithfulness		
Gentleness		
Self-Control		

Holiday Tradition Planning Sheet

Holiday or Significant Event	We will celebrate this occasion by establishing these traditions and practices.
Birthdays	
Our Wedding Anniversary	
Valentine's Day	
Easter	
Memorial Day	
Mother's Day	
Father's Day	
Fourth of July	
Thanksgiving	
Christmas	
New Year's Eve	

Behavioral Truths in Action

Recognize that in this early stage of parenting, you need to give yourself a ramp-up time that is necessary to establish your opinions about child training and to synthesize them with those of your husband. If you determine the basics early, you will give yourself and your child a firm foundation in how to communicate with one another as well as how to correct your child firmly but with love.

➤ **Scripture to ponder**: *And now, dear lady, I am not writing you a new command but one we have had from the beginning. I ask that we love one another. And this is love: that we walk in obedience to his commands. As you have heard from the beginning, his command is that you walk in love. II John 1:5-6*

1. **Obedience training** starts at a young age by helping children learn focus and self-control skills early. When they are very young, teach them basic sign language for things like "food", "drink", "more", and "all done" to communicate their needs. Establish a process that you can follow every time for teaching your little one that screaming, arching their back, and throwing food will not get them what they want. As they enter toddlerhood, require them to sit with you for increasingly extended periods of time throughout the day for reading or some other quiet activity to build focus skills. For more information about teaching sign language to young ones, use *Baby Signs: How to Talk with Your Baby Before Your Baby Can Talk* by Linda Acredolo and Susan Goodwyn. Even today, I still use certain signs with my teens to communicate something in public that they can respond to quickly without making a big production of it!

2. Parents-to-be are often eager to take parenting classes but then sometimes do not follow through after the child is born. Take at least one **parenting class** after you actually have a little one at home, and you can more easily the connection between conceptual and practical faith in action. Here are some Christian parenting resources that might be useful to you.

    ➤ *The Complete Guide to Baby and Childcare* by **Focus on the Family** is a useful book to have on hand that not only covers medical concerns that you may have with your child at various stages of development but also covers child training advice.[197] Also look for other parenting resources on

---

[197] http://www.focusonthefamily.com/

the Focus on the Family website for upcoming workshops, resources, and counseling information.

> *Growing Kids God's Way* by **Growing Kids God's Way International** is an intensive training program for parents. The materials assume that you are taking the course with your husband.[198] The course and DVD materials are too expensive to purchase as an individual family, but many churches own these materials and host regular classes.

> *MotherWise: Freedom for Mother, Five Liberating Principles for Victorious Mothering* by Denise Glenn is also comprehensive and encouraging. Again, the **MotherWise** curriculum is a DVD program that you may find hosted out of a church in your local area.[199]

> Another great tool to help frame your thinking for the parenting process that is upon and ahead of you is *Shepherding a Child's Heart* by Tedd Tripp. It is a straightforward alternative for those parents who cannot attend a formal parenting class but need Scriptural guidance in developing their parenting, communication, and discipline approaches with their child.

I also encourage **new moms to "shadow" other moms** who are more experienced for a day and see how they operate within their home environment. Seeing how veteran moms balance child training and discipline throughout the variables that most homes face each day can be invaluable and encouraging input to put a new mother at ease. Now *that* is on-the-job training!

Seek out additional resources and advice about the spiritual, character, and behavioral development of your child during this season from your mentor. Talk to your husband about your thoughts.

_____

_____

_____

_____

---

[198] http://www.growingfamiliesusa.com/ - *Growing Kids God's Way* is now called *Parenting from the Tree of Life.*
[199] http://www.motherwise.org/

K-2nd Grade

As children enter this stage, they have grown and developed exponentially since they were born. Their comprehension and communication skills will often blow you away with how much they know and can do. However, while parents will often try to do too much too soon with their three-year-old child by the time that same child is in kindergarten, they may not take their training efforts as far as the can and should go. **Do not back off too soon from learning about how to parent a young child as your interactions with them change from mostly care giving to training.**

GOD
↓
Parents
↓
Child

Returning to our organizational chart, this is the stage where children really start to understand that Dad and Mom are accountable to God. If you are consistent in your reinforcement of this idea, children in this season have no problems understanding that their parents are not just "making it up as they go along". Rather, they see that you are requiring certain things from them because God requires certain things from dad and mom. So now their chart expands to look like the diagram to the above. God has now been added, and the child no longer thinks that accountability begins and ends with their parents. While their interactions with others outside of the nuclear family begin to expand, they really continue to limit their view of their world to the inside of their home until they start to leave this season. If grandparents or other significant people in their life serve in a care-giver or training capacity for them, they would also be in the "Parents" box. Here are training steps that parents can take at this season in their child's development.

Spiritual Truths in Action

Seek for your child to fill their mind with Bible stories, memorized scriptures and principles that they will have tucked away now and for their later years. In this young season, they are like sponges and can absorb a great deal of information even if they do not quite understand it all yet. Fill the pantry of their mind now so you can draw from its stores now and in later seasons.

➢ **Scripture to ponder**: *I have hidden your word in my heart that I might not sin against you. Psalm 119:11 (NIV)*

1. **Step up the Bible stories**. Even children as young as five years of age can begin to understand time. As they grasp that Bible stories are different from other stories because they actually did happen a long time ago, begin to introduce your child to the flow and order of biblical occurrences and lessons

that the people learned. My absolute favorite Bible for children is *The Child's Story Bible* written by Catherine Vos in 1935. Mrs. Vos was highly unsatisfied with the children's materials that were available at that time to teach children about their Christian faith and the Bible. She felt that most books available to her were too watered down and incomplete to be meaningful to most families. In response, she wrote this unique, slightly abridged text that covers the entire Bible. However, it reads like a story, and she speaks directly to the child about understanding concepts presented throughout, explaining difficult ideas in a way that is both respectful of the child's intelligence as well as age-appropriate in the level of detailed shared. During this season in our home, we cycled through the entire book every two years so that all of the boys constantly received the flow and content of the Bible as it was reinforced over and over again. Supplement your reading time by using coloring sheets from *The Big Picture Bible Time Line* by Carol Eide as well as the dramatized *Your Story Hour* audio CDs called *Bible Comes Alive,* produced by **Your Story Hour Inc.**[200]

2. Add **scripture memorization** by utilizing song and story CD's that your child can listen to during quiet play time or room time throughout the day or even in the car. Another source for scripture memorization is a **child's devotional text** like *Leading Little Ones to God* by Marian Schoolland. Although it is a bit intensive if you do every part of every chapter, it is very comprehensive and can be scaled to meet your needs. Mrs. Schoolland does an excellent job of relating sometimes intangible concepts in very tangible ways. When we went through this program with our oldest son, I would type out the lesson scriptures and then we would cut and paste them on colored paper and then onto index cards that eventually became the "box cars" in a scripture train that we wrapped around his room. We could then review his "scripture train" in a cumulative manner before he went to bed each night.

3. **Help your child learn how to pray** during mealtimes, bedtime, and other quiet moments with you throughout the day. Make it something that becomes part of their regular pattern for the day and that your child learns early how to communicate with God and rely on His presence throughout the week. If he is already at work, "conference" dad into the morning prayer time. *Teaching Your Child How to Pray* by Rick Osborne is a great resource to use for this purpose.

---

[200] http://www.yourstoryhour.org/; Albums 1-5 cover the entire Bible.

4. **Familiarize your child with the old hymns.** So much of contemporary worship, while positive, has replaced many of the old hymns that reflect the wisdom and faith of our forefathers. Make sure to still play them in your home so your children do not miss the opportunity to know and understand the significance of these songs. For example, if your child eventually understands John Newton's history in the European slave trading business during the eighteenth century and then learns that he later advocated against it and then wrote the most recognizable hymn in Christendom, "Amazing Grace", which is a powerful message. Consider Horatio Spafford, prominent lawyer and business man, who wrote "It Is Well with My Soul" after losing his four daughters in a tragic accident at sea. *O Worship the King* by Joni Eareckson Tada, John MacArthur, and Robert and Bobbie Wolgemuth is a great resource for this purpose. It is a book written of compiled articles about the background of a number of great old hymns along with a listening CD.

5. Continue to **stay involved in understanding what your child is experiencing in their church program and encourage appropriate participation.** Although they are not really building too much in the way of a consistent relationship with their group leader or teacher at this point, too often parents, even with children at this young age, are content to drop their child off and pick them up from their church class week after week without knowing what is going on and how or what they are doing. Get to know their teacher and ask them how your child did. Talk to your child and understand what they learned and what relationships they are building with other children during that time. If you have questions or concerns, you should be able to observe the class without it being an issue. If you are not well received in this request, then that is a red flag that you need to pursue until you have addressed your questions.

Character Truths in Action

This is the season where you focus on building a common vocabulary of character element terms with your child. When they learn the word "attentiveness", for example, they will not know what it means. You then need to break that down for them and help them understand it in an age appropriate way. Cut out pictures of eyes, ears, and a heart. Then explain to your child that "attentiveness" is "listening with your eyes, ears, and your heart" while they glue the pictures onto a labeled piece of paper. Then when you use the word later, they will have some tangible point of reference that reminds them what you mean.[201] In other words, help your child to connect the intangible concepts of integrity and selflessness to the physical world around them.

> **Scripture to ponder**: *Then the LORD said to Satan, "Have you considered my servant Job? There is no one on earth like him; he is blameless and upright, a man who fears God and shuns evil. And he still maintains his integrity, though you incited me against him to ruin him without any reason." Job 2:3 (NIV)*

1. **Add character training resources** to your training plans. For this age, *A Child's Book of Character Building (Book 1 and Book 2)* by Ron & Rebekah Coriel is a perfect solution. Filled with black-line coloring sheet pictures that correspond to each story, you can take your child through each character quality discussed from four different perspectives. For each character trait, parents can present a story about that trait in action at home, in the Bible, in a group setting, and at playtime. The texts cover 24 different qualities such as creativity, attentiveness (as referenced in the introduction section above), diligence, faith, honesty, fairness, and love. You can take a couple of weeks to cover each one and spread this project over more than a year. One idea is to purchase a large book of easel paper that your child can use to glue on their four coloring sheets and other drawings or pictures that represent the idea on the page. Then when they are all done, you can put it together into one giant "Big Book of Character" that they can then share with visitors and grandparents. You can also accomplish something similar in a three-ring binder if you are looking for a smaller solution.

2. Another great resource at this age is *The Original 21 Rules of This House* by Greg Harris. This book is a cross between a situational character training tool and a devotional. It is filled with black-line coloring sheets that can be used for the children to color while you talk about each idea and how they put it to practice within the home. One drawback of the program is that they do not note related scriptures for each "rule". However, if you want to tie scripture reading and/or memorizing into the process, you can easily supplement it by making a list of your own to go along with it.[202] It also comes with a handy poster that your child can reference later when situations arise that relate to one of the "21 Rules".

---

[201] *A Child's Book of Character Building Book 1*, Coriell, Ron & Rebekah, Fleming H. Revell Co., p. 9
[202] I have developed such a scripture list that you can access on our private TBH Facebook account under the "Files" section.

Behavioral Truths in Action

As you work with your husband to establish behavioral rules for your home, try to begin with a few basic expectations for manner and conduct. Then build from there. If you start with a list of fifty expectations for your first grader, they will become quickly discouraged and you will become frustrated from managing such a long, complicated list.

➤ **Scripture to ponder**: *And you have forgotten that word of encouragement that addresses you as sons:*
  "My son, do not make light of the Lord's discipline,
    and do not lose heart when he rebukes you,
  because the Lord disciplines those he loves,
    and he punishes everyone he accepts as a son.

  Endure hardship as discipline; God is treating you as sons. For what son is not disciplined by his father? If you are not disciplined (and everyone undergoes discipline), then you are illegitimate children and not true sons. Hebrews 12:5-8 (NIV)

➤ **Scripture to ponder**: *Whatever happens, conduct yourselves in a manner worthy of the gospel of Christ. Philippians 1:27a (NIV)*

➤ **Scripture to ponder**: *An anxious heart weighs a man down, but a kind word cheers him up. Proverbs 12:25 (NIV)*

1. Much of what you will apply in obedience training for this age will naturally flow out of what you started with them when you were younger. It is important to **stay consistent and unified with your husband** as you work with your children in handling problems as calmly as possible and administering discipline. No matter which parent is available, we know that we will make the same decision, so the child can depend on consistency. Decide in advance what kinds of offenses warrant what kinds of punishments. In our home, willful disobedience or serious safety violations warranted spankings, but those were very rare and always administered in a calm manner with plenty of guiding words, hugs, and kisses before and after. So most of what you will want to determine are the other levels of punishment for lesser offenses and problems. They may even vary by child since what one may consider punishment, another may not think of as a big deal. Do you use isolation to remove the child from the scene of the "crime" or should the child be required to do an act of service in the home that corrects the problem they caused? What privileges should be withheld and what restitution might need to be made to an injured party?

These and many other nuances to discipline must be a top priority for you and your husband to define and administer consistently. In addition to any parenting class resources you use, here are a couple of additional books that you will find useful to have on hand.

➤ *Bringing Up Boys: Practical Advice and Encouragement for Those Shaping the Next Generation of Men* by Dr. James Dobson; This book provides parents with extra insight and support in raising boys into Godly men.

➤ *Bringing Up Girls: Practical Advice and Encouragement for Those Shaping the Next Generation of Women* by Dr. James Dobson; This book provides parents with extra insight and support in raising girls into Godly women.

➤ *Creative Correction* by Lisa Whelchel; This is a lighthearted but very practical look at ways that you can go beyond the basic and often overused standard discipline methods.

➤ *The Five Love Languages for Children* by Gary Chapman; After you have had an opportunity to go through the original title with your husband, this is a great follow-up on how to apply the same "love language" concepts to your children.

➤ *The New Strong-Willed Child* by James Dobson; Let's face it. If you have a strong-willed child, you will definitely know it by this early season of their life! As Dr. Dobson transparently points out, "some children are tougher to raise than others". If you are challenged with a child who fits into this category, take heart that Dr. Dobson can provides insight into establishing a system of "checks and balances", utilizing love and control as your tools.[203]

2. You have already naturally begun to teach your child many important manners for how they talk with others or behave at the dinner table. Continue to build on these points by **incorporating other manners training materials** in your home. One great resource that you can use is *365 Manners Kids Should Know* by Sheryl Eberly. Instead of going in order, we actually took a copy of the table of contents and cut them up into small strips and placed them in a bowl. Then at the dinner table, the boys would take turns selecting a topic, and we would go to that topic in the book and discuss it. Sometimes we would even role play after dinner, showing how *not* to demonstrate that

---

[203] http://www.focusonthefamily.com/parenting/effective-biblical-discipline

manner before role-playing the right way to do it. This is a great way to learn etiquette and build fun family memories at the same time!

3. **Teach your children how you expect them to resolve conflicts with their siblings.** Facilitate conversations between or among your children to show how frustrating behavior should result in each one listening to each other rather than saying unkind words or doing unkind actions. Use a tangible tool that they can go to in order to resolve their issue even before they involve you. A resource like the *Brother-Offended Checklist* by **Doorposts** is a great way for you to teach them about issues of conflict *before* they have an incident so that you are training them and reinforcing these ideas on a regular basis. Reward them as you see appropriate to reinforce the importance of resolving conflicts independently. However, these moments at this young age will be few and far between, so be prepared to step in early as the situation warrants.[204]

Seek out additional resources and advice about the spiritual, character, and behavioral development of your child during this season from your mentor. Talk to your husband about your thoughts.

_____

_____

_____

_____

_____

_____

_____

_____

_____

_____

_____

_____

_____

_____

---

[204] http://www.doorposts.com

3rd Grade – 6th Grade

By this season, children begin to gain an expanded perception of their world influences. No longer is their concept of God's role in the world limited to their immediate family as they also begin to interact with others and see God's hand at work in their lives as well. They start to make connections that their parents' interactions with them, while driven by God's requirements of them, are also influenced by extended family members, friends, and neighbors. This is the season that they also experience influence from other significant adults, such as music teachers, church group leaders, and recreational coaches. They can perceive a two-way relationship of give and take between their parents and the neighbors, friends, and extended family around them as well as between themselves and their friends. However, for most of this season, they still perceive the other relationships on this chart to be mostly one-way roads.

Take a minute now to jot some notes down on the chart here that reflects some of the specific names of the influencers that exist outside of your nuclear family.

Name the primary influencers that impact your family.

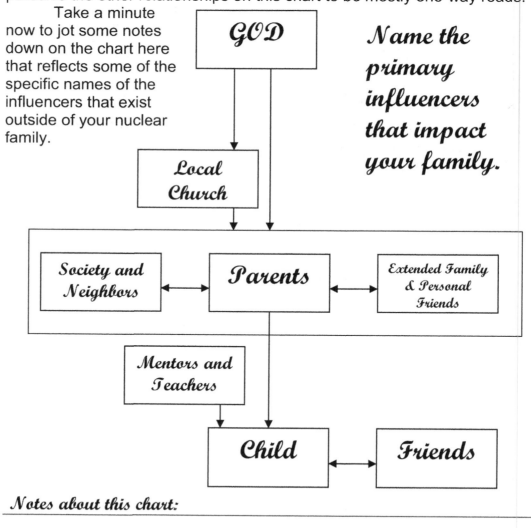

Notes about this chart: _____

_____

_____

Spiritual Truths in Action

"God helps those who help themselves." Quick! Where is that found in the Bible? If you cannot find any such reference in your concordance, do not despair, for this quote is *not* in the Bible! Yet we have heard this saying growing up many times. Where did it come from? I know the first time I stumbled upon it in writing was when I read *Swiss Family Robinson* aloud to my then eight-year old son. There it was as plain as day right in the opening chapter. This is just one small example of how popular sayings can sneak into our belief system before we even realize that it is rooted in our brains. How, then, do we help our child to separate truth from cultural norms? We must continually help them build a method by which to study and understand God's Word so that encounters like this do not confuse them.

➤ **Scripture to ponder**: *Great are the works of the LORD; they are pondered by all who delight in them. Psalm 111:2 (NIV)*

➤ **Scripture to ponder**: *Psalm 119:44-49*

I will always obey your law,
 for ever and ever.

I will walk about in freedom,
 for I have sought out your precepts.

I will speak of your statutes before kings
 and will not be put to shame,

for I delight in your commands
 because I love them.

I lift up my hands to your commands, which I love,
 and I meditate on your decrees.

So now is the time to **add some independent study to the family Bible time.** As they mature during this season, you can continue using the *Child's Story Bible* as your "spine" for the entire family Bible-reading times, assuming you have younger ones too. Your older ones can look up the actual scriptures in their own Bibles to go along with the reading. By the end of 6th grade, children should have their own unabridged text of the Bible in the translation that your church and family most regularly use. You can structure something yourself that is related to your family Bible-reading times or you can tie their study assignment to the teaching priorities that are found in their church program. However, many parents choose a more formal approach by this age. Consider these programs for ideas.

1. *Christian Studies I, II, and III* by **Memoria Press**; If you are looking for a systematic and thorough program, you may be interested in checking out this three-year study. Volume I covers Creation to Moses' Last Words, Volume II covers the invasion of Canaan to Jonah, and Volume III covers Zacharias, Angel's Visit to Mary, Jesus' Birth through Paul's Final Years, Letters of Peter, and the visions of John. The study is designed to be used with *The Golden Children's Bible*: a somewhat simplified King James text. You may also choose to round out your use of this program by finishing with Volume IV, which is an overall summary of the entire Bible and a good way to review/reinforce what was learned in the first three volumes.[205]

2. *Discover 4 Yourself Bible Study Series* by Kay Arthur; This series includes numerous titles that your child can work through independently to study various concepts and figures of the Bible including, *Joseph-God's Superhero, Wrong Way, Jonah!, Abraham-God's Brave Explorer, Bible Prophesy for Kids Revelation 1-7*, and more. If you are interested in this series, start with *How to Study Your Bible for Kids* and *Lord, Teach Me How to Pray, for Kids*. It is written directly to the kids in a fun and engaging manner. If you use this series, I would suggest taking the book to an office supply store and having the binding replaced with a spiral one since your child is expected to write in it. Also, be aware that the Bible translation referred to is the New American Standard Bible. It will be difficult for your child to do many of the exercises if they do not have this translation.

3. *What We Believe Series* by Apologia; This is a beautiful four-volume set of books that help children, ages six through fourteen, navigate modern questions relating to their faith. The titles include *Who is God?, Who Am I?, Who is My Neighbor?,* and *What on Earth Can I Do?*

4. **Add a reliable current events resource to your child's education** to prepare them for world interactions they will encounter in the next season by subscribing to ***God's World News***.[206] Although they publish this monthly periodical beginning with Pre-K and up, your child will get the most out of it during the middle to latter part of this season when they can read and work the various activities, quizzes, maps, and puzzles

---

[205] http://www.memoriapress.com/descriptions/ChristianStudies.html
[206] http://www.gwnews.com/

more independently rather when they are much younger. Articles cover current news events, historical points of interest, and science stories in an interesting, comprehensive, and age-appropriate way while consistently maintaining a Biblical worldview.

Character Truths in Action

As you continue to seek ways to instill positive character traits in your children, this is the season that you can bombard them with biographical stories and fictional situational stories that clearly demonstrate the difficulties that they will face in following God's Word. As they learn about how both children and adults have opportunities to follow their own thinking versus God's principles, you will begin to help them learn how to "see around corners", which also relates to the discussion we will have in the "Behavioral Truths in Action" section.

➤ **Scripture to ponder**: *There is a way that seems right to a man, but in the end it leads to death. Proverbs 16:25 (NIV)*

1. To instill positive character traits in your children, **study about real heroes of the Christian faith.** The best series I have encountered are the *Hero Tales* volumes by Dave & Neta Jackson of **Overcomer Books**.[207] These books are excellent devotional as well as character training tools as your children learn about various Christian missionaries and leaders that have furthered God's Word in their own way. They bring alive historical figures like Florence Nightingale, Gladys Alward, Harriet Tubman, Eric Liddell, Martin Luther, George Washington Carver, George Muller, and many more. Each chapter introduces the hero followed by three stories about the person that illustrates a different character trait for each situation. Scripture references and follow-up questions are provided for each section. Their historical fiction *Trailblazer Books* series is a great follow-up for older children to continue their reading about these great heroes of the faith.

2. Promote informal character discussions with your child as you "do life" together. Whether you "people watch" at the mall or encounter various situations at your local church, there are opportunities all around you for your child to see various circumstances unfold around them and how well people do or do not respond to them. However, at this age, their exposure to the variety of behavioral situations is still quite limited. So, an

---

[207] http://www.daveneta.com/

informal way of promoting character development discussions in your home is to utilize dramatized story media.

3. The *Your Story Hour* audio CDs produced by **Your Story Hour Inc.** mentioned previously also has an *Adventures in Life* series of adventure stories that presents **dramatized stories of various "life" situations** that has a specific lesson or moral attached to it.[208] Their history stories are similar in concept but are based on real figures in history (i.e. *Patterns of Destiny, Heritage of our Country, Exciting Events,* and *Great Stories*). These are great resources for the car or for them to listen to during a quite activity or play time throughout the week.

4. Another informal way of promoting character discussions is to follow the **Adventures in Odyssey** series, produced by **Focus on the Family**.[209] Your child can follow the lives and decisions of various recurring characters as they struggle with compelling circumstances that range from the ordinary to the, of course, adventuresome! You may purchase story media in a volume set, listen to on-line episodes, or purchase an all-access digital membership.

5. Another effective way to incorporate character concepts into your child's training is to **relate life lessons from the literature that they read and the media they encounter**. No matter what your child is reading or what you are reading out to them, there are lessons all around us to be learned. In *Charlotte's Web*, Wilbur learns about the various aspects of friendship from an unlikely relationship with a wise and generous spider. In the *Wizard of Oz,* we see along the way that Dorothy's companions really possessed everything that they were seeking all along but just needed someone to reinforce it so that they could believe in themselves. In *Pilgrim's Progress*, we journey with Christian to the Celestial City and experience his encounters with the allegorical figures of the encourager Hope, the know-it-all-do-nothing Talkative, and the false Flatterer, just to name a few. The *Chronicles of Narnia* are full of endless opportunities to discuss Jesus' relationship to man and the Pevensie children's ability to exercise free will in choosing right or wrong. In *The Hobbit*, Bilbo and his dwarf friends learn the importance of "staying on the path" when they nearly lose their lives in Mirkwood Forest. So, you can see that there is no shortage of opportunities to develop concepts of character, right and wrong, and God's role in man's life as you walk through your child's

---

[208] http://www.yourstoryhour.org/
[209] http://www.whitsend.org/; http://www.focusonthefamily.com/

reading list together. One final point about discussing literature is that, although watching a movie version is fine, there are two things you will want to keep in mind about it before you make any viewing decisions.

➤ First, make sure they have read, or you have read to them, the original. There is nothing like experiencing **original, unabridged, literature** firsthand without having a heavily edited and often incorrect interpretation of the story from the movie swimming around in your child's head.

➤ Second, make sure that you have previewed the movie or have researched it thoroughly first. Sometimes even the most seemingly innocuous film can lead to big regrets when you review it through your Christian worldview perspective. This is especially true for films we may have seen as kids and realize now that they were not that Godly! Websites like **Christian Spotlight on Entertainment, Common Sense Media**, and **Plugged In** can be very useful for this purpose.[210]

Behavioral Truths in Action

Obedience training at this age starts to **shift away from concrete rules to providing the child the tools necessary to make good decisions in a variety of circumstances.** Towards the end of this season, children not only expand their perception of the world around them but also become capable of relating the concepts of "cause and effect" easily. They begin to understand how to "see around corners" and make judgments about, "If I do *this* then *that* might happen, so should I do it or not?"

➤ <u>**Scripture to ponder**</u>: *Listen, my son, to your father's instruction and do not forsake your mother's teaching. Proverbs 1:8 (NIV)*

1. The best method I have found for teaching children how to start thinking critically about life choices is one I created and named called the **"Four Steps to Freedom".** No matter what the issue is, whether it is a reoccurring problem in math, an attitude issue with one of their brothers, or even something more serious, this process is useful to teach children when they enter this season and then throughout it as they encounter various problems, big or small. I have the children envision four circles on the ground. You can also reinforce this by having a physical prop of some

---

[210] http://www.christiananswers.net/spotlight/; https://www.commonsensemedia.org/; http://www.pluggedin.com/

kind. I have them face me and stand in their first "circle" called, **"There *is* a problem"**. Then we discuss how it does not matter if the person causing the problem or involved in it does not agree with the statement that there is a problem, the fact is the problem *does* exist. This problem is reality, it is truth, it is fact. The second "circle" is the most difficult one to face, for this is where the person causing the problem or involved with it must **personally *recognize* that there is a problem that involves them.** This acknowledgement step is critical. Without recognition, no progress can be made. If they can hold my hands and communicate to me how they are responsible for the issue, we have achieved the goal. Once ownership of the problem is established, then they can commence with the third circle. This is the step where the person *plans* to **address the problem.** This is where you, as the parent, are able to work with them on creative ways to address the issue at hand. While this can be used in all areas of life, let us now look at some academic examples. Are they having neatness issues with their

Four Steps to Freedom

There is, in fact, a problem

Recognize they are involved in the problem

Make plans to address the problem

Solve problem and maintain desired outcome

handwriting? Have them trace sample handwriting so they get the look and feel for what they are trying to achieve, showing how neat penmanship can come out of their own hand! Are they having problems remembering certain math facts for geometry? Have them make their own fact cards that they can use to not only reinforce the rule to themselves but that they can use as a reference during their assignments as needed. Perhaps they have difficulty projecting when they are speaking out loud. If so, come up with a safe "public presentation" setting in the home that they can use as practice, either reading something to the family after dinner or even recording themselves so they can critique their own presentation. Whatever the issue is, work with your child to come up with creative solutions that you can live with and that they have demonstrated ownership in deciding. The fourth step is that the **problem is solved and now it becomes a matter of maintaining the desired outcome.** Remember that it is not just enough to solve it, it must *stay* solved!

2. **Grab the teachable moments with your child, even if it is not convenient for you.** One morning, I came into the kitchen and our two younger boys were prepping the breakfast and putting clean dishes away. At first, it was a serene scene to behold—and then came the silverware. For whatever reason, neither child wanted to put the pieces away. The youngest said, "You always make me put it away. I'm tired of putting silverware away. You do it!" Then the other child retorted," No! You do it. I did a lot of these other dishes and I don't want to!" Back and forth it went, and I did not say a word. In the meantime, our oldest son entered and right away admonished them to work it out or there would be no chocolate in their future (see chapter four about incentives for your child)! Still the disagreement raged on, and the silverware lay untouched in the basket. In the meantime, everything was out and ready to go. We all sat around the kitchen island looking at one another when finally, our youngest said, "Mommy, will you pour milk on my cereal?" I looked at him very quietly and said, "No. I don't feel like it." You could have heard a pin drop! Then I went on to say, "In fact, I don't want to get your juice either and I am also tired of making sure you get your vitamins." Another long pause and blank stares of shock passed. I continued bluntly, "I am actually tired of cooking dinner every night: day after day after day. You know, when I think about it I could use a long break from doing laundry because I am tired of making sure you have clean underwear and clothes to wear. While we're at it, could you just figure out a way to teach yourself today? I don't think I want to

do that either." By this time, they were all "getting it", and the smiles and giggles began. I went on a little longer with my feigned speech of exasperation, and then I pulled out my Bible and read to them the following passage:

> *"Do everything without complaining or arguing, so that you may become blameless and pure, children of God without fault in a crooked and depraved generation, in which you shine like stars in the universe as you hold out the word of life—in order that I may boast on the day of Christ that I did not run or labor for nothing." Philippians 2:14-16 (NIV)*

As we talked through the situation, the kids were suitably humbled and aware of what they had sounded like. We talked about how their behavior needs to "shine like stars" so that they set good examples and that they do not "labor for nothing". Were we late starting school that day? Yes and no. The academics were delayed, and regular Bible time was derailed. However, what they walked away with was valuable, for we had not allowed a teachable moment to pass, and it is an experience that they can still remember today. It also helped them to see that God's Word is suitable for any circumstance that they will face. There is nothing that they deal with or that happens to them that Scripture does not address. Be willing to be interrupted to help them figure these things out in real-time.

3. "Seeing around corners" not only translates to physical outcomes related to behavior, but also to **controlling the tongue.** So, at some point during this season, you will want to do a thorough study of the book of James with your child, particularly focusing on chapter three. Another good activity to do with your child that also gets the point across about the importance of the words we use is to compare and contrast Psalm 119:103 with Proverbs 10:26. Using the NIV, these verses read as follows:

> *How sweet are your words to my taste,*
> *sweeter than honey to my mouth! (Psalm 119:103)*

> *As vinegar to the teeth and smoke to the eyes,*
> *so are sluggards to those who send them. (Proverbs 10:26)*

Experiential learning for young children is a very useful tool when getting across spiritual points. In this case, have a teaspoon of white vinegar and a teaspoon of honey available. Then discuss with your child how positive words from our mouth tastes like honey to the Lord, but bitter words taste like vinegar. Have your child taste each one to get the point across. Then, as needed, remind them that "vinegar words" are not allowed or complement them when they use "honey words".

4. For more information about understanding your child's development and **helping them make good personal choices**, check out these additional resources.

  ➤ *The Five Love Languages for Children* by Gary Chapman; If you have not read this book already, now is the time to do it! Filled with practical information on how to "speak your child's love language", Gary Chapman also provides parents insight on how best to discipline and train children based on their primary love language: physical touch, receiving gifts, words of affirmation, acts of service, and quality time.

  ➤ *Manners Made Easy* by June Hines Moore; This is a workbook for students and parents that provide more insight and practice in manners training.

  ➤ *Personal Help for Boys* and *Personal Help for Girls* by **Pearables** are unique texts and workbooks that provide parents additional support in helping to instill good habits into their daily interactions with others. Although some of the writing is a bit "old fashioned", the heart of the content is challenging and valuable.[211]

  ➤ *Preparing for Adolescence* by Dr. James Dobson; If you are looking for a tried and true resource to help prepare your child for their next "season", this is a helpful book to use with your child. Only parents can decide when the right time is to share information with their child about the "facts of life". However, in this culture of ungodly media exposure, parents usually find that they at least need to reveal certain information to their child bit-by-bit so that they are not blindsided or inappropriately "educated" by their peers.

  ➤ *The Power of a Praying Parent* by Stormie OMartian; In the end, or really at the beginning, we must daily place your school plans and your children's progress in the hands of the One who made them. Pray for discernment, wisdom, creativity, and perspective. This book serves as an excellent aid and reminder for parents to do just that.

---

[211] http://www.pearables.com/

5. Finally, make sure to research and **employ Internet filtering and monitoring software** as soon as you allow your child to access computers or personal devices. Even the most innocent of searches can result in unwanted spamming, popups, and links that are inappropriate. Technology options change often, so always research before selecting your tool of choice. At a minimum, utilize parental control options provided to you at the time of purchase (i.e. Microsoft, McAfee, Norton Antivirus, etc.).

➤ **Circle** was developed in partnership with Disney. This device that looks more like a rounded square than a circle helps parents to filter personal devices that are in their home.[212]

➤ **Covenant Eyes** is an Internet accountability service that works with Windows and Apple devices and PC's as well as Kindle Fire HD. It also includes age-based filters and additional resources for parents. [213]

➤ **Ever Accountable** is another Internet accountability product that works across most platforms and provides detailed activity reports for parents. [214]

➤ **Forcefield** works with Apple devices. It allows parents to set up timing controls on your child's device so that they can only access apps, etc. certain times of the day. It gives parents access to see all websites viewed and photos posted by their child. It also allows parents to lock YouTube Restricted Mode and SafeSearch. [215]

Seek out additional resources and advice about the spiritual, character, and behavioral development of your child during this season from your mentor. Talk to your husband about your thoughts.

_____

_____

_____

_____

_____

---

[212] https://meetcircle.com/
[213] http://www.covenanteyes.com/
[214] https://www.everaccountable.com/
[215] https://forcefield.me/

Junior High, High School, and Beyond

For older children, their concept of God and the world and people around them expands to what we know to be true on an adult level. So, **although they will lack the maturity and experiences necessary to navigate the full implications of this adult system for many years yet to come, they can and do understand the structure of it.** They now see how the pieces fit together even though the content of what awaits them in each one is not fully understood. Therefore, you will find that your parenting role will begin to **shift from a training to more of a coaching function** sometime during their seventh and eighth grade years as they enter their teens.

Referring to the "spiritual organizational chart" on page 264, you will begin to help them see that in all of these areas, there is a give and take, bi-directional relationship of communication that takes place. Consider each one of these relationships and how you will coach them to exercise Godly and confident interactions with each entity of influence that they encounter. Not only are friends, family, society, and neighbors a part of the picture now, but they also realize that the Christian body is not simply limited to their own church but that we are connected globally with other believers around the world. They will see keenly at this age how government systems and employers work and what our role as Christians are with these institutions. They will see how other cultures and countries influence society, government, and international businesses and how those cultural nuances trickle down to them. In addition, they will comprehend how choices they make today are influenced by the expectations of their future employers and also influence the health and success of their own future family. Most importantly, as you coach them through these relational and societal waters, **parents must emphasize the importance of the *direct* relationship they have with the Lord in making it all work together.**

This is also the time where teens begin to understand the wisdom and reality of submission. **Submission is really a network of relationships working in Godly harmony.** Reading the following passage, help your teen to understand the essential roles that we all play in our family and in society and how we are illustrating Godly character when we fulfill the role that He has designed for us. Also emphasize that we do not just end at submission but are admonished to "put on the full armor of God". As parents, we must help our child to understand that their training, teaching, and now mentoring time with us is all about equipping them in this "full armor" so that they can effectively stand for but also submit to Christ when they reach adulthood. Consider this passage below and share it with your child.

➤ **Scripture to ponder**: *"Do not love the world or anything in the world. If anyone loves the world, the love of the Father is not in him. For everything in the world—the cravings Submit to one another out of reverence for Christ*

Wives and Husbands

Wives, submit to your husbands as to the Lord. For the husband is the head of the wife as Christ is the head of the church, his body, of which he is the Savior. Now as the church submits to Christ, so also wives should submit to their husbands in everything.

Husbands, love your wives, just as Christ loved the church and gave himself up for her to make her holy, cleansing her by the washing with water through the word, and to present her to himself as a radiant church, without stain or wrinkle or any other blemish, but holy and blameless. In this same way, husbands ought to love their wives as their own bodies. He who loves his wife loves himself. After all, no one ever hated his own body, but he feeds and cares for it, just as Christ does the church— for we are members of his body. "For this reason a man will leave his father and mother and be united to his wife, and the two will become one flesh." This is a profound mystery—but I am talking about Christ and the church. However, each one of you also must love his wife as he loves himself, and the wife must respect her husband.

Children and Parents

Children, obey your parents in the Lord, for this is right. "Honor your father and mother"—which is the first commandment with a promise— "that it may go well with you and that you may enjoy long life on the earth." Fathers, do not exasperate your children; instead, bring them up in the training and instruction of the Lord.

Slaves and Masters

Slaves, obey your earthly masters with respect and fear, and with sincerity of heart, just as you would obey Christ. Obey them not only to win their favor when their eye is on you, but like slaves of Christ, doing the will of God from your heart. Serve wholeheartedly, as if you were serving the Lord, not men, because you know that the Lord will reward everyone for whatever good he does, whether he is slave or free.

And masters, treat your slaves in the same way. Do not threaten them, since you know that he who is both their Master and yours is in heaven, and there is no favoritism with him.

The Armor of God

Finally, be strong in the Lord and in his mighty power. Put on the full armor of God so that you can take your stand against the devil's schemes. For our struggle is not against flesh and blood, but against the rulers, against the authorities, against the powers of this dark world and against the spiritual forces of evil in the heavenly realms. Therefore put on the full armor of God, so that when the day of evil comes, you may be able to stand your ground, and after you have done everything, to stand. Stand firm then, with the belt of truth buckled around your waist, with the breastplate of righteousness in place, and with your feet fitted with the readiness that comes from the gospel of peace. In addition to all this, take up the shield of faith, with which you can extinguish all the flaming arrows of the evil one. Take the helmet of salvation and the sword of the Spirit, which is the word of God. And pray in the Spirit on all occasions with all kinds of prayers and requests. With this in mind, be alert and always keep on praying for all the saints." Ephesians 5:21 – 6:18 (NIV)

This is a lengthy passage to digest. What elements covered in Paul's words do we struggle with in our family? What current relationships are positive influencers and which ones are negative?

_____

_____

_____

_____

_____

_____

_____

_____

_____

_____

_____

_____

_____

_____

_____

_____

_____

_____

Take a minute now to jot some notes down on the chart below. They should reflect some of the **specific names of the influencers** that exist outside of your nuclear and extended family and friends. Also use the space below to write down notes and ideas about other influencers that you see in your child's life that you also want to include on your diagram. Talk to your husband and mentor about additional sources of influence.

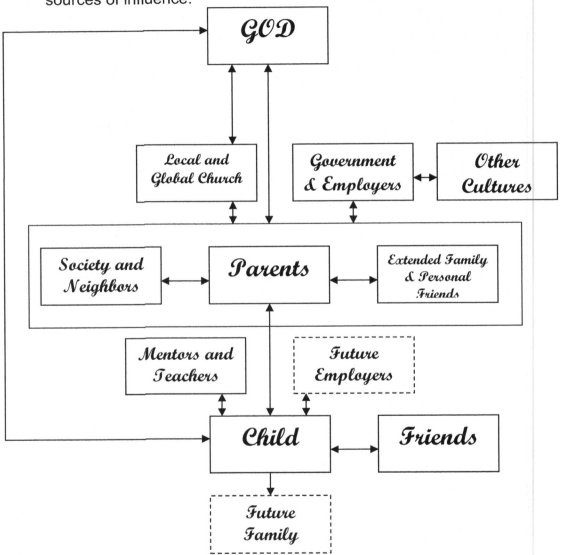

What other influencers have I identified that need to be added to this chart or modified from the previous "season"?

_____

_____

_____

_____

Spiritual Truths in Action

In chapter four, we already established the importance of making sure your child engages in an intensive apologetics course to ground their confidence in their personal belief system and their knowledge of culturally relevant issues. Similarly, **understanding the major aspects of other cultures around the world is also essential element of your teenager's growth.** As they learn how other countries and cultures impact our government, businesses, and overall societal attitudes and trends, they need to have resources to guide them in understanding specific details about these various cultures rather than just forming assumptive, vague opinions. Also share these scriptures with your child, helping them to see that we are called to be "in" the world and not "of" it.

➤ **Scripture to ponder**: *Do not love the world or anything in the world. If anyone loves the world, the love of the Father is not in him. For everything in the world—the cravings of sinful man, the lust of his eyes and the boasting of what he has and does—comes not from the Father but from the world. The world and its desires pass away, but the man who does the will of God lives forever. I John 2:15-17 (NIV)*

➤ **Scripture to ponder**: *Therefore, I urge you, brothers, in view of God's mercy, to offer your bodies as living sacrifices, holy and pleasing to God—this is your spiritual act of worship. Do not conform any longer to the pattern of this world, but be transformed by the renewing of your mind. Then you will be able to test and approve what God's will is—his good, pleasing and perfect will. Romans 12:1-2 (NIV)*

➤ **Scripture to ponder**: *Be strong and very courageous. Be careful to obey all the law my servant Moses gave you; do not turn from it to the right or to the left, that you may be successful wherever you go. Do not let this Book of the Law depart from your mouth; meditate on it day and night, so that you may be careful to do everything written in it. Then you will be prosperous and successful. Have I not commanded you? Be strong and courageous. Do not be terrified; do not be discouraged, for the LORD your God will be with you wherever you go. Joshua 1:7-9 (NIV)*

➤ **Scripture to ponder**: *Remind the people to be subject to rulers and authorities, to be obedient, to be ready to do whatever is good, to slander no one, to be peaceable and considerate, and to show true humility toward all men. Titus 3:1-2 (NIV)*

In addition to the worldview resources mentioned previously on pages 160-161, be sure to **consider these following resources** that contain additional information to support you as you spiritually guide your child through the high school years.

1. *Already Gone: Why Your Kids Will Quit Church and What You Can Do About It* by Ken Ham and Britt Beemer; No matter how spiritually grounded you believe your child to be, this is a "must-read" for every parent. Based on research done by **The Barna Group,** this book shows the reality that two-thirds of children walk away from the church at some point, even if it is just for a short period of time and even if you think that they are spiritually grounded just because they are coming to church now.[216] While the research shows that this issue starts to reveal itself in fifth or sixth grade, read why this is happening and what you can do about it as your child navigates the high school years. It comes in a DVD format as well that is great for sharing with friends or church leaders. Their follow-up book, titled *Already Compromised*, provides an assessment of how Christian colleges vary greatly in their statements of faith on a variety of theological points.

2. **Answers in Genesis** does not just cover apologetics and creation science but has great DVD and book resources that cover various cultural, evangelical, and societal hot topics.[217] Their resources addressing these and other issues are too numerous to list, but below are some examples that pertain to this "season".
   ➢ *The New Answers Books 1, 2, and 3* by Ken Ham
   ➢ *Cloning, Stem Cells, and the Value of Life* by Mike Riddle
   ➢ *The Culture Wars* by Voddie Baucham
   ➢ *Escape from Darkness* by Daniel Shayesteh
   ➢ *Genesis: The Key to Reclaiming the Culture* by Ken Ham
   ➢ *Global Warming: A Scientific and Biblical Expose of Climate Change* (DVD)
   ➢ *Go Into All the World: Evangelizing a Modern Culture* by Ken Ham
   ➢ *God of Suffering?* by Dr. Tommy Mitchell
   ➢ *Great Debate on Science and the Bible* by Ken Ham, Jason Lisle, Hugh Ross, & Walt Kaiser
   ➢ *How Can We Raise Godly Children?* by Ken Ham
   ➢ *How Do We Know the Bible is True?* by Brian H. Edwards

---

[216] http://www.barna.org/
[217] http://www.answersingenesis.org/

> ➢ *It Doesn't Take a Ph.D.! The Cure for a Culture in Crisis* by Dr. A. Charles Ware
> ➢ *Remote Control: The Power of Hollywood on Today's Culture* by Carl Kerby
> ➢ *Why is There Death and Suffering?* by Ken Ham
> ➢ *Why Won't They Listen? The Power of Creation Evangelism* and *Why Won't They Listen? Reaching a Lost Culture* by Ken Ham

3. **BibleGateway.com** is a good website to familiarize your child with at this age. They can look up scriptures quickly in any number of translations while they are doing their personal Bible study.

4. **God's World News Publications**, as mentioned previously, are great resources for current events information presented from a Christian worldview.[218] *The Top Story* issue is designed for children 6th to 9th grade and then children are transitioned to their regular adult publication of *World News* by 10th grade.

5. *Window on the World* by Daphne Spraggett is an easy-to-read reference about most of the **major people groups and countries around the world**. It tells the reader about the cultural norms and religious beliefs of that country. This book is a great way to easily expose your child to elements of other cultures that you study about and how to pray specifically for each one.

Character Truths in Action

Life coaching is a role that is not a comfortable one for many parents. Dads and moms both may have a difficult time recognizing the point at which to transition their hands-on training role to one of side-line coaches. This does not mean that you are disengaged. Rather it is quite the opposite. You are helping your child step up to expectations and responsibilities that they must prepare for to successfully operate as a Godly adult. You are also realizing at this stage that you *must* rely on the Lord's guidance, protection, and development of your child so that they can possess the healthy confidence necessary to take on all aspects of life in their young adult years.

---

[218] http://www.gwnews.com/

> ➤ **Scripture to ponder**: *Perseverance must finish its work so that you may be mature and complete, not lacking anything. James 1:4 (NIV)*

> ➤ **Scripture to ponder**: *But even if you should suffer for what is right, you are blessed "Do not fear what they fear; do not be frightened." But in your hearts set apart Christ as Lord. Always be prepared to give an answer to everyone who asks you to give the reason for the hope that you have. But do this with gentleness and respect, keeping a clear conscience, so that those who speak maliciously against your good behavior in Christ may be ashamed of their slander. I Peter 3:14-16 (NIV)*

1. Discipling is different than mentoring, which we will discuss in the next section. **Discipling involves steeping your child in God's Word and helping them understand their Christian faith and walk.** Although much of this is addressed in their apologetics training we discussed in chapter four's "seasonal" section, discipling is the follow-up process that ensures the content "sticks". So, start a focused discipleship course with your sons and daughters at this age. Ideally, the discipler role will be fulfilled by your husband, regardless of whether you have a son or a daughter. While it is true that sons need their fathers to mentor and train them to be Godly men, fathers also need to build deep, spiritual bonds with their daughters to ensure a positive self-image and confidence that will leave no holes in her heart that she may later seek to fill elsewhere.

   > ➤ *Experiencing God: Student Edition* by Henry Blackaby and Claude V. King; This student edition based on the classic original can be truly life-changing for your teen as they discover how to "hear and follow God in [their] daily life and how to experience God's power as He works through [them]."

   > ➤ *Intensive Discipleship Course: Developing Godly Character* and *Intensive Discipleship Course: Being Useful to God NOW* by Vinnie Carafano; Courses tie your child's spiritual development and connects it to practical action. They teach your child how to study the Bible, how to pray, and how to hear God.

2. Here are some **additional resources** to aid in the discipling process with your child.

> ➢ *Start Here: Do Hard Things Right Where You Are* and *Do Hard Things: A Teenage Rebellion Against Low Expectations* by Alex and Brett Harris; Written directly to teens and based on I Timothy 4:12, your child will be inspired to take on specific responsibilities and projects that will encourage them to consistently look for ways to challenge themselves as they express their spiritual believes and prepare for adulthood. It is not so much a study as it is a way to have them read the text and then to discuss their thoughts with Dad and Mom. The authors also conduct speaking tours and visit the major cities regularly.[219]

> ➢ *The Power of Praying for Your Young Adult Children* by Stormie OMartian; Even though your child is still in your home, start recognizing that your goal is to help them navigate these years successfully into their young adult life. This book guides parents through how to pray for their child's sense of direction, career choices, marriage, other important relationships, spiritual commitment, prayer life, and many other essential areas. This is the follow-up book to *The Power of a Praying Parent*.

Behavioral Truths in Action

During this time, parents want to intensify or add the concept of mentoring to their relationship with their child. Parents also must make specific and clear decisions about the ideas of dating, courtship, and social networking so that expectations are understood far in advance of any encounters their child may have with a teen of the opposite sex.

> ➢ **Scripture to ponder**: *Be very careful, then, how you live—not as unwise but as wise, making the most of every opportunity, because the days are evil. Therefore do not be foolish, but understand what the Lord's will is. Ephesians 5:15-17 (NIV)*

> 1. **Consume positive media** and not just mainstream options. The reality is that our teens and young adult children will eventually experience certain popular movies as they mature. However, when you have other options available for them to view, it can be the seed to meaningful discussions and development that may not otherwise occur. Check out **Pureflix** or **Rightnowmedia** for these types of options.[220]

---

[219] http://www.therebelution.com/index.php
[220] https://pureflix.com/; https://www.rightnowmedia.org/

Vidangel is also a powerful filtering service that enables families to watch mainstream movies, controlling down to a detailed level the violence, language, and sexual content allowed.[221]

2. **Mentoring** is really the focus in working with your teen to help them understand the impact that their behavioral choices have on their present and future course. Parents can help their teens navigate these difficult waters by being prepared and staying the course. Use these resources as general guidance on this concept.

   ➢ *The Balanced High Schooler: Getting Parents and Homeschooled Teens "On the Grid" for College and Beyond* by Carol Gary. While I know that I have mentioned this resource twice before, it just touches on so many areas relevant to this "season"! **Plus, the heart of my purpose behind writing this forty-day conversationally-styled tool is to support parents in their efforts to personally mentor their own teen in every major area of life prior to their launch into the world.** It is a resource that can be used repeatedly throughout the teen years, adjusting and crafting responses, conversations, and observations until you have not only equipped them successfully for their post-high school life, but you have also forged a relationship of mutual trust and open communication that will last a lifetime!

   ➢ Be sure to **continue your quest to understand and speak to your child's primary love language as they navigate through the teen years.** *The Five Love Languages for Teenagers* by Gary Chapman is a natural read for you at this point if you have followed his previous books I have recommended. As with the *Five Love Languages for Children*, this book will also provide valuable insight to you on how to best love and communicate with your child as you enter this final at-home parenting season. This book will translate for the parent which of the five love languages is most effective to exercise when communicating with their teen and also gives special attention to the issues of anger, independence, and responsibility.

---

[221] https://www.vidangel.com/

> ➢ *Boy's Passage, Man's Journey* by Brian D. Molitor; Great resource for helping dad to create a **"rite-of-passage" ceremony** for your adolescent son. With an emphasis on equipping him for God's service and navigating universal pitfalls of adolescence, this book is both inspiring and practical.

> ➢ *Girl's Passage, Father's Duty* by Brian D. Molitor; Emphasizes the importance that dad plays in the **healthy development of your daughter's identity** and ability to have positive relationships later in life.

> ➢ *Raising a Modern Day Knight: A Father's Role in Guiding His Son to Authentic Manhood* by Robert Lewis; This powerful book takes fathers through a journey of instilling Godly character in their sons by **establishing their "knight's" purpose**, planning the ceremonies to lead him from one stage to the next, and connecting him to the community around him as well as the ultimate legacy he will leave.

3. To date, or not date, that is the question. This and many other issues involving your child's sexual and relational development await you very early in this season. You must decide with your husband in advance what steps you will take to **guard and nurture your child's purity**. You must have unity with your husband on your position on **dating versus courtship** and how to understand the difference between the two. One way to look at it is that courtship involves families getting to know families with a future possibility of a mutually beneficial, romantic commitment of one's daughter to another's son in the context of marriage whereas dating involves one male individual knowing and interacting in isolation with one

> **Note to Leaders and Mentors:**
>
> *If you have a teen group within your support group, be cautious and thoughtful about the kinds of programs that are organized for them. The last thing you want to do is to create awkward and inappropriate situations by allowing certain boy/girl relationships to develop in an unhealthy manner. Instead, create a fun and safe family-oriented environment where teens can mix, and their parents can get to know each other in the process. Game nights, barbeques, and even parent co-op classes are all good ways to achieve this goal.*

female individual, having no particular future goal in mind. Courtship involves relationship openness with parents and family whereas dating can lead to relationship ownership that largely excludes the family's input on the match. One is a deliberate plan to explore suitability for marriage, the other is typically more casual and noncommittal in nature. Of the many resources available on the concept of purity, dating, and courtship, my favorite resource center continues to be **Generations of Virtue (GOV)**. Run by Julie Hiramine and specializing in the mission of purity, **GOV** has a vast number of resources to address these difficult subjects including books, DVDs, workshop recordings, purity merchandise, and movies. You will find these and many other resources available for review at their website.[222]

➢ Sex Education Resources for Parents:
  o **Focus on the Family**: In addition to a variety of resources relevant to a Christian family, they have articles that help parents navigate this topic with their teen.[223]
  o **SeanMcDowell.org**: As the son of Josh McDowell, Sean is passionate about taking the teaching of biblical truths to the next generation. In addition to co-authoring an update to his dad's classic, *More than a Carpenter*, Sean has a wealth of resources on his site about a myriad of subjects pertinent to parents, including sex.[224]
  o *The Talks: A Parent's Guide to Critical Conversations about Sex, Dating, and other Unmentionables* by Barrett Johnson; Written from a Christian perspective, this resource breaks down the various pieces of the puzzle into fifteen different conversations that parents can initiate with their teen. Six companion videos are available on **Right Now Media** to complement the book.[225]
  o *Total Health: Choices for a Winning Lifestyle* by Susan Boe; This is an excellent academic text written from a Christian perspective that is designed for use in 10th grade and up. In additional to **all aspects of health and well-being**, it covers the anatomy of both male and female reproductive systems, definitions of sexually transmitted diseases, and relationship considerations for marriage-minded teens. It does not cover the actual mechanics of sex since the author leaves that

---

[222] http://generationsofvirtue.org/
[223] https://www.focusonthefamily.com/lifechallenges/love-and-sex/purity/what-your-teens-need-to-know-about-sex
[224] http://fervr.net/teen-life/8-answers-to-tough-questions-about-sex & http://seanmcdowell.org/search/results?q=sex
[225] https://www.rightnowmedia.org/Content/Series/191764

piece of the discussion up to the parent's discretion. So, to fully cover the subject, parents will want to supplement the material with additional resources and conversations. It is recommended by **My Father's World** as a one semester course for credit, and they have developed a syllabus to go with the student text for that purpose.

➢ General Courtship and Relationship Resources:
  o *I Kissed Dating Goodbye* by Joshua Harris; Although this is a good text for girls too, boys will benefit immensely from this book. This is because the author uses his own life experiences to illustrate the **danger of giving one's heart away at an early age** and contrasts it against what authentic love and purity are all about. He also has an emphasis that focuses on purposeful singleness, which is a great perspective for boys-becoming-young-men to have as they seek to establish themselves in God's purpose for their life.
  o *Boy Meets Girl: Say Hello to Courtship* by Joshua Harris; A sequel to his *I Kissed Dating Goodbye* book, this title focuses on the various aspects of **Godly courtship**.
  o *Meet Mr. Smith* by Eric and Leslie Ludy; This book is written in unique, allegorical format that takes the reader on a journey with the authors who seek to interview "Great Sex". Along the way, they encounter Purity, Sacred, Feminine Grace, and Mr. Marvelous as they learn about **God's design and plan for intimacy between spouses**. Recommended for ages eighteen and older.
  o *When God Writes Your Love Story* by Eric and Leslie Ludy; While this book does not specifically advocate the concept of courtship over dating, it does focus on developing a **"forever kind of love"** in your child's future relationships in a God-honoring way.

➢ Additional Resources for Families with Boys:
  o *Hero: Becoming the Man She Desires* by Fred and Jasen Stoeker; Follow this father/son team as they explore all of the difficult issues and conversations that need to be faced in pursuing **God's plan of purity for your son**. This book is for ages seventeen and up.
  o *How to Ruin Your Life by 40* by Steve Farrar; The author makes frank connections for your child in the **"reap what you sow" principle**. This is a very practical and highly recommended book!
  o *Preparing Your Son for Every Man's Battle* by Stephen Arterburn and Fred Stoeker; This is a must-read resource for parents of boys who are eight to thirteen years old. This text

helps you address issues of **sexual purity** as well as handling negative societal and media messages. The book is divided into two parts; one for Dad only and one for Dad and his son.

> ➢ Additional Resources for Families with Girls:
> - *Answering the Guy Questions: The Set-Apart Girl's Guide to Relating to the Opposite Sex* by Leslie Ludy; Recommended for girls sixteen and older, the author challenges young ladies to **focus on a Christ-centered life as a first priority** to later on set the stage to attract a Godly man into their life.
> - *Before You Meet Prince Charming* by Sarah Mally; The author addresses how your daughter can **commit herself to a pure life as she seeks for God to fulfill His purpose in her.** She gives practical advice to modern teens on the most common questions while taking the reader through a fictional, fairytale setting: humorous and thought provoking.
> - *Gift-Wrapped by God: Secret Answers to the Question "Why Wait?"* by Linda Dillow and Lorianne Pintus; As the authors of *Intimate Issues*, they have created this eight-week Bible study program that covers issues of defining **"the gift"**, recapturing "the gift", saving "the gift", guarding "the gift", waiting for "the gift", and defining the "higher gift". Although it is not exclusively designed for teenagers and is intended to be used with single adult women as well, this text is challenging and practical to girls in the later teen years.
> - *The Guy I am Not Dating* by Trish Perry; This is a humorous novel that follows protagonist Kara in her **journey towards God's plan for romantic relationships.**
> - *Lady in Waiting: Becoming God's Best While Waiting for Mr. Right* by Jackie Kendell and Debby Jones; Again, girls are encouraged to **focus on their relationship with the Lord as their primary responsibility rather than on pursuing temporal relationships with boys** when they are both too young to create something meaningful and lasting.

3. Related to your teen's purity is also the whole issue of how you **manage social networking and technology tools** in your home: computers, cell phones, MP3 players, iPods, and so forth. You need to not only educate yourself on appropriate tools and filters to protect your child, but also establish relational guidelines that will address the root desire to misuse these tools in the first place.[226] Start by making sure that no technology items are allowed in your child's bedroom at night that has Internet or cellular capabilities. If your child has a personal e-mail account, come to an agreement

---

[226] https://www.generationsofvirtue.org/internet-101/#.Wk1o1t-nF3g

with them that you can log in and check this e-mail at any time. If there are violations of the rules that you establish and agree upon in advance, the technology item must be taken from the child indefinitely. While Facebook and Google Plus have made improvements over recent years to ensure privacy, caution and boundaries should still be exercised when allowing your teen to join a group or to "like" a friend. **Homeschoogle** is an interesting site designed to connect homeschooled teens to meet other homeschoolers, create specialized groups, study together, and engage in virtual chat sessions.[227] It also provides pre-screened resources and sponsors to consider. However, it is still a fairly new tool and the same cautions and boundaries should apply to its use as with other social media options.

Seek out additional resource advice from your mentor and discuss your overall concerns with your husband about the spiritual, character, and behavioral development of your teen.

---

[227] http://www.homeschoogle.com/

More Chapter Notes...

Chapter 6

Getting Your Finances in Order

*Suppose one of you wants to build a tower. Will he not first sit down and estimate
the cost to see if he has enough money to complete it? For if he lays the
foundation and is not able to finish it, everyone who sees it will ridicule him,
saying, 'This fellow began to build and was not able to finish.'
Luke 14:28-30 (NIV)*

"Plan to Fail if you Fail to Plan"

This is the gist of a common saying attributed to Benjamin Franklin about
the **importance of planning** that many of us have heard. Most people do not
want to involve themselves in a project or some other commitment if they know
they will not be able to fulfill their obligation. If a child has no intention on
practicing his violin pieces for an upcoming concert yet gives a false impression
to their music teacher that they are well prepared, they would be lying to
themselves and to their teacher if they were to go through with the performance
without changing their practice behavior. If an employee accepts a task to finish
within the next three hours knowing that they cannot complete it by the end of the
day, they are setting themselves up for failure. And if a parent carelessly
commits to play a game with their child at a certain time and that time comes and
goes with no game in sight, disappointment and hurt feelings are sure to come.

When we look at these fictional examples and think of endless more
variations of the principle at work here, most of us will agree that these are not
desirable circumstances for anyone involved. It is not a positive experience for
the student or the teacher, the employee or the employer, or the child or the

parent. The **undesirable principle of "over-commit" and "under-deliver"** is at work here, making everyone miserable. Yet many of the same people who can see the shortcomings of the decisions that occurred in these small illustrations have a hard time seeing it when they manage their own finances. They over-commit to debt and obligate their pocketbook far beyond what they can deliver out of it. Sometimes it is intentional, leading to an unending cycle of interest payments and mental stress. Other times, it is simply a lack of proper planning or due diligence. Still other times, it is the result of a crisis.

As we discussed previously in chapter one, according to **NHERI**, the average homeschooling family spends about $600 per year per child on home education curriculum and materials. Therefore, **not only do homeschooling families need to be concerned about managing their finances wisely to be good Christian stewards of what God has given to them, but they also need to find additional funds to homeschool that are beyond a typical household budget.** This can be especially challenging when most homeschooling households have only one income to support household *and* educational efforts. In addition, families must prepare to face not only the short-term goals associated with saving money for curriculum, but they also need to focus on savings and investments that will support their long-term goals for themselves and their families.

Now take another look back at the opening scripture. Do you and your family members do their part to manage family finances wisely, or is this a source of constant stress within your home? Are you and your husband in agreement on what your short, mid, and long-term savings goals are, or are you both on totally opposite ends of the opinion spectrum? None of us wants to be ridiculed like the fellow in the passage above who set out to accomplish a great task but then had to give it up later due to poor planning. **Remember what *your* great tasks are**, recognizing that you do not want those plans to be interrupted or terminated.

Finally, make sure that you *both* **thoroughly discuss the financial information addressed in this chapter with your husband regardless of who handles the money in your home on a regular basis.** I have personally witnessed families who have been nearly devastated financially and otherwise when one spouse decides to leave the marriage or even perhaps passes away and the remaining spouse (usually the wife) has not a clue about what to do or where to start. If we handle the finances in our family and are going to submit to our husbands, we must be up front with him on all major and minor financial details that occur on a regular basis. Conversely, if your husband manages the finances in your home then he needs to take steps to meet with you regularly and discuss plans, goals, and concerns with you so that you are both part of the management process. This is part of how he demonstrates his love for you just as Christ loved the church—sacrificially and with your best interests at heart.

Here are some **additional general resources** for homeschoolers looking for creative ways to limit family spending on homeschool-related expenses, including curriculum.

1. *Easy Peasy Curriculum* by Lee Giles; Reviewed more thoroughly in chapter three under "Text Book Approach" options, this curriculum covers all ages and stages of homeschooling while remaining completely FREE to users.[228]

2. *Homeschooling on a Shoestring* by Melissa Morgan and Judith Allee; The authors share their views on sourcing affordable curriculum and teaching tools. They also extend into inexpensive options for field trips as well as money-saving tips for home management.

3. *Homeschooling Your Child for Free: More than 1200 Smart, Effective, and Practical Resources for Home Education on the Internet and Beyond* by Laura Maery Gold and Joan Zielinski; Written in 2014, be aware that some of the links will be outdated. Yet resourceful parents will be able to find the information she references by applying normal search efforts.

Record other thoughts on general financial management resources and/or concerns you have:

_____

_____

_____

_____

_____

_____

_____

_____

_____

_____

_____

_____

_____

_____

_____

[228] https://allinonehomeschool.com/ and https://allinonehighschool.com/

Principles of Tithing and Giving

The first thing that every Christian family must put in order is their tithe. Often, this is the last item on the list that gets addressed. However, if you wait until you "have enough money" to tithe, you will never get around to it! So what is a tithe? **A tithe is an undesignated giving to God of the first ten percent of what you and your husband bring into the household.** It is undesignated because we are to bring the "whole tithe into the household" and not specify to our church leaders where it is to be used. This principle of freely giving the tithe is so important to God that the following passage is interestingly the only place in scripture where he challenges us to "test" Him.

> ➤ **Scripture to ponder**: *Will a man rob God? Yet you rob me. "But you ask, 'How do we rob you?'" "In tithes and offerings. You are under a curse—the whole nation of you—because you are robbing me. Bring the whole tithe into the storehouse, that there may be food in my house. Test me in this," says the LORD Almighty, "and see if I will not throw open the floodgates of heaven and pour out so much blessing that you will not have room enough for it. I will prevent pests from devouring your crops, and the vines in your fields will not cast their fruit," says the LORD Almighty. "Then all the nations will call you blessed, for yours will be a delightful land," says the LORD Almighty. Malachi 3:8-12 (NIV)*

You have heard of the principle of the 80/20 rule where 20% of a business's customers make up 80% of their revenue or we use 20% of our home 80% of the time; really the idea can be applied to just about anything. Similarly, in the principle of tithing, you can think of it like a 90/10 rule. God gives us 90% and asks for 10% of it back. It may sound strange, but you will find over time that **you can accomplish *more* with that 90% when you are *with* God than you can when you are using 100% *without* God.** This does not mean that tithing automatically ensures your husband will "get that promotion" or that a sweepstakes representative will be knocking on your door next week with a big, fat check made out in your name. Rather, it means that you are opening your heart and life to be blessed by God in ways you never imagined, even during hard times. This scripture teaches us that, while He does have the power to "open the floodgates of heaven", He can also "prevent" catastrophes from happening and cause material items to last longer. Consider another scripture from Nehemiah which recounts the way that God cared for the basic needs of the Israelites when they wandered in the desert with Moses for forty years.

> ➤ **Scripture to ponder**: *You gave your good Spirit to instruct them. You did not withhold your manna from their mouths, and you gave them water for their thirst. For forty years you sustained them in the desert; they lacked nothing, their clothes did not wear out nor did their feet become swollen. Nehemiah 9:20-21 (NIV)*

So, God can make your car last longer before you must replace it, your major appliances function well past their normal use dates, or your family's food budget stretch further. The Lord also works through people to bless other people, especially in times where there is hardship involved. When someone gives you an unexpected financial gift during a time when you are stressed to make your monthly payments, God is blessing you through those givers. When other homeschooling moms loan you curriculum or books to use that you cannot afford to purchase, God is blessing you through them. Similarly, when people prepare meals for your family while you or one of your family members are in the hospital, God is blessing you through them. Take a moment now and list all the ways that you have observed God's tangible blessings in your life over the past year and then go through the same process for blessing, you received even further back. Try to think of situations that you had perhaps not connected as God blessing you, but now you see that it is true.

God has blessed my family in these ways during the past year:

_____

_____

_____

_____

_____

God has blessed my family in these ways during the past ten years:

_____

_____

_____

_____

_____

In our family, my husband and I have tithed from the very beginning and have been **blessed in many ways during the course of our marriage**. One of the most incredible blessings we experienced came through the generosity of several of my cousins at a time that was much appreciated. We had been pricing air-conditioning replacements for our two units for a few years since they were no longer operating efficiently and were reaching the time in service where they would need to be replaced soon. However, costs for two new units plus the labor to install them were going to run us around $18,000. This is not something that most families, much less homeschoolers such as our family, have lying around in the bank just waiting to be used. On his visits to Arizona, my husband often talked to my cousin, who happens to own his own heating and cooling company, about how we could get the units we owned to behave more efficiently. My husband would implement various ideas that, while helpful, did not have too much impact on reducing our electric bills. Eventually, during one of his visits, my cousin told us he had two brand new units in his shop that he would not be able to sell since they no longer met the performance ratings required in California but that they *did* meet performance requirements for Arizona. In the months that followed, he arranged for another cousin of mine to drive them out to us from northern California to Arizona and still another cousin, who worked in the air conditioning business in Arizona, to come and help us move them to a better location than where our old units had previously been. He worked with my husband to install them and then took away the old units. We were not only blessed with newly installed air conditioners, but we eventually realized a monthly savings on our electric bill of nearly 30%! The kindness and generosity shown by these different family members to look outside of themselves and work to address a need that they could do something about was so humbling and awesome that we will never forget God's hand in the entire process. This is just one of many blessings we have received over the years as we have had the privilege of seeing how God works through His people.

So, the first order of business, then, is to tithe. **Tithing is not just an outward sign of obedience but is also a spiritual act of worship that will ground you in your relationship with the Lord.** It is a tangible way that we express to God that we know He owns 100% of it all anyway and that He comes first.[229] We have the

> ### Note to Leaders and Mentors:
>
> *If you are able, consider organizing a support function within your group that can work to care for your member families in times of need. Whether it is providing meals, transportation, or child care, homeschooling families are in a unique position to help each other in times of difficulty by staying connected with each other and being informed of major life events, such as a difficult pregnancy, death in the family, or a severe medical problem.*

---

[229] Psalm 50:9-12 (NIV)

I have no need of a bull from your stall
    or of goats from your pens,

for every animal of the forest is mine,
    and the cattle on a thousand hills.

I know every bird in the mountains,
    and the creatures of the field are mine.

If I were hungry I would not tell you,
    for the world is mine, and all that is in it.

responsibility of bringing the first fruits to God of what we regularly receive.[230] Again, do not wait and give Him leftovers. If you do, there will never seem to be enough. Instead give Him His due portion from every paycheck without fail.

Sometimes, however, this is easier said than done depending on your husband's viewpoint. First, some of you may have husbands who perhaps give to the church but do not really tithe while others may have husbands who will not support any level of giving. If this is so, make sure that you do not bring discord into your relationship by pushing this issue. Instead, pray for discernment. Then see if you can talk to him about starting with a regular, small amount that you can grow later as you see God's blessing on your efforts. God is not an accountant, and He knows your heart so allow Him to work on your husband in His timing.

The second issue you may be facing is that your finances are really tight. Perhaps there has been a job loss or a severe pay cut, and every dollar counts. You just cannot see a way to make it happen and still meet all your obligations. If this is your situation, please allow me to encourage you in love to *still* make the decision to tithe. Within a four-year period in our household, two different jobs that my husband held were eliminated and we were out of work for eight months one time and four months the second time. Each time, we had a new baby in the house and honestly did not know what the future was going to bring for us. The most difficult tithing checks I ever wrote were those $21 obligations from our $210 unemployment checks. At first you think, what could $21 possibly do for God's Kingdom? But that is when you learn that God does not need your money; He wants your heart. Be faithful in times of hardship *and* in times of plenty. You will see that He *will* take care of you through the difficult times and that you will later see the wisdom of what He was allowing to happen in your life during that time.

So how does the tithe compare to giving or offerings? Are they not the same thing? I was posed this question once by a friend and fellow homeschooling mom. So, I expressed to her that my perspective is that **tithes and offerings are *not* the same thing.** While the tithe has the "undesignated" nature mentioned previously, giving or offerings usually specifies a gift that you set apart for a specific purpose that you control. The use of the tithe goes into a general fund that is then determined by the elders of your church where it will be spent whereas the use of a gift or an offering is usually directed by you.

Be faithful with your tithe in times of hardship and in times of plenty.

Scripture also makes a distinction between the two in the Malachi scripture previously discussed when he admonished the people about robbing Him of tithes *and* offerings. Elsewhere in Deuteronomy and Nehemiah, the concepts of tithes, offerings, sacrifices, and special gifts are also given distinct and separate identities.[231] If you and your husband want to sponsor a child in

---

[230] We also assume responsibility for bringing to the house of the LORD each year the first fruits of our crops and of every fruit tree. Nehemiah 10:35 (NIV)

[231] Deuteronomy 12:6,11; Nehemiah 10:37 & 13:5

a food program, donate funds to a friend raising money for foreign missions, or give to a worthy non-profit who is doing the work of the Lord, that is excellent and good. However, be **careful not to assume that the extra, designated gift or offering you make** *replaces* **the tithe; for it does not.** Similarly, if your church holds a special offering for a need or project, this also does not *replace* the tithe. Think of it this way; the tithe is your starting point and additional opportunities for offerings or gifts are your "above-and-beyond" opportunities to grow.

Take some time now to look at tithing. **Use the following worksheet** to figure out what your monthly and annual figures look like for your household's salary and current giving levels. If you currently tithe, are you hitting the ten percent goal, or do you still have a gap to bridge in meeting the tithe? Once you have established that, make a list of other worthy causes or organizations that are doing God's work and that you wish to sponsor. See what creative things you can do to make your financial support of them a reality. Also, make notes about how you can pray for each of these important agents of the Lord's work or organizations that you believe are making positive community contributions.

Talk to your family members about the goals of these groups and see what sacrifices or concessions your family can make into order to make a small monthly commitment to them. Follow up your work with a discussion with your mentor and make notes about additional thoughts and ideas that they have about the principles of tithing and opportunities for giving. We will touch on this idea again in chapter eight when we consider family involvement in the local community and beyond.

Write down some initial thoughts and questions about tithing and designated giving here. Use the space to jot down initial information about this topic and then transfer your final information to the given worksheet. Talk to your husband and ask your mentor how they handle this issue.

_____

_____

_____

_____

_____

_____

_____

_____

_____

Our Tithing Worksheet

Figure Descriptions	Operation	Annual Figures	Monthly Figures (Annual / 12)	Prayer Focus for Our Church
Our Annual Income	(Monthly Salary * 12)			
10% Annual Tithe Goal	(Gross * 0.10)			
(less) Current Annual Church Tithe	(Current Monthly Tithe * 12)			
Additional Annual Amount Needed to Meet the Tithe	(Goal - Current)			
Additional Monthly Amount Needed to Meet the Tithe (Annual / 12)	(Additional Annual Needed / 12)			

Our Giving Worksheet

Designated Organization or Missionary Doing God's Work	Program Description	Annual Donation Goal	Monthly Figures (Annual / 12)	Prayer Focus for This Ministry or Missionary

What other thoughts or experiences does my mentor have about tithing versus giving? What are some other creative ways they have found to free up more money for giving?

_____

_____

_____

_____

_____

_____

_____

_____

_____

_____

_____

_____

_____

_____

_____

_____

_____

_____

_____

_____

_____

_____

_____

Once your family's position on tithing is firmly established, be prepared to turn your attention towards the following sections that cover household budgeting, short-term savings, and midterm investing goals as well as long-term investing plans and taxes. Do *not* make the mistake of thinking that once you take care of budgeting that you must wait to address the savings and investing questions until you feel like you have extra income to do it. If you wait, it will never happen, and you will continue to lose valuable time needed to make your saving and investing efforts pay off. **Cover them one at a time while doing as much as you can with all the following areas now.**

Principles of Household Budgeting

So now let us turn our attentions towards the 90% that God has entrusted to you to manage. We will start with the area that is closest to your radar and then later work through issues that impact long term, future goals. We will begin with the "b" word: budget. I have known many people over the years to cringe at just hearing this word. Budgeting has received an undeserved "bad rap" as the cause for why families argue over everything from whether to go into debt for that new toy their child just "has to have" for Christmas to whether it is a better value to buy one or two-ply toilet paper! **However, just as money is *not* the root of all evil, neither is budgeting the cause of all financial arguments between spouses.** Instead, we should view budgeting the same as Scripture instructs us to view money. Both are tools to be used for God's purpose and have no intrinsic negative or positive value. Rather, the value to money and the value to budgeting are both tied to how you can and do use them.

> ➤ **Scripture to ponder**: *No servant can serve two masters. Either he will hate the one and love the other, or he will be devoted to the one and despise the other. You cannot serve both God and money. Luke 16:13 (NIV)*

> ➤ **Scripture to ponder**: *People who want to get rich fall into temptation and a trap and into many foolish and harmful desires that plunge men into ruin and destruction. For the love of money is a root of all kinds of evil. Some people, eager for money, have wandered from the faith and pierced themselves with many griefs. I Timothy 6:9-10 (NIV)*

So, to create a workable and comprehensive budget that will help you maximize positive stewardship of the resources you have been given, you will want to consider several points throughout the process.

Define Essential vs. Discretionary Spending

The first item of business when establishing a budget is to **decide what expenditures are discretionary and which ones are essential.** This is important not just because you and your husband need to be unified on what type of expense you consider to be one versus the other, but also because it will help to prepare you when difficult times arise. It is hardly ever a question of "if" but more of a question of "when" difficulties will come. When it does, you do not want to be wading through paperwork trying to get a handle on your finances in the middle of a job loss or some other such crisis. Instead you want to know with confidence at any given point what commitments you have that are essential and what expenses you have that are discretionary and could be cut out or substantially decreased: at least for a period of time. Although the way you may want to organize these categories will vary from what I have listed, it is a comprehensive starting point for you to consider. Please note that items one through nine are considered mostly "essential" expenses whereas items ten through twelve are largely "discretionary".

1. **Giving**: We have addressed this topic at length already but, just as a reminder, the total for this category should be at least 10% for tithe and above and beyond that for other charitable giving. In times of financial crisis, still meet the tithe of whatever income you do receive. However, you may consider suspending charitable giving, unless you have made regular giving commitments to them in advance. If that is the case, try to fill out the term of that commitment or work with them on reducing your monthly donations until your income is restored.

2. **Savings**: We will discuss short versus midterm savings goals in more detail within the coming sections. At this point, however, try to make sure that the total amount going into these categories, including college funds and retirement accounts, are totaling at least 10% with a continuing goal towards 15%.

3. **Financial Management**: Any services or subscriptions you use to manage your finances and investments goes here. I am not in support of financial services that will nickel and dime you to death on fees. However, for a nominal annual maintenance fee, you may

> ### Note to Leaders and Mentors:
>
> *If you have several families who are interested in going through a financial management discussion class, consider hosting a Financial Peace University workshop by Dave Ramsey. You do not need to be a financial expert to facilitate these DVD programs. Anyone can easily host a group and go through the 13 lessons with them to learn about many of the items discussed in this chapter.*
>
> *For example, attendees can learn about the "Debt Snowball" method of eliminating consumer debt. Using this approach, families concentrate on paying off smaller debt amounts first and then they take those payments they were making to the now-paid-off smaller debt and apply them to the next biggest debt due. Then when that one is paid off, that amount is also added to debt reduction payments on the next debt and so forth until all consumer debts are paid in full.*
>
> *For more information or to find an existing Financial Peace group meeting in your area, visit www.daveramsey.com*

want to consider having a line of credit available that you could draw from in case of an unexpected job loss. The percentage interest you pay on a **home equity loan** is a low rate based on prime when you absolutely must borrow money. Take time to also **reevaluate your checking account** and understand the fee structure. If you are regularly being charged fees, it is probably time to change banks. Also, be careful about fees that can sneak into minor accounts you may have for your child. We closed our boys' minor accounts and just keep a separate log of how much of our account is designated to them since we get a better interest rate for them and do not get charged accidental fees. The final item I would like to mention under "Financial Management" is **insurance**. Make sure you shop your insurance options annually to verify that you are getting the best rates and to ensure that you have proper coverage. Even though we cover medical insurance elsewhere in detail, I mention it here along with other types of insurance because shopping the insurance is usually done as one annual event. Also, be sure to purchase your umbrella, home, and auto insurance from the same company so you can maximize your multiple policy discounts. In addition, take time to ensure that your information is easily accessible regarding all your policies so that both you and your husband know how to put your hands on the proper documents, policy information, and phone numbers at a moment's notice. If you do not already have something like this in place, I have provided a worksheet for you at the end of this section.

> ➤ **Term Life Insurance:** While I do not recommend whole life insurance as it costs too much for what it provides, I see term life insurance as a must. This is particularly true for homeschoolers who often have only one income source that they must rely upon to live. Ask yourself this question, "If my spouse passes away, will we be able to continue to maintain our lifestyle and homeschooling choices, or will I be forced to reenter the workplace?" In most cases, we would want the option of keeping our child's life as stable as possible, if given the choice. The problem that many families face on this issue, especially when they have young school-aged children at home, is that there is either not a term life insurance policy at all on their husband or, if they do have one, it is inadequate. While you may be thinking, "My husband's employer provides life insurance, so I don't think I need it"; think again. Usually these work-provided policies are typically only $10,000 to help with funeral expenses and that is it. Instead, the general rule of thumb for husbands who want to make sure their surviving dependents have enough to live independently in the years to come is to have a policy that equates to at least ten times their annual salary. So, for example, if your spouse makes $60,000

a year, you would want a term policy that equals $600,000 in value. As your children graduate and leave your home, then you can drop or dramatically reduce the value of that policy, which is usually only good for 20 years anyway. You should also have a policy on yourself so that in the untimely event of your death, your husband can count on some additional resources to help him not only with arrangements but to assist him with additional in-home help until he figures out how he should pick up the pieces and move on. A $150,000 to $250,000 term policy is a good minimum range to purchase for this purpose.

➤ **Short and Long-Term Disability Insurance**: Often times, your husband's employer will provide short and/or long-term disability benefits. Be sure to find out if one or both are provided. If not, consider whether it makes sense for your family to have it. Short-term disability is usually not a huge deal since it typically only covers two or three months at the most for lost wages. However, long-term disability is certainly worth a look. If your husband is disabled past the short-term period, this insurance kicks in to replace pretty much the salary level that your husband was making at the time of the disability. How long this term lasts varies by policy, but it usually goes for at least two years and can go up through retirement age. This insurance pays out even if your husband is able to take another job elsewhere because it covers the fact that he can no longer do the exact work he was previously doing.

➤ **Umbrella Liability Insurance:** I know we all hate to buy insurance, so you may be wondering why I would add another one to the list that is not standard. However, of any policy you purchase, this is hands down the best value that you will see. Usually for only a couple of hundred dollars a year, give or take, you can carry an umbrella liability policy for a $1-million-dollar value that will protect your family's assets in case you are sued. Yes, we do have certain amounts of liability coverage on our auto and home policies. However, in this environment of excessive lawsuits, it is better to be safe than sorry. This is especially true if you are in business for yourself and your personal assets could be at risk if there is a problem in your relationship with one of your customers.

➤ **Homeowner's Insurance**: When shopping homeowner's insurance, be careful to make certain that the comparisons you are provided are comparing "apples to apples". Also, ensure you have adequate coverage to actually replace or repair your home in the event of severe damage. You have probably heard frightening stories of homeowners who lost everything in a fire or flood only to find out that their loss was either not covered at all or not covered enough to truly replace the home "in kind".

> **Auto Insurance**: The same is true for auto insurance. Make sure to compare identical or similar services when shopping for insurance. Also, consider whether you need additional medical liability coverage provided or if you already have medical insurance that would cover these types of claims.

4. **Debt Retirement** – Debt retirement includes any mortgage, school, car, or home equity loans as well as credit card debt. Make it a priority to get out of debt by having a plan. Some recommend consolidating debt to the lowest interest rate possible and then pay your highest percentage interest debt first. Others, like Dave Ramsey, suggest starting with your smallest debt first, then your next largest, and so forth, using a debt "snowball" method. For those who do not have any consumer debt or school loans, make it a goal to pay your mortgage off early. It *is* possible. When we owned our first home, we both worked outside of the home for several years and we only ever lived on my husband's income for our monthly expense needs. Within six years, we were able to pay off our first home in full and were in a great financial position when we sold it and moved to our second home many years later. Start by making an additional principle payment of $25, $50, or $100 extra a month. Another option is just to make an extra mortgage payment to the principle at the end of the year every year. You would be surprised to learn how quickly it adds up. Every little bit helps. Some people question the wisdom of paying off mortgages early, saying that they have missed out on the tax benefits of paying interest and that such money could have been put to work elsewhere. However, unless you have a guaranteed investment that will bring in more than the interest rate you are paying on your mortgage, paying off your mortgage early is still the best investment you can make since it is usually better than paying out interest all year with the anticipation of getting just *some* of it back during tax time, especially given the recent tax law changes. There is also a certain peace of mind that comes from knowing that you own your home free and clear when times of financial difficulty arise. So, if you think that you will never be able to pay your mortgage off early, take heart. Make it at least a goal to pay it down so that you have more than 20% equity in your home. Then you can at least drop any **PMI (Private Mortgage Insurance)** that the lender has been obligating you to pay up to that time, and you will have started a good habit of making additional principle payments that you can continue while adding the PMI money to your early payment plan when those funds become available.

5. **Household and Utilities**: It never ceases to amaze me that young couples purchasing a home will often only look at their monthly payment, which includes principle, interest, insurance, and property taxes, to decide how much house they can afford. The fact is that these obligations of home ownership, although representing a great deal of the cost, are not the *only* costs. As you will see on the sample budget sheet, many other variables go along with the expenses of owning a home. Homeowners must also account for regular expenses to maintain the home and the yard, alarm monitoring services, pest control costs, utilities (gas, water, and electric), and association fees, just to name a few of the common extras. Furthermore, if you are having a *new* home built, do not obligate yourself to a loan that will max you out and leave you cash poor. This is because you need to plan on an *additional* cash amount that you can access to put in new ceiling fans, window coverings, garage door opener system, additional pieces of furniture, and landscaping, which can be *very* expensive. So, a good rule of thumb is to keep all of these home-related expenses around 40% or less of your total monthly income with a max of 25% going towards mortgage, home insurance, and property tax expenses.

6. **Auto Expenses**: Expenses associated with your vehicle or vehicles can also be very high. This is another area that you need to search your heart and discuss with your husband so that you can come to an agreement on how much of your household budget you want to go towards transportation. In general, it is usually not a good idea to lease a vehicle since you are essentially renting it and never build any equity in the car. Now it is true that cars are not like homes and do not appreciate in value. However, when you purchase and own a car, you do have the ability to decide whether you want to be saddled with perpetual payments, just pay cash for it, or make payments for a short period of time and be done with it. Look at the table below for an additional perspective on buying versus leasing.

Leasing	Purchasing
Likes to have the latest and greatest car every 2-3 years	Content with driving a good car until cost of repairs outpace the value of the car: usually around 10 years or so.
Do not want to hassle with selling and trading process.	Does need to deal with selling and trading process when new car is needed.
Able to drive a car they would not be able to afford otherwise.	Usually needs to drive a more practical model.
On average, leasing costs 20% more than purchasing the same vehicle outright.[232]	Produces an average savings of 20% over a lease option on the same vehicle.

---

[232] For a full article explaining these options see https://www.edmunds.com/car-leasing/should-you-lease-or-buy-your-car.html or see Dave Ramsey's summary at https://www.daveramsey.com/askdave/posts/10367

Also, seriously consider purchasing a new-to-you used car and you will avoid the enormous depreciation "hit" that you get by driving a new car off the lot while still having the warranty benefits of driving a fairly new car. In addition, when considering the cost of your vehicles, consider what the insurance, maintenance, and fuel requirements will be before you purchase so that you know its true cost of ownership.

7. **Household and Utilities**: Living in Arizona, we learned about the wisdom of equalizing our utility payments years ago. Most of us have static salaries and have a difficult time swallowing those increased summer electric bills or winter gas bills. In addition, have your payments automatically paid out of a designated checking account to save you time and hassle in making sure that all your bills are paid on time throughout the year. Here are four great ways to save money on your household and utility expenses:

   ➢ **Go green.** I know that many, including myself, get tired of hearing this overused phrase by those who value the created over the Creator. However, in most cases, the efforts you take to make your home greener will reduce energy costs. Purchase energy efficient appliances that use less electricity and have higher efficiency ratings. Also, if you have gas available in your home, consider converting your dryer to a gas unit instead of an electric one. It is not only going to save you money, but gas is much easier on your clothing than drying with electric. Finally, go through your home and make the investment to change over all of your lighting from regular to florescent or LED bulbs, and be sure to check out special versions for dimmer switch lights. Making this one change several years ago in our home saved us over 20% on our electric bill!

   ➢ **Use timers.** If you do not have timers on your air conditioning system, outdoor lighting, and watering systems, consider having these installed and then adjust the programming on them throughout the year.

   ➢ **Do it yourself.** In an outsourcing environment such as what we experience today, DIY may seem outdated. However, if possible, try to do your own yardwork, pest control, etc. You will save a great deal of money and be able to involve your child in helping with many of the yard duties while teaching them about responsibilities of home ownership along with many practical life skills. This goes for handling basic home repairs as well.

> ➢ **Evaluate your phone, cable, and internet service plan.**
> Some families have dropped their land line in favor of only using
> a cell phone so that their expenses can be reduced, and they
> are not managing two separate numbers. However, be cautious
> about a couple of issues with this. First, if you have a monitored
> alarm system service, make sure it does not require a land line
> to do its job of dialing out to the central system. Otherwise, you
> will need a special cellular adapter for your system, which can
> be obtained for your security service. Second, be aware of what
> risks or limitations you may face regarding emergency services
> when you need to phone 911 from your cell phone. Since many
> companies bundle phone, cable, and internet service plans
> together, shop around and ask yourself what you really need
> and if you can drop or lower some of those services to reduce
> your overall monthly expense.

8. **Groceries**: Regardless of where you purchase these items, all food,
   paper goods, cleaning supplies, vitamins, and over-the-counter
   medicines go here. This is a category that can easily get out of control
   as not-so-essential purchases are made at your local grocery store,
   supercenter, or club warehouse. Try to reduce the amount of
   processed and pre-packaged food products to minimize your food
   expenses while improving the nutritional value of the foods you
   purchase. Also look for opportunities to purchase in bulk the paper
   products you use frequently while at the same time buying cleaning
   products that are "greener" and safer for your household. Another
   consideration is to purchase the generic brand of products from your
   favorite store and to make sure and shop meat specials.[233] You may
   also enjoy couponing or grocery games that help you maximize your
   food budget. See chapter seven for more great ideas about planning
   your meals.

9. **Medical**: Track any medical expenses you have here, including **co-
   pays** as well as **expenses incurred that you must pay to meet your
   yearly deductible**. Do not forget about dental cleanings and eyeglass
   care. Remember that, even though you must have medical expenses
   exceeding 7.5% of your taxable income to deduct it if you itemize on
   your federal return, in some states like Arizona all medical expenses
   are considered deductible at the state level of reporting. So be sure to
   report all of these expenses for tax purposes if it is an advantage in
   your state. This includes any special travel expenses you incur,
   including mileage to and from your health care provider. You should
   also try to **manage your family's prescriptions through the same
   pharmacy** so that you can easily track your expenses for tax purposes
   by logging on at the end of the calendar year and printing your records

---

[233] We will discuss the idea of buying meat in bulk and freezing it for later use in chapter seven.

for each family member who used prescription medications that year. Finally, as mentioned previously, you will want to **shop your family's insurance choices annually,** so use a no-cost brokerage service like **eHealthInsurance** to shop several health insurance providers at once so you can compare costs and coverage options from plan to plan.[234] Even though Obamacare has greatly diminished market options, do this even if your husband's company offers family health insurance coverage since covering your entire family through your husband's job may be cost prohibitive. If separate plans are more economical, then the other benefit is that your family would not need to deal with losing insurance for the entire family in case of a job loss or change. One other point to know is that if your husband is in between jobs right now, consider going through at least **eHealthInsurance** or other brokerage service to shop for short term insurance so that you have catastrophic coverage. Even though this kind of insurance usually only covers major medical and not regular visits, you can usual postpone standard medical care appointments until you have a new plan while at the same time protecting your assets in the event of a major medical issue or accident that occurs during this in-between time. One final consideration is for those families who do not want to go with the traditional healthcare route and would rather look at a medical expense sharing company. For more information about this non-insurance concept, check out **Medi-Share** or **Samaritan Ministries**; both are Christian medical sharing programs.[235] Of course, with the never-ending changes in national healthcare polices, it is wise to review and research options annually.

10. **Personal Discretionary**: Certain expenses in this category are not incurred every month at the same amount. So, **estimate your yearly output for these categories and write down an average monthly amount that must be set aside to cover these expenses.** For haircuts, consider learning how to cut your child's hair to save time and money over the years. For clothing expenses, find a great thrift store like **Savers** to obtain a good deal of your clothing since you will pay a fraction of the price and can find some very high-quality items in the process that your whole family can use. For other shopping needs, focus on only two or three stores you like to shop at and then really learn about their sale structures and periodic markdowns so that you can stock up at the right time of the year and save a great deal of money. Some people do not enjoy doing this because it often involves purchasing out-of-season clothes. However, if you get the hang of it, you will be able to obtain quality clothes for a great bargain well before you need the items. For the boys and my husband, we shop mostly the perpetual clearance sections at various department stores as well

---

[234] http://www.ehealthinsurance.com/
[235] http://medi-share.org/; http://www.samaritanministries.org/

as value stores like **Ross**. Then we go to **Wal-Mart** for basics or items we cannot find elsewhere. I am also very familiar with the sale and clearance opportunities at **Dressbarn** and have probably paid full price for only one item that I can remember! **Payless Shoesource** is where we purchase most of our family's shoes. Another way to save money is to align yourself with a health and beauty company whose products you like to use. Any other expenses that you have for individuals in your family that are purely discretionary should go here, such as recreational items or media. Since expenditures for this category tend to be vague and can get out of hand quickly, it is good have a dollar figure that you and your husband agree upon in advance that is a maximum that can be spent before needing to consult the other person. For us, we use the figure of about $50. If we have an unplanned or personal discretionary expense we know is going to exceed that amount, we consult with each other and then decide on whether to make the purchase or wait.

11. **Entertainment and Hobbies**: Make your husband's lunch as much as possible to save on his non-reimbursable eating out expenses at work. Only take magazine subscriptions that you will really read and that are suitable for Christian homes. Unread magazines sitting around the house add unnecessary clutter and pressure in your life: making you sense that you are "behind" all the time when they are not read. Also, instead of renting movies from pay-per-view system or rental service, consider using the $1 rental boxes or the library for these occasions. Basically, you and your husband need to re-evaluate expenditures on *all* hobbies and entertainment choices every year. If you find that there is an area that is too high, think about how you can work to reduce that expense. For example, if you like digital scrapbooking, host a **Heritage Makers** party where you can earn free product towards your hobby. If you enjoy cooking, host a **Pampered Chef** party and if you want to work towards some new jewelry, host a **Silpada** party. Maybe your husband likes to golf and there may be an opportunity for him to work a few hours a week in the pro shop in exchange for greatly reduced or free green fees. The options to fund your hobbies are only limited by your own imagination!

12. **Education, Lessons, and Classes**: While most of these expenses can be considered discretionary and postponed for a time, some of your curriculum expenses must be incurred depending on where you are at in the year. However, when money is tight, consider alternatives to extra things like outside classes and lessons. For example, in 2008 when our family weathered our nation's financial crisis and suffered a significant pay cut, as many did, we worked with the boys' piano instructor to only have two lessons for each per month instead of four so that we could afford to keep them moving on their program but cut

the expenses in half. Since I was very familiar with their piano program, I was able to adequately coach them in the interim and we still communicated questions and show video clips of progress to their teacher via e-mail as needed. Also, instead of investing in expensive private lessons for your children in activities like karate or dance, having your child take these classes at a local community center. They will enjoy similar programs and get a flavor for what they are all about while you are able to pay a fraction of the cost of most expensive, annuity-structured programs. This is especially true when the children are young and still exploring their interests. One final option to consider is that you may have an opportunity to help as a volunteer or coach in a class or lesson setting that your child is taking from a private organization that would allow you to receive a discounted rate for your child.

13. **Special Projects and Vacations**: No budget of regular categories can account for every possibility. Therefore, if you have a vacation you are saving for or a large expense that you know is coming, you can set aside a certain amount each month over a period of time until you reach your goal. Braces, career exploration camps, improving your home or yard, or replacing your vehicle or a major appliance all fall under this category. When estimating vacation costs, include transportation, food, lodging, attraction fees, and any special supplies or equipment you need to address for in your budgeted figure.

Make notes about any other ideas you, your husband, or your mentor have about identifying and controlling essential versus discretionary expenses. Then be sure to fill out the "Insurance Policy Information Sheet" on the following page.

_____

_____

_____

_____

_____

_____

_____

_____

_____

Insurance Policy Summary Sheet

Policy Type	Policy #	Policy Description of Coverage	Company Contact Information
Term Life Insurance			
Umbrella Liability Policy			
Home Owner's Insurance			
Auto Insurance			
Medical Insurance			
Dental Insurance			

Regularly Audit and Adjust Your Categories

Once your categories are defined, you must regularly audit the actual expenses you have incurred and compare them to what you originally designated for each one. When you discover a category that has actual expenses that have exceeded budgeted expectations by a concerning amount, **dig into it and find out why the actual was so out of proportion to the expected figure.** Have both of you made expenditures in that area without realizing it, or are there issues with impulse purchasing habits that need to be addressed? Has the cost for related products or services of the category in question significantly changed so that your budgeted figure is no longer a realistic one? Or perhaps you or your husband have made several discretionary purchases that were not planned for and have, therefore, cut into the funds you have available for your essential expenses. Whatever the reason, be willing to consider it and find out what is going on and then discuss it calmly with your husband. Figure out not just the dollar expenses for each category, but also compute the percentage of your total income that the expense represents. Use the guidelines suggested and see what areas might pose problems for you and your family.

The bottom line is that **no subject or spending category should be off-limits or taboo to discuss.** If one spouse is hesitant about sharing information, consider what spiritual issue may be taking root that needs to be addressed so that there is indeed open communication in your marriage, the lack of which can be one of the most stressful problems you can deal with as a couple.

The next section has a list of expenses that can help prompt your thinking about how to define essential spending (i.e. our needs) versus discretionary spending (i.e. our wants). They reflect the various categories that we have just discussed, and the assignments that I have given to each expense is just a general distinction. You could move even more expenses to "discretionary" from "essential" if you need to take it all down to the "bare bones". You may either use the *"Monthly Budget Planning Sheet"* provided or use it as a springboard from which you will create your own unique budget. Also use the *"Expense Categorization and Audit Sheet"* provided to define budget allocations by percentages, identifying patterns and potential issues.

This is also the time when you need to decide whether to use a cash system. For those who have struggled with consumer debt in the past, consider using **a debit-card-only or cash-envelope system**. Any cash not used for the originally designated purpose can then be reallocated towards a savings goal or used to pay down existing debt. We use our card for most everything we do so we do not lose the cash and can earn points towards the generous rewards program we have. Also, using a card helps us to very specifically track where our money has gone for the month. However, if you use a credit card, *always* pay each month's balance in full. Never carry it over, and work to avoid finance charges or fees. **So, if you use a credit card, make sure you utilize it wisely and pay it off every month!** Otherwise, stick to just using a debit-card or cash envelope system.

Most of the line items noted on the following sample budget are common to many families. However, there are some I have listed that may not apply to you or you may find that some category is missing that you would need in order to make your budget complete. Take some time to list information that is unique to your family's budget. Look at the sample on the next page and then figure out where you would classify these unique expenses so that you can begin to conceptualize what your budget may look like. Review it with your husband and come to consensus on how you want to classify your budget. Then use a spreadsheet tool to define and refine your own budget categories.

Monthly Budget Planning Sheet

Income - Salary and Bonuses (Net of Taxes)	$	Other Income Sources (Net of Taxes)	$
		TOTAL INCOME (ALL SOURCES)	

Essentials Expenses		Discretionary Expenses	
GIVING	$	**PERSONAL DISCRETIONARY**	$
Tithe		Children's' Clothes and Shoes	
Charity:		Parents' Clothes and Shoes	
Charity:		Monthly Haircuts*	
SAVINGS		Presents & Cards (Christmas, Graduations, Birthday, etc.)	
College Fund - Total Monthly Contributions		Professional Studio Photos	
Short to Mid-Term Savings*		Decorating, Office Supplies, other Household Expenses	
Retirement Savings		Other:	
Other:		Other:	
Other:		**ENTERTAINMENT OR HOBBIES**	
FINANCIAL MANAGEMENT		Eating Out Lunch Expenses for Work	
Term Life Insurance Coverage		Entertainment (Meal, movies, etc.)	
Umbrella Liability Policy		Magazine Subscriptions (Parents)	
Safe Deposit Box - Annual Fee		Photography and Digital Scrapbook Expenses	
Annual Line of Credit Fee		Other:	
Sound Mind Investing Web Subscription		Other:	
Stamps		**EDUCATION, LESSONS AND CLASSES**	
Checks		Homeschool Materials and Curriculum*	
Other:		Homeschool Supplies	
Other:		Standardized Testing Fees (IOWA)	
DEBT RETIREMENT		State, Conference, and Local Support Group Fees	
Mortgage		HSLDA Membership	
Other debt:		Magazine Subscriptions	
Other debt:		Music Lessons	
Other debt:		PE or Sports Classes	
HOUSEHOLD & UTILITIES		Summer Swim Lessons	
Property Taxes		Library Membership	
Home Owner's Insurance		Other:	
Home Repair and Improvement*		Other:	
Yard Maintenance Expenses*		**SPECIAL PROJECTS OR VACATIONS**	
Alarm Monitoring Service*		Vacation Account	
Pest Control Expenses*		Other:	
Association Dues		Other:	
Electric Utilities Company		**TOTAL Discretionary**	
Gas Company			
City Water Company			
Cable, Internet, and Phone Services*		**TOTAL INCOME**	
Cellular Phone Service		**(less) TOTAL EXPENSES**	
Other:		**NET BALANCE****	
Other:			
AUTO EXPENSES (ALL CARS)			
Car Payment+			
Cost Co. Auto Insurance			
Car Registration			
Gasoline			
Car Repairs & Maintenance			
Other:			
Other:			
GROCERIES			
Monthly Health Food Store			
Monthly Warehouse Store			
Food Warehouse Membership			
Monthly Grocery Store			
Make Up and Beauty Products			
Other:			
Other:			
MEDICAL			
Medical Visits and Copays			
Family Medical Insurance Premiums			
Family Dental Insurance Premiums			
Regular Medical Prescriptions			
Medic Alert Membership			
Other:			
Other:			
Other:			
TOTAL ESSENTIAL EXPENSES			

**In a zero-based budget, the net balance would be "0" each month since the income is totally distributed across all categories, including savings.

If a balance is left, you can incorporate it into your short-term savings acccount or maybe a special savings account for vacation. Then start at "0" again the next month.

If, however, your balance is negative then it is time to examine your individual category expenses to see what expenditure habits or commitments are making you out of balance. Use the percentage chart below to see what your culprit may be and then take steps to address it.

	Percentage of Net Income
GIVING	
SAVINGS	
FINANCIAL MANAGEMENT	
DEBT RETIREMENT	
HOUSEHOLD & UTILITIES	
AUTO EXPENSES (ALL CARS)	
GROCERIES	
MEDICAL	
PERSONAL DISCRETIONARY	
ENTERTAINMENT OR HOBBIES	
EDUCATION, LESSONS AND CLASSES	
SPECIAL PROJECTS OR VACATIONS	
TOTAL	100%

Expense Categorization and Audit Sheet

Expense Type & % Goal*	Expense Category	Expense Description	Is this expense under control? List problems.
E – %	Giving	Total at least 10% for tithe and above and beyond for other charitable giving.	
E – %	Savings	Total at least 10% across all forms of savings.	
E – %	Financial Management	Any services or subscriptions you use to manage your finances and investments goes here. You may choose to have a line of credit available that you could draw from in case of an unexpected job loss.	
E – %	Debt Retirement	Includes any mortgage, school, car, or home equity loans as well as credit card debt. Make it a priority to consolidate debt to the lowest interest rate possible and then pay your highest percentage interest debt first.	
E – %	Household and Utilities	This category plus your mortgage should equal no more than 40% of your overall monthly income. Items marked with an * can be dropped or at least reduced greatly in times of financial crisis.	
E – %	Auto Expenses	Estimate an average monthly amount to set registration fees based on whether you do a one or two-year renewal for your vehicles. The + for Car Payment means it could also be moved to the Debt Retirement section. However, leaving it here will show you the true value of what your vehicles are costing you every month.	
E – %	Groceries	All food, paper goods, cleaning supplies, vitamins, and over-the-counter medicines go here.	
E – %	Medical	Try to manage your family's prescriptions through the same pharmacy so you can easily track your expenses for tax purposes. Shop your family's insurance choices annually using www.ehealthinsurance.com	
D – %	Personal Discretionary	Certain expenses in this category are not incurred every month at the same amount. Estimate your yearly output for these categories and write down an average monthly amount that must be set aside to cover these expenses. Any other expenses that you have for personal individuals in your family that are purely discretionary should go here.	
D – %	Entertainment & Hobbies	Make your husband's lunch as much as possible to save on his non-reimbursable eating out expenses at work. Only take magazine subscriptions that you will actually read and that are suitable for Christian homes. Re-evaluate expenditures on *all* hobbies every year.	
D – As needed	Special Projects and Vacations	All other major expenses that you know are coming can be planned for and tracked here.	

*D = Discretionary; E = Essential; Write in goals as a percentage of income. A blank form is provided in the Appendices.

Money Management & Organizational Tools

Use this information on the Monthly Budget Planning Sheet as a basic guideline when creating your own personal budget. If you have pets, you will want to include the expenses required to care for them. If your children are involved in league sports or other specialty club activities, include those fees as well. Perhaps you have unreimbursed business expenses that you need to track for tax purposes. Essentially, you can go through your checkbook and banking accounts to gain an understanding of what *your* regular expenses are and then figure out how to classify and then categorize them. Here are some additional tools that you can use to create and maintain a household budget.

1. However, another great tool to consider is **Crown Financial Ministry's** various budgeting tools.[236] It is designed for helping families manage their bill paying responsibilities by treating their activity as an envelope system, even though it is a computerized, secure, online service that you can access from any system with Internet access. It helps track how much you have obligated to your credit cards for any given month and deducts related expenses from the proper category so that you will then have enough money to pay the bill off in full at the end of the month rather than being caught off guard by unnecessary expenses that tend to put you over your budget. You can set up automatic investments, payments, and saving deposits.

2. If you prefer just a paper system, **Crown Financial Ministry** also publishes *Family Financial Workbook: A Family Budgeting Guide* to help you define and manage your budgeting categories. This text uses a guided worksheet approach to lead you through the budgeting process.

3. **Every Dollar** is a popular budgeting tool produced by Ramsey Solutions.[237] The basic tool is free. However, users have an option to tie to their financial accounts by upgrading to *Every Dollar Plus*.

4. **Intuit's** *Quicken* is an excellent industry standard that serves to track all aspects of your household expenses and keep on top of bill paying responsibilities.[238] It is easy to perform associated updates and "talks" well with the company's *Turbo Tax* product for tax preparation we will discuss later. You can also conduct "what if" scenarios and track investments as well. Several handy calculators are built into the program and the information you will track will help

---

[236] https://www.crown.org/resources/category/budgeting/ & https://www.crown.org/how-to-use-the-envelope-system/
[237] https://www.daveramsey.com/everydollar
[238] http://quicken.intuit.com/

you with tax planning and compare investing options. However, I like the ability to write out our own budget, so I personally use both **Microsoft's Excel** spreadsheet tool and *Quicken* together to manage our finances and find the combination to be a good one.

5. **Mint** is a free budgeting tool that also enables users to tie directly into their financial accounts for real-time information.[239]

6. **You Need a Budget (YNAB)** combines financial planning methods with their software for real-time financial management.[240]

The second type of money management resource is to go through a **Christian financial management course** where you are encouraged to maximize your stewardship of God's resources and to take specific steps to improve your financial decisions and handling processes. Remember that the more you save and make, the more you will have available to expand God's Kingdom while meeting your own family's financial goals.

1. **Crown Financial Ministries**: Founded by Larry Burkett, this ministry provides my favorite resources to help families and businesses with their budgeting and financial planning needs.[241] They also have several helpful resources and tools on their website that you will want to check out for you own purposes as well as for your children, many of which I mention later in this chapter. Mr. Burkett wrote many useful books about financial management during his life, including *Debt-Free Living.*

2. **Dave Ramsey's Financial Peace University**: As mentioned previously, Dave Ramsey has developed a comprehensive teaching program about financial management decisions and tools that we need to employ consistently in our homes to bring the "peace of mind" we all desire to have from financial concerns.[242] He is known throughout the nation as a financial author, syndicated radio show host, and national speaker. There is even a junior version of this program for young children through age twelve.

Lastly, **make sure that you have a household filing system** that works for both you and your husband so that either one of you can find what you need at a moment's notice. When the mail comes into the house, we set it on my kitchen desk. Then later that day or the next, it gets sorted into one of five places.

---

[239] https://www.mint.com/
[240] http://www.youneedabudget.com
[241] http://www.crown.org/
[242] http://www.daveramsey.com/

1. Most of the mail and envelopes are **recycled,** so I open the mail right next to the recycle can.

2. Mail that I do not need but has personal information on it goes into a **"to-be-shredded" pile**.

3. Although most of our regular bills are set up automatically to pay, bills that I do need to process are then placed in my **"to-be-processed" file box**. I do not take care of it right when it comes in. Instead, I process them later. Then they are subsequently either filed in the accordion file mentioned in point four or the permanent cabinet, also discussed below.

4. Paperwork that I need to keep but do not need to do anything further with at that time are filed in my current, **annual accordion file**. This is just a regular, monthly accordion file used mostly for monthly billing statements that you can source at any office supply store. I then clean this out at the end of the year and evaluate whether I need to file or shred the documents, depending on what is warranted. The reason I do not file these items right away is that some of them will not be needed by the end of the year and I do not just want to file everything permanently. I usually only keep a year's worth of information on the bills unless it relates to our taxes or investments, which are kept for a much longer period.[243]

5. Paperwork that I need to **keep permanently** for warranty, insurance, taxes, or other such purposes are placed in a separate filing area rather than the accordion file. Then I will place those into the filing cabinets in their proper places the next time that I do the filing. Again, I do not take time to do it right then and there. I have one drawer dedicated to product purchases and the related manuals, receipts, and warranty paperwork associated with them. Another drawer is dedicated to tax files and work checks while still another drawer is used for all of services information, medical files, and bills current from the previous year.

Write down other ideas that your husband or your mentor has about processes and tools for money management. _____

_____

_____

_____

---

[243] https://lifehacker.com/5977082/what-documents-should-i-shred-and-what-should-i-keep - See this article to decide what information should be kept and what information should be shredded throughout the month and after each year's evaluation of papers for tax purposes.

Short-Term Savings and Midterm Investing

Once you have a handle on budgeting and auditing your regular household expenses, you will be able to discuss and **plan special projects and vacations** that will require more than just a minor shift in the regular budget to accomplish. When you know you would like your family to take a trip together or your refrigerator or even your car needs to be replaced, you will need to do more than just shuffle a few line items around to be able to afford that large expense without going into debt. Upcoming expenses like this can either be in the short term (i.e. less than a year away) or in the midterm (i.e. usually five years or sooner). There are also those unplanned expenses that cut into your short-term savings when something unexpectedly breaks down or an unforeseen illness or injury brings medical expenses to your door that you did not anticipate occurring.

In addition to the money management tools listed previously, you can also check out **Crown Financial Ministry** for guidance and information related to short and midterm savings goals.[244] Also, **Dave Ramsey's site** has specific guidance and resources available for you to consider when establishing your investment strategies and plans.[245] However, my absolute favorite resource for advice on investing and tax planning is **Sound Mind Investing**.[246] Endorsed by Crown Financial Ministry and founded by Austin Pryor in the late 1990's, his book by the same name, *The Sound Mind Investing Handbook,* is a "must-have" for any Christian home. To receive full benefit from the time you take to read *The Sound Mind Investing Handbook*, subscribe to their monthly newsletter and receive excellent, readable articles as well as monthly investment advice for a modest fee of $14.95 a month, less if you pay annually. Their website is a wealth of resources, particularly for subscribers, so check out the website's "Visitor's Center" for a full understanding of the overall structure, concepts, tools, and performance data related to the Sound Mind Investing (SMI) services.

> ➤ **Scripture to ponder**: *Do you not know that in a race all the runners run, but only one gets the prize? Run in such a way as to get the prize. Everyone who competes in the games goes into strict training. They do it to get a crown that will not last; but we do it to get a crown that will last forever. Therefore I do not run like a man running aimlessly; I do not fight like a man beating the air. No, I beat my body and make it my slave so that after I have preached to others, I myself will not be disqualified for the prize. I Corinthians 9:24-27 (NIV)*

While Paul is discussing the goal of running for a spiritual "prize", we can see that being **good stewards** of what God has given us and making sure to act purposefully and not "aimlessly" with our finances also builds a positive result for our families while providing a Christian witness for others, including our children. So here are some sequential steps to consider as you seek to bring structure and planning to your short and midterm financial goals.

---

[244] https://www.crown.org/
[245] https://www.daveramsey.com/blog/daves-investing-philosophy
[246] http://www.soundmindinvesting.com

Establish an Emergency Fund

The first priority is to **establish an emergency fund** that you can draw out quickly in the event of an unplanned expenditure: a large car repair bill, a broken air conditioner, a fallen tree that you need to remove, a termite invasion, or an unexpected trip to the emergency room. We have personally had *all* of these issues happen at some point and sometimes one crisis is followed immediately by another one! So, if you do not have a fund at all, set aside $1,000 as an initial goal; $3,000 is even better. A high-yield savings account or money market account is an appropriate parking place for this type of money, and then build it to cover at least three months of income in the case of a job loss. The point is that, even though decent yields are difficult to find these days, your emergency fund needs to be secure and readily available.

Consider Setting Up a Home Equity Loan

I am not a fan of debt. However, if your husband is in a volatile industry and you do not have a decent emergency fund set aside, **consider setting up a home-equity line of credit (i.e. HELOC)** that you would *only* draw out of in case of an emergency. As mentioned previously, you can set one up for a relatively low annual fee and minimum paperwork that would then give you a peace of mind that if you *did* have financial difficulties later on, you could draw upon this relatively low interest option to keep your family afloat. Remember that you cannot establish a home equity loan once your husband has lost his job or is not working for some reason, so do it while your husband is gainfully employed. The terms on these types of loans are usually 10 years at which point you either just let it close and you are done, or you can decide to have a new home-equity loan issued. Also, know that as of 2018, interest paid on HELOC's are no longer considered tax deductible.

Build an Income Replacement Fund

After the initial emergency fund is set and you have considered opening a HELOC, the next priority is to take steps to **set aside an income replacement fund in case of an unexpected job loss or change** that would set you back financially. Ideally, you would have a minimum of three months of income set aside for this purpose, but six months is even better. Remember that this figure will *not* equal what you normally have as your budgeted monthly expenditures that you have already determined. Instead, you would only need to make sure you could cover the "essentials" and should be able to discontinue or at least greatly reduce any "discretionary" expenses since you would have already figured out which is which. As I mentioned previously, we have personally experienced two different job losses over the years when we had no income and new babies in our home—once for eight months and another a few years later for four months. So, we definitely understand the wisdom of having an income replacement fund. Also, **keep in mind too**

that usually when your husband *does* secure a new position, he is often taking a pay cut just to get working again, so be flexible on your budget. Again, have this kind of money in a very liquid account as discussed with your emergency fund. If the family does not have enough money to bridge the gap, then consider drawing funds from your HELOC to cover that period and then work on paying it back quickly when he is working again.

Define Short to Midterm Savings Goals

Once an emergency fund and an income-replacement strategy have been established, **evaluate any short or midterm savings priorities that you have for special projects or vacations you wish to take.** If you know that braces are soon coming into your child's life, start setting aside resources for that. If your washing and drying machines are acting up, know that you need to start making plans to replace them. If you dream of taking your family on an educational trip to Washington D.C., a major national park adventure, or a tour of the famous expedition landmarks of "Lewis and Clark", research the related expenses and allocate the needed amount each month until you have it fully funded. Since you usually have a bit more time to address these large expenses that you are planning on making, you can consider additional savings instruments like **CDs** (i.e. Certificates of Deposit) or even a **short-term bond fund**. CD's have set and variable terms and related interest rates so that you can set up multiple CD accounts and have them come due every six months so that you are maximizing your yield options while at the same time, remaining liquid with the CD's that are coming due. This is often referred to as a "CD Ladder". Short-term bond accounts can also be effective savings tools, but they do carry higher risk than CD's and do not have the stability of interest that CD's have. However, since they are really designed to be set aside for at least two years or longer, they may give you a higher overall yield than CD's in the end.[247]

What other ideas do you, your husband, or your mentor have about the importance and the methods of short-term savings and midterm investment options? _____

_____

_____

_____

_____

_____

---

[247] For an excellent article covering various short-term savings instruments, read this article
https://soundmindinvesting.com/articles/view/at-long-last-rates-for-savers-begin-to-rise

Long-Term Investing

Long-term investing plans are just as significant to **establish now** as your budget and short to midterm savings and investing practices were to address. Once you discuss your long-range plans, you will have a better idea to figure out what your life with your husband will look like once you are "empty nesters" and all the other issues that go along with that season of life, like helping aging parents and making sure that we have done due diligence on our own "estate planning" efforts. But first, we will discuss saving for college, which may be more of a short-term goal at this point if you have not addressed this issue when your child was younger. Consider for a moment the "Parable of the Talents" (NIV).

> **Scripture to ponder**: *"Again, it will be like a man going on a journey, who called his servants and entrusted his property to them. To one he gave five talents of money, to another two talents, and to another one talent, each according to his ability. Then he went on his journey. The man who had received the five talents went at once and put his money to work and gained five more. So also, the one with the two talents gained two more. But the man who had received the one talent went off, dug a hole in the ground and hid his master's money.*
>
> *"After a long time the master of those servants returned and settled accounts with them. The man who had received the five talents brought the other five. 'Master,' he said, 'you entrusted me with five talents. See, I have gained five more.'*
>
> *"His master replied, 'Well done, good and faithful servant! You have been faithful with a few things; I will put you in charge of many things. Come and share your master's happiness!'*
>
> *"The man with the two talents also came. 'Master,' he said, 'you entrusted me with two talents; see, I have gained two more.'*
>
> *"His master replied, 'Well done, good and faithful servant! You have been faithful with a few things; I will put you in charge of many things. Come and share your master's happiness!'*
>
> *"Then the man who had received the one talent came. 'Master,' he said, 'I knew that you are a hard man, harvesting where you have not sown and gathering where you have not scattered seed. So I was afraid and went out and hid your talent in the ground. See, here is what belongs to you.'*
>
> *"His master replied, 'You wicked, lazy servant! So you knew that I harvest where I have not sown and gather where I have not scattered seed? Well then, you should have put my money on deposit with the bankers, so that when I returned I would have received it back with interest.*
>
> *'Take the talent from him and give it to the one who has the ten talents. For everyone who has will be given more, and he will have an abundance. Whoever does not have, even what he has will be taken from him. And throw that worthless servant outside, into the darkness, where there will be weeping and gnashing of teeth.' Matthew 25:14-30*

As this story illustrates, **God expects us to put His resources to work not only for the short but also for the long term**. This kind of planning requires visionary thinking and self-discipline so that when the time comes, you will not be anxious about your budget, and you will be in a good position to not only live comfortably but, more importantly, to be able to give an even greater portion of your money and time away: money because you will have more resources available to you and time because you will be able to spend your time doing the Lord's work more so than finding ways to scrimp by and still earn income when you are well into the retirement years. As with short and midterm investing, the best resource for Christian advice and sensible direction about long-term investing is **Sound Mind Investing**.[248] Remember to understand what your allocations across various types of funds should be and how they should shift to more a more conservative mix as you are within ten or fifteen years prior to your retirement season.[249] Place most of your investing resources into well-managed stock or bond funds (i.e. collections of other funds and stocks/bonds) and always be careful about investing in highly volatile, individual stock options unless you have a keen understanding and confidence in the performance of that individual company.

College Planning

College expenses are huge and rising at rates disproportionate to inflation. The College Board states that, as of 2016/2017 data, the average annual sticker price for a four-year state school (tuition, fees, room, and board) is a little over $21,000. A private institution averages $46,600.[250] These are annual estimates, so each should be multiplied by at least four. I say "at least" because data also shows that most students take longer than four years to complete their undergraduate degree.[251] Even worse, just over half of the students who start college ever finish.[252] So many are winding up with the debt and no degree plus no way to secure a higher paying job to clear it. Though sticker prices are usually not reflective of what families pay, the cost is still substantial. Therefore, the first job we must do as parents is to ensure that the traditional education route for college is the best path for our child to follow.

If your student is indeed college-bound, plan with your spouse and communicate expectations often and early with your child. For, of all the

---

[248] http://www.soundmindinvesting.com

[249] Fund types can vary but usually differ based on the size of the company they are invested in as well as the types of industries they represent and whether or not the mix is mostly allocated to domestic or primarily international companies. Various fund profiles bring with them a tradeoff between risk and reward so be sure to research your allocations thoroughly by following good financial advice. Once you have your plan and have your advice resource identified, then stick to it and do not be swayed by the constant stream of "noise" that is out there surrounding what you should do with your money.

[250] https://www.collegedata.com/cs/content/content_payarticle_tmpl.jhtml?articleId=10064

[251] https://www.nytimes.com/2014/12/02/education/most-college-students-dont-earn-degree-in-4-years-study-finds.html

[252] https://www.nbcnews.com/feature/freshman-year/just-over-half-all-college-students-actually-graduate-report-finds-n465606

long-term savings priorities a family can have, saving for your child's education can often bubble up to the top of the list in terms of the added stress a family can have over it. This is largely because it is the first long-term savings goal that most families withdraw from when the time comes since retirement is usually still quite a way off compared to when your child graduates from high school. The other reason that college planning can lead to stress is that many families are at either one end of the spectrum or another. Either they have not saved *anything* for their child because there was never enough "month left at the end of the money" to set it aside for this purpose, or they have spent years over-sacrificing other essential areas of life to put everything they could into their child's education fund, strapping their family beyond what is reasonable. The key, then, is to **achieve the right balance between these two extremes.**

Here is the bottom line when it comes to saving for college; whether for short, mid, or long-term purposes, **of all savings priorities mentioned in this manual, saving for college is the least important**. I know. It is shocking to see it in print, right? I am not saying that you should not set aside funds for your children and, in fact, we personally established a fund for each of our boys the moment we received social security numbers for them. However, what I *am* saying is that saving for college should *not* replace or overtake the importance that retirement, short-to-midterm savings, or monthly budget needs have in our lives.

We decided from the beginning that we were not going to even attempt to try and fully fund a four-year education for each of our boys. Instead, we automatically deposit an amount in each child's account every month that will provide each one of them a hefty portion of what they will need when the time comes to cover tuition, knowing that part-time work, grants, student loans, and/or even possible scholarship opportunities may also be available to them. In contrast, **you have no such options as these when saving for retirement, so you should not allow saving for college to overshadow your retirement goals.** You also only have a short season of living with your children while they are in your home, so make sure that you are not sacrificing too much in other key areas of living just to make sure that the almighty college fund is overflowing.

So, what can you do? First, make sure that you **constantly dialogue with your child** as early as middle school the expectation that they will attend an in-state school that is within budget. Unless a full-ride scholarship emerges, staying in-state is mandatory. Also, choose an option that would make commuting possible. As you start to research, you will realize that annual costs for room and board are usually half or more of the total bill. Private schools are only an option if scholarships, etc. make them affordable, and community college may be the first step after high school rather than stepping directly into a four-year university. Making sure your child is on the same page as you and your spouse in such expectations is half the battle.

Also, as mentioned earlier in chapter four, there are many websites that can aid you in your search for **scholarship information**.[253] However, your best source of information still rests with the institution of choice that your child would like to attend. Find out what they offer and figure it out early since some universities and colleges also have grants and scholarships that are exclusive to their institution. So, make it your child's part-time job in high school to research and apply for as many scholarships as possible, particularly the smaller ones as many of these often go unclaimed every year.[254] Another organization parents can utilize to research, plan, and track scholarship opportunities is **Scholly**.[255]

Even with the aid of possible scholarships, however, most families will need some source of additional aid to help their child navigate the financial obligations of college without going into a crippling level of debt. To figure out what college savings instrument is best for your family, the best resource I have found to use is **Savingforcollege.com**.[256] It thoroughly explains the most common instrument used today to save for college, which is the **529 plan**. Most all states have these plans and you can usually purchase an out-of-state plan as well, no matter where you live or where your child goes to school later in their life. There are many benefits to a 529 plan including the following:

1. **Parental control of the money** with a designated beneficiary is great so that funds are used for the intended purpose of higher-education. Also, in case of scholarships, parents may withdraw the amount awarded in the scholarship without penalty. Even so, always work with your tax advisor before making your withdrawal decisions.

2. **Tax advantages** come with this type of plan since the money is eventually taxed at the child's income rate rather than the parent's rate. Also, many states, including Arizona, now allow a certain portion of your yearly contributions to a qualified 529 plan to be tax deductible.

3. **529 plans are transferrable** so that if one child in your family winds up receiving a full-scholarship and will not need the full amount you have saved for them, you can change the designated beneficiary to a different child. You may also simply leave it there in case the "scholarship" child decides to use the funds for qualified expenses later in life, such as to earn a master's degree, Ph.D., or other higher education option later in their life.

---

[253] http://www.scholarships.com/
[254] https://www.fastweb.com/financial-aid/articles/over-2-point-nine-billion-in-free-college-money-unclaimed-by-students-why
[255] https://myscholly.com/
[256] http://www.savingforcollege.com/

For additional options to save for college as an Arizona resident, visit **AZCollegePlanning** to sign up for a local, free workshop and learn how to access scholarships and grants.[257]

Discuss other thoughts and options regarding the importance of retirement planning versus saving for college with your husband and your mentor.

_____

_____

_____

_____

_____

_____

_____

_____

_____

_____

_____

_____

_____

_____

_____

_____

_____

_____

_____

_____

_____

_____

_____

_____

_____

[257] http://azcollegeplanning.com/

Retirement Planning

With rare exception, unless you or your husband has served in the military, the days of expecting company pensions are long gone. In addition, as our nation ominously marches towards national bankruptcy, you might as well not count on Social Security either. Even if it is still around by the time that most of us can draw from it, it will probably be greatly reduced from the current benefit levels, and it may not be around at all when our child reaches retirement. For more information about this issue, set aside 30 minutes to view the video on the **I.O.U.S.A. One Nation. Under Stress. In Debt.** website.[258] It will open your eyes and educate you in an accessible and straight-forward manner about the imminence of our country's situation.

So, what is a Christian family to do? As in the "Parable of the Talents", the worst thing we can do is nothing. Thus, do not despair over what cannot be controlled. Instead, take steps to do what you *can* do with what God has given to you.

First, **if your husband's company has a 401K matching plan, fund that fully before looking at other investment options.** Even though fund choices are limited, you can figure out the appropriate allocations among fund types by learning about basic percentage guidelines based on your and your husband's ages and performance goals. Fund it up at least to the point where you maximize the advantage of the dollar matching from his employer.

Next, **take any extra funds you can invest in your retirement and have your husband open his own IRA** (Individual Retirement Account) or **Roth IRA** with you named as the beneficiary. Children can then be named as secondary beneficiaries in equal portions if you both pass away. Also, as many of us moms worked in the private sector for some period of time before transitioning to our stay-at-home status, if you personally have a 401K that is still lurking around at your old employer, roll that over immediately into your own personal IRA, naming your husband as the primary beneficiary and so forth. Make sure your husband does the same with any 401K plans he has from a previous employer as well.

There are a few reasons to do this. First, previous employers may have financial difficulty themselves which may pose a risk to any investments you have tied up with them, especially if some of the value of the 401K is tied up in company stock. Second, even if the previous employer is financially solid, most 401K plans are quite limited in their fund offerings and you are better off going with a large, reputable brokerage house like **Fidelity Investments**, **Charles Schwab**, or **Scottrade** that are reliable and have plenty of investment choices. [259]

Once you have your 401K and IRA's in place, **regularly manage them** so that you can make sure allocations among fund types maintain

---

[258] http://www.imdb.com/title/tt0963807/; *I.O.U.S.A. The Movie* can be streamed from Netflix, Amazon, etc. Though made in 2008, it still holds a good deal of relevant information for us today.

[259] https://www.fidelity.com/; https://www.schwab.com/; http://www.scottrade.com/

the appropriate percentages you want them to hold in your portfolio as you trade funds over the course of the year. Remember that rolled-over IRA's cannot be contributed to anymore, and you just manage what you have. However, if you open a new IRA, you can set up regular contributions to that account. For more information about what investing approach to follow, specific fund recommendations, how to manage your monthly trading activities, rebalance your portfolio annually, or whether to open a regular or a Roth IRA, visit **Sound Mind Investing (SMI)**.[260]

Remember that any gains you have from dividends paid or value in share price gained is not taxable until you withdraw the money at retirement. It is wise to use other savings options rather than prematurely tapping into retirement so that, for your IRA funds, you can wait until the IRS forces you to start making minimum withdrawals at age 70 ½. That way, you can maximize the amount of money you will have in the years that follow, and your funds will not run out too soon. Also, keep in mind that if you take this money out *before* the minimum age for distribution (i.e. 59 ½), you will not only have to pay taxes on the amount you withdraw but will also be hit with a 10% penalty. There are some exceptions but generally the penalty applies. Since that is a "one, two punch" of negative impact, you will want to avoid that at nearly all costs and make sure your other savings options are in place to cover unplanned expenses as we previously discussed.

Discuss other thoughts and options with your spouse regarding your plans for retirement savings.

_____

_____

_____

_____

_____

_____

_____

_____

_____

_____

_____

[260] SMI has an excellent program of "Just the Basics" investing for families who have a total savings portfolio of under $25,000 versus families who can use the "Upgrading" strategy when they have funds in excess of that amount. http://www.soundmindinvesting.com/

Wills and Estate Planning

Wills and estate planning are topics that most people do not wish to deal with. Yet, of any plans you and your husband make for your family and your finances, **specifying both of your wishes in the event of your and your spouse's death is the single most important thing that you need to address**. Do it right from the beginning as soon as you start having children. You may be thinking, "Wait! We don't have enough money to be considered as having an *estate*!" But the fact is, if you own property or have bank accounts of any kind, you have an estate.

None of us wants to think about it, but **if you and your husband die without a will in place and without specification as to who you wish to act as a guardian to your children or executor of your estate, you are not fulfilling your obligation as the responsible parent that you want to be to your child.** Do not think that having even casual arrangements are enough to address this issue as you never know what unforeseen problems may arise that will interfere with your assumed plans and desired wishes. Putting these items in place does not cost that much in time or money, so just get it done as soon as possible with your general attorney. Even more, it is a tangible act of love.

1. **Establish a relationship with a reputable estate attorney**. If you do not have an attorney who can handle these basic services, obtain a referral from a trusted friend or relative. You will also want to have an established relationship with one to help you with issues your aging parents may have, if they do not already have one. If using an attorney is not financially feasible, then utilize resources from a reputable service like **U.S. Legal Forms** to create your state-specific document needs.[261]

2. **Draft a will.** Even though your investment accounts have designated beneficiaries and do not get counted in your estate as far as the courts are concerned, your regular bank accounts, home, and other property all fall under the jurisdiction of a will. You may specify your wishes for the distribution of your wealth down to very specific details with any combination of contingent beneficiaries.

3. **Establish a durable power of attorney next**. This document is necessary for you to have on file in the event that you are unable to make financial decisions, as in the case of being in a coma or having suffered a stroke and being unable to communicate clearly. In practical terms, this legal document gives your designated person the ability to manage your finances, pay your bills from your checking account, and so forth while you are unable to do so. Typically, your husband holds your durable power of attorney, but

---

[261] https://www.uslegalforms.com/

you also name a secondary person if your spouse is unable to fulfill those duties.

4. **Establish a healthcare power of attorney as well.** This document is like a durable power of attorney but applies to medical decisions that need to be made on your behalf.

5. **Put in writing your wishes for the care of your children in case you and your spouse die with minor children at home.** This can be as simple as writing out a letter specifying your guardians of choice and your reasons why you wish to select them. Be sure that you have a conversation with your child's intended guardian(s) first before you put it in writing. Just because you think your sister or brother *should* take your child in the event of your and your husband's death does not mean that they necessarily want that responsibility. Also, do not always assume that a relative should take them. You should prayerfully consider what adult, or preferably a married couple, in your life has a great relationship with your child and holds the same values as you do. So, if you are in a family of non-Christian relatives, seriously consider talking to your trusted friends who are Christians about your desire to have them act as your child's guardian in the unlikely event of your and your spouse's untimely death.

6. **Put in writing your wishes for who would act as the executor of your estate in case you and your spouse die with minor children at home.** Ideally, the ones that you choose as guardians for your child should also serve as the executor of your estate in making financial decisions for the benefit of your children who are left behind. However, there may be a good reason to separate this function off to someone else. For example, perhaps you have one sibling who is younger, more energetic, and would serve as a great guardian for your child. But perhaps that same sibling is not that good with money. Maybe you have an older sibling who would not be able to raise your young child but would be happy to help manage the finances for them and send your other sibling the money necessary on a regular basis to help cover your child's expenses and so forth. That is a good example of why you would have one person designated for one job versus the other.

7. **Consider pre-paying at least part of your funeral expenses.** This is not a decision that everyone can make when they have young children at home. However, if you can make these kinds of arrangements yourself, you will always make it easier on your remaining loved ones while at the same time saving them from making these difficult choices and incurring even greater expenses

in the future. Consider investing in an endowment property where, no matter what happens to the ownership of the memorial park, the property will be forever set aside for its current purpose.

Whether determining your wishes for guardianship or the executor responsibilities for your estate, be sure to have notarized copies of these sent to your attorney as well as the individuals that you have designated to hold those positions so that there is no confusion about it later. Also, if you have a reason that you do *not* want a certain family member taking over either or both roles who you think might contest your decision, you should specify those wishes and reasoning in writing as well in case the matter should need to go to court.

Show your love to your minor child by putting in writing what you wish to have happen in the unfortunate event that both you and your spouse die.

In the end, you need to trust that God will take care of your child in the best manner possible under the circumstances. However, we still need to do our part to send a message loud and clear to our child that even though we are not there anymore, we cared about them enough to make sure that this difficult time would be as smooth as possible for them. When they are older, your child will understand how **these diligent acts of service were additional ways that you expressed your love for them while you were alive.**

Explore the topic of wills, estate planning, and pre-paying funeral expenses with your spouse.

_____

_____

_____

_____

_____

_____

_____

_____

_____

_____

Tax Planning

Most of us have basic enough investments, property holdings, and earnings such that doing our own taxes every year, although sometimes unpleasant, is a manageable task. However, even if you have an accountant or service who prepares your taxes for you, you still need to do a certain amount of preparation in advance and tracking throughout the year so that you can give them everything they need to calculate the lowest possible tax obligation that can be achieved. Therefore, here are some fundamental items to keep in mind when tracking information to process your taxes each year. This discussion assumes that you itemize your deductions rather than just take the standard deduction. Although under the new tax law that took effect in 2018 most families will not itemize, I have still covered the topic since you may still wish to itemize, and the tax cuts are currently only valid through 2025.

1. **Have a central filing system.** As you obtain documents that you know will be needed to process your taxes the following year, have one place that both you and your husband know is the central file for keeping those documents until the time to organize them comes. Be sure also to **periodically copy important computer files** to a CD or USB memory stick that you can then place in your lock box as an off-site back up. You can also use a cloud storage account for this purpose.

2. **Track medical, dental, & eye care visit information** including mileage driven, co-pays and deductibles paid, as well as prescription and eyewear expenses. Set up a special category in your budgeting program that allows you to easily pull medical expenses that you have paid out during the previous year, but also keep receipts or credit card charges that proves those amounts were paid. Remember that the receipts you get from the doctor's office often times fades over time so having a back-up credit card statement or even making a photocopy of the original receipt will ensure that you have back up information if you are audited in the future. **Keep a spreadsheet of the places you visited for any medical purpose that shows the date, the location, the mileage traveled, the reason, other travel fees, and the money paid for the visit** so that you can easily transfer the information to your tax program the following year. Use a mapping site to get an accurate idea of the mileage driven if you are not sure. Once you have done this one time, you can use that distance information from year to year since most of us stick with the same healthcare providers for many years. I have included a sample form at the end of this section and in Appendix B to help you with this tracking, if you need it. I also make sure to highlight any medical appointments in green on our calendar so that I can go back through it the following year to see if I missed any appointments on my spreadsheet before finalizing the numbers.

3. **Track monetary donations carefully** by issuing checks or paying by card rather than cash. That way, you can ensure the non-profits you contribute to throughout the year send you the documentation necessary to support your reported figures the following year.

4. **Track non-cash donations** of clothing and other household items through a thorough system of documentation. Families will often take goods to a donation center throughout the year and not take time to track the value of those donations which can help to lower their overall tax burden the next year. While many household goods and electronics do not hold much value to claim, donated clothing in like-new or good condition can add up more quickly than you realize. To easily track and value your donated goods throughout the year, follow these steps:

    ➤ Have a **central collection tub** in your house for toys, clothing, and other items that you know you want to donate. Three to six times a year, go through this plastic tub and any other closets and cabinets you want to clear out and place everything out on the floor or a large bed where the can be easily spread out and seen.

    ➤ Write down a **description and condition of the items** by category using the distinction of "high" (like new) or "medium" (very good) quality. Anything in poor condition is not counted in your tracking and should just be tossed.

    ➤ Once you have your log of what you are donating, **photograph the items** that you can then put with your list of items donated.

    ➤ Gather the items all up in boxes or large plastic garbage bags and **deliver them to your drop-off location** of choice. Make sure that they give you a **receipt**, acknowledging the donation. Write the date and a short summary of what you donated on this receipt and put it with your paperwork for this donation.

    ➤ To **value your donation**, use **Intuit's** *It's Deductible* tracking system for non-cash donations.[262] It is a free, on-line service that you can use and access all year and keeps track of your donations from previous years. Type in the information from your log as well as the basic information requested about the organization you donated it to, and then you can print out the summary reports that show what you donated and their estimated values.

---

[262] http://turbotax.intuit.com/

This may seem like an excessive number of steps to follow, but you would be surprised how quickly the value of non-cash donations adds up within a year's time. If your donations exceed $500 in value, the **IRS** becomes very particular about your documentation support. Therefore, since you do not know at the beginning of the year how much value you will donate throughout the year, it is better just to follow the same process for all non-cash donations. Visit the **IRS** website and review *Publication 526* for more specifics about cash/noncash donations.[263]

5. Although this is by no means an exhaustive list, **other common items that you will want to track** and keep in your tax file are copies of any registration fees you paid to register your vehicles during that tax year, contributions made to a qualified 529 plan, property taxes paid, mortgage interest paid, and, of course, any W-2 or 1099 forms you receive documenting your family's income for the year.

6. Finally, **select a reputable service to process your taxes for a reasonable fee or, better yet, just process them yourself. Intuit's** *Turbo Tax* is a great industry standard that steps you through each aspect of reporting your taxes for state and federal purposes.[264] It covers every eventuality, including major life events like buying and selling property, investment gains and losses, and so forth. On-line support is available as well as an extensive help system. Once you have completed inputting the information and running the error checks, you can submit your taxes electronically. It is very easy to do, and if you are receiving refunds, you can have them automatically deposited into your account of choice, usually receiving it in a relatively short period of time.

Discuss other thoughts and ideas regarding tax planning with your spouse. _____

_____

_____

_____

_____

_____

_____

---

[263] http://www.irs.gov/publications/p526/ar02.html
[264] http://www.turbotax.com

Medical Driving and Expense Log for _____

Date	Description	Purpose	Round Trip Mileage	Fees Paid

Teaching Financial Responsibilities to Your Child

When teaching financial responsibilities to your child, take advantage of every life opportunity that comes up since children usually retain information you teach them when they have a need to know it or specifically ask about it. However, there are other specific steps you can take to equip your children to be good financial stewards along the way—long before they would ever think to ask you about specific questions related to money.

Little Ones

During this season, children have little understanding of money and the way it works. However, towards the end of these years, a three or four-year-old can understand that when we go to the store, we are not allowed to just take what we want. We need to be able to give the store enough money to pay for the items we need, and if we do not have enough money, we cannot get that item. So, **have conversations with your child when you are in the store and let them in on your thinking process as you make purchasing decisions.**

For example, if you are purchasing a pair of shoes for them say, "These two choices are nice and would work for you. That pair over there is nice also, but they cost too much money and we cannot afford those. So, let's choose between one of the first two pair." If you are looking at an appliance for your kitchen and you do not have quite enough money yet for the item, say to your child, "I would really like to buy that mixer, but I don't have enough money for it yet. I will need to save a little longer before we can buy it." When you send them to their church class, give them some pocket change or a dollar and say, "Now when we go to your class, the first thing we need to do is that put that money in the church offering so that God can help the people to use it to pay for things that you use at the church. The craft supplies, snacks, and books you use all cost money, so we want to be sure and help to pay for the things we use and to make sure that they are available for new children to enjoy too." So, make a habit out of explaining things to your child even if they do not quite understand it all now and you will **establish the necessary groundwork for open and healthy communications with them about money as they mature** and are able to take in more information about it.

K-2nd Grade

This is the age that you want to **consider instituting an allowance system**. Now some parents do not believe in giving out allowances, and if that is your opinion, that is fine. However, consider this. If a child is not allowed to have any money on a regular basis, how can you make sure that they have an opportunity to practice how to manage and handle it responsibly? Play money is good for learning about the value of money: how to make change, count it out, and so forth. But it really does not help to solidify practice in learning how to use money since it does not represent anything of real value. When they start to see that taking money to the store can then be exchanged for something they want, they gain experience in the emotional side of working with money. "Do I buy that less expensive toy now just so I can buy something, or should I wait and put it towards something I *really* want?" That sort of tough choice cannot be easily wrestled with unless they are using the real thing. So here are some points to consider regarding allowance.

1. **Determine what constitutes a regular allowance for your child**. Dave Ramsey calls it "commissions" while others call it "chore money" or, in our case, "allowance". Whatever you call it, make sure first that it is given for fulfilling regular daily expectations. In our home, they need to do their schoolwork, music practice, and daily chores in a complete and cheerful manner. Daily and weekly expected chores include things they are personally involved with, such as taking care of personal hygiene, helping make their bed, putting away their used dishes, picking up after themselves, keeping their schoolwork tidy, sorting dirty laundry, putting away their weekly clean laundry, and cleaning up outside toys that they use. Each child also must rotate participation in setting the dinner table and has one additional weekly housecleaning chore they are expected to do based on their age and ability. If they have not done so or have done so with a poor attitude, then they receive a reduced or no allowance. This rarely occurs but since it *has* happened on occasion, they know that they do not want to be in that position of missing out, so it is a good incentive for them to approach each day in a positive manner.

2. Also, **we model the payment schedule that their father is on for his work.** Since he receives payment for work done twice a month, they too receive allowance twice a month. Write it on your calendar and be diligent about keeping their "pay days" consistent. We pay out twice a month on Mondays if each child has demonstrated diligence and a good attitude in their schoolwork and basic chores.

3. **Make your amount chosen easily dividable among spending, saving, and giving categories**. You want them to be able to easily divide their money, so give it to them in such a way as to help them to see the percentage relationship among these three items even though they are too young to understand percentages. To make it easy when they were young, we gave each child $2.50 every allowance period using two one-dollar bills and two quarters. This way, 10% (i.e. one quarter) can be allocated towards giving and another 10% (i.e. the other quarter) can be allocated towards savings. Then the remaining

$2.00 goes towards their spending. Again, they will not understand the math behind it all yet, but they will start to see the relationships among the value of each category. They will see that this is how Christians handle money and it is then an easy conceptual transition when they get older and have more income to manage. It is their introduction to how if we live off 80% of what we make, we can give 10% to God and still have 10% to put into savings.

4. **Give them an opportunity to earn extra money**. As children can physically do more, they should be allowed to participate in extra chores that allow them to earn extra money. Yardwork tasks, like raking leaves, helping to plant new plants, weeding, picking up rocks out of the grass, and sweeping off the porch, are all good examples of extra chores. Cleaning baseboards, organizing kitchen drawers, cleaning out their closets, or helping a parent with a special project are also opportunities for earning additional money. If they help above and beyond their expected personal responsibilities and weekly housecleaning chore, they might also earn extra money for that.

The second priority you want to establish during this season is to have the proper tools in place needed to make allowance management an easy system to administrate. If it is too complicated or takes too much time to manage, you will not follow through with it and the teaching points will be lost on your child.

1. **Purchase or make a three-way savings bank**. These banks should have slots for "Giving", "Spending", and "Saving" so that as they receive money, you can help them understand how to split it up. The *ABC Learning Bank* from **Crown Financial Ministries** is one option, though it is no longer in production.[265] Each of the three components can be separated from each other so the child can take that part of their bank with them, depending on where they are going. **Crown Financial Ministries** also made the *My Giving Bank*.[266] This is also a great tool. It is their older version of this type of bank and is an all-in-one unit, but it is still sold through Amazon.com. If you have trouble locating one, consider making your own version.

2. Be sure to **have plenty of cash on hand in a safe place** in your home for helping to make the appropriate change when necessary and to pay allowances regularly. You will need both

---

[265] http://crown-322355.hs-sites.com/childrenscenter
[266] http://www.amazon.com/My-Giving-Bank-Faith-Kids/dp/9834502702

paper and coin money on hand to be able to work with them on their finances at a moment's notice.

3. If you are overwhelmed by the idea of tracking everyone's chore "to do's", **make a chore list** for each child on your computer that you can post for your benefit to track and see if they are keeping up with expectations. You could also make one that covers what jobs need to be done for the whole house and then just rotate who is doing the different jobs each week. If you need more assistance in this area, consider purchasing *Choreganizers* by Jennifer Steward. This is a visual system that you can use to post a card holder strip for each child that then holds the cards you expect them to complete each day. There are also blank ones that you can use to put some of your unique chores on that you cannot find represented in the pre-printed cards. It comes with "Mom and Dad Dollars" to give out in exchange for things later, but we also found it to be easier just to use cash rather than converting the values later.

4. For a more formal tool, a good Bible study resource for this young season is *The ABC's of Handling Money God's Way* by **Crown Financial Ministries**.[267] Designed for ages 5-7 and divided up into 12 lessons, your child follows the adventures of four children who work together to save enough money for a puppy. Along the way they learn about various principles of handling money as their work towards this goal.

3rd Grade – 6th Grade

During this season, you are building on what you already established in the previous one regarding chore expectations and allowances. Perhaps at this age, you are increasing the dollar amount of that allowance, if you would like. However, in our home, we just continued to use the same base amount for allowances knowing that children in this season have the option to perform more extra chores that they could not physically or safely do before, such as mowing the lawn, washing windows, or moving, running the washing machines, shredding old documents, and organizing and moving heavier items.

A good study you can take your child through at this season, specifically designed for children ages 8-12, is **Crown Financial Ministries'** *The Secret of Handling Money God's Way*.[268] Lessons are divided up over twelve chapters and include simple Bible stories plus a guided prayer journal. Keep reading for additional ideas and resources that you may want to consider instituting during this season.

---

[267] http://www.crown.org/
[268] http://www.crown.org/

1. **Allow your child to do additional work outside of the home for family and neighbors** as you feel comfortable. Perhaps your child could wash their cars or help manage their home while they are away on vacation doing chores such as picking up their mail and newspapers, keeping their porch clear of advertising papers and delivered boxes, and setting out and putting away their trashcans. Another thought is helping to take care of some regular need that their grandparents have. For example, at one time, we cleaned their Grandma's home once a month, which also allowed them to earn extra money while helping her do what she could not do for herself. At the same time, we got to spend more time with her. She loves to reward them with some money at the end of their stay for both cleaning and extra projects, and everyone feels good about it all the way around.

2. **Before going to a store, always make sure your child articulates *in advance* what they want to buy.** Even if they do not have an exact name of a toy, they should be able to say whether they want a doll, building set, outdoor toy, game, and so forth before you go. Be clear with them that they are not allowed to buy something just to buy it. If that store does not have what they want, they will need to save their money and wait until another day.

3. **This is also the age where children should learn about sales tax and shipping charges.** When your child wants a particular item that is $19.99, for example, let them know as they are saving for it that they will need to actually save $21.84 to purchase it if the sales tax rate where you live is 9.3%. Make sure that they understand this early and that you are not just paying the difference every time they go to make an on-line or catalog purchase. This is also true of shipping costs for special items ordered online that cannot be sourced locally.

4. **Allow your child to experience various "life truths" about the way money works in the safety of your home and under your supervision.** Always keep in mind that you would rather your child learn difficult life lessons while under your care than for them never to deal with the issue until they are out on their own. For example, we were at a toy store one time for our oldest and youngest sons to make purchases with the money they had each been saving. Our middle son, who is always the one to save for months at a time towards a bigger purchase, was visiting his Lego kit of choice he was saving towards while we were there. He knew he was still $13 short of his goal but

just liked to go and look at it while we were there. When we got ready to go, we noticed that he was particularly distressed, not because he could not buy and use the kit that day but because there were only a couple of them left and he was afraid they would all be gone before he could save his money. Right or wrong, we decided to buy it and told him we would put it away for him until he had saved the additional money and could finish paying us for the toy. He would need to do this *before* he received the toy. Happy with this decision, we all left the store. During the ride home, however, his older brother generously offered to loan him the $13 so that he could pay what he owed us, and the toy could be enjoyed that day rather than waiting. My husband and I glanced uneasily at each other with the words of William Shakespeare's *Hamlet* ringing in our ears: "Never a borrower or a lender be." Of course, we had essentially arranged a layaway with him, but we knew allowing him to enter into this sort of borrowing arrangement with his brother was going to lead to trouble. Yet, we let them do it. We are such bad parents, right? Well I am sure not all parents would have allowed this arrangement to take place, but we thought that somewhere in the days to come a valuable life lesson was going to be learned. Yes, we had already had all of the discussions about making sure older brother knew that it was going to take younger brother awhile to pay the $13 and we reminded younger brother that he would need to stay cheerful about knowing that he owed the money and not resent his debt to his brother. However, it did not take but three weeks for it to all come to a head. Older brother had made up a chart so that he could track any payments he had received and started to make it an every two to three-day habit of asking younger brother if he had any more money to pay towards his debt. Frustrated because his opportunities to make extra money were not matching his desire to pay back the debt, a rift began to form between them. What began as a well-intended gesture was quickly turning into resentment and frustration on both ends. This was the point that Dad stepped in with individual discussions with them both. Now the "life lesson" about not going into debt and about the dangers of loaning family members money could be well understood. Although God's Word does not prevent us from loaning money, He does give us guidelines about it and their dad was able to discuss these principles on both sides. In the end, both learned valuable lessons about the stress of owing as well as loaning money that they could not have learned if we had not allowed them to experience it firsthand. They were able to go through the process and see how much more gratifying it is just to wait and earn the money first *before* getting what you want, using it, and yet still owing money on it. They also learned how family relationships can be strained if money is loaned instead of just given as a gift. So, do not miss out on those teachable moments that allow them to sometimes "crash and burn" in the safety of your own home.

5. Finally, this is the age to institute **money management board games** that can be both fun and educational. Start with games like *Monopoly Jr.* by **Parker Brothers** or *Cashflow for Kids* by **Rich Dad**.[269] Later, move to games like the full *Monopoly* game by **Parker Brothers** or *LIFE* by **Milton Bradley** that will add more complicated concepts of money management and life issues that can arise. It is a great way to learn about principles of borrowing, purchasing, career choices, and so forth while building relationships and having fun with each other.

Jr. High, High School, and Beyond

This is the age where everything starts to come together for your child on how to manage money. The best thing you can do during this season, then, is to incorporate them into every aspect of what it takes to run your own personal household. **Use <u>everything</u> that was discussed earlier in this chapter as your guideline for the minimum principles you want them to understand before they leave your home.** Allow them to interact with your bills and paperwork to see how to manage the monthly, quarterly, and annual demands of running a real household. In addition, consider incorporating these experiences into your teaching plans with them.

1. **Allow them to open their own, minor checking account**. Be sure to tie it to your account so that your child is not charged "low balance" fees. Teach them about debits and credits and how to make sure that they never overdraw their account.

2. **Teach them how to financially run a home.** Look at your household budget and think about how you could divide up the topics to discuss how you handle the elements of each different section. By the end of this season, you should give them the assignment of literally running your home for a time to reinforce financial principles while experiencing issues that arise.

3. **Teach them the concept of confidentiality** and that they are not to discuss your household's personal information and financial status with others, including younger siblings. Show

---

[269] http://www.richdad.com/apps-games/cashflow-for-kids

them proper filing techniques and how you keep your personal documents secure, including the use of a bank lock box. Teach them also the importance of protecting their identity and how to secure important paperwork and shred others so that such critical information is never compromised.

4. **Mentor them in your business dealings.** Regardless of whether own your own business or not, every adult must deal with business matters. Working with repair personnel, medical offices, insurance companies, and shopping other potential service providers are just a few areas that your child needs experience and guidance in handling. Teach them how to deal respectfully, clearly, but firmly in all matters. They also need to learn how to ask for information in writing and how to keep a log of their interactions in certain situations that require multiple contacts. Even showing them how to negotiate terms is a valuable lesson that will come in handy later on when they need to purchase a car or arrange a competitive interest rate in their future business dealings. A helpful tool to help coach your child in their communication skills at this level is *Communication and Interpersonal Relationships* by David Marks.

5. **Still use games or other books and resources to instill more advanced principles.** Take your child through the classic economics book called *Whatever Happened to Penny Candy? A Fast, Clear, and Fun Explanation of the Economics You Need for Success in Your Career, Business, and Investments* by Richard Maybury. You can also use the **Rich Dad's** *Cashflow 101* board game that is designed for children ages fourteen to eighteen.[270]

6. **Provide special guidance in career choices for your daughters.** Many Christian homeschooling families raise daughters who have a heart to become a wife and mother early in their life. So, parents need to be sensitive to listening to their daughters and understanding that their single, young adult daughter still needs guidance in this area even when the high school days are far behind them. Please know that my comments should not be misconstrued as support for the **"patriarchal movement"** that some support in the homeschooling community.[271] After all, I hold a master's degree

---

[270] http://www.richdad.com/apps-games/cashflow-boardgame

[271] Much controversy has arisen in recent years over this issue as some families believe that daughters should not pursue education past high school and simply work and reside in their father's home until she is married. For an overview of this movement and its issues, read Michael Farris' article disavowing it here:

myself and worked outside the home for many years, so I am certainly in support of young women attending college or earning a degree in a field of interest that can provide fulfillment and needed support. However, if your daughter's greatest wish is to be a wife and mother, consider whether she needs to attend a full four-year college program, or if an associate's degree or a vocational program would be more appropriate instead. For those who do pursue a college degree, encourage her to think about focusing her higher education in areas that can be easily facilitated out of the home later in life in case she wants to be able to produce some income while she is a homemaker, wife, and mother. Freelance writing, graphic design, or bookkeeping are flexible options that could be done out of the home, for example. Counseling or tutoring are other options that may be able to work part-time for those who hold degrees in education or psychology. Those who are more entrepreneurial by nature may even want to consider starting their own home business. For more information about these concepts and the issues consider these materials:

➢ *Business Boutique: A Woman's Guide for Making Money Doing What She Loves* by Christy Wright; Part of the Ramsey Solutions brand, Christy provides very practical advice on **how women can identify a niche, create a business plan, and streamline efforts to fulfill that plan in their home business.** In addition to her book, she has a whole host of resources and coaching services available on her site.[272]

➢ *Women Leaving the Workplace* by Larry Burkett; Although you may have a daughter who does intend to work in the corporate world and later needs to transition out of it, this is an excellent read for any young woman. By reading it, your daughter will **see what eventualities she will face when she does become a mother and glean wisdom from what she can do now to prepare for that time.** It will also encourage young couples to live within the means of one income so that having your daughter stay home with the children eventually is a very doable option for her rather than having to work in the marketplace just to keep financially afloat.

---

https://hslda.org/courtreport/V30N2/V30N202.asp?utm_source=&utm_term=&utm_content=&utm_campaign=&utm_medium= Please note that HSLDA membership is required to access this article.
[272] https://www.businessboutique.com/

7. **For adult children in the home, work out a reasonable support arrangement with them.** I do not believe that all children, once they have graduated from high school or even college, should have to pay rent to their parents. I believe that there is a "ramp up" time that should be allocated to each child, depending on their situation and circumstances. For example, if your child is going to college as a full-time student after high school, you may not be able to do as much financially for them as you wish but you *can* help them with the living expenses. Come to an arrangement that they will continue to respect the rules of the house as well as maintain their grades and, as a result, room and board will be of no additional cost to them. I believe the same goes for a child who has decided to go into missions, full-time church work, or even if they have entered a trade after high school. Help them out for the duration of their time in training (i.e. vocational training or college) and within the year following their entry into the adult workplace. Then sit down with them and discuss what the next steps are. If you have a son, talk about the need to establish himself as an independent man and provider so that he may have an opportunity to eventually court a Godly woman who may become his wife. If you have a daughter, explain to her that, while she can strike out on her own, that she also has the option to contribute to her home with her parents and do any additional work that God has called her to do in that setting until the time comes for her to marry and leave the protective environment of the family.

Discuss other thoughts and options regarding other ways you can teach your children to exercise responsible financial stewardship. Talk with your husband about this and also obtain insight from your mentor.

_____

_____

_____

_____

_____

_____

_____

More Chapter Notes...

Chapter 7

Managing Life's Physical Interactions & Demands

So I find this law at work: When I want to do good, evil is right there with me. For in my inner being I delight in God's law; but I see another law at work in the members of my body, waging war against the law of my mind and making me a prisoner of the law of sin at work within my members. What a wretched man I am! Who will rescue me from this body of death? Thanks be to God—through Jesus Christ our Lord! Therefore, there is now no condemnation for those who are in Christ Jesus, because through Christ Jesus the law of the Spirit of life set me free from the law of sin and death. Romans 7:21-8:2 (NIV)

Valuing and Honoring Relationships

Is this scripture reflective of what we struggle with every day? Yes, it is! We want to follow God's law and do the right thing in training and discipling our children, managing our finances, and so forth, but **our body is weak**. We also want to do all of the right things physically, like eating right and exercising. But sometimes it is just so hard to make that as important as the other demands that are pressing in around us. So how do we do everything we want to accomplish with our family and our household while living wholesome, positive lives?

First, of all the healthy priorities you want to focus on, **build positive relationships within your family**. You can have the perfect meal on the table, less than 3% body fat on your frame, and a spotless home, but if your relationships are unstable, you do not have a healthy household. So, recognize that, while meeting all the demands of life are important, nurturing positive relationships and communications with your husband, your child, and others in your life are *the* most important priority.

Encourage Direct Relationships

Encourage your child to **build direct relationships**. Too often dad or mom set themselves up to be the "go-between" for the child and the other parent. Once Dad or Mom have been labeled in the child's mind as being difficult to talk to or work with, they will choose the path of least resistance and work through the approachable parent to be their mouthpiece. If you tend to be the one your child comes to, resist the urge to translate your child's questions or frustrations to the other parent and encourage them, instead, to work directly with them.

Also talk to your husband about your child's concerns and encourage him to be proactive in developing a positive, one-on-one relationship with them. Work with him to create moments that are just for him and your child to be together; for **quantity time creates opportunities for quality moments**. Even if it is just taking one child

> *Note to Leaders and Mentors:*
> *Too often homeschool support groups offer every social and activity opportunity under the sun for moms and children but leave dads out of the picture completely. Consider having some gathering events that rely on dad's participation, like hosting a "Backyard Ballistics" contest or child/dad relay competitions that will create those bonding opportunities while networking whole families together with each other.*

to the hardware shop or going down to the grocery store to share a treat together, having dad spend one-on-one time with each child on a rotating basis throughout the month just "doing life" together creates opportunities for bonding and conversation that cannot otherwise be achieved.

1. Have dad spend time with your child working on **involved craft projects or science experiments** that have time requirements beyond the normal school day.

2. If possible, arrange a time where your **child can go to your husband's work for a day**, or even just a half day to see what he does all day and to promote conversations about work ethics and other issues that arise on a regular basis in the work environment.

3. If your husband enjoys outdoor activities, arrange a time where **just the two of them** can go hiking or camping out with each other. If nature activities are not his style, then even a trip to the hardware store or down to the park to fly a kite or remote-control plane would be a great use of time.

4. Have several **fun project books** on hand that they can grab and use together at a moment's notice. These projects mostly appeal to boys, but you can also encourage your husband to spend time with your girls by focusing on an area of interest they have, such as going to a concert, playing sports, building models, or doing some other special-interest activity together.

> *Backyard Ballistics* by William Gurstelle guides families in how to make catapults, potato cannons, fire kites, and more![273]

> *Sneaky Uses for Everyday Things* by Cy Tymony has a whole series of these books that are fun and fairly easy to do including *The Sneaky Book for Boys* and *The Sneaky Book for Girls*. [274]

Actively Listen to Others

Most of the daily communication we engage in is nonverbal, so actively listen and face your child when they talk to you. If you are busy cooking, reading, or working on the computer, **stop what you are doing and turn to face them eye to eye**. Resist the quickest method of communication by nodding empty "uh-huh's" while you continue doing what you are doing. If you model this method to them, they will be more likely to do the same thing to you when you wish to address them. I speak from experience when our youngest son, who was about five at the time, had to take my face in his little hands to get direct eye contact with me!

When they share a concern with you, **repeat it back to them** to make sure you follow what they are saying. For example, if they are having difficulty with a school assignment say, "So you are not sure how to memorize your multiplication table for the 'eights' and you need some help, is that correct?" When they say "yes", ask them if they have any ideas as to why they might be having trouble and then that will help you work together on a plan to address the issue. You can follow this approach for any concern or problem they have, making sure that you are on the same page with them. Be sure to **require them to actively listen to you** also when you are giving instructions and have them repeat it back so there is no confusion about what is expected of them. Active listening saves frustration down the road and demonstrates respectful communication skills they will need when they mature into competent adults.

Model appropriate communication behaviors

---

[273] http://www.backyard-ballistics.com/
[274] http://sneakyuses.com/

Consistently Resolve Conflict

As your children start grasping the unpleasantness that goes along with sibling disputes, instruct them right away how you expect them to handle their disagreement by teaching them the essence of this scripture.

"If your brother sins against you, go and show him his fault, just between the two of you. If he listens to you, you have won your brother over. But if he will not listen, take one or two others along, so that 'every matter may be established by the testimony of two or three witnesses.' If he refuses to listen to them, tell it to the church; and if he refuses to listen even to the church, treat him as you would a pagan or a tax collector. Matthew 18:15-17 (NIV)

Unless there is a serious safety issue at hand, we expect our boys to try to **work things out between and among themselves first**. They have learned by now that if Dad or Mom needs to involve themselves in the resolution process that probably both of the quarreling brothers will not necessarily be pleased with the outcome. The most common issue when they were younger stemmed over the use of a toy that they both wanted. They learned quickly that the toy often goes away when they cannot work out a sharing arrangement, so we have trained them that working it out with each other first is usually a better route. As they have gotten older, arguments stem more from issues of bossiness or perhaps disrespectful tones that need to be addressed, which can be harder for them to recognize as a conflict until they are deep into the problem. In this case, we have drilled the "Matthew" resolution passage noted above into them to the point that they know if one brother tries to handle it in a biblical way and the other one does not follow suit that they will be at risk of losing their privileges. The "Four Steps to Freedom" covered on pages 255-257 is also an invaluable tool for resolving such relational issues.

> *Make sure to point out what __both__ of them did right and what __both__ of them did that was wrong.*

For those times that you *do* need to step in, **avoid comparing them** in such a way to where one is the golden child and the other is the wrongdoer, for this is *rarely* the true picture of why the conflict occurred. Make sure to point out what *both* of them did right and what *both* of them did that was wrong so that learning can occur from both perspectives. For example, if one child took another child's toy without asking. "Taking" child was wrong for doing this, but "violated" child made the mistake of leaving the special toy out in a public area in the first place. If one child calls the other child a negative name, "negative name" child was wrong for saying the words, but "violated" child was wrong for provoking a conflict in the first place. Always positively acknowledge them when a child comes to you with the truth about a situation or says to you that they honestly could not work it out. They will still receive appropriate punishments but praise them for their honesty and let them know that punishments and consequences are *always* worse when the child does not tell the truth or tries to hide it. Always end with a time of reconciliation or an agreed upon plan of restitution to the "violated" sibling if something has been broken in the process.

The bottom line point for this issue is to make sure that your children know how you expect them to resolve issues with their siblings and friends. Talk about it in advance of the problem and role play out some scenarios to "make it stick". Know that problems *will* arise, and you will not always be around to prevent every possible negative encounter they have. So, your goal is to **train them ahead of time to recognize conflict when it occurs and to take a step back, trying to solve it in a biblical manner so that the best possible outcome is reached.**

Here are some additional resources that will help you with the issue of sibling rivalry and conflict resolution.

1. A good resource to read that will aid you with the issue of addressing **sibling rivalry** is Rick Boyer's book called *Raising Cain Without Killing Abel*. As a father of fourteen, he and his wife, Marilyn, certainly have a lot of experience on the subject!

2. *Making Brothers and Sisters Best Friends* by Sarah, Steven, and Grace Mally is another great tool for addressing sibling rivalry. Divided into 12 lessons, this material focuses not just on preventing bad behavior and tolerating each other but really coaches families how to **ensure that siblings are "best friends"**. There is a companion coloring book for younger children and a DVD format as well.

Confidently Manage Stress and Anger

There are volumes of books and essays available to you to read that are written about managing stress and anger. This topic is so far reaching that I cannot attempt to address every aspect of it here. However, there are three crucial observations that I would like to share with you about this issue that may be of use to you.

First, recognize that **anger by itself is not wrong or bad**. Most of us are probably familiar with the New Testament passage covering Jesus' entry into the Temple during Passover time.

> *Jesus entered the temple area and drove out all who were buying and selling there. He overturned the tables of the money changers and the benches of those selling doves. "It is written," he said to them," 'My house will be called a house of prayer,' but you are making it a 'den of robbers.'" Matthew 21:12-13 (NIV)*

We know that Jesus never sinned, and we see that out of His anger came a right admonishment towards those who were violating the use of God's temple. His first emotion appears to be one of righteous indignation, which brought the second one of anger. In turn, this anger in turn resulted in firm action needed to correct the problem. In the same way, we must recognize that **anger is always a follow-up emotion** that stems from an initial emotion, which must be identified in order to act in a way that is constructive and appropriate. Fear, pride, jealousy, and other sins are all ripe examples of trigger emotions that can lead to anger.

Second, realize that **angry parents produce angry children**. It is like that story we have all heard where Dad has a rough day at work and then comes home and is short with Mom. Mom, hurt by this, is in turn upset with the children about some minor infraction. The children then begin to fight with each other over whatever issue is nearest at hand and then the youngest of them all gets pushed around the most by the older ones who, in turn, kicks the family dog. Out-of-control anger is like an evil bank account, snatching deposits and overdrawing itself before you even realize what has happened. Then you must work *ten times* as much to replace what was carelessly withdrawn. So, if you or your husband have unmanageable anger issues, get professional, Christian counseling and **never** administer spankings to your children until you have this issue firmly under control.

Lastly, recognize that while reasons vary dramatically from one person to another as to what triggers anger, try to **understand what your personal triggers are** and work to manage those issues so that you remain in control of your tongue and your actions. For many moms, particularly homeschooling ones, **interruptions are a large part of why anger occurs**. After all, our whole day is centered on the successful management of interruptions. The more you have on your plate to accomplish that is separate from your teaching and home management priorities, the higher your sense of frustration will be and the anger that follows. This will always happen when your personal priorities conflict with your daily responsibilities, and we will discuss more about addressing this issue in chapter nine when we cover scheduling.

So, for now, be aware of this universal issue of motherhood and take steps now to reduce outside expectations and stresses on your life, particularly when your children are very young. When you are a homeschooling

Out-of-control anger is like an evil bank account; snatching deposits and overdrawing itself before you even realize what has happened.

mom, **you *cannot* continue to do all the hobbies and church activities that once were a large part of your life.** Non-homeschoolers often do not "get it" and think, "Well, you're home all day, so why can't you do this or that?" or "Why can't you come to this weekday morning Bible study since you don't have to go to work?" The fact is that you *do* have a full-time job, teaching and mothering. If you try to maintain all those things you once did *plus* add even more to your plate, you will hit a wall at some point—most likely at your family's expense.

Another common trigger for moms is the stress that comes from a **lack of preparation**. While it is true that some moms are very structured in their teaching approach and others are more naturally free flowing, there are certain aspects of preparation that can benefit us all. When you have plans to cover certain experiments or art projects within a specific timeframe, be sure to shop for supplies in advance so that you have them on hand when needed. If your curriculum relies on copies to be made or pages to be printed, just go ahead and have that done prior to when they are necessary. Whatever you can do in advance and have ready to go, the less stress you will have in that moment. This means less opportunities for triggering anger!

So, learn to manage stress in your own life as well as that of your child through advance planning, understanding that interruptions will happen and that plans will change sometimes. Also **help your child learn the benefits of praying regularly, taking deep breaths, and engaging in physical activity on a consistent basis to managing difficult experiences and disappointments,** which will avoid major meltdowns and tantrums in the process.

What anger issues are you presently coping with? What other issues related to anger exist in your home?

_____

_____

_____

_____

_____

_____

_____

_____

_____

_____

Gently Help Your Child Cope with Grief

Although your child may not have experienced grief firsthand in their young life, loss brings with it a tremendous amount of stress. So, knowing that the day will come when they will need to deal with it, think about ways that you can **prepare them in advance with more removed experiences**, discussing concepts of life and death openly and calmly. For example, if a neighbor has a friend or relative who passed away recently, talk about it in clear, simple terms with your child. Use word pictures like **"the glove" analogy** to explain what death to a Christian means and how, even though we will not see them any more on Earth, we will see them one day in heaven. To explain this concept, take a glove and place it on your child's hand. Explain to them that the glove is the person's body while the hand inside is the person's spirit and unique personality that was created by God. Talk about how our "gloves" wear out eventually and that a person's body stays on Earth when they die. Then talk about how the "hand" is that Christian person's spirit, which is immediately ushered into the presence of God to live with Him forever.

Before continuing this section, take a moment to write down your own personal experience with loss as well as any thoughts regarding how to talk to your child about it.

_____

_____

_____

_____

_____

_____

_____

_____

_____

_____

_____

_____

_____

_____

In our family with young children in the home, we have experienced death in three very different ways that each required a unique approach to help our children cope. **Our first loss occurred when our second oldest son died half way through my pregnancy with him.** It was very distressing for all of us and our then 18-month old son had a difficult time understanding what was happening. "Why is Mommy in the hospital so long? Where did brother go?" It was agonizing for us and our sadness often transferred onto him. So, one of the ways that we coped with our loss was to arrange a memorial gathering in his honor. We invited our friends and family to the memorial park where they could come and view his designated niche area and tiny urn. We had a separate time with our immediate family and then open gathering time with others who came and went during a two-hour period. The niche has other special items in it and a plaque commemorating his short life with the following words.

We commit you into God's hands our sweet son and look forward to the day when we shall meet you in eternal glory. We are grateful to the Lord that you are our son and how you have so deeply touched our souls and the hearts of those around us. We love you.

Love,

Mommy & Daddy

Benjamin Patrick Gary

"Son of My Right Hand"

Promoted to Glory: 8/3/99

"Before I formed you in the womb
I knew you,
Before you were born
I set you apart."
Jeremiah 1:5

Going through this time was painful. Yet it was amazing to see **God's hand at work even during that difficult period**. I was overwhelmed by the outpouring of love from our friends and family who supported us through that time and was so surprised to learn from many of my mother's friends that they had experienced similar losses as well as the death of their infant children for a variety of reasons. Even at that time—decades after they had experienced their own personal losses—they welled up with tears and told us how wonderful they thought the memorial gathering was to attend. They had felt so alone after their experiences during a time when you "just didn't talk about it". We were so blessed by the healing that began to occur during that time for us as well as the benefit that it provided to our friends and family.

The process to cope with grief from miscarriage is no different than other grief experiences, and I utilized other methods in the months that followed, like making a small scrapbook and putting together some pictures that a friend took at the memorial gathering. Even though our oldest son was quite young at the time, I have these memories and items that later testified to him and his other brothers, who were not yet born when it happened, how Dad and Mom processed this loss and how **a family can come out on the other side of grief stronger and more committed to God and each other than ever**.

For more information about coping through the loss of miscarriage or infant death, consider these books. Also, contact your church and ask if there is a support group or contact available to you as regular grief groups are inadequate to help a grieving mother in this situation.

1. *I'll Hold You in Heaven* by Jack W. Hayford; This is a very helpful, biblical look at the confidence you can have in knowing that your **child was ushered directly into the presence of Jesus** when they died and that you will know them one day.

2. *Empty Arms: Coping After Miscarriage, Stillbirth, and Infant Death* by Ilse Sherokee; This book is a very practical look at how to **cope with the specific aspects of daily life** during and after the loss of your child.

3. *A Deeper Shade of Grace* by Bernadette Keaggy; This is an inspirational and **encouraging book of comfort**.

4. *Preventing Miscarriage: The Good News* by Jonathan Scher; This exceptional book gave us many solid answers and resources. The **specific medical information and insight** it provided eventually led me to pursue the diagnosis and treatment of our issues related to reproductive immunology. After eighteen months of treatment, blood work, and travel we were able to have two more healthy sons!

Our second loss since we become parents came to us when my father passed away seven weeks to the day after our third son was born. He had gone in for a somewhat routine surgery and wound up having cardiac issues—dying unexpectedly in the hospital at the age of seventy-one. It was a great shock, and none of us were prepared. We were still adjusting to life with balancing a newborn child and a toddler. On top of it all, we were out of work at the time and my husband was attending a night school technical certification course. This seemed like an impossible season for us and, frankly, much of it was a blur. However, there are four observations I now have about our life during that time and also as a result of the previous loss of our son that I hope may support you in some way, either now or in the future.

First, just like we found with losing our infant son, **we obtained great comfort in "doing" whatever we could to properly honor my father while caring for my mother at the same time**. Just like we discussed in chapter five, sometimes you need to behave your way through difficult seasons, forcing the logic of your mind to overrule the devastated pieces of your heart. My husband and I were with my mother during the entire process, both during those serious days in the hospital as well as during the time that followed my father's death. We helped her out with every conceivable concern and arrangement that we could, aiding her to focus on what the next step, the next day, or even the next hour needed to entail. We also took on the role of communicating and working with my brother, who was living out of state at the time, as well as other concerned friends and family members.

Second, **reach out to a trusted family member or friend who can help you through this time by providing you essential logistical support.** There would have been no way we could have been as helpful to my mother as we were, nor could we have had the time we needed ourselves to digest what had transpired if we had not had reliable friends who could jump in and help us out with life's details at a moment's notice. One family in particular served us in such a way that it still makes me emotional today to think about their generosity. When we received a call from my mother in the middle of the night that things were not going well with my father, my husband went to the hospital to understand what was going on. Later, when he called to tell me I needed to come, I did not hesitate to call my friend, and she rushed over to stay the night in our home with our son so that we would not have to wake or distress him. He was not quite four at the time. She essentially took him into her life for a couple of days while we were coping with everything at the hospital and, eventually, at the funeral home. On top of that, even her parents, who also lived near us at the time, came over to go with me and our new infant to the hospital in the middle of the night since my husband had already left to be with my mother. Her dad followed me while her mother rode with me in our van and comforted me all the way there. I will never forget their kindness or the way that they blessed us during such a season of crisis.

In the days that followed, we also had other friends who offered to make us meals and help with various aspects of the arrangements, all of whom blessed us as well. So, **know in advance who your "go to" friends are who will always have time for you in a moment of need.**

Third, **be willing to talk about your deceased loved one in a way that will both honor them and educate your child about life and death truths** in a positive and healthy manner. Some families become hesitant to discuss loved ones who have died for fear of making their child sad. However, more often than not, it is not the child who is uncomfortable talking about them, but the parent. Learn to work through your grief in such a way that talking about how much that person meant to you in a way that helps your child to understand the positive impact they had on others while they lived on Earth. My husband *still* finds replacement parts even over a decade after my father passed away that he took care to make sure he had on hand to fix various items around my parents' house and yard, serving to once again testify to the care he took to always be prepared and to think ahead to the future needs of others. He did the same thing in planning with their finances so that my mother would not have to worry about how she would continue to live after he was gone. These are the kind of qualities we have discussed and shared with our boys over time as they now witness these experiences from their own perspective.

Lastly, reassure your child that **we will see our Christian loved ones again for all eternity** when we all meet in heaven again someday. Reinforce to your child the reality that this life is but a mist and that we are training now for our eternal life in heaven. [275]

One more thought I would like to share is this; **always take advantage of the opportunities you have now to be with your parents while you can**. I have little patience for adult children who do not take time to support and engage with their aging parents. We all know people in our community and sometimes even in our own families who do not give their parents the time of day or treat them with the respect they deserve until they want something from them. Seek to be an adult child, then, who honors your parents in a way that will not only minister to them and to yourself but will also serve as a good example to your child.

Even when one accounts for the usual bumps that accompany most parent/child relationships, I have always had a reasonably good relationship with my father that only continued to improve after I left the home to get married. He was always interested in what was going in my corporate job and became even more interested in our lives once we started having children. He was very supportive during the loss of our

---

[275] Why, you do not even know what will happen tomorrow. What is your life? You are a mist that appears for a little while and then vanishes. James 4:14 (NIV); "Do not let your hearts be troubled. Trust in God; trust also in me. In my Father's house are many rooms; if it were not so, I would have told you. I am going there to prepare a place for you. And if I go and prepare a place for you, I will come back and take you to be with me that you also may be where I am. John 14:1-3 (NIV)

infant son and the subsequent work we did to address our issues with an out-of-state specialist. I remember one very pointed time when I needed to make one last trip to Los Gatos, California for a final treatment, making make sure that I would carry our third son to term as some of my routine bloodwork showed that one of my numbers had unexpectedly spiked. I was about thirty-two weeks pregnant and it was just after the "9-11" terrorist attacks in 2001, so now the security procedures for air travel made it just about impossible to do a turnaround trip like I had always done. Still, I had to fly out within forty-eight hours. As I was arranging child care with my mother for our oldest son, my father got on the phone and expressed that he wanted to go with me. I was taken aback at first thinking how expensive it was going to be for him to purchase a non-refundable, full-fare ticket since I was using the last of my "free" tickets I had earned. I also felt bad that he would be taking an entire day out of his life just to travel around with his very pregnant daughter and just sit there while I was having a treatment done for three hours. But, in the end, he was not comfortable with me traveling in my advanced stage of pregnancy by myself and wanted to come, so I just went with it. I will say that I later realized the significance of that day once he was no longer with me. Not only was he a huge help and comfort to me that day, but we talked about everything and nothing for eighteen whole hours of traveling there, doing the treatment, and then traveling back. We discussed just about every topic you can think of, and he also shared stories with me that I never heard before, including one where he was doing an engineering job on board a large commercial ship early in his career and got in big trouble for unknowingly "eating the captain's pickles"! We also talked about his future with Mom and his "end of life" wishes; little did I know at that moment how timely that was going to be in just a few short weeks. So, while most of us do not have the opportunity to spend eighteen straight hours with our mom or dad as an adult, **we *can* carve out significant times that are just between you and them** that will serve to carry you through the rest of your adult life and will testify to your child how important parents are for their whole lives.

For more information about helping you or your child cope with grief and understand life after death issues, check out the many resources available from **Focus on the Family** or **Lamb and Lion Ministries**, a Bible prophesy ministry that does an excellent job tackling many difficult issues like this.[276] If you are in need resources personally, please consider the following recommendations. Also, if you have a friend who could benefit from one of these titles, please consider gifting one to them during their season of grief.

---

[276] *Coping With Death and Grief* by Patricia Johnson; http://www.focusonthefamily.com/lifechallenges/emotional_health/coping_with_death_and_grief.aspx; http://www.lamblion.com/

1. *Death and the Life After* by Billy Graham; This is a great "classic" to have in your home; **full of practicality and compassion.**

2. *How Could a Loving God? Powerful Answers on Suffering and Loss* by Ken Ham; This book looks at more of the **global issues surrounding life, death, and the Christian faith.**

3. *Jesus is Coming Again* by David Reagan; Excellent, easy-to-read **book for children** that explains what will happen in the end times when Jesus comes for the second time.

4. *My Friend is Struggling With the Death of a Loved One* by Josh McDowell; This book is designed for to **help teens who have a friend coping with grief.**

5. *One Minute After You Die* by Erwin Lutzer; **Addresses nearly every pointed question** one can have about this subject.

6. *Wrath and Glory* or *God's Plan for the Ages* by David Reagan; These titles cover **end-times and "life after death" issues** for teenagers and adults. The first concentrates more on Revelation and the second covers all aspects of Bible Prophesy.

Our third and most profound loss occurred when our oldest son passed away at the age of fourteen in the fall of 2012 after a two-year battle with an aggressive form of leukemia that also involved his lymphatic system. He had been diagnosed at the age of twelve in the fall of 2010 and was mostly treated at Phoenix Children's Hospital (PCH) over his twenty-five-month treatment journey.

It was believed that the initial eight months of treatment at PCH had cured him. However, when he relapsed shortly thereafter, it became clear that he never really achieved a quality remission and that he needed a bone marrow transplant. So, we made plans to take him to Seattle Children's Hospital in the fall of 2011 since PCH's program was not versed in cord blood transplants. Neither of his brothers were a match and none of the sixteen-plus million listed donors were even close to his type, so doing a double cord blood transplant was his best option.

Yet, he was never able to have that transplant since he had issues with fighting infections while also continuing to try and keep the cancer under control. After three clinical trials there to get him back into remission had failed, we then took him to the NIH (National Institutes for Health) in Bethesda, Maryland and spent four months pursuing three more clinical trial options. These trials were based on promising new anti-body therapies since he was quickly becoming resistant to standard chemotherapy options.

When those eventually failed, we then spent a month at St. Jude Children's Research Hospital in Memphis, Tennessee on another antibody trial option there. This ultimately failed as well. So, after nine months of traveling and living in communal housing situations, our family returned to Phoenix and to PCH to regroup and continued to pursue other options there as well as with Texas Children's Hospital. In his final few months, however, we were not able to pursue any other treatment options as he continued to cope with mounting issues in fighting a variety of infections as well as the advancing cancer.

As he bravely battled leukemia and the problems that accompany treatment in these various settings and circumstances, our son continued to homeschool and excel in most everything he did while maintaining a positive attitude and an eternal perspective on life. Once a person met him, their life was changed forever and for the better.

The evening before he passed away, ultimately succumbing at the age of fourteen, he declared, "I am going to serve Jesus and Him alone. I am going to focus on what is right. How about you?" Into the loving arms of Jesus, we committed him on November 28th, 2012.

It is difficult to convey in the limited nature of this manual the depth of anguish that a parent experiences when their child endures a long-suffering illness such as cancer and then cannot ultimately overcome it. So, I will not attempt to do that here, particularly as our entire journey has been chronicled on his **Caring Bridge** that I invite you to read.[277]

However, I will say that three additional points jump out at me about coping with grief that I wish to share with you. First, **all the previous observations I have already expressed regarding our previous losses were also true of our experience with our oldest son.** We had the privilege of sharing our son's legacy with the untold number of supporters who visited his Caring Bridge site as at his memorial service and subsequent placement gathering. Through the creation of the Evan C. Gary Memorial Scholarship administered by the Grand Canyon University Scholarship Foundation, we **continue to honor our son's memory** while encouraging homeschooling graduates to faithfully pursue a vocational calling that reflects the nature of his interests (i.e. engineering, science, or medicine).[278] Even this mentoring program is a way to honor him. I remember once asking him when I was in the midst of first constructing this program if he was doing okay with the amount of time it was taking me to write it and get everything launched. In response he said, "I think it's cool that my mom is an author and has a website! I also want other families to have what we have. I want everyone to homeschool. I think it's great!" Thus, it is for him and our other sons that I continue to share what I have learned about the gift homeschooling with others—from the seekers to the strugglers and everyone in between.

---

[277] http://www.caringbridge.org/visit/evangary
[278] http://gcuscholarshipfoundation.org/donor-recognition/

I remember the very first thought that I had after the doctors had confirmed the worst. I remember thinking, "I have no idea what is going to happen, and I don't understand anything about this horrible disease. But I know, no matter what, I have no regrets."

We also relied heavily on the **logistical support** of loving friends and family and even those we did not know who reached out to us in a variety of ways: encouragement, meals, childcare, and financial support. Through them as well as the support of organizations like **The Ronald McDonald House Charities**, **The Children's Inn**, and **HSLDA Compassion** (formerly the Home School Foundation), we received not only practical assistance but also love in many settings and circumstances that could have easily been discouraging without them.[279]

In addition to these points, we also **regularly encourage our two youngest boys and other family members and friends to speak freely about our son** and what he meant to all of them. Our boys also enjoy looking through our family photo albums and yearbooks so that they may remember all the many facets of their relationship with their brother and not just the cancer that ultimately took his life. They also love watching old video clips and home movies of different experiences we all had with each other. We particularly focus on our oldest son on his birthday each year, engaging in activities that he enjoyed or would have enjoyed. We eat at his favorite restaurant and then bring home a memento from our day's outing that will remind us of that special day. In these and many other ways, their brother is always a part of our life even though he is no longer physically present with us.

The **second main point I would like to make is that even in difficult situations such as this, homeschooling was the one primary constant we had that kept us together and focused as a family unit.** In fact, I remember the very first thought that I had after the doctors had confirmed the worst. I remember thinking, "I have no idea what is going to happen, and I don't understand anything about this horrible disease. But I know, no matter what, I have no regrets." Just ten years after hearing Marilyn Boyer speak the message of "No Regrets" to me in that very first homeschooling conference I attended that I relayed to you back in chapter one, I found myself coming full circle

---

[279] https://www.rmhc.org/; https://childrensinn.org/; https://www.homeschoolfoundation.org/

as we sought to cope with the very same situation her family had endured. Yet we knew God had called us to be our boys' parents and we moved forward each day, knowing that we never had to give up a day with him or each other. My husband was able to work remotely and no matter where we were living as a family or what was happening with his medical needs. Every day, we were together. They never felt "behind" in their work, and we took advantage of every unique and new experience that we could embrace during our travels. As I have recounted in these subsequent articles included in the footnote, they may not have had all of the schooling experiences that I had originally planned during those times, but they certainly received an education.[280]

Finally, I will say **that Scripture became the absolute authority to all that we did.** While I recommend that grief materials and coping-though-crisis books be used for practical help, the Lord taught us that the sufficiency of Scripture must be upheld above all other pieces of advice. Even biblically-centered materials must not be allowed to replace the direct impact, authority, and reliability of God's Word in our lives. In addition, we realized that while many hold Christian ideals as true in theory, all of us were being daily pressed to apply it. We were constantly searching Scripture to strengthen our understanding of why we believe what we believe and then sought to make it all real and consistent in our daily decisions. The best resource we found to help us keep Scripture supreme when grieving for our son was *"Gone but Not Lost: Grieving the Death of a Child"* by David W. Wiersbe, which **emphasizes the importance of praying through the promises of God.**

We are forever grateful to the Lord for our son and the blessing that we had in him for those fourteen-plus years. We continue to be blessed by having loved, parented, and taught him and look forward to the day when we are once again together—this time for eternity.

Write out a prayer of thanksgiving for the child(ren) God has entrusted to you and your husband. If you have a child who is with the Lord, thank them for the time you parented them on this Earth, and praise God that you will be forever united with them one day.

_____

_____

_____

_____

_____

---

[280] https://www.homeschoolfoundation.org/index.php?id=219
https://news.gcu.edu/2016/03/art-soul-evan-garys-crafts-faith-live-on/

Purposefully Leave a Legacy

Did you ever stop to think about the fact that once you have left this Earth, all your child will have left of you are the memories they have in their heart and the "stuff" you leave behind? Like it or not, the items we leave to our children say a lot about us, so consider these principles.

First, **if you have items in your home that you would be embarrassed for your loved ones to find one day, get it out of your home now.** Spiritually assess *why* you have that movie, book, or other questionable item in your home and seek God's guidance on cleansing it out of your heart and home now rather than when your children and grandchildren come across it later. When your child goes through your things later in life, you want it to be a lesson of discovery that will continue to reinforce the values and ideas that you worked so hard all those years to teach to them rather than a time that disappoints them or leaves them to question the truth of your values. Even years later, I *still* found myself going through some of my dad's things and continued to peel back the onion of what a great man he was. *That* is what you want your child to someday experience when they eventually go through your things.

Second, **make purposeful efforts to ensure that your thoughts, feelings, and memories are immortalized for your child and their descendants**. Make a scrapbook, video yourself sharing thoughts with your family, or write letters to your child. How many of us have handwritten notes and letters from our parents? I hardly have any from my father and cherish the very few I have, and I certainly appreciate the ones that my mother has written to me over the years. When our children were small, we wrote letters to each of them on their birthdays and then put them away in our bank box for them to have later in life. I also spent time making them special baby books when they were each little and have since created annual family yearbooks, using a digital scrapbooking service called **Heritage Makers**.[281] What is so great is that you make the book one time and just order the number of copies that you need. I have also appreciated the work my mother has done to put together some information about the **history and genealogy of our family** and know that our boys will appreciate it when they are older as well. She has also created special **memory quilts** for each one of us.

In addition, I have chosen to write this mentoring manual largely out of my motivation to **share my heart with our boys and their future families** about these issues of life that every parent copes with at some point in their journey. Perhaps I will not have the privilege of being with them as long as I would like, but I know that my heart can continue to mentor and speak to them through the words I am now writing. Even if you just keep journals or make videos that log your thoughts, prayers, advice, and love to your children that they can later read or view, you would be leaving them and your future grandchildren a great gift.

---

[281] http://www.astorytoremember.com

Even if you cannot devote the time or energy to creating annual yearbooks or other involved documents, at least consider writing a **newsy Christmas letter** every year that includes thoughts about the year's happenings and includes a few pictures and a summary of what your family experienced that year. Then you could place these letters in a book later as a keepsake for them and a way for them to remember the timing of when certain significant events took place. We have done this each year for the past several years. Not only does it start to build a nice memory log for your children, but it also serves to reach and minister to friends and family that you may only contact once a year. Every year, we receive many positive comments from loved ones about how much they appreciated our letter and how nice it is to keep in touch with what the boys are up to doing.

Lastly, think about the legacy you are leaving them about what it means to be a "Smith", or a "Brown", or, in our case, a "Gary". Your **family identity is a huge part of the message you want to leave your child.** Family identity is different than your family mission statement we discussed way back in chapter one. Instead, it is a collection of descriptors of what your family is known for and how you relate to others that can easily be communicated to the outside world. **For us, a Gary is known for helping others, speaking respectfully, following through, being fair-minded, planning carefully, and solving problems.** So, when your child is behaving in a way that does not reflect your family's identity, remind them of who they are in Christ and how your family should handle that issue. For example, if we have a child who is melting down over some small, surmountable issue, I remind them who they are by saying, "Hey! We are Gary's and we solve problems, so let's figure this out together!" Or if one boy demanded something from a reluctant brother, I reminded them that Gary's are fair-minded and that there are *always* two sides to every issue. Look at it from your brother's point of view and recognize his concerns. Focus on having a right relationship rather than being "right" all the time.

Jot down some key words and thoughts that you can use to describe your family's identity.

_____

_____

_____

_____

_____

_____

_____

Discuss with your husband and your mentor other thoughts and opinions regarding the importance of building and maintaining healthy relationships, leaving a legacy, and helping to establish and to craft as well as reinforce your family's unique identity.

Balancing and Planning Meals

Here is a truth we should face. Whether we enjoy cooking or not, making sure to have meals prepared three times a day and providing snacks can be a huge burden! Plus, if you are nursing or have very young children at home, there are times when you feel like all you do is feed the people in your home. By the way, that feeling returns when they are all teenagers! Each of us has made meals on the fly with whatever we have around, frantically assembling options together sometimes with better results than others. Instead, what most families need are **easy, nutritious options that can carry them through the school week with minimal preparation time and hassle.** So, in order to ensure that "winging it" is not a daily occurrence, pre-planning is a must.

When we were first married, much to my mother's distress, I knew how to scramble eggs, make a sandwich, and do some baking, but that was about it. I had never really worked with raw meats and seasoning food was something I did not understand very well. It was not that I was unwilling to learn while growing up. My mother was just always pressed to produce perfect meals, so I had never really had the opportunity to learn the basic principles about working with food much less how to pull off an entire meal when I was younger. Suffice it to say, however, I *did* learn how to do it and my family is pleased with what comes to the table every night. Ultimately, then, I would say that I successfully learned how to plan and make meals that are both good to eat and good for the body. So, if you consider your culinary responsibilities to be an insurmountable challenge and that your family is doomed to a life of take-out, frozen dinners, and sandwiches, take heart. If I can learn how to cook with minimal effort, good results, and a reasonable amount of enjoyment, you can too!

Rotating Meal Plans

Even if cooking for your family is no trouble at all, you will find a time in your homeschooling season where taking that extra hour or so to prepare and cook a meal at night will just seem like it is too much. You will either still be helping a child with a school assignment or project or you may be so busy grading and doing other household duties that stopping to prepare dinner will completely derail you. Although we will discuss lunch and breakfast planning as well, it is the dinner meal that tends to be the most challenging to plan and deliver. So, consider incorporating the following ideas, all of which are based on the principle of planning in advance.

Breakfast: Limit choices to fruit, non-fat dairy and high-fiber options.
Lunch: Quick-fix meal rotating same five balanced meal choices a week.
Dinner: Use balanced, three-month rotating meal plan. Quick-fix meals as needed.

First, create a list of your family's favorite meals that you make. Ideally, you will want to **select 24 dinners so that you can develop a rotating meal plan that will cover a three-month period.** Even half of that number is a good start! Have your family participate by voting on their favorites if you have having difficulty narrowing down your list. On the other hand, if you do not have that many meal options, you could just do a two-month planner to start with, but three months is better since it keeps the variety rotating for longer cycles. You can also contact a few of your homeschooling friends and talk with your mentor about favorite recipes their families enjoy and that they would be willing to share with you. Be sure to also research plenty of **slow cooker options** since having your meal already prepared and cooking during the day is an awesome feeling of accomplishment when you do not need to take time later in the day to do it.

    Post a printed list of your rotating meal schedule, like the form I have shared with you on page 362, so that everything you need is in one place and you do not have to constantly keep searching for basic information about the recipes you are going to make. I keep mine to a one-page reference list that can be taped on the inside of one of my kitchen cabinets as a quick and easy reference. When preparing the list, I like to note the main protein that is being used for each dish so that I can make sure to rotate food types for variety and so that I can plan ahead and make sure I have everything I need for that month's meals when figuring out meat purchases. List the main dish and the sides you intend to make along with any recipe locations so that you can grab it at a moment's notice to refresh your mind on the steps or ingredients required to make the dish. In the final column, I have a place where I list non-standard ingredients that I will need to include in my shopping list. I do not bother with listing staples like salt, flour, milk, and so forth that I always have on hand.

    When planning your list, follow three important principles. First, **make sure that your meal selections are balanced**. Look to include one protein, one starch, one vegetable, and one fruit. If possible, add a small salad or fruit option onto most all your meals, which tend to provide high-water content bulk foods that are filling. This encourages dinner portions of reasonable sizes, and your family will rarely want or need "seconds" of the higher calorie, etc. foods. Be careful, however, to avoid full-fat dressings and add-on products with processed ingredients to your salad as it defeats the point!

    Second, **be careful about the drinks that you select for your family.** Avoid sodas and sugary or artificially sweetened drinks as a rule. Over thirty years ago, I virtually eliminated caffeine since it was causing a variety of health problems for me, though my husband still likes to have an occasional soda or cup of caffeinated coffee or tea. However, he has even cut way back, which has improved his sleeping habits and overall wellbeing too. Our sons mostly have low-fat milk with their lunch and dinner meals, having water once they drink the milk that they are given. Another great option for your family is naturally flavored seltzer water that contains no aspartame, which is good since aspartame can lead to a host of health problems.

Lastly, to build your three-month rotating meal plan, **become a label reader and try to purchase food and ingredients that use natural products**. For example, not all yogurts are the same. By looking at the packaging, you can quickly tell which ones contain just non-fat cultured milk and pectin versus ones that are full of additional and unnecessary ingredients and sweeteners. In general, the more you stick to shopping the outer perimeter of your store in the produce, dairy, and meat sections and the less pre-made, processed food you buy, the better off you will be. I am not saying we never buy processed food. What I am saying, however, is that we do not make a habit out of doing so. You will also find that your food bill lowers as you begin preparing more foods yourself.

I also have a similar list and process for what I call "quick fix meals" that take very little planning to prepare. Again, you can include the same information you have noted for your three-month rotation list except this collection of meals can be thrown together quickly with ingredients that you have readily available. These can be used for dinner, but you can even include your lunch plans on this list as well. In their younger years, our boys rotated through five different lunch meals every week. It made it easy because they knew what to expect based on what day it was and they would even help prep the lunches when I was busy helping one of their brothers. This was possible since we always had the right ingredients on hand. For an example of the difference between a "Quick Fix" and a regular meal, look at the following chart.

Rotating Meal Planner	Quick Fix Counterpart Option
Slow Cooked Lasagna, salad, pears, green beans, and whole wheat rolls.	Spaghetti, salad, pears, and leftover vegetable of choice
Mile-High Chicken Pot Pie, salad, applesauce, and peas.	Speedy Chicken Enchiladas, salad, grapes or fresh melon, and organic corn chips and salsa
Pork Chops with Orange Rice, salad and broccoli.	Grilled pork tenderloin, salad, pears, mixed vegetables, and quick cooking brown rice
Meatloaf, salad, fresh fruit, green beans, and a side of cottage cheese.	Hamburger Hot Rice, salad, pears, leftover vegetable of choice
Chicken Parmesan, salad, side of whole wheat pasta, and soybeans.	Chicken Rice Vegetable Soup, salad, grapes, and whole wheat rolls.
Slow Cooked Smoky Beef and Beans Chili, salad, pears, green beans, and whole wheat rolls.	Grilled Hamburgers, fresh fruit, carrot sticks, and low-fat chips or crackers.

Notice on the page 362 that you basically need to identify twenty-four full meals that you and your family regularly enjoy, creating your own three-month rotating meal plan. In our family, we typically make **new**

meals on Monday and Tuesday and then have Monday's leftovers on Wednesday and Tuesday's leftovers on Thursday. Friday we make pizza for our movie night, and we keep it simple on the weekends: chicken and rice, stir fry, chicken salad, paninis, or turkey sandwiches. Sunday morning, my husband likes to make a special breakfast and that evening is usually soy nut butter sandwiches, fruit, and popcorn. So that is it, and I only really need to cook two or three times a week! Of course, there will be variations and times that you will go out to eat, so you can plan your rotation any way you like. But following a consistent plan like this is a solid, minimum starting point that will give you the peace of mind that you are providing good, home-cooked meals for your family for the week without exhausting yourself.

I have not used these services, but if you find yourself in need of additional meal planning support, consider something like **e-Meals** or **Plan to Eat**.[282] We have, however, recently added **Yummly** as our planning tool of choice.[283] I can easily use it with our teens who help cook family dinners, and it gives us an endless supply of new meal ideas based on our preferences.

Take a moment to jot down some of your family's favorite recipes that you can put on your three-month rotating list and collect into a book or recipe box for your children. Ask your mentor and others in your group if they wish to do a recipe exchange!

_____

_____

_____

_____

_____

_____

_____

_____

_____

_____

_____

_____

---

[282] https://emeals.com/; https://www.plantoeat.com/
[283] https://www.yummly.com/

Rotating Meal Planner - 3 Months

Meal Number	Protein Base (Pork, Chicken, Beef, Beans, Fish)	Main Dish	Side Dish	Recipe Location(s)	Beyond Basics Shopping List Needs
1					
2					
3					
4					
5					
6					
7					
8					
9					
10					
11					
12					
13					
14					
15					
16					
17					
18					
19					
20					
21					
22					
23					
24					

Quick Fix Meal Options

Meal Number	Protein Base (Pork, Chicken, Beef, Beans, Fish)	Main Dish	Side Dish	Recipe Location(s)	Beyond Basics Shopping List Needs
1					
2					
3					
4					
5					
6					
7					
8					
9					
10					
11					
12					
13					
14					
15					
16					

Notes:

_____

_____

_____

_____

As you narrow down your rotating meal list over the years, **consider consolidating all your family's favorites into a family cookbook that you can pass down to your children.** My oldest son gave me the idea when he exclaimed one day, "Mom, do you have all of your recipes written down somewhere? I sure hope you do. I want to make them all when I grow up!" That little motivation was all I needed! I started taking photographs of the standard favorite meals that we eat from our rotating list, and I have been compiling them ever since. My plan is to utilize my digital scrapbook program through **Heritage Makers** and compile a cookbook that each son can have someday when they are out on their own.[284] Food is intimately connected with family memories and experiences. So, putting together something like this or even a recipe box of handwritten cards is yet another way to leave a legacy for your family, as we discussed earlier in this chapter.

Planned Purchasing

Now that you have your three-month rotating meal and quick meal lists figured out, it is time to go shopping! Since you already have your information put together, you can **just make a copy of your meal lists and simply highlight what items you are lacking.**

I also **create special shopping lists** that contain the food that I normally shop for at that store. I have one for the club warehouse we use, one for a regular grocery store, and one for a specialty health store. That way, I pre-fill all the information regarding the items we normally purchase and then print a copy of each to keep in my calendar. Then I just highlight the things that we need as we use them throughout the month. I also went so far as to try to organize it similarly to the way that the store is laid out so that if I need to give the list to my husband, he can easily find everything I have noted on the list. I have provided blank lists for you to reference on the following pages and in Appendix B. Notice how they are structured differently to reflect each store's layout. Keep this in mind when creating your own lists.

If you are interested in using an app instead of a paper system, my favorite choice is **Grocery IQ**.[285] You can maintain many different lists and even digitally scan a product when you are finished with it and want to replenish it in your pantry. It allows you to mark off your items as you shop and also keeps a history of your frequently purchased items so that you can easily build a new list for the future.

When you create your lists, be sure to **include several healthy "fantastic foods"** that you want to have on hand throughout the week for snacks or supplements to your meals. What do you have on YOUR "fantastic foods" list?

---

[284] http://www.astorytoremember.com
[285] http://www.groceryiq.com/

The Balanced Homeschooler

"Fantastic Food"	Benefit
Apples	Encourage your child to eat it with the skin on for the full nutritional value of the fiber.
Applesauce (unsweetened)	Just add some honey and cinnamon and you have a simple way to get your children to have another serving of fruit. It is also an excellent substitute for vegetable oil when you are baking cakes, cookies, waffles, or pancakes.
Avocadoes	Although they are high in fat, it is the "good" fat that we need to protect our hearts. In moderation this is a great food to serve mashed on sandwiches and wraps. It is high in potassium, vitamin A, and other essential vitamins.
Bananas	Excellent source of potassium and great in smoothies, cereal, or for a snack.
Beans (lentils, black, chickpeas, etc.)	Another good source of fiber that can add bulk to many stews or soups. Consider purchasing canned organic, vegetarian chili to have on hand when you want to quickly add substance to another recipe.
Blueberries	Fresh blueberries can be expensive so buy them in season and then freeze them. They are packed with antioxidants and are great in cereal, oatmeal or yogurt. Avoid the dried ones that are full of sugar.
Dark Chocolate	Use in moderation, but this food has the potential to lower blood pressure and is a useful antioxidant.
Green Tea	Full of antioxidants and very little caffeine, try to have two to three cups per day, even in the summer!
Honey	Okay; so honey does not have a lot of nutritional value. However, when you consider what a great job it does substituting for sugar in cooking and in your tea, it is definitely a "fantastic food"! Great for sore throats too!
Hummus	This is a terrific snack product; spreading on crackers or as an alternative to high-fat vegetable dips. The primary ingredient in it is mashed chick peas (also known as garbanzo beans). Check your local health food store for alternative flavors like garlic or red-roasted pepper.
Lemons	Try to have fresh lemon or plain lemon juice on hand to add to your water. Adding it to the water you drink has more of a cleansing impact than water alone gives you.
Pomegranate Juice	This is another excellent antioxidant source. However, be careful only to purchase a brand that is 100% pomegranate juice and not one with a lot of other additives. Also, it is high in calorie so just have one small serving a day if you are watching your weight.
Soy Nut Butter	An alternative to peanut butter, this is also an excellent source of protein but usually contains one more gram of fiber per serving than peanut butter. The Wonderbutter brand is processed in a dedicated, peanut-free facility. Serve it on whole wheat toast or with a banana for a great snack.
Walnuts	Nuts in general are good for you but walnuts in particular have very high levels of Omega-3 fatty acids in them that are good for your heart.
Whole Grain Wheat Breads, Pasta, and Tortillas	Great source of fiber and a healthy way to get your good carbs in. Make sure that the first ingredient listed is "whole wheat flour" and that it is not "enriched" in anyway, which is a bleaching process that removes a great deal of the nutritional value of the grain.
Yogurt	As mentioned previously, yogurts vary on their nutritional quality so be sure to purchase one that is just plain non-fat yogurt and then add fruit and honey for flavor. Have it at least once a day to regulate digestion. A great source of calcium too!
Yogurt (Greek)	Another yogurt product is Greek yogurt, which tends to be smoother and creamier than its regular counterpart. It is higher in protein and lower in carbohydrates and sodium than regular yogurt. However, it is not as high in calcium as regular yogurt.

Shopping List – Grocery Store

Produce:

Deli:

Meats:

Breads:

Breakfast Foods:

Coffee/Tea:

Baking:

Mexican Foods:

Canned Fruits:

Canned Veggies:

Pasta:

Boxed Foods:

Soups:

Cleaners:

Paper Products:

Condiments:

Drinks:

Snacks:

Dairy:

Frozen Foods:

Hygiene Items:

Medicine:

Misc. (Cards, etc.)

Shopping List – Health Food Store

Hygiene Items:

Medicine:

Coffee/Tea:

Condiments:

Canned Fruits:

Pasta:

Canned Veggies:

Soups:

Spices:

Baking:

Boxed Foods:

Crackers/Cookies:

Drinks:

Cleaners:

Frozen Foods:

Paper Products:

Dairy:

Produce:

Meats:

Deli:

Breads:

Bulk:

Misc. (Cards, etc.)

Shopping List – Warehouse Store

Breads:

Chips:

Deli:

Produce

Paper Products:

Frozen Foods:

Refridgerated Foods:

Drinks:

Baking/Spices:

Other Foods:

Canned Foods:

Snacks & Dried Fruit:

Breakfast Foods:

Food Wraps:

House Cleaners:

Clothes Cleaners:

Children's Items:

Hygiene Items:

Medicine:

Vitamins:

Misc.

To Buy in Bulk or Not to Buy in Bulk; that is the Question!

Purchasing in bulk can be a double-edged sword. On the one hand, per ounce or pound pricing of buying in bulk cannot be beat. But on the other hand, do you really need the quantities that they provide for that item? So, ask yourself this question, "**Is this a common enough staple item that I will use no matter how long I have it, or does the item have a limited shelf life and some of it might go bad?**" Be realistic about what you will use so that you do not waste resources on items that you will never get around to consuming before it goes stale or bad. Also, be careful about buying products in bulk that are unknown to you. If there is a good chance that the product will not work for you, do not buy it.

The second question to ask yourself is, "**Do I have adequate storage to purchase in bulk?**" If purchasing in bulk makes sense, look for opportunities to add shelving in your garage for extra paper products or in your laundry area for extra dried or canned foods. Also, if you have space, consider investing in an extra refrigerator or full freezer. If you do not have space inside your home for one, there are units that can tolerate the heat, even in Arizona, if you place it in your garage. This way, you can pre-cook and freeze meals, and you can purchase quality, all-natural meats when they are on sale, packaging them yourself and freezing them in usable units. We have both an extra full-size refrigerator and freezer, and I would not want to manage without them!

Such planning also helps to **minimize store trips** by making one warehouse trip a month, one major trip to regular grocery store a month, and then one trip to a specialty health food store. For the meats, I watch the specials and when, for example, ground beef is on sale and I am getting low on my supply, we go and purchase twenty pounds and then we use a food packaging machine to seal and freeze the meat in one-pound packages for later use.[286] We do the same with chicken and pork purchases. Following this process, we only need to go to any given store two, maybe three times a month with my husband helping to fill in occasionally on small needs on the way home from work. Also, consider joining a well-run food co-op, like **Bountiful Baskets**, to improve the quality of your produce while buying larger quantities but lowering your overall food bill at the same time.[287]

There are **many resources** out there about saving money in the home with frugal and healthy cooking, so here are just a few useful books to further aid your exploration on these concepts.

1. *Deceptively Delicious* by Jessica Seinfeld; This cookbook contains another good reason to purchase an extra freezer. The author shows you how to prepare vegetable purées that allow you to add extra nutrition to dishes. For example, puréed

---

[286] We have used the FoodSaver vacuum sealing system that is available to purchase in most major stores. See http://www.foodsaver.com/ for more information.

[287] http://www.bountifulbaskets.org/

cauliflower can easily be added to mashed potatoes with no change in taste or texture to the dish. Similarly, chickpeas added to homemade chocolate chip cookies add texture and fiber without interfering with your child's enjoyment.

2. *Frugal Mom's Guide to Once-a-Month Cooking* by Candace Anderson; This is a good starting place to explore the option of cooking the bulk of your meals monthly and then pulling them out of the freezer as you need them.[288]

3. *Healthy Meals for Less* or *Miserly Moms* by Jonni McCoy; Miserly Moms covers many additional household money saving ideas beyond the choices you make for your kitchen pantry. Both are filled with great information and ideas for every mom and homemaker.[289]

The Thirty-Pound Experiment

I will close this section about nutrition and meal planning by sharing my experience with you from 2015. That spring, one of our sons was doing *Apologia's General Science* course. The last half of the book deals a lot with the human body and one day we were talking about how the body first uses carbs before it looks to burn fat. When the fat is not there, then the body has no choice but to burn proteins.

Reflecting later about our discussion, I decided that I was going to become living proof of these facts by losing weight myself. Pounds that I had gained during our years spent in and out of hospitals in support of our oldest son during his illness had remained even though we were living more actively again. Couple that with metabolism changes and the continued aging process, those middle-aged pounds were not going to leave unless I intentionally changed my habits.

Sure enough, just by adjusting the balance of my diet to exclude unnecessary simple carbs, replacing them with low cholesterol proteins, high-quality plant products, and reduced sugars, the weight consistently came off and has stayed off. **With absolutely no changes to my physical activity, I safely and healthfully lost over thirty pounds within about four months.** I have also since learned from various sources that weight loss is dependent on about 80% of what we do nutritionally and only about 20% of what we do physically. I am certainly not saying that exercise is not important, and we will address that in an upcoming section. However, when it comes to sustainable weight loss, it is what you eat (or do not eat!) that will make the huge difference. There is that 80/20 rule at work again that we talked about in chapter six![290]

---

[288] http://www.frugalmom.net/

[289] http://miserlymoms.com/

[290] To count those calories, check out a tool like this: https://www.verywellfit.com/calorie-counts-and-nutrition-facts-4157035

What other ideas do you or your mentor for preparing meals, planning in advance, and purchasing in bulk? What great recipes can you share with each other this week that both your families can enjoy? What input does your family have on these topics?

_____

_____

_____

_____

_____

_____

_____

_____

_____

_____

_____

What personal goals do you have for your own health, and what research steps do you need to take to make a plan?

_____

_____

_____

_____

_____

_____

_____

_____

_____

_____

_____

Dealing with Allergies

As a mother of a son who had a severe allergy to peanuts, I know the concerns that you have if your child has a food allergy. **If you even suspect that your child may be allergic to a specific type of food, talk to your child's pediatrician and determine if testing is right for your child.** Severe allergies to foods like peanuts can be life threatening as anaphylactic shock leading to respiratory distress may occur, so you want to be prepared with the proper medications and **EpiPen Jr.** or regular **EpiPen** if necessary.[291] Even if you do not have an allergic child, please read this section so that you can be educated and sensitive to interacting with your friend's child who may have some sort of food allergy.

First, **be extremely vigilant about making sure your child's environment is safe when they are young.** Until they get to be *at least* eight years old, you really need to take control of managing their allergy for them. **Communicate with all the child's caregivers**, including grandparents, church nursery workers, and other teachers about your child's allergy, making sure they understand the severity of it. Ensure that the medication stays with your child, that caregivers can reach you by cell phone in case of an emergency, and that they can and are willing to administer the medicine, including the **EpiPen Jr.** or **EpiPen,** if necessary.

As our son was diagnosed when he was only two, I played an important role in making sure that the **nursery policies** at our church were changed to prevent parents from allowing **outside food** to be brought in for their child. Even skin contact with peanut butter inadvertently smeared on a table or still on another child's hand could have triggered a reaction for him. Check the snacks provided each week, and also be aware of crafts that they may do that involve food products. Read all labels and if you cannot verify the safety of what is being offered, have an additional red dot or alert sticker that can be placed on their name tag to show that they cannot have that snack. Most churches are much better about food policies like this these days, but you still need to make sure you understand what they are and how they will help your child in case of an emergency. Even many emergency service vehicles still do not consistently carry epinephrine with them, so make sure your child's medicine is always with them. Include an antihistamine like **Benadryl** with them so that they can take that as well in case of an accidental exposure.

When they get older and they go to a friend's home, church, family camp, or a VBS program, give them a small waist pack to carry their items with them. **They should be 100% responsible for managing their allergy by the time they are twelve**, remembering to take their pack with them always and what questions to ask about food items when they are out in public. Here are some other considerations to be aware of at this age as well as when they are younger.

---

[291] http://www.epipen.com/

1. **Make sure to set your child up with a Medic Alert bracelet.**[292] You want to make sure your child's medical provider, medication dosages, and allergy information is available at a moment's notice to anyone who is providing care to your child. Medic Alert also keeps track of all your child's contact information so that you will be notified right away in case there is a problem. Having the bracelet on also helps emergency personnel to know what the issue is immediately. Our son was also allergic to penicillin, so that was also noted on his bracelet.

2. When eating out, **check with the restaurant about the oils used to fry certain foods or other general cooking purposes.** For example, if they use peanut oil to prepare their French fries or cook certain Asian dishes, you will want to avoid those items for a peanut allergy. Even having your child's food cooked in a pan that was not properly cleaned out from the use of peanut oil used in a previous dish can cause a problem. Soy, milk, and eggs can be used in many kinds of recipes that you may not suspect, so make sure you know what your child is eating. If the restaurant staff cannot adequately answer the questions, you probably should choose a different place to eat.

3. **If you have a dog, be mindful of the treats that you give them.** For example, if the treat biscuits they have contain a food allergen for your child and the dog then licks your child, they will most likely have a reaction. We had this happen when we were visiting our family one time. Their dog had eaten treats that continued peanut butter, so when the dog licked his face, he immediately broke out and required Benadryl.

4. **Also pay attention to additives in hair and skin care products.** Again, for the same reason you want to check the ingredients on the pet treats, check ingredients for other products your child will use on their hair and skin. Often if your child cannot tolerate regular products, you will find a good organic alternative at **Sprouts, Whole Foods,** or some other source for health products. Our youngest son has always had tendencies for dry skin. When he was very young, it was more severe and even his scalp would peel and flake when using regular shampoo products. Taking him to a neem-based product was what it took to address the issue properly, but the only way we knew what to do was by talking at length with an expert in the natural products section at Sprouts, who then connected us with the right products.

---

[292] http://www.medicalert.org/

5. **Read <u>all</u> food labels, including vitamins and bakery items, for cross contamination warnings.** Probably your child's most likely area for unwanted exposure is in a cross-contaminated item. You would be surprised to learn how many processed foods and even children's vitamins are "also manufactured in a plant that processes peanuts", or whatever other allergen is of concern to you. So, no matter what the food allergy is that your child has, **be a label checker and make sure that your child understands how to read them**. Bakery items are also famous for being an issue. Even something that you think is totally safe is usually prone to cross-contamination. For example, one time we were to bring cupcakes to a homeschool support group event. Pressed for time, I picked up a dozen bakery cupcakes (white with white frosting) on the way. Sure enough, when I checked the package later, there was the warning, plainly written. This was the day I learned to **always check labels** and make sure to **have a snack with you that they can have** in case this type of thing comes up in a public setting. **Be careful about participating in potlucks.** Unless you know without a doubt where the food came from and that it is safe for your child, do not allow them to have it. Since desserts tended to be the big issue for us, I usually

Note to Leaders and Mentors:
*Potlucks and similar gatherings can be very unnerving for a family who has a severely allergic child. However, make sure that you are clear with your families that food allergies are ultimately the **parent's** responsibility to manage.*

Support groups can take reasonable precautions, such as suggesting that parents have product packaging available for review by other parents for the food they bring. However, the group but should not have to "jump through hoops" to accommodate a child who has a food allergy. Even if that parent brings their child's lunch to the park, you can bet that there will be other foods floating around that could be potentially hazardous to them. However, this is no different than the parent needing to manage the child's allergy in other public places.

*If the parent needs additional information and support in helping to manage their child's allergy in public settings, do not feel like you need to be an expert. Instead, refer them to **The Food Allergy Network**.*

volunteered to bring one so that he could be sure to have at least one treat he could eat!

6. Be aware that even if you do everything you should do, there may be an item you purchase that has an **undeclared product** in it that may trigger an issue for your child. So, stay registered and connected with food advocacy groups, like the **Food Allergy Network**, who will equip you with excellent newsletters, recipes, and books to help you manage your child's allergy while staying up on the latest medical news.[293] They will also notify you of any product recalls due to undeclared allergen products.

7. **Have your child retested at various times throughout their life to see if their severity changes**. If you find that their allergy lessens, speak to their allergist about how that translates to their child's food options. For example, when our son was younger, the allergist advised us to avoid all nuts, even though he tested negative for tree nut allergies. This is because there is a 30% crossover of proteins in all nuts and he could have still developed an allergy to those nuts too if he had too early of an exposure to them. When he was older, he was able to introduce tree nuts into his diet. However, we still needed to make sure that the ones he ate came "straight from the farm" because of cross-contamination issues that exist in pre-packaged options.

What other concerns or questions do you have about dealing with allergies or planning meals for your family?

_____

_____

_____

_____

_____

_____

_____

_____

_____

_____

[293] http://www.foodallergy.org/

Physical Concerns

At one point or another, every parent wrestles with their concerns for their child's physical health. Very few of us get the kind of physical activity we need every day without making extra effort, particularly since we are in the home more than most and live in an age that is tied to the sedentary enjoyment of media. However, since we are at home so often, creating a safe and healthy environment as well as making sure that the whole family gets enough exercise needs to be a top priority.

Exercise for Life

The first and most obvious area of concern is physical exercise. Ensuring that there is enough quantity and variety of activities available to your child can be a tall order to fill, especially if your child is not naturally inclined to participate in sports and outdoor activities. The key is to be flexible throughout their life on the programs that they are involved in without allowing any one activity to dominate the family's schedule.

Model positive habits so that your child will know the importance of living an active life.

However, before you think about this issue for your child, consider your and your husband's activity level first. **If you do not model an active lifestyle, then it will be difficult for you to emphasize the importance of it to your child.** Even though I am personally lukewarm on structured exercise, I must consciously decide each week that physical activity will be a part of our regular routine in some way! Just like studying your Bible, habits like this are "caught" more than "taught". So, if your child does not see you making physical activities a priority, any instruction you give them to do so will fall flat.

1. When your child is young, **provide them exposure to different activity options through your local community center.** This is an inexpensive but comprehensive way to allow your child to try different physical activities without investing too much money in any one choice while they are still "exploring" their options. If you have more than one child, look for programs that they can both participate in or try to have them in separate classes during the same time to make the most efficient use of your schedule. **City sports leagues and local teams** are also a great option for those families who have children who are very interested in pursuing a specific sport. However, do be aware that the commitment required to these organizations can easily take over your daily home life during the season for that sport. So, be careful to protect your family's time from being negatively impacted by any single outside activity.

2. Have some sort of equipment and/or **area in the home that is designated for deliberate exercise**. Most of us cannot dedicate an entire room to exercise. However, we typically can find a space where an exercise mat can be rolled out and used, either as we facilitate them through a routine or if you have a children's workout video that you like. Use the **Presidential Fitness Standards** as a guideline for what your child should strive to do and keep tabs on their progress by making a tracking chart for each child.[294] Help them build endurance with a treadmill or a recumbent bike that Dad and Mom can also use, making it a family event. Just taking a fifteen or twenty-minute brisk walk can serve this purpose as well. A good rule of thumb is to shoot for twenty minutes of aerobic activity followed by at least ten or fifteen minutes of strength building exercises. If you have your child do this at least three or four days a week, you will be helping them build good exercise habits for life. You will also find that they can concentrate better during school hours and will sleep more soundly. If you wish to assign high school credit for health or physical education, be sure to have your teen log their exercise hours in a journal.

3. **Get out and about as a family.** Physical activity does not always mean aerobic activity. Sometimes it just means getting out into a nature environment so that you can bike, hike, fish, or just enjoy the views together as a family. Also have dad plan one-on-one times with each child in this type of environment for the relationship growth benefits as well.

4. **Attend or volunteer your time as a family at a local camp**. Attending a Christian family camp in your area can be a great opportunity to build relationships as well as challenge each family member physically over the course of the various activities available. Many life lessons can be absorbed during these occasions that also contribute to the emotional stability and well-being of each member of the family. In addition, if you can volunteer your time during an off-season weekend to help out around the facility. Your contributions will surely be appreciated while still having the opportunity to enjoy many aspects of camp life together.

5. **Consider investing in a Wii U system** or other technology that requires physical exertion. Even though my husband has worked in the information technology field for most of his working life, we are conservative about bringing new technology into our home. However, if you look at the **Wii Fit and sports**

---

[294] https://www.pyfp.org/

line of products, you and your family can engage in physical activity and relationship building fun at the same time.[295] Be careful, however, about investing in the other game products for your **Wii U** system, which are more sedentary by nature and can expose your child to inappropriate content. As with your family's home computer system, always screen every piece of technology that comes into your home.

6. If your child is getting regular activity, it will help them to sleep more soundly and wake up feeling more rested. **So, as important as exercise is promoting overall wellbeing for your child, making sure they get enough sleep is also important**. When children do not get a proper night's sleep, you will both pay for it the next day. They will have difficulty concentrating or completing work, and they will have an overall moody attitude. So, avoid having regular late-night commitments on school nights or allowing them to stay up past a reasonable hour. Most young children (and teens!) function better when they have had at least nine hours of sleep. Our sons are early risers, usually getting up between 5:00 and 6:30. So, on school nights, they need to have everything done and ready for nighttime reading by 8:30 p.m. so they can be sleeping by 9:00 p.m. or so.

What other concerns or questions do you have about increasing your family's activity level? What schedule changes do you need to make to ensure that your child gets a good night's sleep. Ask your mentor for input and new ideas.

_____

_____

_____

_____

_____

_____

_____

_____

_____

_____

_____

---

[295] http://wiifit.com/

Communicate Your Medical History

Another important subject to consider is how and when to communicate your medical history to your child. Often, we develop medical issues later on in life, like diabetes or heart problems, that may be passed on to your child to some extent. Be sure, then, to **keep the appropriate medical records and details so that you can provide it to them later in life**. Placing certain records in a bank box, for instance, is a good plan so you can be sure the information eventually gets to them even if they are too young to hear it now.

In our family, my husband and I had quite a medical journey to cope with as we researched and treated our miscarriage issues that were related to the field of reproductive immunology. My husband and I worked very closely for nearly four years with the founding physician of the **Alan E. Beer Center for Reproductive Immunology and Genetics** as we successfully managed our lives, travel schedules, and medical requirements through two additional pregnancies that followed the loss of our infant son in 1999.[296] Consequently, I have documented thoroughly the information and issues related to our experience so that, when the appropriate time comes, our sons will be informed regarding what we dealt with in the journey that God led us on to grow our family.

As mentioned previously, I also documented our oldest son's journey with cancer on his **CaringBridge** site that is still available today to inform and encourage our own sons as well as other families who continue to cope with leukemia and are interested in the technical and medical issues we encountered.[297]

What medical conditions or concerns do you have that you want to communicate to your child one day? What about your husband? Depending on the issue, you may even want to include medical information related to both sets of your child's grandparents.

_____

_____

_____

_____

_____

_____

_____

_____

[296] http://www.repro-med.net/
[297] http://www.caringbridge.org/visit/evangary

Personal Safety

In this age of living in an increasingly hostile society, teaching your family about personal safety and self-defense is essential. It is also important to practice good safety procedures in the home so that your family knows how to respond in event of an emergency.

> *Do not assume that your child will intuitively understand issues related to personal safety. Instead, prepare them!*

1. **Consider having your child participate with you in a self-defense course.** There are plenty of good martial arts or self-defense class options around through your community center and other venues that can benefit your entire family's health as well as safety. Sometimes Christian parents are concerned about the spiritual issues associated with a martial arts class, but there are several out there that do not promote any particular spiritual set of beliefs, merely emphasizing the importance of developing focus, confidence, and safety skills. **Role play situations** your child may find themselves in and then coach them through what to do if such a problem occurs. This is **particularly important for families who frequent public park areas** since this is a common location where child predators will seek out their next victim.

2. Have a **home monitoring security system** installed or at least security signage in the front yard. Most burglaries occur as a last-minute decision. So, given a choice between one home that has signage and another home that does not, a potential thief will go for the one that does not have signage. If you have it monitored, be sure to list a trusted neighbor on your contact list who has a copy of your key and a code to enter the home in case you are gone in case the alarm goes off. In addition, keep in mind that having a system in place typically lowers your home insurance premium. Getting involved with your local **Block Watch** or your neighborhood association group is also a good way to prevent crime.[298] In one of our previous homes that was up for sale, burglars entered the home and stole our expensive kitchen appliances! Where were the neighbors when they backed up their truck into our garage and helped themselves to our property? Awareness is half the battle!

---

[298] Just research "Block Watch" on your computer to find the chapter that pertains to your community.

3. Another investment that can potentially lower your home insurance premium is having **working fire extinguishers** and **working fire alarms** in key areas throughout your home. The kitchen and master bedroom are two essential spots to have extinguishers, and every room in the house should have a working smoke alarm. Also, be sure to **develop an overall escape plan** for your family in case of a fire or other emergency. **Practice evacuating your home by doing periodic fire drills.** Finally, always have a central location meetup location in case you are separated from each other.

4. Attend an **emergency preparedness class** with your child to learn the basics of CPR and first aid through an organization like the **Red Cross**.[299] You can visit their website to locate a class in your area. This type of training is especially important if your child is going to have responsibility for a younger sibling or is going to offer babysitting services to other families in the neighborhood. Even young children can also be trained on how and **when to call 911**or even **Poison Control** for an emergency.[300]

5. Regardless of whether you own a pool or not, **make sure that your child is comfortable swimming and being around water.** For most of their young lives, we did not own a pool. So, we went to an indoor swim school when our oldest son was learning to swim, and I had a baby to watch. I liked having them in an indoor environment out of the Arizona sun, but I can tell you that they did not really learn how to swim. Going once a week just does not cut it, no matter how good the instructor is. So, when all three were old enough and needed to *really* understand how to swim, I signed them up through the city's Red Cross swim lesson program. After the first week (i.e. four lessons a week), they all knew how to swim, and it cost a tenth of what the indoor swim school charged. So, it really is just a matter of doing the lessons several days in a row that makes the techniques stick while also building the child's confidence.

6. One other area of safety you may want to consider is involving your teen in a **hunter's safety course** provided by your state's local game and fish department. Even if your child (minimum age of 10) is not going to hunt, consider having Dad take them through this experience so they can learn about gun safety and discuss related life issues that center around the concept of

---

[299] http://www.redcross.org
[300] http://www.911forkids.com; http://www.poison.org/

hunting and conservation. In Arizona, see the **Arizona Game in Fish Department** for this and other useful courses on topics like fishing and boating.[301]

What other concerns or questions do you have about personal safety? Ask your mentor for input and ideas. Talk to your husband about establishing certain safety measures in your home.

_____

_____

_____

_____

_____

_____

_____

_____

_____

_____

_____

_____

_____

_____

_____

_____

_____

_____

_____

_____

_____

_____

[301] http://www.azgfd.gov/i_e/education_programs.shtml

Create a Safe and Healthy Home

The last areas of physical safety to consider are the potential hazards that may exist inside your home as well as opportunities to improve the purity of your home. Sometimes these priorities are obvious while other times we just need a regular reminder to make sure we take care of them.

1. **Minimize dust and change out your home's air filters every month**. You may be surprised to learn how much dust build-up can occur within just a few short weeks in your air vent so keep a supply of filters on hand that you can change out regularly. If your child is particularly sensitive to dust particles, consider purchasing a personal filtration system for their room and clean that filter out regularly as well. Have a consistent schedule to take care of dust on high shelves, window treatments, and under the beds, which tend to be neglected collectors of unwanted dust. Cleaning ceiling fans regularly and running stuffed toys through the dryer helps too!

2. **Clean your carpets once or twice a year with a rented cleaning machine**. If you have ever had your carpets professionally cleaned, you know how incredibly expensive it can be. So, during the spring and fall seasons, just work with your husband to do it yourself over a weekend when it is pleasant. That way, you can open the windows to air the house out as it dries. Keep n non-toxic spot cleaner on hand throughout the year for those inevitable spills that occur.

3. **Replace your standard cleaning products with "green" alternatives**. Although they may cost a bit more in some cases, using non-toxic cleaning products are safer for your child and any pets you have in the home. In addition, you can feel good about your child helping you with the chores when you know that they are using a safe window or surface cleaner rather than products that contain bleach or other harsh chemicals. There are many good products on the market, so try different ones until you find a brand that you like.

4. **Seal door and window openings** to reduce the possibility of bugs entering your home and to make your air conditioning system work more efficiently. Spray regularly with a concentrated substance you add to water and spray on for better coverage, reducing pest problems for children and pets when they play outside.

5. **Install a reverse osmosis system** for your drinking water and change its filter regularly rather than engaging with a water service. Install your own system, ensuring that you have good tasting water in your home. Be aware, however, that fluoride is one of the elements that is taken out

Take the extra time yourself to do the work necessary to make your home as safe as possible.

when water is filtered so you may want to have your child use an **anti-cavity, fluoride rinse** at night just before bedtime.

6. **Regularly maintain your vehicles and have emergency supplies.** This may seem like an obvious point, but I have known people to drive their vehicles and never change the oil until their engine dies. It is also easy to forget to have your tires regularly rotated and checked, leading to an unwanted blowout on the freeway when it is 115 degrees in the shade and you do not know how to change out to the spare or do not have a service to come and do it for you. Even more than keeping a regular maintenance schedule, you will want to be prepared to handle emergencies. **Along with tire change tools and jumper cables, keep flares and extra water with you at all times.** Also, keeping a **battery-operated drill** in your car, especially if you are going on a long trip, is handy to easily spin the scissor-jack up and down when changing a tire rather than cranking it by hand. Carrying a fuel substitute in the car for emergencies is also smart, especially if you are on a travel trip and find yourself in a remote area without a nearby gas station.[302] Finally, of your child is young, be sure to **keep a spray bottle of water with you in the car during the summer months always.** Particularly in hot environments like Arizona, children are susceptible to receiving bad burns from metal car seat belts and plastic parts. A simple spray bottle helps you to spray hardware and seats down to avoid this problem and can make the steering wheel more comfortable for you. It also helps to cool down the dash and steering wheel areas as well.

7. **Connect with a trusted advocacy group like Consumer Reports** so that you can stay apprised of product safety and recall issues. In addition, when you need to purchase a major appliance or replace your car, they have independent reviews that make the process easier.[303]

---

[302] http://www.mymagictank.com/
[303] https://www.consumerreports.org

What other concerns or questions do you have about creating a safe and healthy home? Ask your mentor for input and share some ideas. Inventory your current cleaning products and decide which ones may need to be replaced.

More Chapter Notes...

Chapter 8

Community Outreach & Service

Let us not become weary in doing good, for at the proper time we will reap a harvest if we do not give up. Therefore, as we have opportunity, let us do good to all people, especially to those who belong to the family of believers.
Galatians 6:9-10 (NIV)

Ministry Begins at Home

Most of what we have discussed so far has centered on creating a healthy, **Christ-centered home and homeschool environment for your nuclear family**. We have covered all aspects of your educational choices and homeschool planning options as well as delivery priorities. We have also talked about several items to consider when seeking to successfully disciple your child, manage your finances, and handle a variety of relational and physical requirements for your household and family.

But what about the rest of the world around you? This chapter is designed to deal with that question. As the opening passage indicates, we should not grow "weary in doing good", and we want to focus on doing "good to all people". Therefore, we are not only to minister to our family, although it is our top priority. Rather we are to **seek to find ways to influence and bless people beyond our four walls** and past the reaches of even our own neighborhood.

Now I know what you may be thinking, "How can we possibly do any more than what we are *already* doing? Goodness knows we have many areas to improve and work through before we can even *think* about reaching outside of our own family! I want to do it, but how?" My answer to these concerns may surprise you. For it is my opinion that **community outreach and service is not something that should take a high priority until all your children are in primary school or olde**r. Perhaps in very large families, this can be adjusted. However, most homeschooling families I know are just functioning through the day with little ones at home who need a great deal of physical care and routine is the most—even more—that many families can handle.

So, when it comes to ministering outside of your home, do not try to do too much too soon. Try instead to **first focus on all of the concepts we have discussed in the first seven chapters**. Make them your priority now as you seek to establish a good footing in these areas when your children are young. There will be a season when you can look outside of your home for ministry opportunities, but now is not that time if you still have children in the "Little Ones" season or even if you have a kindergartner at home. Essentially, **when you have very young children, your ministry should be mostly limited to your family.** Furthermore, even with older children, if many of the concepts discussed so far are new to you, focus on those things first before trying to make yourself available to the outside world of ministry opportunities.

This means you will need to **learn to say "no" or "not at this time"** to the many people around you who will want you to be involved in church volunteer and other outreach opportunities. This also means that you will need to limit other activities that may even include your ladies Bible study group or leadership responsibilities within your local homeschool support group for a season as well. You just cannot do everything at the same time when your family is quite young and you are working hard to establish so many important principles and routines with them. You also cannot expect yourself to take on more responsibilities when homeschooling is quite new to you.

Note to Leaders and Mentors:

Homeschool support groups appreciate new volunteers who are enthusiastic and wish to contribute in some significant way. However, in my experience, it is best to discourage families with very young children from doing too much during this season. This is also true for any family who is new to homeschooling or has not participated in the group for at least a year. Even for moms who are veteran homeschoolers, if they have not been part of your group for at least six months, they will not yet have a full sense of the processes, expectations, and vision that defines the group's structure and culture.

We know all too well the potential burnout and frustration that comes from trying to be all things to all people and would rather that families have a positive first year, establishing good habits in the home before overcommitting. Not only is this true, but you also do not want to have overextended people running a key area of your support group's structure only to have them quit part way through the year.

There is always next year or even beyond that where they can get involved and it will be a positive experience for their whole family and the support group.

Your Place in the Circle

As your family matures, however, and your **whole family can play a role in outside ministry opportunities,** then you will be able to take the next step and start to look outside of your nuclear family. First, realize that your nuclear family exists inside the center of five concentric circles of influence and outreach opportunities. So, as you seek out ways to minister to others, one logical approach is to start with the innermost circle closest to you and work your way out. The circle that surrounds your nuclear family is the one designated for "Extended Friends and Family". Following that is your "Local Community" which is then followed by opportunities to support "National Organizations". Finally, your family also has the prospect of being involved in work that has the potential to influence and minister to others involved in "International Missions".

The importance of looking at your world in this way clearly relates to the **"Great Commission"** when Jesus said spoke these points.

"All authority in heaven and on earth has been given to me. Therefore go and make disciples of all nations, baptizing them in the name of the Father and of the Son and of the Holy Spirit, and teaching them to obey everything I have commanded you. And surely I am with you always, to the very end of the age." Matthew 28:18-20 (NIV).

In other words, Jesus does not want us to keep the Good News and the associated works that go with our faith to ourselves.

So, take a moment to consider this diagram and **mark where you think your family is involved in ministry at this season in your life**. Most families will not have representation in all five areas yet. Then use the space on the next page to note the ways you are currently involved in ministering within these various areas as well as ideas you have for expanding into new ones.

Notes about Nuclear Family Ministry:

_____

_____

_____

_____

_____

Notes about Extended Family and Friends Ministry:

_____

_____

_____

_____

_____

Notes about Local Community Ministry:

_____

_____

_____

_____

_____

Notes about National Ministry:

_____

_____

_____

_____

Notes about International Ministry:

_____

_____

_____

_____

Your Reach Outside of the Circle

You are already aware of the work you need to do within your nuclear family and have made notes and plans throughout our time together to address those items. Continue to make this your top priority.

For the remainder of this chapter, then, we will focus on the other areas of ministry influence that you can consider as your school-aged children mature to a point that they are able to participate with you. **Always look for ministry opportunities that can be shared by the whole family or fit with a particular "season" of your life** rather than having each family member going off in different directions—the right hand not knowing what the left is doing. You have probably heard the saying that "the family that prays together stays together". Similarly, I say that "the family that serves together matures together"!

Also, be careful about doing ministries out of obligation rather than out of a sincere desire to make yourself available to contribute. If you wrestle with this issue of trying to "do things *for* Jesus" instead of allowing Jesus to "do things *through* you", I highly recommend the book called *Grace Walk: What You've Always Wanted in the Christian Life* by Steve McVey. We should find freedom and pleasure in serving, not burden and exhaustion.

Extended Friends and Family

Starting here is the **best first place to begin your ministry efforts outside of the home**. It is easy for your children to see the benefits of treating friends and family members with kindness and being available to help them, especially when you think about the posture of the early church recorded in Acts.

> *"All the believers were together and had everything in common. Selling their possessions and goods, they gave to anyone as he had need."* Acts 2:44-45 (NIV)

That willingness of heart must first be firmly established within the home and with extended family and friends. Then they can later translate these intentions to organizations and work that is more removed from their personal daily life but no less important.

Write a Variety of Letters

Anything that you can do to promote "otherness" in your child's mind is useful in helping them to see that the world does not singularly revolve around them. There are other people in the world, and they matter to God, so they should matter to us. One of the most powerful tools that you can employ, even with young children at home, is to write personal letters. Children should see you writing letters, and they should **always write thank you notes**

After you have your ministry to your family firmly established, look to how you can serve your extended family and friends next.

when they are given a gift, even if they have said "thank you" in person. Help them with this task until they are old enough to do it themselves. Unfortunately, personally written "thank you" notes are a lost courtesy in our society, so make it a priority in your family's courtesy practices that such generosity *always* deserves a written acknowledgement.

Related to this concept is the idea of **writing letters of encouragement**. If you have a friend or relative who is ill or just needs a note of kindness, you should write to them. E-mails and texts are fine, but a personal, handwritten note is even better. As your children get older, have them also write encouragement and regular **"update" letters** to out-of-state relatives themselves, especially to interested grandparents.

Involve Them in Your Homeschool Experiences

The next easy way to reach out to your friends and family is to share the progress your child is making in their school work while involving them in your homeschool experience. **Schedule special presentation days** for them or have your child send copies of papers and photos of projects to more distant relations so that they can see firsthand how your child is progressing. Better yet, **invite them as a guest to your home** so that they can be a part of your school for a day and see the depth and breadth of what you do with your child every day. If you use them, be sure to also **consider sending written progress reports** on your child to grandparents and other key friends and family members annually.

Also invite them to any public presentations that your child participates in, including local plays, debates, presentations, music recitals, and graduations. You may even consider inviting them to your state's annual homeschooling convention and curriculum fair so that they experience firsthand what homeschooling is all about. At many annual conventions and curriculum fairs, grandparents are welcome to attend with their grandchild's family for free.

Also utilize video conferencing tools like **Skype** so that your child can share their progress directly with friends and family or just visit "face to face" with them.[304] **Facetime** and **WhatsApp** are also great options.[305] If you cannot arrange a video conference contact time easily, **sharing video clips and photos or scanning and sending written work** to your friends and family to enjoy is another great option.[306] Even the most skeptical observers can be quickly softened by the "fruit" produced by your child, both academically and relationally, and you will have blessed your extended family or friend in the process with this kind of personal contact.

---

[304] http://www.skype.com – You will need to purchase a web camera, if you do not already have one;
[305] https://itunes.apple.com/us/app/facetime/id1110145091?mt=8; https://www.whatsapp.com/ – This tool is interesting since it easily enables communications using Wi-Fi, including overseas video calls!
[306] https://www.dropbox.com/ - You can create a free Dropbox account that allows you to upload up to 1 GB for free. Specifically, for videos or a photo presentation, you can also consider setting up a family YouTube channel (https://www.youtube.com) that only certain people can access for privacy reasons.

Practice Hospitality

Another great way to minister to your friends and family is to **practice hospitality** by inviting them over to share a meal or to visit with them. Create a welcoming environment by having your family participate in the clean-up and preparation activities. However, be careful not to place unrealistic expectations on everyone by expecting everything to be perfect. It is better to just grill hamburgers and hotdogs and have people over than to try to plan a complicated meal and you get so discouraged with preparations that you never invite them over. For larger events, consider having an "**open house**" where people can drop by over a two or three-hour period. You will have the opportunity to spend more one-on-one time with your guests while at the same time making it more convenient for your invitees to attend. For more ideas about practicing hospitality and creating a welcoming environment, read *The Hidden Art of Homemaking* by Edith Shaeffer. Although she has very detailed thoughts about a variety of household subjects and you may find yourself becoming overwhelmed by it, chances are you will pick up many great nuggets of advice along the way that you will be encouraged to employ.

Be Available to Help

Another way to minister to your friends and extended family is to **be available to help them in times of a crisis**. Scripture tells us in Ecclesiastes 4:9-10 says, *"Two are better than one, because they have a good return for their work: If one falls down, his friend can help him up. But pity the man who falls and has no one to help him up!"*

So be available when your friend or family member calls to share a trouble or unexpectedly has a loved one in the hospital. Try to loan out items to them that will help them when their own household items break or have problems. Be available for unusual needs, like offering to hold household items for them in your home if they need to have their home tented and fogged for termites. Take them to the airport at the last minute when their other transportation arrangements have fallen through. Be available to help them with involved landscaping or home improvement projects, lending your time, tools, and expertise where you can.

Also, **be available to provide regular support and assistance to aging parents, relatives, and friends** who need it. In addition, to helping my widowed mother with her ongoing house maintenance needs, my husband is also regularly available to help her widowed neighbor, who is also our friend. Whether sprinkler heads need replacing, a toilet needs fixing, the computer is acting up, or some improvement is needed that will make their lives easier, he regularly makes himself available to address these concerns and opportunities. As mentioned previously, we also had a season where we cleaned my mother's home monthly and I always make myself available to help her with financial management and tax planning questions as needed. So just be cheerfully available and that alone will minister to your aging loved one or neighbor.

Develop Adult Friendships Wisely

When you have school-aged children at home, **neither your or your husband will be able to spend as much one-on-one time with your adult friends as you used to do.** This does not mean that you never take separate time to be with them, but only that the occasions to do so will be few and far between. So, make sure that as you develop friendships with other adults that you do not spread yourself too thin. Follow that 80/20 rule again **by investing 80% of your available time with the adults who represent 20% of your closest friends.** Make sure your girlfriends understand that your time is very limited and that you would like to come up with a communication plan that will work for you both, especially when you are homeschooling a young family.

Some of my closest friends live outside of the Phoenix area or in another state altogether. So, we do not see each other as often as I would like. However, through periodic phone calls, e-mail messages, texting, and personal notes, we can **stay connected** and supportive of each other throughout the year. Other friends I have in the homeschooling community all share this common issue of limited time. So, we are all on the same page of not expecting too much of each other regarding social time. However, we do try to make the most of every conference, field trip, or other group social activity that we attend with our families to interact with each other at that time. Ultimately, personal e-mails or texts are preferable social media as the best tool to use between personal visits, keeping in contact with each other in a way that fits both of our varying schedules.

Additionally, try to **develop friendships with other couples and their families that benefit both you and your husband.** If you can practice hospitality by having them and their children come to your home, you will be able to more regularly interact with them than if you just try to arrange one-on-one time.

Also, this probably goes without saying, but **if you have a friend who is of the opposite sex, you should not have a relationship with them that exists separately from your husband.** The same goes for him. For these friends, again, make sure that *both* of you develop a relationship with *both* of them. Just as your husband should not be in a one-on-one situation where he is alone with a female who is not a family member in the workplace or any other environment, you should not continue to maintain an independent, non-family relationship with a male who is outside of your husband's presence. This goes for social media as well so that if you want to "friend" a male who is not family, only do so if they are married and their spouse is your "friend" as well. In other words, come to consensus with your husband on this point and be above reproach in all areas of your life for obvious practical reasons and to set a good example for your children.

Share other ideas with your mentor about ministering to your extended friends and family. Discuss them with your husband too.

Local Community

The next logical focus for ways to minister to others is to get out in the community and show your children firsthand how they can make a difference in the lives of others. They may not ever even meet the people they serve in the local community. However, they *will* understand from their experiences with ministering to their extended family and friends that people *do* benefit from whatever work they are doing as they serve with you in their neighborhood and their city.

Be Aware of Neighborhood Needs

Be aware of who your neighbors are and understand what their routine, ongoing needs are. This is easier said than done when many neighbors close their automatic door as soon as their car squeaks into the garage and rarely come outside for any reason. However, over time if you look and pray for opportunities, you can **find ways to interact with and even help them.** When they go out of town, offer to take in their paper, collect their mail, or take care of their trash cans. Help them "jump" their battery when their car is dead or offer to help them run a wheelbarrow in and out of their backyard when you notice they have sod or other landscaping material that needs to be moved. If their home has been vandalized, go over to help clean it up and when you have not seen your neighbor in a few days, especially a single elderly one, go over and knock on their door to make sure they are okay. When your child is older, they can offer to pet sit or take their pet on walks for them. They can also offer to babysit for a family with young children.

Also keep a **sharp eye out for any safety or possible criminal activities** that may be happening in your neighborhood. Join or implement a **Block Watch** program, as mentioned in chapter seven, that encourages neighbors to know one another and to understand when a suspicious car or person is hanging around your neighbor's home.[307] This is a particular area of opportunity for homeschoolers since we are home more than our average neighbor.

In addition, if there are **mutual neighborhood areas of interest that need clean up help,** like a common area park, empty field, or even a neighborhood school parking lot, consider organizing an effort that will serve not only to beautify your neighborhood but also to connect neighbors with one another. The more people understand about the families that live near them, the better off everyone is.

Carefully Choose Adult Mentors for Your Child

Way back in chapter one when we discussed the issue of "socialization" for homeschoolers, we talked about the importance of being mindful when you select adult mentors and teachers for your child. One way to manage this responsibility carefully is to **volunteer your time in**

---

[307] http://www.blockwatch.com/

helping within your kids' activities that they enjoy within the community. Whether it is a church activity, sports league, or specialty club or class, find a way to work as a volunteer in this setting. This way, even though you are not the adult giving the primary instruction, you can be involved in seeing how the instructing adult interacts with your child and the other children. You will have the opportunity to make observations and then work with your child "offline" to instruct and nurture them, looking to the wisdom and authority of other key adults in an independent but still somewhat controlled setting.

Volunteering will also give you an opportunity to have input into various aspects of the program as well as the ability to provide feedback to the instructor or coach about their interactions with your child. If you are just dropping them off and picking them up from these kinds of extracurricular experiences, you miss out on these valuable opportunities. Examples of how to involve yourself in the child-related programs your son or daughter takes include music lessons, sports, fine arts classes, VBS (Vacation Bible School), and other church programs for children.

Involve Yourself Strategically in Church Programs

Another obvious area of potential involvement for you and your family is within the context of your **local church home**. Hosting and leading church Bible studies and being involved in other ministries are all common options that can be great learning and relationship building opportunities. But there are also many concepts to consider along the way as you structure your family's involvement in church-related activities.

The first caution is to **be careful about involving yourself in everything your church offers.** For example, in the mega-church we attend, many of the activities are designed to attract un-churched people to the various programs and offerings as they become comfortable with being on the church campus. If we did everything that was offered, we would never be home. So, while our sons participate in weekly worship, small groups, volunteer work, service projects, and family-oriented events, they do not usually attend the large, purely social activities. This is because we do not have time to commit our schedule to include every possible opportunity, and we also recognize that the purpose of certain events and programs do not always fulfill what God's personal plan is for our family. If one of our sons has an un-churched friend that they could bring to such an event to help them in their spiritual walk eventually, that is one thing. But just to go for the fun's sake does not reinforce our family's values.

Instead, we **participate in ministry programs that fit our season of life and the areas where God has gifted us**. From its inception, I was involved in the leadership of a large homeschool support group for twelve years. Since it was a ministry within our church at the time, this was an area that made sense for me to be involved in, as I was able to serve other people while also meeting the needs of my own family and that of our local community at the same time. For many years, my husband was involved in teaching a weekly Bible study that we hosted in our home. It worked for us while our kids were very young, and we would retain a babysitter. However, when they became older and we wanted to involve them in the study and interaction process with other families who were in our same season of life, we had to restructure our involvement.

So, remember that not every program offered by your church will fit every need you have in every season. Alternatively, **seek to create what God has laid on your heart as a priority for *your* family while at the same time guarding your heart against the mistake of withdrawing from your church home altogether.** Remember what we discussed back in chapter five from the book of Hebrews.

> *"Let us not give up meeting together, as some are in the habit of doing, but let us encourage one another—and all the more as you see the Day approaching."* Hebrews 10:25 (NIV)

We also extend this concept to church camps and believe that this is an area of life where a conservative tact is best. For **Jesus needs to be first and foremost sought, taught, and caught in the home environment.** While camp for older teens can be beneficial for building relationships and fostering independence that is appropriate to that season, camps for the younger set are largely focused on entertainment and can potentially lead to negative peer influences that will do more harm than good. I have spoken to various homeschooling parents over time who have shared heartbreaking stories of regret over this issue. As a homeschooler, you have worked all these years to coach them on good behavior, establishing a positive self-image helping them put Christian principles to work. **Why give away all of that hard work in a week?** Remember that just as private Christian schools can sometimes be a central repository for children coping with difficult behavioral and emotional issues, some Christian youth camps can be the same way. So, if you do want to send your child to a camp before they are in high school, especially if they have an un-churched friend they want to invite, your heart is in the right place and you want to make sure that your child has a good experience. Even so, be sure to **check out the program thoroughly and even volunteer to help at the camp yourself** so you can understand firsthand how the program works, keeping in touch with how your child is coping with their experience throughout the week.

Another thought to discuss with your husband is to determine the appropriate time to involve your child in ministry. When our boys turn twelve or thirteen, we **seek to have them volunteer their time in some capacity at the church with us.** Our oldest, for example, loved to work with young children and always had a gift for interacting with them. So, he and I volunteered during the summer months to run a class with preschoolers so that the regular workers could take a break. He gained the volunteer experience while at the same time we continued to develop our experiences and relationship with each other. Our two youngest sons are not as inclined to work with younger children, but they both play piano and guitar, so they regularly serve in the student worship band. We also all serve as greeters together on a weekly basis. So, although you can involve kids to take on individual duties like this at a younger age, we find that they are not ready from a maturity standpoint to appreciate the full responsibility that goes along with why they are doing what they are doing in this capacity until they are entering junior high school.

Also, **do not always think that you must limit your participation in the local Christian community to only what your church offers**. Sometimes we get stuck in a "school spirit" mentality of thinking that our church is the only church around and that we are almost in competition with other Christ-centered churches. However, you will do your family better on this subject if you seek to participate appropriately with other local Christian organizations as you and your husband feel led. For example, as our home church did not offer such an option, we were involved for many years in participating and helping with the **VBS (Vacation Bible School) program** at a small church that was in our previous neighborhood. They did an excellent job with it, and our boys absolutely loved the week-long program of singing, crafts, recreation, and Bible study. I helped with the program by working in one of their classes not only because volunteers were needed but also to stay in touch with what the boys experienced throughout the week. We all enjoyed it very much and it came to represent the official beginning of our summer break that we all looked forward to doing. If you do participate in a community **VBS, AWANA, or RA/GA** program, be sure to provide a financial donation to at least cover your child's participation in the program.[308] We usually donated at least enough to cover our sons' expenses and then enough to cover a scholarship for another child whose family may not be able to donate towards the program. This is another way to promote a positive relationship between your family and other Christian organizations in your community.

Also, we have enjoyed going as a family up north to **help at a Christian family camp** run by two very good friends of ours, even though it is not connected with the camp program that our home church facilitates. Though they have now retired, it was such a special opportunity to learn new skills while experiencing new joys. Whether climbing the rock wall, playing games, chopping wood, or cleaning dorms, we loved it all. We appreciated the work we were able to do for them and liked the various aspects of camp life we did as a family and with our friends. It was a good fit for us, and our time spent serving the broader Christian community proved to be mutually beneficial to everyone involved.

---

[308] http://www.awana.org/; http://wmu.com/index.php?q=children; WMU Missions for Life has a "Royal Ambassadors" program for boys and a "Girls in Action" program for girls that is similar to AWANA but focuses on introducing children to the work that missionaries do around the world.

Similarly, even when a homeschool group is formally associated with a church, they can be designed from the beginning to welcome homeschoolers from all around the county without requiring church membership or attendance. For example, well over half of the families involved in the homeschool group where I served did not attend our church that provided oversight. It was truly an **outreach ministry to the community**, and we will explore this element further in chapter ten.

The Christian community extends past your local church.

So, do not always think that your church's campus is the only way to involve your family in ministry and look at it as another way you can **teach your child about the vastness of God's purpose in the local Christian community**. Yet in these areas, *do* make sure that you and your husband are in one accord on where God is leading you to serve—both inside and outside of your local church home.

Be Aware of Local and State Political Involvement Opportunities

We have all been stopped on the way into the library asking for our signatures on one ballot measure or another. Usually we are annoyed and in a hurry. However, **take time to consider these propositions and individuals who are trying to get into the voting ballots.** Often, they are individuals who have your same interests at heart and just need your help in getting a chance for people to consider their candidate or proposition during the next election cycle. Be careful about voicing your irritation over these volunteers since that response sends a negative message to your child about what should be viewed as a privilege. Of course, it goes almost without saying that you need to **regularly participate in the election process** and make sure your child knows what you are doing.[309] Many of us enjoy the convenience of just voting by mail, which also gives you time to share your decision-making criteria with your child as you go through your selections and explain things to them.

For those who are ready to take the next step, you can **become involved in helping your preferred candidate or proposition get on the ballot** and become one of those annoying volunteers collecting signatures yourself! For more ambitious families, you can run a call campaign, host a fundraising event, or involve yourself in other "hands on" opportunities to work to make a difference in your community. You can also encourage your

Network with reliable local advocacy groups.

---

[309] http://www.azvoterguide.com/; Use a voter guide like this in your state to make wise voting choices.

child to get involved with the local political process by involving them in programs like **Generation Joshua** or **TeenPact,** both discussed previously in chapter four.[310] Also take an opportunity when your children are old enough to appreciate it to go with them on a **tour through your state capitol**. Learn about what processes are involved to turn a bill into a law and get to know your local representatives, who love to hear from supportive and concerned citizens in their district. Again, involve yourself as a parent participant or volunteer in these activities and you too will benefit while modeling positive behavior in this area.

Another strategy is to stay in tune with local social and family policy issues that may be on the horizon by staying in touch with your state's local, family-focused "watchdog" organization. In Arizona, the **Center for Arizona Policy** with the motto of "Protecting the Family; Preserving the Future", is an invaluable resource to connect with, staying current with problems and successes that occur in maintaining personal freedoms, valuing all life, protecting marriage, supporting school choice, and other family-friendly issues.[311] Get on their mailing lists, donate to them if you can, and respond promptly to any community "calls to action".

Finally, since laws governing homeschooling are issued at the state level, be sure to **stay in tune with the efforts and issues that occur in your state that relate to the maintenance of homeschooling freedoms**. Even if your state is "easy" to homeschool in, be vigilant in helping to maintain homeschooling freedoms for all families. As discussed in chapter one, align yourself with your state support organization and they will usually keep you informed of opportunities to advance and even defend our homeschooling rights. They, in turn, stay connected with national organizations like **HSLDA** to ensure that they are keeping track of potential issues at the state as well as national level. This is because often when other states, like California for example, experience problems with homeschooling freedoms, it will not be long before that spills over into Arizona and other states as well. Then, when your state organization or HSLDA *does* give you a "call to action", make sure to follow through and involve older teens in the process.

> *Even if your state is "easy" to homeschool in, be vigilant in helping to maintain homeschooling freedoms for all families.*

---

[310] http://www.generationjoshua.org/; This is a Christian, civic responsibility club with chapters throughout the country that is under the organizational leadership of HSLDA; http://www.teenpact.com/; Also a Christian civic responsibility organization but it is centered on annual workshops and training camps.
[311] http://www.azpolicy.org/

Consider Other Local Community Programs

Finally, consider other worthy community programs that you can involve your family in that may not be associated with your church or neighborhood groups. Perhaps you would like to volunteer at a local food bank or answer phones at a **Pregnancy Resource Center**.[312] Maybe you could spare a day a week to rock babies in the NICU or qualify your dog to participate in a patient therapy program at your local hospital. Think about local leadership, sports, and church groups that your child participates in and consider if you or your husband can volunteer your time in some way to ensure their success. What about visiting an assisted living center for the elderly and giving a lonely man or woman a spiritual boost for the day? You can even have your child play an instrument or sing for them in a public gathering place at the facility as an extra treat. Have your support group visit your local Christian radio station for a tour and then present them with a collected amount of funds or other items that you would like to give as a group donation. Even making cookies and visiting recently widowed ladies in your community is a great way to show the love of Jesus by putting your faith into practical action.

> **Note to Leaders and Mentors:**
>
> *Group experiences do not need to be limited just to your typical field trips. Find ways within your homeschool support group to create opportunities for families to serve in the local community. Do be aware, however, that some organizations like food banks, blood banks, or the local library require children to meet minimum age requirements.*

Share other ideas with your mentor about ministering to people in your local community. Discuss them with your husband as well.

_____

_____

_____

_____

_____

_____

_____

_____

_____

_____

---

[312] http://www.choicesaz.org/ or http://www.optionline.org/

National Organizations

Many opportunities that exist outside of our local community are monetary ones as you align yourself with groups and organizations that work to advance a policy or concept that is important to you and your family. Most national organizations need **financial as well as prayer support** more than anything else. So, consider what national non-profits groups you would like your family to partner with and support. Consider the following scripture from II Corinthians.

> *"And here is my advice about what is best for you in this matter: Last year you were the first not only to give but also to have the desire to do so. Now finish the work, so that your eager willingness to do it may be matched by your completion of it, according to your means. For if the willingness is there, the gift is acceptable according to what one has, not according to what he does not have.*
>
> *Our desire is not that others might be relieved while you are hard pressed, but that there might be equality. At the present time your plenty will supply what they need, so that in turn their plenty will supply what you need. Then there will be equality, as it is written: "He who gathered much did not have too much, and he who gathered little did not have too little." II Corinthians 8:10-15 (NIV)*

So willingly seek to provide the funds necessary to support national organizations financially, above and beyond your tithe as we discussed in chapter six. Identify organizations that advance the cause of Christ in a way that is important to you and even make sacrifices on your part to give to them, if you can. Also, look for positive ways that you can share and market information about your favorite charitable organizations to **build excitement and support from other people** in the community about the work that they are engaged in doing to benefit their recipient base.

In our family, we have provided support to several different organizations over the years, including national ones. Here are examples of gospel-advancing ministries that we have chosen to support in one way or another.

1. **Answers in Genesis (AIG)**: Mentioned previously, AIG "is an apologetics (i.e., Christianity-defending) ministry, dedicated to enabling Christians to defend their faith and to proclaim the gospel of Jesus Christ effectively. [They] focus particularly on providing answers to questions surrounding the book of Genesis, as it is the most-attacked book of the Bible. [They] also desire to train others to develop a biblical worldview, and seek to expose the bankruptcy of evolutionary ideas, and its bedfellow, a "millions of years old" earth (and even older universe)." [313]

---

[313] http://www.answersingenesis.org/

2. **HSLDA Compassion**: Formerly known as the Home School Foundation, this organization serves as the hands and feet of Christ to help families continue to homeschool through hard times, helping thousands of families since 1999.[314] During our oldest son's illness, they were not only a point of financial support for our family but also a refreshing source of encouragement through letters, e-mails, and unexpected gifts. We have not only provided them financial support, but I have volunteered as their AZ State Ambassador since 2013. My husband is a Community Ambassador for them and our oldest son is a Youth Ambassador.

3. **Homeschool Now USA**: This organization promotes the growth of the homeschooling movement.[315]   In association with School Choice Week, Homeschool Now USA provides opportunities to host or attend meetings that discuss the option and benefits of home education.[316]

4. **Lamb and Lion Ministries**: They produce resources and programs to proclaim the imminence of the Lord's return.[317] They inspire Christians to look to Bible prophesy to be excited about their future in Christ and motivates them to share their faith in the present. They also do an excellent job of building awareness in the Christian community regarding the biblical implications of current issues surrounding culture, cults, and international politics.

You can also choose to support various national political organizations that represent your political beliefs or other national citizen awareness groups. National groups that provide relief assistance are also an important part of our community and can sometimes serve as an extension of the church body.

5. **Alliance Defending Freedom:** This AZ-based organization is the one that Michael Farris left HSLDA to lead.[318] This organization advocates for religious freedom, the sanctity of life, and marriage and family by funding legal cases that deal with such topics through a network of allied, professionals, attorneys, and various like-minded organizations.

6. **ParentalRights.org:** As a homeschooler, protecting parental rights should be a top priority.[319]   This non-partisan organization seeks to protect the "vital child-parent relationship" by working to "secure a constitutional amendment that defends the rights of parents to direct the upbringing and education of their children." In addition to donating money, you can sign the petition and work to lobby your local legislators to support the initiative.

---

[314] http://www.homeschoolfoundation.org/
[315] http://www.homeschoolnowusa.com/
[316] https://schoolchoiceweek.com/
[317] http://www.lamblion.com/
[318] https://www.adflegal.org/
[319] http://www.parentalrights.org/

7. **Manhattan Declaration:** Like the Center for AZ Policy previously mentioned, every state has access to several other national organizations that provide opportunities for state-level action to support family values and conservative principles. For example, the Manhattan Declaration is a national "call to the church" via a petition to support sanctity of life, dignity of marriage, and freedom of religion.[320]

Another option is to support various medical organizations that have been essential to your family. We support or have supported the following groups because they directly impacted us in life changing ways, particularly having had a child who was highly allergic to peanuts and later treated for leukemia/lymphoma. Others of you may wish to support the **American Cancer Society** or the **American Heart Association**, for example, if they have positively touched your life in some way. The possibilities of worthy organizations desiring your support are endless, so you need only seek your personal connection with the right one or ones to make it meaningful.

8. **Food Allergy Network:** As an advocacy organization for people with severe allergies, this organization has been useful to us over the years through their newsletter and important research work that they continue to push forward in a never-ending quest to successfully manage and maybe even one day cure many life-threatening food allergies.[321]

9. **MedicAlert:** "MedicAlert Foundation is a nonprofit organization providing 24-hour emergency medical information and identification service."[322] We were very grateful to have received their essential support services for our son during our journey with him.

10. **Leukemia and Lymphoma Society:** "Since 1949, LLS has been dedicated to curing leukemia, lymphoma and myeloma. LLS is the world's largest voluntary (nonprofit) health organization dedicated to funding blood cancer research and providing education and patient services."[323]

11. **Phoenix Children's Hospital:** As most of our son's care was provided by the local children's hospital, we started a team (4R_EVAN) that annually participates in and raises money for the "Run to Fight Children's Cancer" 5K/10K event organized by the Children's Cancer Network. It is held every March at Grand Canyon University to benefit PCH and CNC.[324]

---

[320] http://manhattandeclaration.org/#0
[321] http://www.foodallergy.org/
[322] http://www.medicalert.org/
[323] http://www.lls.org/
[324] http://www.phoenixchildrens.org/ and http://runtofightcancer.com/

12. **Ronald McDonald House Charities:** As a family who received services from two different Ronald McDonald Houses during our travels to obtain a cure for our oldest son, we know first-hand the incredible service that this selfless non-profit provides.[325] We cannot praise this organization enough and have designated McDonald's as our favorite fast food establishment!

When you start to add it up, you **realize how many organizations have been essential to you** and how you have also been blessed by striving to support their important work just on the national level alone. Even if you cannot monetarily support every organization that you would like, continue to make a list of ones that you think are valuable in sharing the love of Jesus as well as in providing practical support to families in some vital area of life. Stay connected with them and get on their e-mail newsletter or alert lists. Then pray for involvement opportunities and see what the Lord may open for you and your family to work more closely with that organization or others like it in the future.

What other ideas do you and your husband have about the various worthy national organizations that you would like to support? What ideas does your mentor have about it?

_____

_____

_____

_____

_____

_____

_____

_____

_____

_____

_____

_____

_____

---

[325] http://www.rmhc.org/

International Missions

      Opportunities for involvement in international missions are like national ones in that prayer and financial support are much needed resources and are often in short supply. **Bible translators and overseas missionaries associated with your church often have very little to work with, so they just wind up doing without.**[326] However, many times it is within our power to help if we just look for opportunities. So, check out options for mission trips and have your family **attend any local missionary meet-and-greet opportunities** that your church hosts so that you can learn more about the work that they are seeking to accomplish firsthand.

      Another type of international support opportunity is **one that focuses on feeding hungry children around the world or ministering to them in some other significant, physical way in the name of Jesus**. Building new schools, installing fresh water supply systems, and providing medical support are all great examples of what certain international ministries can do to be the "hands and feet" of Jesus. In addition to church-sponsored work within the context of local and international missions, we have supported the following such organizations with our time and our money.

13. **Compassion International:** This organization focuses on providing children in struggling countries with needed food, medical care, education, and spiritual support from a Christ-centered perspective.[327] Their model largely centers around monthly sponsorships and also provides a great opportunity for your child to learn more about the country that your sponsor child lives in as well as the daily challenges that they face in their culture. Families are also encouraged to write letters and provide special gifts to their sponsor child throughout the year.

14. **Feed My Starving Children:** Not all food program ministries are legitimate, so be careful with who you work with. **FMSC** is unique because well over 90% of their revenue goes directly to their food program to provide much needed, nutritionally balanced meals to devastated areas of the world like Haiti and many other countries including El Salvador, Indonesia, and Uganda.[328] They are a Christ-centered organization and have worked with leading scientists to create a balanced meal packet of food that helps to turn around a starving child to a healthy one in just a few short months. In addition to providing money, families with members as young as four or five years old can help in the food packing process.

15. **Samaritan's Purse:** Franklin Graham, son of evangelism great Billy Graham, is the president and CEO of this organization.[329] They provide relief and medical support to needy communities around the world and are

[326] http://www.wycliffe.org/
[327] https://www.compassion.com/
[328] http://www.fmsc.org/
[329] http://www.samaritanspurse.org/

well known for their "**Operation Christmas Child**" program. Our sons enjoyed those years of putting special boxes together for boys their own age many times over the years. They especially loved knowing that the box they took care to fill and pack went to a child who rarely, if ever, received nice new supplies and toys.

Another opportunity to minister to others on an international scale if you have an older child in the home is to **consider hosting a foreign exchange** student for a time. Since it can be difficult to sort out what organization to work with, contact your local church for more information and guidance on the one they suggest. You can also work with a local college or school of business in your area known for its emphasis on attracting students from around the world[330] and **offer your home as a host site** for one of their students or a married couple. If you have a child ages twelve through seventeen, you can also involve them in a **German-American ePal Program** that is endorsed by **HSLDA**. Homeschoolers in Germany have been severely persecuted in recent years, so encouragement from an American student is a great ministry opportunity.[331]

One final type of **international support opportunity organization** that homeschoolers will want to consider is **HSLDA**. Although we have discussed this organization many times, it is one that is worth your consideration when thinking about where to designate a gift above your normal tithe to your church and membership with them (HSLDA). Remember that even if your state is a relatively easy one to homeschool in that there are parents around the world, particularly in Europe, who are being threatened constantly with the removal of their children or even jail time for taking a strong stand in support of home education. HSLDA works tirelessly to help such families, which ultimately benefits us, as they continue to successfully defend homeschooling families and lobby for protection of homeschooling freedoms. It truly is a mission of global proportions.[332]

Just like the national organizations you support, you see how easily you can build a list of international missions that have also captured your attention. There are so many worthy causes that we cannot possibly support them all. Therefore, **listen carefully to the burden that God has placed on your heart, and He will guide you** into the areas that can be of greatest impact to your family personally as well as to the supported organization(s) of choice. Also, return to your tithing and giving worksheet back in chapter six. Think about the updates you may want to make to it based on your work in this chapter and finalize you goals and plans for your giving.

---

[330] In the Phoenix area, you can connect with the Thunderbird School of International Management (now part of ASU) or Grand Canyon University; both emphasize international management programs.
[331] http://www.homeschoolamericainc.org/programs.php
[332] https://www.hslda.org/hs/international/

What other ideas do you and your husband have about the various worthy international organizations that you would like to support? What ideas does your mentor have about it?

_____

_____

_____

_____

_____

_____

_____

_____

_____

_____

_____

_____

_____

_____

_____

_____

_____

_____

_____

_____

_____

_____

_____

_____

_____

_____

_____

_____

_____

A Word of Caution...

When deciding which organization(s) you will connect your family with to support, I encourage you to exercise caution in your selection(s). Not all non-profit (i.e. 501c3) organizations are well-run, nor do they all put a majority of their funds raised into the cause that they are supposed to represent. So find out about the financial structure of any organization you consider supporting before you make your decision, researching executive salaries and overhead expenses compared to the funds that actually get into the hands of the people who need the assistance. All non-profits have a certain amount of expenses for overhead and marketing purposes. However, when that figure becomes disproportionate to the amount that goes directly to the people who should benefit from their program offerings, such a discovery should raise a red flag of caution.[333]

What questions or concerns do you have about any organizations you currently support or would like to consider for support?

_____

_____

_____

_____

_____

_____

_____

_____

_____

_____

_____

_____

_____

_____

_____

_____

_____

_____

---

[333] https://www.consumerreports.org/charities/best-charities-for-your-donations/

More Chapter Notes...

Chapter 9

Scheduling for Life

There is a time for everything, and a season for every activity under heaven.
Ecclesiastes 3:1 (NIV)

Who Rules Your Home Anyway?

When our oldest son was still quite young, I remember attending a weekly ladies Bible study group. Leading our table was a young but capable mother of four whose husband was one of the leaders of the church. I marveled at her thinking, "Wow, she's got four kids! How does she do it all?" However, as she began to share about herself and her life with her children, it quickly became clear that her concerns and daily interactions with her kids were *not* centered on discipleship and child training as much as it was about schedules and driving. I am sure that they worked to be the best parents they could be. However, the emphasis and discussion that she presented about the "taxi" requirements of taking this child to this program and the other one to that appointment clearly clouded over any quality interactions that she had with her children on a daily basis. It was all about the schedule all of the time. I remembered leaving that day thinking, **"If there is one thing that my children will not say about me, it is that I was a great chauffer."**

Sure, we all do a fair amount of carting our children around from one place to another. I heartily support that schooling in the minivan is sometimes necessary and can be beneficial from time to time for a change of pace and focus. However, if the heart of the day centers on running from here to there

Who, or what, is running your home?

every day of the week, who rules your home? Well, in this case it is not so much a "who" but a "what". **For those who are attached to the goal of getting to this place or that place on time or having this assignment or that task done at a certain hour of the day, it is the clock who rules your home.** The clock rules because you have given it that authority and, if it seems like it is a cruel taskmaster, it is because you have loaded the day up with so many expectations that you have built in zero margin for traffic jams, lost shoes, and sick tummies. There is no time to take care of that discipline issue here or that unmotivated attitude there because stopping the routine would take too much time away from "the schedule" to address. **So, if you find that keeping the schedule is the goal of your day at all costs, it is probably time to reevaluate who *should* be running your home.** Like the opening Scripture says, there is "a time" and "a season for every activity under heaven". Eventually, the important "stuff" *will* get done, so proper scheduling is really a matter of getting the most important items done in the most efficient *and* low-stress manner possible.

Who or what is running your home? Gain insight from your mentor about how to figure out what the driving force in your day is and how you can manage it to keep it from managing you!

_____
_____
_____
_____
_____
_____
_____
_____
_____
_____
_____
_____
_____
_____

"If It Isn't on the Calendar, It Isn't Going to Happen!"

Much to my husband's embarrassment and even though I am technically savvy in many areas, it was with great reluctance over many years before I transitioned my scheduling tool from a pocket wall calendar and pen to a digital option! Many of you, as do I, use **Microsoft Outlook** or some other technology tool with wonderful results; but I still say there is something satisfying about the tactile experience of pen to paper followed by coloring coding with a highlighter. Perhaps it was all those years of practice I had carefully filling in my favorite coloring books as a child—remember that I am a textbook SL (Structured Learner)! Maybe I am just paranoid that my computer will die, or the "cloud" will blow up taking my entire scheduled future along with it. Whatever the reason, I do still like having a physical tool along with the technology.[334]

So, if you have not already settled on a favorite approach, **start with or change over to some simple organizational solution** that helps you to integrate your homeschooling with your home life priorities, like errands, doctor's appointments, cleaning, meal prep, laundry, and other activities. **Recognize that there are *only* twenty-four hours in a day** (really only sixteen to eighteen hours when you factor in sleeping) and if it does not have a space on the calendar, it is not going to get done! Remember that homeschooling, while an efficient teaching method for your children, *will* take a good portion of your time each day and something else that maybe you have been used to doing regularly will have to give. Laundry, meal preparations, and housecleaning are all basic tasks that consume a certain amount of time each day or week, so those should be noted as well. I know it may seem unnecessary, but if you color code every category so you can see what the balance is of things to accomplish that month "at-a-glance", you can get a feeling for where most of your time has gone that particular week or month.

The following chart shows the coloring system I have for noting certain categories of tasks on my calendar. Take a moment to review these now.

Highlighter Color	Related Meaning
Pink	Any school-related task including teaching, library trips, school preparatory duties, grading, music practice, and private lessons.
Blue	Any household task including meal preparation, grocery planning, cleaning, special organization projects, and laundry.
Green	Any medical appointment or related tasks. Noting appointments and so forth this way also provides a helpful summary for tax planning.
Orange	Any financial planning duties including paying the bills, updating investments, paying allowances, evaluating finances, shopping for insurance, preparing taxes, and inputting computer information.
Yellow	I use this color to represent any "out-of-the-house" activities so I can quickly see how much we will be driving around that week. Some items have two colors associated with them if it relates to one of the above categories *and* takes place out of the home.

---

[334] I have used a "Simply Organized Pocket Calendar" by Current (www.currentcatalog.com) for years. I love that it has a double page layout with oversized date spaces to log plenty of information about the day. I am also able to keep event tickets, receipts, and other essential documents in the generous pocket that is built into every month.

When I have a lot of yellow on the calendar, for example, I realize that we have too much scheduled outside of the home and need to adjust. If I have a lot of blue noted, then perhaps I am trying to do too many home-related tasks while still trying to accomplish important school priorities and should be moved something to the following week or month.

So, just as you and your husband needed to come up with an agreed upon filing system in chapter six, pick or adjust your calendaring system together and stick with it. Also, **try to use only one main calendar** so you do not run into issues of multiple commitments that conflict with each other or noting an important task on one calendar and then forgetting to transfer it to the other ones. When you will be out at the doctor's office or someplace else where you think you might need access to your current month's information, you can always make a quick photocopy of a calendar page before you leave if you feel you must have the information with you. If you do use an electronic calendar, be sure to synchronize it regularly to your primary computer or your "cloud" account so that information is up-to-date in all areas of your home. I also send myself e-mails to make sure to transfer new appointments or remind myself to do something when it is not convenient to note it any other way at the time.

You will eventually note school assignments separately, as discussed later in this chapter, but the word "school" should still be noted on your family calendar since it represents a big part of your day. Similarly, put down basic tasks like "laundry" or "meal preparation" or "housecleaning" since they literally take up time as well. **This is an important step** because so many moms just think or assume in the back of their heads that they are going to get the daily tasks done with no problems while also loading up their day with many non-standard or recurring commitments that collide with their ability just to do the basics. So, you may think it is ridiculous to **write the daily tasks down**, but since they physically take up several hours in your day, they need a space on the calendar to keep you and your family mindful of the reality of their existence. Also, be sure to use your family calendar to note what meal you are making on which day, so you can easily reference your three-month rotating meal plan throughout the month that we discussed in the chapter seven.

What centralized family scheduling system do you or will you use?

_____

_____

_____

_____

_____

_____

_____

Embrace Flexibility by Prioritizing and Building in Margin

You may have heard that cattle ranchers need to have at least a couple of acres of grazing land to support just one cow. However, in a recent conversation with a rancher in the Badlands of Montana, I learned that in desert environments, the ratio **is twenty-four acres to one cow!** In other words, the more desolate the place, the greater the land margin must be to ensure survival of the cow! Thus, just as acreage supports the cow, margins make the written page readable, and rests make music melodic and pleasant to hear, **margin in our schedules creates an enjoyable flow to the priorities that you seek to accomplish each day** with your child and your home. As you prioritize and discern between what is good and what is best, figure out how much extra time in a day you *really* have compared to what you think you have.

Many of us tend to overestimate what we can do in a day and underestimate what we can accomplish in a year. This may sound odd, but it really indicates that we are more comfortable engaging in easy busy work than we are in setting and working intentionally towards ambitious, long-term goals. The distracting "small stuff" seems easier to do than the challenging "big stuff", which just feels too overwhelming and unachievable. However, the fact is that if we can **create more margin in our day by eliminating unnecessary busy work,** then we can build in activities that will help us accomplish our significant annual goals while still getting all the daily "stuff" done.

For our home **in any given school weekday, I typically only allow <u>one</u> other non-standard or weekly item to be scheduled.** This is because every day has school, music practice, and meal preparation requirements as a minimum. Add that to everything else that needs to be done in a day and I *maybe* have a couple of undesignated hours a day to "play with". The "one other" activity I might put in this two-hour window could be a doctor's appointment, grocery shopping, library trip, laundry, house cleaning, ministry work, scrapbooking, field trip, private lesson, or some special or seasonal project task. However, **be aware that most days the "one other" activity is broken up throughout the day and not able to be completed in two uninterrupted hours.** In any case, if I need to have more than two hours to accomplish a "one other" task, I will need to trim down a daily task area or I simply will not have enough time to do it. This is partly what the section titled "Seek Out Time Savers" is intended to address later in the chapter.

But first, notice that I have provided two lists on page 421; one gives examples of typical **daily tasks** that while the other is a listing of **"one-other" activity** examples. You will notice that many of the items we have discussed throughout this manual until now are represented here and are particularly noted in the "one-other" activity section. This is also why I placed this chapter about scheduling at the end of Part II of this manual, **for everything else we have discussed**

We tend to overestimate what we can do in a day and underestimate what we can accomplish in a year.

so far in chapters one through eight now comes together in one final plan of execution. Certainly, your list and related schedule will vary from mine as I have not included everything that could possibly be of concern to every family, including my own. However, it *does* address the most common and not-so-common tasks that most of us face. By doing this, it will help get you started on how to look at the **two camps of responsibilities** that you have on a regular basis so that you can prioritize and schedule them for successful completion. I have also provided you two different versions of this form in Appendix B.

What are some of your current scheduling challenges?

_____

_____

_____

_____

_____

_____

_____

_____

_____

_____

_____

_____

_____

_____

_____

_____

_____

_____

_____

_____

_____

_____

_____

Daily Task Example *(Complete Entire list every day)*	"One Other" Activity Examples *(Select and complete ONE of these a day)*
Mom's Daily Exercise or early morning reading – 45 min.	Working Towards a Long-Term Goal or Project. (continuing education work, running a personal business, major home improvement project)
Morning Activities (daily grooming for entire family, make beds) – 1 hour 15 min.	Ministry or Community Involvement Work (preparation activities and fulfilling scheduled duties)
Preparing Breakfast & Cleanup – 15 min.	Weekly House Cleaning and Yard Work Duties (dusting, sweeping, mopping, scrubbing, trash, mowing, gardening, tree/bush trimming, changing linens)
Daily Devotionals with Breakfast– 45 min.	Periodic Cleaning & Organizing Tasks (blinds, baseboards, dusting hard-to-reach shelves, ceiling fans, silk plants, windows, or touch up painting; organizing a room, drawer, garage, storage box, or closet)
Teaching School and Coaching Music (includes periodic breaks and grading time) – 5 hours	Business Correspondence (evaluating and answering e-mails, returning business calls, and going through the regular mail)
Preparing Lunch & Cleanup – 1 hour	Corresponding with Family or Friends (cards, sending video clips, e-mailing sample work, phoning, video conference calls)
Teaching School and Coaching music (includes periodic breaks and grading time) – 3 hours	Homeschool Activities (researching new curriculum options and teaching concepts, weekly preparation, updating school plans, prepping new homeschool help tools and worksheets, or preparing grade cards)
Preparing Dinner, Having Family Dinner & Discussion, & Cleanup – 1 hour	Grocery and Meal Preparation (inventorying pantry, preparing shopping list, researching new recipes, shopping, and training boys (cooking & nutrition)
Children's Nighttime Routines (includes sharing schoolwork with Dad and grooming activities) – 30 min.	Outside Activities (field trips, weekly park day, helping Grandma, PE class, sports programs, private lesson or class, planning a trip or vacation)
Nighttime Reading & Discipleship Training – 1 hour	Managing Finances (budgeting, paying bills, managing investments, shopping insurance, shredding, filing)
Next Day Preparations (picking up room, getting school items ready) – 30 min.	Health and Medical Activities (appointments, in-home therapy activities, physical training for boys, related phone work to physician's office or insurance company).
Sleeping – 7 hours	Hobbies and Family Social and Activity Time (board game, Wii system, date night, digital scrapbooking, photo shoots, photo editing, etc.)
TOTAL HOURS SPENT ON DAILY ITEMS = 22	**TOTAL DAILY HOURS AVAILABLE FOR "ONE OTHER" ITEMS = 2**

So, what did you come up with using the blank task list found in Appendix B? Do you have two or more hours to spare for your "one other" activity a day or are you hard pressed even to come up with that much? Also, recognize that if your family is committed to a host of **evening activities**, such as church obligations or multiple days of sports practices and games, you are most likely overextended in your schedule and are not able to accomplish many additional "one-other" activities or even basic tasks easily. This is especially true when our families are young. Like the "one-other" activity that can be done during the daytime hours, families usually only have one evening a week that can be devoted to some activity that is outside the home if they really stop to evaluate their schedules. Flexibility on this issue increases somewhat when your children are teenagers, but you even need to be mindful of potential burnout during that season as well.

Notice on the previous page that I also recorded an average estimated time for each "daily task" in fifteen, thirty, or forty-five-minute increments as well as hourly blocks. See that I have put down a total of eight hours for teaching and music coaching time; **homeschooling really is a full-time job**! However, the eight hours a day are noted largely because I am teaching different boys who, at times, have been on different curriculums. Even though our oldest was very independent in his middle school and junior high seasons, I continually taught all morning and into the afternoon a good deal, even though each individual child was *not* doing anywhere near eight hours of school and music a day. This category also has periodic breaks and grading time built into the estimates, so it is not continual teaching or coaching for those eight hours for me either. In other words, **I have built margin into those noted eight hours.** The same goes for the other categories. I have estimated the times conservatively knowing that I will have extra time throughout the day as we move efficiently through those tasks. However, if we *do* get bogged down for one reason or another or wish to read an extra book or do an additional activity with one of my boys, my day will not be completely off track because of have padded the times to allow for such a cushion, if needed. If you receive an emergency phone call, your child gets ill, or you have a discipline issue crop up that you need to stop and correct, you do not want to feel like the clock is pulling you to take shortcuts in working through these inevitable interruptions.

One last point of scheduling advice is to **be careful about overbooking your weekends.** Sometimes we look at the weekend as our time to "catch up" on everything that did not happen during the week. However, this is a potential recipe for disaster if you make it a regular practice. In our home, we usually devote the first half of our Saturdays to errands, home projects, yard work, or weekly school preparation tasks. Then the last half of

Learn how to build margin into your life. Not every second of every day should be committed to some task or appointment.

the day is set aside for family time. We then work to **protect the rest of our weekend**, worshiping with our church body, resting and relaxing, enjoying extra time with our sons, visiting with family or friends, reading, or just hanging out together.

How good of a job do you do now in building in margin? When you add up all of the time you spend on required daily activities, how much margin is left over for your "one other" activity?

_____

_____

_____

_____

_____

_____

_____

_____

_____

_____

_____

_____

_____

        One final perspective I would like to share with you about the importance of building in margin is that our biggest daily frustrations tend to come from our irritation with interruptions. Because our days are usually too packed, interruptions are viewed as necessary evils at best. However, if you think about it, interruptions are a natural occurrence in every life, in every job, and in every home. So, since your child will never get away from interruptions their whole life, is not it better to help them learn how to manage and cope with them positively than to be setting an example of perpetual irritation about them? Therefore, **building in margin is not just about estimating time conservatively or padding your schedule**. It is also about **helping to train your child to graciously and confidently handle interruptions and crises** that are going to occur each day.

        Can we minimize interruptions by training our children to save their questions for a more convenient time? Yes, and we should do this. However, know that when you and your husband decided to have children, you were also signing up for about twenty years of interruptions! So be approachable, make the best of it, and **realize that with every disturbance usually comes an opportunity:** an opportunity to praise, an opportunity to correct, an opportunity to mother, an opportunity to mentor, an opportunity to suggest, an opportunity to instruct, an opportunity to coach, or an opportunity to simply express your love to them. When we begin to realize that interruptions can equal opportunities, our perspective changes from the negative to the positive.

> *With every disturbance usually comes an opportunity.*

Take a moment to note what your biggest interruption-related frustrations are. How many of them can be avoided by retraining your family to present their needs to you differently? How many of these interruptions can perhaps be viewed, instead, as opportunities that you do not want to miss? Discuss ideas and concerns with your mentor and your husband. How many opportunities have you missed?

_____

_____

_____

_____

_____

_____

Begin with the End in Mind

Regardless of what you would like to accomplish, always begin with the end in mind. **This principle applies to small tasks and lofty goals alike.** For example, if you need to have your child at the dentist's office by 8:00 a.m. in the morning, figure out what time you need to leave your home to get there ten minutes or so early so that you can find a parking space, update paperwork, and so forth. Build in the margin we discussed in case there are traffic issues and then consider the other household items that need to happen before your child and you are ready to go. Do as much of it in advance the night before as possible, such as laying out clothes, gathering schoolwork to take with you, and so forth. Then have a small list ready to remind you of what else needs to happen before you walk out the door. Back up from there to account for grooming and breakfast tasks so you can determine when to have your child up and ready to go. This is a simple example of how to begin with the end in mind when scheduling your time.

For a large home project, an aggressive financial goal, or a discipleship plan for your child, just follow the same process. Start by articulating what the end goal is and when it must be achieved. Then, working your way backwards, set the necessary milestones and define the related activities along the way to successfully pull it all together. Keep doing this process and define supporting activities that need to be completed until you **understand what you need to do** *today* **in order to support the fulfillment of that long-term goal**. Again, build in margin and allow for setbacks while staying focused on the end goal. Also, if you do not completely know all the steps involved to meet your goal, then build in some additional, upfront time to research the unclear information so you can fill in the gaps and achieve the desired result.

Seek Out Time Savers

Before creating an actual schedule, it is also useful to take some time to look for ways to save time or "kill two birds with one stone" when you are making commitment decisions about the upcoming week or month. So, consider some of the thoughts in this section and see if you might not find it useful to incorporate some of these ideas into your planning. Often, finding ways to reduce time requirements to complete certain tasks comes from **looking at the issue in a new way or simply knowing when to ask for assistance.**

Once upon a time towards the end of a school year, I sent my husband this e-mail message while he was still at work.

> *Dear Grant,*
>
> *I taught, discipled, laundered, coached, facilitated, organized, directed, cooked, cleaned, scrubbed, swept, wiped, vacuumed, fluffed, e-mailed, shredded, glue gunned, supervised, printed, wrote, stacked, phoned, prepared, distributed, and dusted today. Would you mind stopping at the store for me on the way home?*
>
> *XXOO*
>
> *Carol*

If it sounds like I am rattling off this host of accomplishments from the day to justify my request, that is exactly what I was doing! We often sense that we need to give a million reasons why we need help before we simply ask for it. Instead, **know in advance that sometimes you just need help** and you usually have key people in your life who would love to give it! Grandparents, aunts, uncles, trusted neighbors, and good friends are also often untapped resources. We try to "do it all" ourselves in an effort to prove that the life we have chosen is not too much for us to handle. However, if you think about it, any family, whether they homeschool or not, can occasionally benefit from assistance. So, do not be embarrassed to make a few well-placed requests for help throughout the month and certain times of the year.

Similarly, if we want to accomplish as much as we can in a given day or week, we also need to **find other creative ways to make the best use of our time** while moving efficiently towards the completion of our goals. Here are several additional such suggestions that you may want to consider employing in your home.

Homeschooling & Traveling – Related to Part I (Chapters 1-4)

Prior to looking at homeschool schedule options in more detail in the "Detailed Homeschool Schedules" section, here are some time saving concepts that you may want to keep in mind as you establish your daily, weekly, monthly, and annual teaching priorities.

1. The first point is just to **be prepared**. Not only should your child know exactly where all their books are to get going each day, but they should also have the extra paper, pencils, tissue packets, and so forth available, ensuring they are not getting up every five minutes to get this or that. Consider having a portable clipboard with a built-in carry box to help them keep supplies in one place that can travel around with them. Make it their responsibility the night before to make sure everything, including their clothes, is ready to go the next day. Also, **have small snacks and water available** to give them at strategic points in the morning and afternoon when energy or interest is waning. Since we do most of our school in a common area, I make sure to have these issues addressed so we are not constantly running in and out of the kitchen to retrieve these things.

2. As your child gains independence in their schooling, recognize that their learning capabilities typically outpace their motor skills for writing or their perception on how to logically set up a paper. By third grade, then, **consider creating any useful forms or templates** that your child can use to cut down on the amount of time it takes to set up a paper for a written assignment. Write up a sample experiment sheet for science that gives them an idea of how to structure it or give them a writing check list that clarifies to them what you are looking for when you grade a paragraph they wrote. Make up a form they can use to practice difficult spelling words or keep a chart for them on their exercise goals that they want to track and improve.[335]

3. Like what I will cover again in point two on page 432 of the section called "Correspondence and Financial Duties", use a **designation and rotation system** when scheduling your child's school work. This means that, while your child may not do the same assignment related to a school subject every day, they can do work that relates to the same overall topic. For example, instead of having your child work through the same kind of writing assignment every day for the same length of time, you can organize it where your child engages in various types of writing-related activities within other subjects that are not necessarily completed in one continuous lesson. In

---

[335] Several useful templates designed to increase efficiency and reduce frustration are available for your use on our private TBH Facebook.

addition, they are not doing the same assignment every day but are instead engaging in a variety of methods and activities that relate to one teaching subject, which helps to increase their interest.

When you look at the chart at the bottom of this page that uses the example of writing, you see that are several ways to create a writing program that will teach them what they need learn in their content subjects like science and history while at the same time teaching them writing skills. This is true for math or any other kind of skill subject as well. You want to **have them spend a certain amount to *time* practicing and reinforcing concepts in the various major school subject areas**. So, do not be as concerned about finishing a complete assignment in every subject, every single day. Instead, decide what the reasonable time is for that skill and then limit them to that time. You will be surprised to see the variety of methods you can cover and resources you can utilize in teaching your child a subject if you employ this in even one or two few key areas. At the same time, you will feel in control of your schedule by having them move onto something else when they have spent enough time on that area, even if they are not completely done with what they were working on that day. So, unless you have a reason to require a hard and fast deadline, try to be flexible to occasionally move assignment due date expectations within reason and let them enjoy a variety of ways to reinforce their skills. Here is a sample of different writing assignments a middle school child could have during the week:

Daily Writing Requirement	Assignment Variation Examples
Monday – Total of 1 to 1.5 hours throughout the day	*Dictation Work:* Pre-record a passage from a book that your child is reading and have them write it down or type it out by ear. *Work in Handwriting Book*. *Writing Assignment for History*.
Tuesday – Total of 1 to 1.5 hours throughout the day	*Formal Writing Program Assignment* OR *Book Report Assignment*. *Work in Handwriting Book*. *Writing Assignment for Science*.
Wednesday – Total of 1 to 1.5 hours throughout the day	*Dictation Work:* Pre-record a passage from a book that your child is reading and have them write it down or type it out by ear. *Work in Handwriting Book*. *Writing Assignment for History*.
Thursday – Total of 1 to 1.5 hours throughout the day	*Formal Writing Program Assignment* OR *Book Report Assignment*. *Work in Handwriting Book*. *Writing Assignment for Science*.
Friday – 30 minutes	*Literature Mechanics Discussion* and *Story Charting*

Notice also that by doing a "designation and rotation" system, that you will be able to **take advantage of overlapping learning opportunities**. For example, the writing that they do for science or history does not just relate to science or history but also connects to the concept of writing. In addition, your child can either do a science *or* a history paper every other day on Monday through Thursday, which means that they are taking the same amount of time each day for either science or history and for writing, but they are not doing both major subjects on the same day. Particularly when they were younger, this worked much better in our home than in trying to do a little bit in every subject, every day.

4. When possible, also **find appropriate ways for your oldest child to help with teaching a younger sibling**. If your oldest is a CL (i.e. Community Learner) or just simply enjoys having this type of responsibility, it can serve as a great motivator for them to complete their work in a timely manner throughout the day so that they can be part of the teaching process for their younger brother or sister. An older sibling can easily read to a younger child, aid them on an assignment, help to quiz them on memory work, assist with a craft, or give them a spelling test. Be careful, however, that if you do engage your older child to fulfill one of these duties, set proper expectations for them as well as with the younger sibling on what you want them to accomplish. The younger child needs to understand that the older child is helping them because Mom asked them to do so, which will go a long way in facilitating cooperation on both ends. They are acting as your "agent", so they need to give them the same attention and respect they give to you. At the same time, the oldest child needs to be careful about being "bossy" with the younger one, so guide them in how they can encourage and interact with the younger sibling in a positive and productive manner.

5. Although I mentioned these tools in chapter four, they are worth mentioning again! Be sure to **make good use of a household timer and the voice notes feature of your cell phone** or other convenient recording device. Use a timer to help keep you and your children on task when you are busy teaching one of them, managing breaks, or guiding an independent student who is working on an assignment and may have gone way over on the amount of time that should be devoted to it. Similarly, being able to record your child's spelling lists, dictation assignments, or any other instructional information you need to give them is a great time saver. This is because often you are sitting down to teach a younger child who needs more hands-on attention when your oldest child pops up and is ready for their spelling test. Since no

one else can really give your oldest children their words, you may sometimes try to juggle it with your other teaching job with frustrating results! You also do not want to put the older one off since they need to keep their day moving too. Instead, have these sorts of aids recorded and ready to go when they need them. Ambitious parents can even utilize a video recording device for the same purpose or, for a change of pace, even have Dad record a dictation passage or spelling list!

6. **If your child takes music or art lessons or needs a foreign language tutor, consider "Skyping" them** into your home at regularly scheduled times to work with your child within the area of interest that you would like them to develop.[336] Several years ago, our boys' piano teacher moved out to the East Coast to engage in ministry work at a Christian camp. However, she was able to continue teaching our boys via the Internet and by sending e-mails and video clips back and forth with us. She even came into town three times a year to conduct group lessons and recitals since she had to come anyway to periodically check on their Arizona rental property. We were very pleased with the arrangement for those two years, and the boys make just as much if not more progress than having regular in-person lessons. Even though we are with a new piano teacher today since our previous one retired, we still do lessons on Skype. We also utilize this tool for most of their guitar lessons and their Spanish as well with great results![337]

7. Since homeschooling often involves park days or field trips, be sure to **plan ahead and complete as many preparations as possible the prior evening.** Even doing pre-work the night before you know you need to take your child to the dentist or some other doctor's appointment will prove productive and efficient. If you will be out for a long period of time, always plan to bring a suitable snack and plenty of water. Pack lunches if you know that your activity will cut into their normal lunch hour since it is always costly to eat "on the go" and is not always convenient to take the time to stop. This is particularly important if your child has a food allergy and you do not want to run into issues with them becoming exposed to an unwanted allergen, like we covered in chapter seven. Also **have a "to go" tote bag available to grab** when you need to go out for any reason. Keep this bag stocked with writing instruments, a notebook, a box of crayons, a coloring book or blank sheets, a current book you are working on, a deck of cards, learning drill cards, current assignments or books your children are working on,

---

[336] http://www.skype.com
[337] http://travelinglessons.com/, http://www.nickjensenmusic.com/, http://www.homeschoolspanishacademy.com/

and a fun travel game. Our boys' favorite is **20Q**, a classic "twenty questions" guessing game that was given to us by a friend many years ago. It will be convenient to have this bag when you wait in a doctor's office or need to occupy a younger child when an older one is in a class at the community center or taking a music lesson.

8. If you do a regular bit of traveling during the year, **create a standardized packing list** on the computer that you can easily update and reference as needed. Have a section for clothing, grooming items, personal items, supplies needed, and snacks you are going to take, especially if it is a driving trip. Also, try to **vary the destinations of your trips so that you can fulfill teaching and educational experience priorities** that you have along with your husband's use of his vacation time. For example, when we studied about Earth science, we took the boys to Tucson to visit nearby examples of both "live" and "dead" caves. When we studied about rocks and minerals, we visited Jerome, the "largest living ghost town" in America where they have a rich history of copper mining. In addition, we made a trip to Tucson's famous rock and mineral show. Other historically or scientifically rich expeditions we have experienced include the Washington D.C. area, Ark Encounter, Creation Museum, and Vanderbilt Castle as well as several national parks, including the Grand Canyon, Yellowstone, Yosemite, and Sequoia. We even did a "dino-dig" in southeastern Montana![338] These are just a few examples of how to incorporate learning into a family trip.

9. Share with family members who may expect you to travel to see them annually, or even more frequently, that you may have other plans that year and that they are welcome to meet you at your chosen destination, if they would like. However, **let them know that your travel plans will change regularly as the kids grow, and you will need to decide from year to year what those plans are going to entail.** This may be an uncomfortable conversation to have. Yet, all family members need to face the fact that everyone's time and resources are limited, and your family cannot be expected to use a good portion of your money and vacation time to make the same trip annually while the years and travel opportunities with your nuclear family continue to slip away from you. Instead, have out-of-state relatives come to stay with you during the school year so that they can peek into your child's world and see what they do all day long. You can also show them around your hometown and enjoy areas of local interest together. These "staycations" can be

---

[338] http://www.northwestrockandfossil.com/ - Northwest Treasures is a family-owned, Christian organization that writes geology curriculum and coordinates spectacular tours and experiences, including their annual "dino-dig" field trip to Glendive, Montana!

budget-friendly, great ways to build new memories without even leaving town! Then plan your travel trips as a separate event to fit your relationship development goals and teaching priorities with your child. **Remember that you cannot always please everyone at the same time and that you only have limited resources and a short season with your children while they are still in the home with you before they are grown and gone.**

Spiritual Discipleship – Relates to Chapter 5

1. **Have dinner together as a family most every night.** Although it may not always happen based on your husband's schedule and the commitments involving your children, make it a goal and use that time to connect everyone with each other. Go around and have each person tell something about their day that went well and then something that could have gone differently. Use these times to reinforce character qualities and spiritual expectations. Then have everyone participate in the clean-up process so that "many hands make the load light". If dinners do not work out, then have breakfast together!

2. Instead of allowing media to consume an inordinate amount of your evening, take time to disciple your child after dinner, setting aside time for conversation, Bible study, and other important one-on-one activities, particularly with Dad. Television programs and the commercials that invade our homes often become viewed as almost members of the family that must be on all of the time, taking priority over the living and breathing people in your home. Instead, **limit your media time only for good family programs** that can be recorded and watched together later, leaving your weekday nights free from television.

3. Occasions to spiritually nurture your child can only come when time is set aside to do so. However, in addition to formally sitting down and teaching your child a life concept as discussed in chapter five, provide opportunities for significant interaction by using a **"divide and conquer"** approach. This means that you and your husband can take errands that need to be done and go your separate ways: each getting the jobs completed that need to be done while giving your husband a "one-on-one" opportunity to be with and mentor your child. This also gives you time with your other child and serves to mix things up a bit from what they are used to all week long. Trips to the local home improvement store, the auto repair shop, or even a journey to the dump after a morning's worth of yard work trimmings can provide great opportunities for your child to share and talk to Dad.

Correspondence & Financial Management Duties —Relates to Chapter 6

1. As I reviewed in chapter six, the mail and the various destinations it goes to, based on the type of correspondence it is and retention requirements each piece has, will vary. However, I do not stop and *process* them right at that time. I only filter the mail and then at a regularly scheduled time, I deal with it. So, even though the mail comes in almost daily, **I only process bills and other correspondence once a week** thereby avoiding the problems of being distracted from the priorities that should take precedence that day.

2. **Other duties like managing investments or filing, I usually only process them monthly.** However, there is still a space on my calendar that is for "processing finances" once a week. So each week, the *task* of what I do varies while the *topic* of doing something related to finances does not. For example, the first time I will update the checkbooks and get bills paid. Then the next week, I might update information in our tracking system. The following week is usually for updating anything related to our investments and the last week could be set aside for filing or related reading. This concept is like what I discussed earlier in your home school about a **designation and rotation system.**

3. If you have not done so already, set up **automatic bill paying** so that you do not need to take time to write checks for your regular expenses. Put your electric bill on an **equalizing plan** that calculates your payment based on your usage during the past twelve months, which will determine an average monthly bill rather than paying extraordinarily high bills during the summer, especially when your income is usually static throughout the year. That way your monthly bill processing activities will be streamlined, and you will only need to take extra time to process those nonstandard, periodic expenses that arise. Finally, **stick to using only one debit or credit card**, if you can manage it, so that you do not have to spend a lot of extra time managing and processing payments and logging transactions for multiple accounts. For credit card users, do not neglect to pay it in full *every* month!

4. Even though it is supposed to make our lives easier, reading your e-mail can take a huge chunk of time out of your day if you let it. So, **set up e-mail filters** to automatically deliver certain messages into appropriately designated folders that you can then review at a separate time. If you are on a lot of unnecessary e-mail lists, go through the process to "unsubscribe" from those that you do not need. You can also automatically delete or reject e-mails from

unwanted solicitors. This concept also applies to social media, applying the appropriate filters and notifications. Finally, if you have a friend or family member who is constantly sending you unwanted material and potentially hazardous attachments because you are on their group delivery list, you can either set up a rule to delete it right away or kindly ask them to only send you information that is personally directed to you.

5. **Keep pen and paper handy by your bedside table** so that you can jot down ideas or concerns about things you need to do when you are going to bed. You do not want to forget them but, do not at the same time you do want to avoid dwelling on these kinds of things in the middle of the night. So always have a way to write your thoughts down so that you can then address them fully in the morning. Similarly, **set up future dated messages to yourself through e-mail** for items that you want to make sure to do at a specified date in the future. A good example of this is to set up a future e-mail to deliver to you regarding library book renewals or books you need to pick up that are on hold for you at your local branch. I will also forward myself articles that relate to a future activity or possible field trip idea that I want to consider but know that I will not be able pursue for a while.

Home Management – Relates to Chapter 7

1. As indicated by my earlier story in this chapter, **do not hesitate to ask your husband to stop off at the store** and get one or two important items rather than you taking twenty minutes just to get everyone in the car and twice as long as necessary to get in the store, get what you need, and come home before everyone takes those unplanned trips to the public bathroom! What you *know* takes only 10 or 15 minutes to accomplish winds up taking an hour of your life that you will never get back. So, while you do not want to overdo it on how much you need at the store or how often you need it, *do* ask for help when it makes sense and your husband is available to step in.

2. Perhaps you have a new baby in the home and you are just drowning in undone housework. If that is the case, **have a trusted and reliable homeschooled high school student come to your home one afternoon a week to play with your children and take care of them** so that you can complete tasks that are always eluding you. I say reliable homeschooled student because often a typical neighborhood teenager who is even considered to be a "good kid" may bring immodesty or unwanted technology into your home, missing the whole point of what they are supposed to be

modeling with your child. So, keep in mind that paying a homeschooled high school student a fair babysitting rate is much more economical than hiring a cleaning company to come in, and your children will enjoy the change of pace and benefit from their good example. By having this help weekly or at least twice a month, you will be relieved to know that such a time is coming, and you can plan on using that time for projects or tasks you cannot seem to otherwise accomplish.

3. If your kids are old enough, **put them to work around the house** by assigning them either daily or "one-other" tasks that they can do. Essentially, if they can handle the job, you need to let them do it so that they can regularly train to perform new tasks, increasing their responsibilities as they age. The result might not be as perfect as you want but let them do it anyway. They will receive a sense of satisfaction and over time they *will* get better at it. Praise them and thank them along the way, even finding opportunities to give them extra rewards as the quality of their work and cheerfulness of their disposition warrant it. When you do want them to learn a new task, do not just throw them into it "cold turkey". First, have them see you do it. Then do it with them. Next, have them do it while you watch them on a couple of different occasions. Only then are they capable of doing it mostly unsupervised. Also, make sure to say to them, **"When you think you are done with that task, come and get me so I can check it."** This statement has done wonders in our home to build personal responsibility and to ensure that they have finished the task before they come and get Dad or Mom to check them. It also reduces the possibility of distractions so that they do not go off and do something else, knowing they need to get a "thumbs up" first. In chapter six, we already discussed *Choreganizers*, so use an extra tool like this if you think it will help you communicate your child's responsibilities to them. However, you could also just use the "daily task" versus "one other" list provided in Appendix B and simply modify it to fit what your child is expected to do on a regular versus a rotating basis. Another option for assigning tasks is to put note cards into envelopes that have a "basic" or "one other" written on it. Then, when it is time to do such work, they can choose an envelope to select whatever task they are going to do. Whichever tool or method you use, make sure you can work with it every day and that it is not too much of a hassle to administer.

"When you think you are done with that task, come get me so I can check it."

4. Related to the idea of cleaning tasks, **give yourself grace on your weekly chores and do not try to clean every part of your house every week.** Once a month, we give the house a good cleaning, making sure to vacuum and dust everything. However, the other weeks, I just focus on the basics, like cleaning all the bathrooms, the kitchen, and the floors as well as the furniture in the main common use areas. If I get to more areas, great! But if it does not happen, then that is okay too. The boys are always responsible for doing their own rooms and school areas, but I know that at least once a month, I will get in there with them and make sure that they are not missing key areas.

5. You have probably heard the saying, **"a place for everything and everything in its place".** Another time saver that relates to number three above is to make sure, then, that you have a well-organized home and that every member in the family does their part to keep it that way. There should always be "a place for everything". Allow your home to get reasonably messy during the day. Then, at a certain time during the day, "everything should be in its place." In our home, this time comes usually right before dinner, except for any in-process projects that can stay out until the next day or longer, if necessary. When they were younger, one boy usually helped to set the table on a rotating basis while the others picked up common areas. Each boy was also responsible for picking up their own room. If they had enough time after doing this and before dinner, they played outside, exercised, or enjoyed a game together. That way, after dinner, we spent time doing something as a family. My husband had one-on-one time with one of them, or we just focused on grooming activities before it was time for reading and bed. As teens, their chore charts extended to daily, weekly, and monthly tasks that reflect increasing levels of responsibilities.

6. Related to idea number four above is to have a **centralized "need-to-put away" basket** in a public location. If you have a two-story home, you could locate it on the landing of the stairway as a central drop spot for items that are downstairs that need to go upstairs or vice versa. With building set pieces, game pieces, and so forth floating around the house, this a great way to toss items into a holding spot so that they do not get lost or sucked up by the vacuum but then are still put away on a regular basis without taking that exact moment to put it in its final destination. I usually have the boys work together on a weekly basis to clear out whatever is in there as a required precursor to our Friday movie night or some other important event or outing.

7. If your "one-other" activity involves a trip outside the home to the grocery store, library, or doctor's office, either make sure to **put on a crock pot meal or simply stop by the store to pick up a rotisserie chicken for dinner**. Since this type of "one-other" activity is a continuous two-hour commitment, you really do not have time to do meal preparation on such a day, so just plan on doing what I suggested or make a quick fix meal to save time. Another time saver related to shopping is to consider having your local grocery store deliver your food to you. When the boys were younger, I used **Safeway's** service many times, particularly over the summer when I did not want to be hauling perishable food and irritable children around in 115-degree temperatures![339] They sent so many promotional cards and e-mail coupons to me that I do not think I have ever paid a service charge for delivery. I loved being able to specify exactly what I want and how the system kept my order history for easy list management in the future. The pricing is the same as what is offered in the store, but the only drawback is that you cannot use your coupons for on-line orders. Also, be sure to plan and place your order at least the night before you need the items. If you wait until that morning, you will probably miss the cut off window for having it delivered the same day. Fry's and Wal-Mart are additional examples of stores that now offer delivery or pick-up services. Other moms desiring organic options can enjoy a similar delivery service through **Nature's Garden Express**.[340]

8. **Involve your child in the meal preparation duties as much as possible.** Even very young children can help assemble breakfast foods or lunches with a little guidance. Then when they are older, they can take responsibility for preparing it all from start to finish. By the time they are in junior high or high school, they can even prepare an evening meal from beginning to end if you have taken time when they are young to teach them about cooking techniques and safety concerns along the way. As teens, each of our sons is responsible for cooking one family meal a week.

9. **When you or your child exercise independently, take that same time to expand your minds as well**. One can easily read a book while using a recumbent bike, making the time pass before you know it. On a treadmill, you or your child can listen to an audio book or lecture while getting a good twenty-minute walk done. Also, if your exercise equipment is located near a DVD player, you or your child can watch an educational program that relates to some topic that you have been recently studying.

---

[339] http://www.safeway.com
[340] https://www.naturesgardenexpress.com/shop

Community or Ministry Activities – Relates to Chapter 8

1. If you are involved in a regular ministry or community volunteer opportunity, be careful to make sure that the demands of what you do with them and for them do not spill over into the time you have allocated for teaching and daily household duties. Except for a true crisis, **you should not allow yourself to get bogged down by taking phone calls or answering e-mails during the day when you really need to be doing other things.** So, give a few key individuals in your life your cell phone number for emergencies and allow everyone else to send you e-mails or leave voice messages that you can respond to at your convenience.

2. Related to the first point, then, be sure to **address your ministry responsibilities at a time where your fellow volunteers or homeschool support group families can count on hearing back from you.** Often the reason we may feel that we are drowning in our ministry work is because people will be constantly contacting you for updates and answers to questions. Instead, let them know in advance which day or days during the week they can expect to hear from you and then you, making a better use of your time for you both.

Take a moment now to discuss additional time-saving ideas with your mentor for any of the concepts discussed in this section.

_____

_____

_____

_____

_____

_____

_____

_____

_____

_____

_____

_____

_____

_____

Creating the Family Calendar

So now that you have figured out who is running your home, how to make sure all your plans are documented in a central place, how to prioritize and build margin into your schedule, and how to save time throughout your day, it is **time to transfer this information to your paper or on-line calendar**. This is the easy part since you have already done all the mental work by now necessary to determine what deserves a place on your family's calendar and what does not.

During the last week of every month, sit down with your calendar and begin to document what the following month will look like. Follow these steps every time, and you will be pleased to see how much more smoothly your month will flow.

1. First, **write down all of the basic "daily tasks"** that need to take place every day. See page 421 to refresh your memory about these activities and limit your notation on your calendar to one word to describe them like "laundry", "exercise", "dusting", "school", or "music".

2. Next, **write down any appointments** that you need to make sure to attend and keep any associated paperwork with it handy. These could be commitments that are either outside of the home like a dentist appointment or ones where you are expecting people to come to your home. If you ever need to build margin into your schedule to account for dropping your child off at Grandma's home while you go to an important appointment, make sure to note the time on your calendar that you need to leave your home and not just the time of the appointment itself.

3. Third, **note all "one-other" activities that you wish to see happen that month**. When the boys were younger, I used my Monday "one-other" time for financial management duties that have a different associated task every week. Tuesdays were usually for a special organizing or cleaning job or project. Wednesdays were often set aside for ministry work and Thursdays were used for the regular weekly cleaning duties and laundry. Friday's "one-other" time and any extra time during the week were used to stay caught up on digital scrapbooking or extra reading. If you are on a four-day school schedule or your fifth day is light, it is also a good day to schedule outside appointments, music lessons, park outings, or field trips. Now that our boys are older, our "one-other" activities have changed, but the principle remains the same.

4. Fourth, **plan all your meals out for the month**. Regardless of whether you cook a month's worth of meals at a time or not, all of us can reference our three-month meal rotation list discussed in chapter seven and make a note at the bottom of each calendar day what you plan on serving. If you need to start the dinner in the morning because

it is a crock pot meal, make any notes to yourself that are necessary to remember to do it and also to defrost any frozen meats in advance of when you need them.

5. Once you are done with these steps, now it is time to **look at any holidays or special occasions that will be coming up**. Plan meals, gift giving, and special outings well in advance for the basic holidays and birthdays. Take another look at Appendix D for more ideas about things that you can do to plan a special experience for everyone.

6. Next, **set aside separate time to discuss the upcoming month of shared events with your husband.** Note any of his medical appointments on your calendar and make sure you give him plenty of notice regarding any special commitments that he needs to attend or be home for as well. If you wait until the last minute and just expect him to work around your request, neither of you will have a successful or positive experience. In recent years, we have added a "family calendar" using Microsoft Outlook where either one of us can add appointments while also populating our independent calendars. This has helped to avoid miscommunications and ensure that we receive the same details and reminders related to the family event.

7. Lastly, whether using a paper or electronic system, **color code it** so you understand the kinds of activities that are taking up a good deal of your month. Take time to rebalance and rearrange things before a dreadfully overbooked day is upon you.

This all may sound like a lot of busy work, but it really is not since you do it once a month and then spend the rest of your month "living it" rather than second guessing what you should be doing at what time. Also, as you get used to working with your family calendar, you will find that going through these steps will not take nearly as long as you may think. **Your days will be more enjoyable** in the process because all the decisions for what the month holds will already have been made. Post it in a central location and then your entire family will be unified about the scheduled expectations.

In addition, you will also **be modeling good time management skills** for your child. Even very young children can keep a fun calendar in their room that you can help them update or note special events that are coming. By junior high school, encourage your child to maintain their own calendar by asking them to update it regularly so you know what they see as their important priorities in the coming week and month. After all, just as a budget directs your money, a schedule directs your time.

Of course, **exceptions will arise**, and a crisis may come up that you did not expect. However, knowing what absolutely must happen versus what can be postponed until a later time will make you more at ease in processing through such out-of-the-ordinary occurrences. Remember, margin is important!

What other calendar creation steps do you think you need to do? What other ideas does you mentor have about this topic?

_____

_____

_____

_____

_____

_____

Detailed Homeschool Schedules

Now that you have the family calendar figured out, it is time to put some separate "meat" on the "bones" of the word "School" that you have noted. So, **for your child's school schedule**, ask yourself, "How many days will I teach a week? When will I schedule vacations, other trips, and field trips for the family? What time should we begin and end school each day? Do I want to homeschool all your long with periodic breaks built in, or do I want to take two or three months off during the summer to plan and give the children a continuous break? These are just a few of the decisions awaiting you as you construct your schedule.

The tendency is to ask, "Am I doing this right? Am I allowed to do it this way?" However, instead of fretting, realize that there are no "right" decisions to these choices: only what is the best framework for your family. You will also find **what worked well last year will not necessarily work well this year.** So, allow flexibility to work in your favor by having the freedom to navigate around illnesses, to account for special seasons, and to cope with unexpected life events. Also incorporate flexibility by taking advice from "Ms. Frizzle" of the *Magic School Bus* series: "Take chances, get messy, and make mistakes!" Be open, approachable, interesting, and efficient, willing to spend more time when they need it in a particular area and to move on when they do not.

Before delving into the specific factors to consider for creating your school schedule, I would like to share a planning idea that will also provide valuable input into your decision-making activities. Several years ago, I realized that moms are either off-the-charts excited for the schoolyear to commence or they view it with dread and trepidation. I have yet to meet a mom who was in the middle! So, if you do take a break between school seasons, consider employing a **"preview week"** before your official launch. Implementing this approach enables not only your child to orient themselves to their new books and tools, but it also gives you additional grace to address issues prior to starting your full schedule. For example, you may realize that you are missing some basic school supplies, forgot to prep certain materials, or experience an issue with a DVD program or other technology-related tool. By easing into school one week prior to your full start date, you and your child can enjoy the transition more by having a lower level of anxiety and a higher level of confidence. So here is a suggested schedule to use for "preview week" when reviewing new materials and tools with your student(s).

- Monday: Review math and foreign language
- Tuesday: Review grammar related subjects (i.e. grammar, spelling, writing, handwriting)
- Wednesday: Review history and any music/art subjects
- Thursday: Review science and any other subjects/skills not yet covered (i.e. typing, chore charts, etc.)
- Friday: Take a last summer blast field trip!

Homeschool Scheduling Decisions	Descriptions
Should we school four or five days a week?	If you would like to have Fridays available for doctor's appointments, private lessons, library trips or just to have lighter load to wrap up assignments and finish for the week, then be prepared to have a very focused and structured homeschool environment the other **four days**. Those wishing to have a greater degree of flexibility throughout the week can simply take the **full five days** of school.
What time of day will we begin lessons?	Again, think back to the principle of "beginning with the end in mind". If there is a specific time of day you wish to have everything done by, consider the number of school hours that need to be completed for everything to be done by that time. In earlier years, most of our boys were early risers so we do better if we get the high concentration work done first. **Each boy used an alarm clock** during the school year that was set for 6:30 a.m. or so. This gave them time to get up, groom themselves, make their beds, and pull out the books and things that they will need to use that day. Everyone was then ready by 7:00 a.m. for breakfast and we then do devotionals and get ready to "hit the books" by 7:30 a.m. or so. This allowed us to get math, language work, and music done before lunch, leaving them with the "humanities" like science or history to do after lunch along with some literary reading and occasional art projects. Our youngest still pretty much follows this routine, while our other son gets up even earlier now (about 5:00 a.m.!) to start school and music practice. He just likes it that way! While this may seem too structured for you, it works for us. So find a schedule that works for you and your child and then stick with it.
Will we do school year-round or on a traditional, "summer off" schedule?	Some families successfully school all **year around** with significant breaks built into each quarter and particularly around holiday times. The **advantage** to this approach is that your child does not lose important skills during an excessively long break. On the other hand, there is an **advantage to taking two or three months off** during the summer so that you can plan for the coming year, work on major house projects, get doctor appointments done, and your children can participate in summer programs like VBS and swim lessons without feeling the pressures of a full school load. Families with this approach usually have some drill work and other activities over the summer to keep reading, math, and language skills sharpened.

Another task that will help you determine your family's answers to these scheduling questions is to **look at the curriculum you wish to accomplish in the coming year.** Take the number of lessons and divided it by the number of school weeks you think you will teach this year. See how many of those lessons need to be accomplished each week to meet your family's scheduling goals and then compare that with another option and see which one appeals to you more (i.e. four-day versus five-day or year-around versus summer-break scheduling).

Once you have wrestled with these basic questions, it is time to **look at the actual work your child will be doing this academic season.** Over the years, I have tried many different approaches to school scheduling: some because I was not sure of what I wanted and others because my children's ever-changing maturity levels and needs. I have looked at various ready-made schedules on the market many times, but I have never been satisfied with what is out there, mostly due to their inflexible nature.

Thus, I have been mostly happy with what I developed on my own, using **Microsoft Excel** as my tool. I have always kept some sort of log or list showing what I was going to do with them each year, even when they are young. But I did not keep a detailed log of their day-to-day work, showing a week at a time until about 5th grade. However, beginning in third grade you can provide them a daily schedule and start to help them build an awareness of what it takes to successfully manage through a day's worth of school. So, although you will still want to consider their learning style when you decide what scheduling approach works best for your family as discussed in chapter four, here are some general guidelines that may prove useful to you when you consider your child's age, learning style, and maturity level.

"Season"	Scheduling Tool
Little Ones	No formal schedule is needed. Just keep a list of resources you used with any additional information that will help you remember what you did if you have additional children that will come behind them.
K-2nd Grade	Keep a list of the curriculum you will use and the books you will read this year with your young child. If you have an SL (Structured Learner) and they really like to check things off a list, consider listing just the subject names so that they can mark off each day without logging specific assignments.
3rd – 6th Grade *(See the end of this chapter for samples of a daily assignment list or a detailed weekly assignment list.)*	During this season, especially for your ML (Moving Learner), start by using a **visual scheduling board** that they can manage, showing what subjects they are going to do and providing them a place to store their assignment papers they need to do as well as their completed ones. See our private Facebook group for instructions on making one with a tri-panel foam board. As they move through this season, you can also choose to present your child with a **daily assignment list** that they can then reference throughout the day as they budget their time. Create these in a workbook fashion, assigning each day to a new worksheet so that, after they are done with the year you will have an entire year's worth of assignments completed that can then be used for any subsequent children you have. Towards the end of this season, transition your student to a **detailed weekly assignment list** so they can begin to learn how to budget their time throughout the week. Again, create one week per worksheet and you will have an entire year's worth of assignments completed by the end of the year.

	By junior high, they will continue using a **detailed weekly assignment list** so that by high school, they will be comfortable making up their own schedule. Some curriculum options even provide such a detailed list for you, such as My Father's World or Sonlight. They will be able to do this because you or their curriculum provider will simply give them a rundown of what needs to be completed by the end of the week and then they will need to come up with the plan to make that happen. As they **shift to independent scheduling**, you will find that some children will work hard to get everything done in three to four days whereas others prefer to spread
Jr./Sr. High	their work evenly throughout the five-day week.

Essentially, the more you involve your children in the daily management of their schedule as they grow, the more independent they will become by the high school season. Also, **continually reinforce to your child how their rewards and privileges are directly tied to the quality of their schoolwork** and see how motivation soars!

On pages 445-446, I have provided you an idea of how you can put together either a daily task list or a week's worth of detailed plans for your child to accomplish. It may seem like a lot of work to put these together, but it will save you much time and frustration during the school week if you just get the pre-planning done either the prior Friday before or Saturday morning, particularly if you are trying to juggle teaching priorities for multiple children.

The first sample is a **simple daily schedule** worksheet that you can create for your child if they are younger and you just want to give them a day's worth of instructions at a time. **This sample was right from a schedule that I used with our oldest son when he was in second grade**. Notice that you can also incorporate daily chore information for them so that they have one place to go to figure out what you expect of them that day. Also note how you do not need to have your child do everything every day and that you can rotate priorities throughout the week. In addition, consider using a highlighter to color what activities should be completed before versus after the lunch hour. Particularly for your AL (Analytical Learner), this will help your child develop wise time management habits while still given them flexibility on how to order their tasks.

The second sample shows you how a **detailed weekly schedule** might look that you can give to your child each Monday morning. It comes from a **Microsoft Excel** workbook file that has 42 lesson "worksheets" in it. This sample is from the 25th week of school that our oldest son did during 6th grade. Notice how the details are much greater and you can also log time requirements for each area so that they do not spend an inordinate amount of their day on any one subject or task. See also how you can record the curriculum book that they are using to complete that subject's requirements, tracking what you used with them during each different year. Again, this is particularly useful guidance for you in later years when you can reuse these schedules for any subsequent children you have.

Make sure that your **generally recommended times and order can vary based on your child's needs**. In our home, for example, you will notice that our oldest son had his math and language related subjects (i.e. "grammar" ones like English, Latin, spelling, writing mechanics, math, and the review portion of his piano) done before lunch whereas the "humanities" subjects like history, science, art, reading, and the working part of his piano practice waited until after lunch. This was what worked best for him during that season. However, your child may do better with a different arrangement, so put together a generally recommended format that best suits your child's needs. Remember that the example schedules on the following pages are just that—examples. Thus, the best tool will be the one that you have the most in put in creating so that you can change it as you need to do so over the years. This desire for customization is what has continually led me back to using a simple spreadsheet format.

Note the features that you would like to have in your school scheduling tool. How does this list of requirements compare to the tool you use now?

The Balanced Homeschooler

Daily Things to Do List
Monday, January 2nd

Topic	Description	Done?
Personal Chores	*Get Dressed, Make Bed, Eat Breakfast, Brush Teeth, Comb Hair, Pick up Room*	
Other Chores	*Feed Fish; Organize and File School Papers; Set Table for Dinner*	
Bible	*Review OT and NT Books of the Bible and the Lord's Prayer.	
Character Training		
Art or Music Appreciation or Spanish		
Music	*Note Reading. *Review piano teacher's notes and practice accordingly. *Work on Joy to the World. *Play 1 of your one-handed jar songs. Your lesson is this afternoon!	
History	*Review/re-read ALL of chapter 19. *Take chapter test.	
Science	*Color polar habitat sheet.	
Math	*Compelete Lesson with Mom. *Complete Exercise 54.	
Spelling	*Copy your locker words from the white board on to the space provided (page 73) and then complete the rest of page 73.	
Handwriting	*Complete page 116.	
Reading	*Make narration pages (Robin Hood and the Saracen Maid). *Continue the "The Boy and His Horse" reading with Mom.	
Grammar	*Complete Grammar Lesson with Mom. *Complete copy work page on brown paper.	
Physical Ed.	*Outdoor playtime. *Practice Karate Routine.	

Schedule Color Codes:	Complete before 9:30 a.m. - HIGHLIGHT YELLOW
	Completed between 9:30 a.m. and Lunch - HIGHLIGHT PINK
	Complete After Lunch - HIGHLIGHT GREEN
	Complete After Dinner - HIGHLIGHT ORANGE

Weekly Schoolwork Schedule - 6th Grade

Topic	Additional Instructions & Information	Monday	Tuesday	Wednesday	Thursday	Friday
EYE THERAPY and HAND BALL	Bring pencil to eyes until you see two of them	20 per day; Brach String	20 per day; Brach String	20 per day; Brach String	20 per day; Brach String	
BIBLE		How To Study Your Bible; NT Reading w/ Family	How To Study Your Bible; NT Reading w/ Family	How To Study Your Bible; Hero Tales Reading w/ Family	How To Study Your Bible; Hero Tales Reading w/ Family	How To Study Your Bible; WOW Reading w/ Family
PIANO - 15 min.	Suzuki - Book 2	Daily Practice - Review Pieces	Daily Practice - Review Pieces	Daily Practice - Review Pieces	Daily Practice - Review Pieces	Full Practice Lesson with Miss Cindy
MATH - 1 Hr.	Singapore 6B - Circles	Ex. 12	Ex. 13-14	Ex. 15-16	Practice 2B	Practice 2C
ENGLISH 5 - 1 Hr.	R&S Book 6	Ex. 83	Ex. 84	Ex. 86	Ex. 85 - Stories (2nd Draft)	Practice Worksheets as Assigned.
SPELLING - 30 min.	Spelling Workout H: Use Webster 1828 dictionary to check origin of words as needed.	Lesson 29 - Complete intro lesson to new lesson. Take warm-up test.	Lesson 29 - Practice and check trouble words; Complete one page	Lesson 29 - Practice and check trouble words; Complete one page	Lesson 29 - Practice trouble words; Complete spelling assignment and take final test.	Complete Bonus Words Assignment; Update Prefix/Suffix Chart and Word Root Chart.
LATIN - 1 Hr.	Memoria Press First Form Latin; Lesson 23	New Lesson Intro.; Recitations; Worksheet 1; Cumulative Vocabulary Review	Worksheets 2 and 3; Recitations with Audio	Worksheets 4 and 5; Recitations with Audio	Form Drill 1st and THEN take Weekly Quiz OR Unit Test	
WRITING, LIT. & HANDWRITING - 1+ Hr.	Winning His Spurs Dictation	Handwriting Page; Figuratively Speaking	Handwriting Page; Figuratively Speaking	Dictation Assignment	(see English)	
LUNCH						
HISTORY - 1.5-2 Hrs.	MOH v. 2; Note any memory dates on your cards!	Complete Pretest; Read Lesson 70 about The Great Khans and the Mongol Invasion of China. Complete a fact card about them. Read Lesson 71 about St. Marco Polo Travels East. Complete a fact card about him. Write a contrast/comparison paragraph about the two great Khans.		Read Lesson 72 about Sir William Wallace and Robert Bruce, "Bravehearts" of Scotland. Write a fact card about them and a paragraph about Marco Polo and his role in opening up knowledge of the east to the western world. Complete Mapwork.	Review history fact cards.	Complete Unfinished Work; Take Test; Prepare Timeline Figures.
SCIENCE - 1.5 - 2 Hrs.	Apologia's Exploring Creation with Astronomy		Read Lesson 7: Mars: Write a paragraph about its features and NASA's attempts to explore it. Q & A with Mom. Read any related chapters in "The Astronomy Book".		Make a drawing of Mars. Complete Assigned Activity.	
PIANO - 30 min.	Suzuki - Book 2	Daily Practice - Working Pieces	Daily Practice - Working Pieces	Daily Practice - Working Pieces	Daily Practice - Working Pieces	
READING - 1 Hr.	History-related titles	Famous Men of the Middle Ages - pp. 159-162	Marco Polo for Kids	Famous Men of the Middle Ages - pp. 153-158		
PE - 30 min.		Treadmill or Bike - 1+ mile	Treadmill and Presidential Fitness Program	Treadmill or Bike - 1+ mile	Treadmill and Presidential Fitness Program	Weekly PE Class - 11:30 a.m.
TYPING PRACTICE - 15 min.		Daily Practice	Daily Practice	Daily Practice	Daily Practice	Daily Practice
DINNER						
CORRECTIONS		Correct any problem work.	Correct any problem work.	Correct any problem work.	Correct any problem work.	Correct any problem work.
ARTS SKILLS & APPRECIATION		Drawing Lesson	Drawing Lesson	Drawing Lesson	Read assigned sections of "Art and Civilization in Medieval Times"	
FREE READING		Marco Polo His Notebook	Marco Polo by Strathloch	Kat and the Emperor's Gift	In Freedom's Cause: A Story of Wallace and Bruce	In Freedom's Cause: A Story of Wallace and Bruce

By the time your child is in high school, work with them on coming up with an **independent system** that will work for both of you to ensure that they stay on track while at the same time communicating to you what was accomplished each week. This can be a manual system or a type written form that they use to track their time and log hours for any self-designed courses. It could also be done through an on-line scheduling tool like **Microsoft Outlook**.

Regardless of how old your child is or whether they are on a daily, weekly, or independent scheduling system, recognize that really any subject that they work through has **three phases** that must be accounted for when figuring out your time allocations.

1. **Phase one is learning.** This is where your child is actively self-learning, or you are teaching them directly. Information is being taken in with the goal of understanding it so that it can be applied or discussed later.

2. **Phase two is producing.** This is the time your child needs to complete written assignments, do experiments, work on projects, etc.

3. **Phase three is crafting.** This is when your child is checking their work or self-editing to make their final paper or product even better. Make sure that your child knows this phase cannot be skipped!

So, when you are allocating time for various assignments, **think about creating enough time in their day to move through these three phases for each subject.** For example, if it takes you fifteen minutes to teach a lesson, thirty-five minutes for them to do the assignment and then ten minutes to check their work or look for opportunities to improve what they have done, allocate one hour for that subject. In some cases, you may even want to have one day where they work on the first two phases and then schedule a different day to work on phase three. This is especially useful when your child is writing a paragraph or essay and needs to have multiple days to complete the assignment.

What other items would you like to be able to track on your child's daily or weekly school schedule? _____

_____

_____

_____

_____

_____

_____

Phase Allocation Time Needed by Subject

Topic	Phase 1 (Learn)	Phase 2 (Produce)	Phase 3 (Craft)	TOTAL TIME NEEDED	Comments
BIBLE					
MUSIC					
MATH					
ENGLISH					
SPELLING					
FOREIGN LANGUAGE					
WRITING					
HISTORY					
SCIENCE					
ART					
READING/ LITERATURE					

Another perspective I would like to share is one that may be useful if you are **teaching multiple levels of children.** Our three boys were on three different levels as youngsters but used the same curriculum publishers for much of what they did. This made it easier on me to teach and smoother on them to transition from one year to the next since the structure of what they did largely remained the same. The key to successful multi-level teaching is making sure that each child can keep moving even if you are not available to every child during every moment of the day. Some of the resources you can employ to help accomplish this goal were covered in the *"Seek Out Time Savers"* section for Homeschooling: timers, recording devices, and even older children to help with some of the teaching priorities of the youngest child.

Using **Microsoft Excel**, I created the "**Gary Homeschool Snapshot Schedule**" and provided it to you as a sample of what our homeschool schedule looked like a few years ago. You will see where I employed some of the previously mentioned time-saving techniques that kept the day moving along. The "snapshot" schedule does *not* have specific assignments on them and does *not* replace the other schedule types discussed that you give to your child. Rather it gives *you* an idea of how you are going to move through the day and what timing instructions to give your child. You can, however, provide a copy of your "snapshot" to your older child so that they understand what your overall priorities are for the day and how they fit into the overall plan. An older child who has this understanding will be more likely to work efficiently with you to help make sure that the overall day is accomplished successfully, especially if they are motivated to help teach a younger sibling and want to make sure they complete their own items on time in order to do this. The "snapshot" also helps you to communicate your overall structure, schedule, and teaching priorities to your husband.

Additionally, note that I have **shaded areas of the schedule** where most of my personal teaching time takes place. It is not that I am unavailable to others during that time. Rather, it is that I am mainly concentrating my efforts and that the other knows that they need to hold their questions, if possible. Encourage your children to skip any difficult items that they have honestly tried to work through but cannot resolve on their own. This way, they do not waste time staying "stuck" and can move on to the next problem or assignment. Then, when you finish with the other child, you can step in and help them resolve their issue.

Also, observe that the time frames given are general ones and that I have **built "margin" into the blocks of time** noted to ensure that the allocations are

The key to successful multi-level teaching is making sure that each child can "keep moving" even if you are not available to every child during every moment of the day.

realistic. That way, if we run into issues or problems along the way, the entire day is not sent into a tailspin. As the children move through the day, they being to learn that if they are efficient in their use of time, they can experience more breaks throughout the day or keep moving forward to finish the day earlier than expected, leaving more time to pursue other interests.

What other issues and/or possible solutions do you have teaching multiple levels?

_____

_____

_____

_____

_____

_____

_____

_____

_____

_____

_____

_____

_____

_____

_____

_____

_____

_____

_____

_____

_____

_____

_____

_____

Gary Homeschool Snapshot Schedule

This is a Mon.-Th. schedule with "margin" built into each block of time. Friday is used for completing unfinished assignments, extra practice, special projects, music lessons, PE, etc. The shaded boxes indicate where my primary teaching is done during that time. I am available to all three but primarily focus where the shading indicates I am most needed.

START TIME	EVAN-7TH GRADE	JONATHAN-3RD GRADE	SIMON-1ST GRADE
6:30	Wake up, morning routine, and make beds.		
7:00	BREAKFAST, Bible/devotions, and kitchen clean up		
7:30	**Suzuki 2 Book Piano** *Review Pieces Only; Use metronome w/ headphones*	**Singapore Math 3A** *New Lesson or Review*	**Singapore Math 1B** *New Lesson or Review*
7:45	**Teaching Textbooks; Pre-Algebra** *Review previous day corrections and go through New Lesson Intro.*	Continue Math Assignment	Continue Math Assignment
8:15	Continue Math Assignment	**Suzuki 2 Book Piano** *Review Pieces Only; Use metronome w/ headphones*	**Reading Pathways** *Phonics Practice* **OR** *Oral assigned reading; Can be done with Evan if his math is done early.*
8:30	**Spelling Workout - Level H** *Complete Assignment; Tests Given by pre-recorded audio*	**Spelling Workout - Level C** *Complete Assignment; When necessary, tests Given by pre-recorded audio*	**Spelling Workout - Level B** *Complete Assignment; Tests given to Simon in-person or by Evan or Jonathan if they finish early.*
9:00	This extra time can be used to finish a previous assignment or to work on part of a new writing assignment.	**Zaner Bloser Handwriting - 3** *Complete Assignment* **OR** *do Copywork/Dictation as assigned*	**Zaner Bloser Handwriting - 2M** *Complete Assignment* **OR** *do Copywork/Dictation as assigned*
9:15	BREAK		
9:30	**Rod & Staff - English 7** *Listen to Review Questions on Audio; Complete New Assignment*	**Rod & Staff - English 3** *New Lesson & Complete Assignment* Work on any assigned Literature summaries or drawings as assigned when English is done.	**Story of the World Volume 1** *Listen to New History Lesson on Audio (Mon./Wed.); Listen to Pre-recorded Story Book by Mom (Tu./Th.)* **First Language Lessons** *New Lesson & Complete Assignment*
10:30	**Memoria Press - 2nd Form Latin** New Lesson Intro. Review vocabulary with Audio	**Memoria Press - Prima Latina** New Lesson Intro. Review vocabulary with Audio	**EXTRA BREAK OR** Narration Drawing for Literature as assigned
11:00	Continue Latin Assignment; Evan to help Jonathan as needed. When finished, do assigned reading until lunch.		**Suzuki 1 Book Piano** Full Piano Practice and Music Theory Game
11:30	LUNCH		
12:30		**Suzuki 2 Book Piano** Scales, Working Pieces, and Theory Review	Coloring Sheets As Assigned (History or Science)
1:00		**Story of the World Volume 3** *Listen to New History Lesson on Audio (Mon./Wed.); Read assigned extra book for History, Science, or Literature (Tu../Th.)*	**Story of the World Volume 1** *Narration work with Mom (Mon./Wed.)* **OR** *New Assignment using* **God's Design for Life: The Animal Kingdom**
1:30	**Mystery of History - Vol. 3** *Read Lesson and/or Complete Assignment (Mon./Wed./Fri.)* **OR** *Read Lesson and/or Complete Assignment/Experiment (Tu./Th.) using* **Apologia's General Science**	**Story of the World Volume 3** *Narration Work with Mom (Mon./Wed.)* **OR** *Chemistry Assignment (Tu./Th.)* using **Adventures With Atoms and Molecules Book I** and **God's Design for Chemistry: Properties of Atoms and Molecules**	Finish any uncompleted work and then take a **BREAK**
2:00	Assigned Reading (Literature, history, or science) **OR** Literature-related writing assignment	Work on finishing any assigned Literature summaries or drawings.	Work on finishing any assigned Literature summaries or drawings.
2:30		Finish any uncompleted work or assigned reading.	
3:00	**Suzuki 2 Book Piano** Scales, Working Pieces, and Theory Review		
3:30	**Memoria Press - Traditional Logic I** New Lesson w/ DVD or Continued assignment		
4:00	DONE FOR THE DAY - Collect and organize materials for next day, free time, extra playtime, exercise, etc.	DONE FOR THE DAY - Collect and organize materials for next day, free time, extra playtime, exercise, etc.	DONE FOR THE DAY - Collect and organize materials for next day, free time, extra playtime, exercise, etc.
4:30			
5:00			
5:30	Evening chores, set table, wash up and prepare for **DINNER**		
7:00	Family time, review items and/or discipleship time with Dad, prepare for bed.		
8:00	Read Aloud Evening Story and/or Free Reading		
8:30	Extra Free Reading; Sleep by 9	Bed time	

One final thought regarding scheduling is for those families who have **babies and toddlers** in the home. When you have both school-aged children and little ones, scheduling can be a very difficult priority to accomplish. However, there are some basic principles that you can follow to make the day go as smoothly as possible.

1. **Still go ahead and make out your child's daily school schedule and your snapshot schedule** as we discussed. That way, when interruptions occur, you know how to direct your older child in what they can do while you are busy with your young one. It will help you and your child both have a sense of confidence about what still needs to happen that day and what they can be doing to continue to move the day along.

2. Most young children are content just to be near mom no matter what she is doing. For your toddler, have a **large play blanket and a box of toys that you pull out only during certain parts of the school day.** A play yard works well too. Make this box special that your child cannot have access to except during school time. You may even want to rotate two or more different boxes throughout the week to keep their interest level up. Special puzzles are a great option as well.

3. **Schedule "room time" or "quiet time".** As your young child takes fewer or shorter naps and the "blanket time" is no longer appropriate or working for you, train them to be content in their room for various periods of time. The door can be open, and they should understand that they have access to Mom if they need her. This is a time where you can have them look at books quietly, listen to an audio story with headphones, or listen to Bible songs or other music softly in their room while they play quietly. Start with ten minutes and then work your way up from there until they can easily spend at least 20-30 minutes doing these quiet activities. Remember that young children will not naturally want to do this in most cases in the beginning, so you need to train them just like you did on their "blanket" time. Be consistent and praise them for being "big boy" or "big girl" that they are now ready for this new experience.

4. **As they get older, have them join you and your older children so they can "do school" too.** Give them copies of coloring sheets or maps that you are working on with your older child so that they can color too, even if they are not really following the lesson. Allow them to be a part of any crafts or reading aloud activities that you do as well. It does not matter that they may not be following much of what you are saying. They just like the closeness and they do pick up on more than you think they will take in as they consistently engage with the family.

5. **Have snacks readily available** for your child during the day. Take the time in advance to make small snack baggies of fish crackers, cereal, etc. so that they are easy to grab as you need them.

6. **Take full advantage of nap time**. When your baby or young child takes a nap, use this time to teach your older child a "high-concentration" subject, like math or language arts.

What other questions do you have about teaching multiple ages of children at once? What other scheduling concerns do you have about teaching your older children while younger children are in the home?

_____

_____

_____

_____

_____

_____

_____

_____

_____

_____

_____

_____

_____

_____

_____

_____

_____

_____

_____

More Chapter Notes...

Chapter 10

Participating in & Running a Local Homeschool Support Group

Likewise, teach the older women to be reverent in the way they live, not to be slanderers or addicted to much wine, but to teach what is good. Then they can train the younger women to love their husbands and children, to be self-controlled and pure, to be busy at home, to be kind, and to be subject to their husbands, so that no one will malign the word of God. Titus 2:3-5 (NIV)

Is a Local Support Group Really Necessary?

Now we have come full circle. We started our time together by discussing the purpose of this manual and its close ties with Paul's instructions to how each member of Christ's' body should live, including those of us who have gained experience as wives and mothers over the years. As we have traveled through this mutual journey, you can see what vast opportunities exist to "teach what is good" and to "train the younger women to love their husbands and children, to be self-controlled and pure, to be busy at home, to be kind, and to be subject to their husbands."

Now it is time to look at one more area of life that usually comes into play at some point in the experience of a typical homeschooler: the role of the local homeschool support group. In the final assessment of things, we can see that the fulfillment of Paul's instructions above cannot be fully realized unless we connect ourselves to other families. More specifically, Christian wives and mothers are directed to make themselves available to encourage and guide women who are not necessarily always younger in age but younger in experience. To that end, then, it is easy to see how the local homeschool support group is intended to play a vital role in providing those connections and mentoring opportunities. Yes, one *can* do it all on their own. However, what is possible is not always beneficial. Consider Paul's words.

> *"Everything is permissible"—but not everything is beneficial. "Everything is permissible"—but not everything is constructive. Nobody should seek his own good, but the good of others. I Corinthians 10:23-24 (NIV)*

So, regardless of whether we homeschool or not, God did not intend for Christian wives and mothers to go through life isolated in their own separate silo of existence. Nor are we to try and "do everything" but are to focus on those things that are "beneficial" and "constructive".

Is a local homeschool support group necessary? My answer to this is "yes" and "no".

Looking back at the question for this section, then, "Is a local homeschool support group really necessary?" **My answer to this is "yes" and "no".** I say "yes" for the obvious reason that participating in such a group provides many benefits, including opportunities to be with other families, creating shared experiences, and encouraging as well as learning from others in the various specifics of home education.

However, I also say "no" because a homeschooling family does not have to be a member of a *formal* support group to create their own support system. I have met many homeschooling families over the years who are not part of a formal group and yet have operated very successfully in their educational and relationship development goals by simply seeking out and creating support opportunities with a few other key families on their own. Either approach works, so it just depends on how comfortable you are taking on more responsibilities yourself versus connecting with families in your community who have already found each other and have established some creative and efficient ways to network on a variety of levels. One way or another, however, it *is* important that you connect with other homeschooling families on a regular basis. No family thrives in a vacuum, and that is especially true for homeschoolers.

Do you think being part of a local group will be beneficial to you or do you simply want to create your own informal relationships with a few other families to serve as your support system? _____

_____

_____

_____

Characteristics and Cautions of a Good Support Group

So, if connecting with an existing group is important, what are not only the opportunities but also the potential cautions that exist that you should be aware of in your search for the right group? Although there are many factors to consider, most of what will drive your decision on what existing group to associate with will largely be based on two things.

First, **choosing a group must be first and foremost tied to your understanding of the group's purpose**. Consider what the group is designed to do, what the religious beliefs of the members are, and how it is set up to function. Compare such findings with what your position is on these points and what your motivation is for even connecting with other people. Are you looking for a greater number of shared learning occasions for your child or just purely social opportunities? What about a group that puts their faith into action by engaging in service projects? On the other hand, maybe your main concern is participating in field trips or perhaps all you care about is that your child can attend a weekly park day or physical education class. Whatever you perceive to be as the "hole" in your family's homeschool experience will set the tone for what you are looking for in a local homeschool support group. So, be careful about jumping into a group that has a very loose (or no) stated purpose since such a vague association can lead to a pattern of idleness and serve as a potential breeding ground for gossip and unproductive interactions.

The second driving factor to recognize in selecting the right group for your family is to know that your **personality will play a big role in your final decision.** If you are more of a structured individual, you will absolutely hate being involved in a group that is loosely run and disorganized. On the other hand, if you are more of a free spirit, the idea of rules, reporting structures, and approval processes will drive you crazy. No format is right or wrong, but you must be comfortable with it or you will find yourself dreading events and programs that just do not match the style of how you want to interact with people on a regular basis.

Therefore, now that you understand what the primary drivers are, you can also look to clarify other important areas as well before you make your final choice. Consider asking these questions below and always look for three characteristics in any group you choose: **unity of purpose, clarity of organization, and faithful member commitment**, which will be further reviewed starting on page 467. I have also provided the following information in Appendix C so that you can print out several copies of the "*Homeschool Support Group Interview Form*" as you assess different groups in your local area.

Three important characteristics of any homeschool support group are unity of purpose, clarity of organization, and faithful member commitment.

Homeschool Support Group Interview Form

1. What is the purpose of your group and when were you formed? What is your group's "story of origin", and are you associated with a church? If so, what is the positional statement of that church?

2. What do you require of your members? Do I need to sign a statement of faith, code of conduct, or other such agreement?

3. What is the registration process, and do you charge an annual fee? If so, how much is it and how is that money used? How is money collected for participating in individual events?

4. What are the primary activities that your group does? How does one host or organize and event?

Program	Y or N?	Description
Park Day		
Field Trips		
Mom's Activities		
Family Activities		
Topical Workshops		
Student Clubs or Events		
Dad's Activities		
Other		

5. How are leadership members selected, and what are their responsibilities? How is accountability assessed?

6. What other processes or programs are unique about your group?

7. Bottom line: How would you say your group demonstrates unity of purpose, clarity of organization, and positive member commitment?

So, take the information discussed previously about what characteristics make up a good support group and ask any potential group about their experience or position on those things. If you are satisfied with their feedback to you, then ask if you can attend a park day or other group event open to seekers to attend so you can check them out and see if they will be a good fit for your family. Pray about it, talk to your husband, and "interview" current members of the group. If you discern that the group would add value to your family's homeschool experience, then make the commitment to sign up for a year.

If not, keep researching until you find one that fits your family's homeschooling support priorities. **If you need help finding an existing group** in your area, contact your state homeschooling support group and they can usually provide you with a listing of active groups in the area along with a summary profile of each one. If you do not know who your local state support group is, contact **HSLDA** directly.[341]

What other qualities in a local homeschool support group do you value? What advice or experiences does you mentor have about this subject?

_____

_____

_____

_____

_____

_____

_____

_____

_____

_____

_____

_____

_____

_____

_____

_____

_____

[341] https://www.afhe.org/resources/support-groups/ - This link provides families with the ability to search on local support groups that are available in the state of Arizona. For information about local groups in your area, see HSLDA's site at http://www.hslda.org/orgs/ and search by your state.

Considerations for Leadership

If you are interested in leadership opportunities, you are either considering starting your own group or **you have a group identified where you wish to serve as a leader.** If the latter describes your situation, then your approach is clear cut. You simply contact the existing leadership of that organization and ask about their overall purpose, policies, registration process, and so forth, if you do not already know what they are.

Will you start your own or join an existing group?

Ideally, you will have already participated with that group for a time before you seek to step into leadership and most of the capable support groups will even require that you be part of the group for at least a year and that you have been homeschooling for at least a year before they can consider you for leadership. **Share with the leadership your intentions** and that you would like to be a part of their team in the future. Then **participate in such a way that they can observe your cooperative, helpful, and positive nature** firsthand so it will be an easy transition process when the right time comes. The leadership team will appreciate your enthusiasm and candor in sharing your plans in advance as the end of the current season approaches and they begin setting plans for the following year.

Also, do not always be stuck into thinking that you need to fit into a pre-existing job. If you really want to host a ladies **BUNCO** night at your home and they do not have such a group now, you can be the one to start it.[342] If you want to have a literature discussion group for your teen and they do not have one, express your interest to do that. Remember that homeschool support groups are made up of homeschooling families. So, the best programs are the ones that members are inspired to take on themselves with little direction needed.

Should You Associate with a Church or Not?

If, however, you are **interested in starting your own group**, there are several key points you will want to keep in mind. The first is that you will want to **consider whether you will associate your group with your local church or if it will just be an informal community group.** I have attended the state conference for homeschool leaders for several years and I can tell you that homeschool groups associated with a church, like the one I used to help run, are the definite minority.[343] Nevertheless, regardless of whether you formally associate your group with your church, take a moment to consider the pros and cons of each potential framework as you make your final decision. I have outlined a summary chart of the following page that generalizes the main differences you will find between running a church associated group versus an informal community group.

---

[342] http://www.bunco.com/
[343] While most groups in my area are considered informal community support groups, some can be associated formally with a local church.

Church "Pros"	Church "Cons"	Community "Pros"	Community "Cons"
Mission of the group is plainly articulated, unity is solid, and accountability processes and escalation procedures are clearly stated and tied to church's overall processes.	Not as easily able to formally participate in "social networking" outlets to promote "conversations" since the appropriateness of content may be questionable and dialogue exchanges reflect back on church's community presence.	Able to set up various social networking outlets easily, such as Yahoo Groups, Twitter, Facebook, and so forth to keep families personally connected.	Purpose of the group and related accountability processes are often unclear, leading to undesirable "group fights" and lack of unity. This can be a particular problem if your group grows quickly.
Operational processes are clearly documented in a policies and procedures document. Operational continuity flows even when leadership changes.	Must exercise caution in partnering with other churches, homeschool groups, or organizations for "joint" events. Philosophy and faith perspectives of that organization must be in line with that of the church's.	Greater flexibility in partnering with other organizations (i.e. churches, homeschool groups, etc.) when planning events, leading to a greater variety of activities than what the group could do alone.	Operational processes are often undocumented, personality-driven, "word of mouth" practices that can be confusing or difficult to replicate when a leader leaves their position.
Able to escalate difficult, unforeseen issues to church leadership for resolution. As an agent of the church, leaders have limited if no personal liability exposure.	Often not able to restrict membership, sometimes leading to participation of families who are not traditional homeschoolers (i.e. virtual academy, public-school-at-home program families)	Can determine very specific participation guidelines, often requiring members to sign a "statement of faith" ensuring that all members are "on the same page" about the group's purpose.	Must rely on resolution of excessively difficult circumstances within leadership team. Possible exposure to personal liability.
Able to provide brochure and other publication services for a low cost.	Can seem more impersonal at times since these groups tend to be larger than community groups.	Able to have a "tighter" group experience when groups are smaller and more personal.	Must incur publication expenses at a retail cost.
Group activities can be covered by the church's insurance policy and provide legal support when needed.	Proposed events and programs often must go through additional approval processes, causing potential delays.	Greater flexibility to implement proposed events and programs more quickly.	Need to consider securing independent group insurance and legal support.
Can process registrations and related fees easily through church's on-line system. Group works off a budget run through church and is easily managed. Also able to easily manage related e-mail lists.	Need to ensure that church will allow non-church members to participate in order for it to be a true "outreach" ministry. Although not really a "con", leadership team must be church members.	Able to set participation guidelines without consideration to church policies. Leadership team may or may not be made up of members from the same church, which may be a "con" or a "pro" depending on your view.	Need to come up with funding for an independent website and on-line registration process. Decisions must be made on how to handle money and to budget responsibly. Managing e-mails lists are often a labor-intensive process.
Access to meeting space on church's campus and related resources are readily available.	Not all members are "on board" with having a general outreach focus in addition to their homeschool focus.	Group does not need to incorporate general "outreach" activities and can just stick to what directly supports their homeschooling efforts.	Often times pressed to secure large meeting spaces for various events and meetings.

Remember that the information I shared with you on the previous page are just general observations and what I consider a "pro" or a "con" of one versus the other based on my own experience. These thoughts may not be your experience, or you may not see a "con" I listed as a negative or vice versa. Even so, you have probably found the comparison to be useful as a good starting point and can build on it as you seek to determine which structure is ultimately right for you and your family. Also, as more groups apply for 501c3 status, a blending of some of these "pros" and "cons" listed can lead to yet a whole new category of groups to consider.

One last point to realize is that **some churches do not *want* to support a homeschool group in their church,** fearing that it will offend non-homeschooling members or send a message that the church believes all parents should homeschool. If this is your struggle, assure your church leaders that serving the needs of homeschoolers in the community in no way passes judgment on non-homeschooling families, but simply gives the church one more avenue to reach out to others who might not otherwise ever darken their doorstep. It is no different than offering other specialized support groups that they probably already have in place. Help them see the general outreach benefits of it as well, including the notion of supporting school choice for families, and you will usually be able to come to an agreement with your church leadership about the mutually beneficial nature of the ministry you would like to help create.

So, in general, associating yourself with your local church can provide several resources and support that you would not otherwise have access to use while also providing a solid structure and mission from which to build. Yet the tradeoff usually costs you somewhat in areas such as decreased flexibility and difficulty in personally connecting with your families. Conversely, community groups tend to relate families on a more personal level while at the same time possessing greater flexibility. However, they often fall short on establishing a clear vision and implementing defined operational and communication processes, which can make them more personality-driven than process-driven organizations.

Will you associate your group with your church or not?

Common Considerations for Any Group

The second point to consider is to **be aware that there are some issues common to either type of group**. One of the biggest concerns I have found in either setting is this odd need for homeschool support groups to specifically seek out people to fulfill certain jobs in the group even though no one seems to want to do it. Inevitably, when you pressure moms into volunteering for a job they do not want, everyone will have a poor experience. Instead, allow your members to understand what types of areas are available by giving them involvement ideas, but do not expect to have your members jump up and take every slot that you envision filling. Instead, be open to them coming up with involvement ideas of their own and support them to the extent that their idea is in line with your group's mission. In the end, no group should push to offer a program that no one wants to organize. In other words, **if no one wants to run that program or event, simply do not do it!** There is no "homeschool support group law" that says every group should have a park day, put on an academic fair, or host a mom's-night-out event. Eventually, if that experience is important enough to your members, someone will bubble up to take it over. If not, then it probably was not important enough to pursue in the first place, based on your group's purpose and current interests—interests which tend to change over the years as families come and go. Having this **grassroots perspective** on whether things get done or programs get organized also helps to guard against the potentially harmful **consumer mentality** that so many people, including homeschoolers, fall victim to. It is not all about "what the support group can do for me" but how we can work together to create a mutually beneficial experience for everyone.

Another common issue for all groups to wrestle with is **whether to charge a general fee to their members or to keep it free**. While most groups, including the ones I have belonged to, usually do charge a nominal annual fee, covering the expenses of printing materials, hosting a website, and obtaining basic supplies for the year, some groups may not want to do so. If your group is small and very informal, it is perhaps not an issue for you. However, if you plan on allowing the Lord to grow your group, consider the benefits of having a small charge, like $15-25 per year per family. Charging a fee associates value to what you are doing and tends to "weed out" those who are just looking to absorb what they can and not positively contribute in any way to the group's mission. Also, it will give you some flexibility in being able to host periodic events for your families, whether it is at a weekly park day, a parent's meeting, or other such event that is open to all of the families to enjoy. Aside from that, most of what you will do with your group should be a "pay as you go" experience so that members only pay for what they do: workshops, field trips, etc. Be careful, however, to once again counteract a **consumer mentality** from setting in since sometimes members will pay the fee expecting you to set up a countless number of programs for them instead of them playing a vital role in the implementation of such offerings.

One Group: Many Personalities

Next, keep in mind that, in addition to representing a host of different personalities and opinions, **homeschoolers tend to be fiercely independent**. After all, none of us want the government telling us what to teach, how to teach, and when to teach our kids, right?! So be aware that this persona of independence will spill over into any type of support group that you seek to create. While this trait as an excellent one to have when giving your volunteers autonomy to create programs or host events, it can sometimes be a characteristic that is tricky to navigate.

Be careful about having a group that requires minimum involvement expectations on organizing events or makes participants volunteer for roles that they are neither skilled nor interested in doing. If you take this tact, your group meetings will probably be very short indeed since you may find yourself sitting in your living room all by yourself! Instead, give your families the freedom they need to be involved within the context of the group's policies and structure, when and where they can, recognizing that everyone goes through seasons where they must pull back or even vanish for a while. Eventually, many of these families come back when the time is right, and they are even better for it—both for themselves and for the group itself.

On the other hand, if you have a family whose tendency for independence is so disruptive to the group such that it has turned into an issue of control, you had best nip that in the bud as soon as possible. So, **decide in advance how you will handle group membership and what your practice will be in working with difficult families so that no one is surprised on the back end when actions must be taken.**

In the group I previously worked with, our leadership team consistently applied the Matthew 18:15-17 passage discussed earlier in chapter seven. On the rare occasion when we had an issue, we worked with the person one-on-one first. That usually was enough to handle it. However, if that did not resolve the issue, then we worked with the person along with additional leadership team members as "witnesses" and for support. If that still did not appropriately resolve the problem, then we may have brought in the church pastor to whom we were responsible. Though it did not happen often, we did have to deal with some difficult issues over those dozen years that required the use of this entire process—even one time needing to completely remove a volunteer from their position.

So, when starting your own group, try to anticipate difficult issues like this and clarify expectations to your families in advance. This is a point that clearly makes a homeschool group operating as an extension of your church a benefit. Even families who are involved in your group but are not members of your church need to understand that they have indeed placed themselves under your church's headship to the extent that they participate in a ministry offered by your church.

We're All in This Together

Finally, emphasize to your families that all members and leaders are homeschooling families before anything else, and **the home education of our own children needs to remain the top priority.** Remember that no volunteer is a paid staff member, which can be confusing for member families when your group is associated with a church. Over the years, I had to clarify to people that we who served on the leadership team of the group are not paid employees of the church and that our **time to serve in that capacity was limited**. When push comes to shove, the education of the children and the wellbeing of our families must come before support group priorities.

Similarly, the leadership of a support group should never view their organization as an "us" versus "them" proposition. Rather it should be seen as a God-given opportunity to come alongside other homeschooling families who share many of the same passions and motivations for their family and their child's education as you do. **Therefore, the difference between you and a member family is only that your experience and leadership skills can help them meet the educational and spiritual development goals that they have for their family, which may be otherwise unattainable for them.** That is why we serve. That is why we lead. That is how we show the love of Jesus. That is what ministry is all about. Remember that someone most likely mentored you and showed you the way early on in your own homeschooling journey. So, as a leader in the homeschool community, now is the time to "pay it forward" to someone else in a manner that is loving, encouraging, challenging, and confident.

What other common considerations does your mentor suggest you look at before deciding what your role in leadership should be? What is motivating you to want to serve in this way?

_____

_____

_____

_____

_____

_____

_____

_____

_____

_____

_____

_____

_____

Building a Strong Support Group

Building a strong group does not necessarily mean that you need to have a large one or one that offers every activity under the sun. As long as there is **unity of purpose, clarity of organization, and faithful member commitment** in the inception and facilitation of the group, you will have the opportunity to positively impact your family as well as the lives of other homeschoolers in your community.

Unity of Purpose

This characteristic is the single most important one of the three. **If the leadership team does not have unity of purpose, then everyone might as well pack up and go home**. Unity must be present not only in the purpose that the group exists to fulfill but also in the way it is fulfilled. The leadership team must commit in advance that, while they may not always agree on every point of discussion, they can agree to disagree on points of opinion and still come to a **general consensus** in the end. Decide ahead of time that points that have a scriptural foundation must be biblically resolved in a unanimous manner while other decisions based purely on opinion and common sense can be decided democratically. Remember that, just like we discussed way back in chapter one, **your mission should remain constant even though your strategies to fulfill it will change.**

Closely tied to this point of unity is the **selection of leadership team** members. Be sure to specify and document early on what the process and requirements are for serving in a leadership capacity. Consider even going so far as to write **job descriptions** so that when that person leaves the leadership team, someone else can easily step into their shoes without reinventing the wheel.

Make sure to also **specify performance expectations**. If you are associated with a church, make sure that all key volunteers on the leadership team are church members in order to avoid conflicts of interest and disharmony later on. If your group is a community one, then decide whether you are going to appoint them or allow voting for representation on the leadership team. Also decide and agree upon in advance what is going to be the process if there is a leader who is not fulfilling their agreed-upon responsibilities or is doing so in an inappropriate manner. Even consider having your new leaders fill out and sign a volunteer application that allows them to acknowledge their duties for the year while ensuring that if they need to leave their position that they will help to transition things as smoothly as possible.

Clarity of Organization

This concept is all about the ease with which your group executes its strategies including programs, events, communications, and so forth. When there is clarity of organization, members and leaders alike understand the structure of the group: how it operates and communicates, how registrations and money are handled, how to address problems, and how to organize events. So, **consider writing up an operational manual** to specify processes and to provide your leaders with the proper tools they need to be successful in their roles. You can include any job descriptions mentioned previously as well as guidelines that should specify any important policies and procedures such as the following list of examples. Also specify how your group will handle finances, including budget responsibilities and the tracking of payments for events and registrations. Sample forms that may be useful to you for clarifying some of the areas noted below are provided for you in Appendix C.

1. **Marketing Items:** Whether you have a flyer, a brochure, or even a website set up to tell others about your group, time will need to be spent thinking about the "message" you wish to give to the homeschoolers in your area. Provide your information to the state organization as well and they can also help you get the word out about your group.

2. **Planning Events**: Whether they are home-hosted or held at a public facility, events that involve the whole group take a certain amount of pre-work and communications. Provide a checklist that helps your volunteers to work through basic questions that will help the planning and communications that are sent to the group. Take special note of the **"Event Planner Form"** provided in Appendix C on pages 541-542.

3. **Signups**: It is good to have at least a generic sign-up form available that you can have at a moment's notice when you have a volunteer who needs to gather the names of moms interested in helping with an upcoming event or program.

4. **Medical Release Form:** In the group I led, we generally discouraged members from hosting events that are of a "drop off" nature. However, sometimes it is an issue that must decisively be dealt with by the leadership. So, if you do sponsor any events or classes that will have the parents drop off and leave their children for any period of time, have a release form on file for that child in case of any emergency that takes place during that time. Regardless of whether your group is associated with your church, ask the legal department at your local church for a copy of what they use for their other youth programs and see if you can adapt it to your purpose.

5. **Background Check Form:** Related to number four, if you allow your group to sponsor an event that allows children to be placed into the supervisory hands of another adult, consider having

these adults background checked. This process is easy to facilitate through a church setting since all volunteers who work independently with children must usually submit to a background check in most churches these days. So just ask them for a copy of their standard form that is used. However, having this done in a community group can be more difficult and the expense of it can be hard to absorb. Again, to save grief later on, consider in advance your group's policy on "drop off" programs before any of these types of events are scheduled.

Related to organizational structure is how you will **communicate with the group.** It is usually not practical to communicate with your families through any other medium but e-mail or a private social media site, but you could also simply ask them to regularly visit a website that you have in place if you would rather do it that way.[344] If your group shares information about its members with each other, be sure to put in place a guideline that clearly states the **appropriate use and privacy** of such family information. You would not want your support group's list to be given to a vendor who will inappropriately solicit them or used for someone's personal political purposes. Remember that the families in your group share their information for purposes of support in their homeschooling journey and the sharing of their private information should be limited to the member families.

Always apply the principle to your communications that you will **never put anything in writing that you would not want your pastor to read,** regardless of whether or not your group is associated with your church. When handling difficult issues, pray about it first and even sleep on it if necessary. Then try first to resolve these issues over the phone or in person since e-mail communications can be easily misconstrued and taking out of context. At the same time, e-mail does work well for follow-up and to create a document trail. Be **firm but respectful** when confronting a member on a sensitive issue and, above all, be biblically consistent in the decisions that you and the rest of the leadership team makes. Finally, whenever you are facing a new issue that you have not handled previously, take it to the leadership team first before you jump to conclusions about how to respond; for "two heads are better than one" in most cases and there are always at least two perspectives to the same problem.

Faithful Member Commitment

This final idea of faithful member commitment embodies the attitude that members have about their involvement in your support group. Are they generally friendly and open to newcomers or are they more satisfied with sticking with the original families and do not seek to expand

---

[344] https://mailchimp.com/ - Great FREE option for groups to use when sending out professional e-newsletters or event notifications to their members.

their reach beyond them? Do the members communicate with each other in a positive and constructive manner or do they tend to slip into patterns of gossip, cliques, and critical words? While there are no perfect groups, members can certainly make every effort to embody what the group is all about in a way that is simultaneously **God-honoring and productive** to members and potential members alike. Commend members when you see them going the extra mile to be a peacemaker and support your other leadership volunteers when they need to have a sensitive conversation with someone.

However, no matter how hard you may try to avoid it, there will be **times when difficult attitudes will surface** to the point where it becomes disruptive and negative to the group. To address this, always take the approach to calmly remind your families what the purpose of the group is all about and how they are welcome to communicate comments and escalate concerns directly to you or other members of the leadership team. Otherwise, they may continue to only aimlessly complain about one thing or another, never getting to the root of the matter while at the same time negatively affecting other families. Usually when this happens, there may be something else going on inside their home or personal life that you are not aware of, and their negativity within the group is a way of coping with these kinds of unrelated issues. If you think someone needs help or counseling, connect with your local church to point them to the appropriate resource rather than trying to handle it yourself.

Also, although it is every family's individual choice, generally **discourage your families from being a member of multiple support groups**. While families can certainly benefit from partaking in several on-line informational groups, having families who have one foot in one group and one in another is just like trying to honor membership at two different churches; it does not work well and can quickly become disruptive and lead to scheduling conflicts. Instead, help your families to work through what their most important needs are. If they really want a group that is structured like a co-op and your group is not focused on arranging academic classes for families, redirect them to a group that may be more suited to their needs. If they really want to do a

It is better to have multiple groups out in the community doing a really good job at serving homeschoolers in their own unique way than it is to try and discourage people from leaving your group and finding what they really want and need for their family.

myriad of field trips but your group is limited to park day activities, help them find a different group that will fulfill their desired experience or even give them some guidance on how to start their own group. It is better to have multiple groups out in the community serving homeschoolers well in their own unique way than it is to try and discourage people from leaving your group and gaining what they really want and need for their family. This is especially evident when unity among groups is key for a common purpose, such as accomplishing legislative goals at the state and even national levels. Thus, members who participate in their group of choice in a positive manner will promote shared purpose and cooperation for the whole body of homeschoolers.

Lastly, remember also that, just as within your own families, **you cannot be all things to all people,** so do not even try to do it! No matter what the focus or structure of your group is, you will never make everyone happy. However, did you notice how many times I used the words "in advance" or "ahead of time" in this chapter? So, you *can* ensure that your group has a positive experience with each other by setting expectations and communicating how the group is set up **in advance**. You will not avoid difficulties altogether, but you will minimize them to a great extent if you take a preemptive and proactive approach.

For more resources on helping to start and run a successful homeschool support group, visit Carol Topp's website called **Homeschool CPA**.[345] There you will find resources on organizing co-ops, managing the business of a homeschool support group, and considerations about the IRS and its role in relationship to your group. Other resources for state and other types of homeschool leaders on a national basis can be found through **Alliance** or **HSLDA** via their **annual leadership conference**.[346]

What other elements do you think are necessary to build a strong support group? How formal or informal do you wish to be about the way that your group will operate? Ask your mentor for input on this subject as well.

_____

_____

_____

_____

_____

_____

_____

---

[345] http://homeschoolcpa.com/
[346] https://www.achel.org/login/index.cfm; http://conference.hslda.org/

More Chapter Notes...

Appendices

This page is left blank intentionally

Appendix A:
Part I Forms

This page is left blank intentionally

Homeschooling Approach Planning Sheet

Approach	What I like about this approach…	What I do not like about this approach…	Rank Top 3	What More information do you need? What book(s) will you read?
Text-Book				
Cultural Literacy				
Principle				
Classical				
Common Sense				
Living Books or Charlotte Mason				
Lifestyle of Learning or Relaxed				
Eclectic				

This page is left blank intentionally

Homeschooling Curriculum Planning Sheet by Approach

Highlight Curriculum you are considering by "Approach"	*Can I deliver it CONSISTENTLY based on its structure?*	*Can I interact with it CONSTANTLY, maintaining a high level of interest?*	*Am I CONFIDENT in its quality, benefits, and value?*	*Is it COMPREHENSIVE enough to meet our needs?*
Textbook ▪ A Beka ▪ Alpha Omega ▪ Bob Jones				
Cultural Literacy ▪ Core Knowledge Program				
Principle ▪ Noah Plan Curriculum Guides				
Classical ▪ Trivium Pursuit ▪ Well-Trained Mind ▪ Mystery of History ▪ Tapestry of Grace ▪ Veritas Press				
Common Sense ▪ Dr. Ruth Beechick ▪ Debra Bell ▪ Gayle Graham				
Living Books or Charlotte Mason ▪ Sonlight ▪ My Father's World ▪ Andreola or Levison's Books ▪ Diane Lopez				
Lifestyle of Learning/Relaxed ▪ Hewitt				
Eclectic ▪ Christianbook.com ▪ Rainbow Resource ▪ Cathy Duffy ▪ Booklist Books ▪ Library				

This page is left blank intentionally

Homeschooling Curriculum Planning Sheet by Subject

Highlight Curriculum you are considering by "Subject"	Can I deliver it CONSISTENTLY based on its structure?	Can I interact with it CONSTANTLY, maintaining a high level of interest?	Am I CONFIDENT in its quality, benefits, and value?	Is it COMPREHENSIVE enough to meet our needs?
Math				
Language Arts • Phonics/Reading • Spelling • Grammar • Logic				
Writing • Handwriting • Concepts				
Literature				
History				
Science				
Foreign Language				
Art & Music				

This page is left blank intentionally

What Learning Style Does My Child Exhibit?

Characteristics	Moving Learner "outside the box"	Structured Learner "inside the box"	Analytical Learner "staring at the box"	Community Learner "talking to the box"
Setting Goals	Give your ML the primary "digestible" sections that they will be expected to perform each day but not to the level of detail that you would give to your SL. Set short-term, even daily goals for them.	Keep goals tangible and clear. SL's like to understand the details but are not always as long-term in their thinking as you may assume. Instead, give your SL monthly goals.	Share yearly goals with your AL with the "big picture". Demonstrate how each subject ties to those goals. AL's like to know that each assignment they are doing is purposeful. Set Monthly or bi-monthly goals.	Usually not concerned with plans or goal-setting. So help them understand the importance of meeting short-term goals by tying them to their social interests.
Schedules	Reveal on a need to know basis each day when younger. By middle years, give a physical chart that they can update daily.	SL's love to check things off so give a daily written schedule with flexibility on order and timing of completion.	Give a weekly schedule with flexibility but be sure to follow-up daily to check progress. Help your AL see how to manage their time wisely.	Do not give a formal schedule until later years. Do share what they need to do daily and tie it to their extra-curricular interests.
A Typical Day…	Incorporate physical teaching methods when needed. Include plenty of breaks and allow various "locations" for school.	Provide a single, quiet, undistracted setting. Be prepared to assign very specific tasks since "depth" may not be your SL's strength.	Allow the "mad scientist" in your AL some freedom to be somewhat scattered in their space as long as progress in learning organizational skills and subject content are evident.	Give your CL the opportunity to present their work in front of an audience or one-on-one with different visitors regularly. Use video technology to share progress outside of your home.
Subject Perspectives	Appreciates creative subjects and the arts. Great at observing information. Utilize project forums like science or history fairs to increase interest in difficult subjects. Sports, etc. can be great motivators.	Likes subject with clear cut "answers" like grammar, math, and languages. Dislikes subjectivity and assessing material past the typical answers. Motivate with participation in local "bee" competitions.	Partial to math, logic, and science. Likes to explain more than discuss answers to other subjects from various angles. Allow your AL to become involved in a robotics or chess club as a great motivator.	Enjoys creative subjects but not so "hands-on" as an ML. Able to excel at most any subject. Social clubs, field trips, and community service activities are great motivators for the people-oriented CL.
Best Methods to Apply	▪ Kinesthetic and experiential learning activities ▪ Visual ▪ Auditory	▪ Visual – writing lessons on a white board to promote note taking and creating own reference cards ▪ Drill or memory work	▪ Visual – diagram or draw out lesson information for math, grammar, spelling, etc.	▪ Auditory - delivering lessons, record drill activities, audio books ▪ Role playing ▪ Connect non-public study habits to future public presentations
Overall Strengths	▪ Creativity ▪ Enthusiasm ▪ Flexibility ▪ Physical Ed. ▪ Social Skills ▪ Observation Skills	▪ Organization ▪ Time Mgmt. ▪ Self-control ▪ Efficiency & Details ▪ Independent Learning	▪ Focused & Logical ▪ Thoroughness ▪ Independent Learning ▪ Technical Subjects	▪ Excellent Communicators ▪ Creativity ▪ Confidence ▪ Social Skills ▪ Public Presentations
Potential Weaknesses	▪ Organization ▪ Long-term focus ▪ Planning ▪ Self-control ▪ Independent Learning	▪ Depth ▪ Flexibility ▪ Subjective or Opinion Subjects ▪ Social Skills	▪ Organization ▪ Creativity ▪ Time Mgmt. ▪ Efficiency & Details ▪ Literature & Writing ▪ Social Skills	▪ Focus ▪ Thoroughness ▪ Independent Learning
Child's Name				

This page is left blank intentionally

Portfolio Contents Checklist

Portfolio Contents for _____ *(child's name)*	Notes Section Check When Completed
11. Include any **grade summaries** that you have written for your child. For each of our boys, I prepare a tri-fold report that has the look and feel of a "grade card". It summarizes each of the subjects they completed that year with what grade I assigned to it along with a note on each one for any "areas for development". It makes a great discussion tool to utilize with your husband as well as your child when encouraging them about what they did well that year while looking towards what will be the focus of the development or improvement for the next year.	
12. Include photo copies of the **title** and **Table of Contents pages** from each text used to serve as a kind of syllabus for what was covered that year and what materials were used. Check subjects off when you are done: History Science English Math Logic Foreign Language Spelling Handwriting Writing Other:_____	
13. Keep at least copies of the child's **major tests and exams** for all subjects to show progress and achievement in each area.	
14. Keep at least copies of all of your child's **completed written reports and outlines** that you know took a certain amount of effort to do that is representative of the child's abilities.	
15. Include **special history and science projects or experiments** that your child completed. **Include photos** of related events or large projects that you will not keep for the long term. After all, most homes do not need to have three different models of the solar system or will not keep Viking ship models or adobe home replicas forever!	
16. Include any **formal booklists of literature** that they read that year that you wish to track for your child.	
17. Include a section for keeping information about **field trips or other special events** that your child was involved with. Event programs or brochures as well as earned certificates or other awards would be included here. Other examples include photos and related materials from concerts or presentations that the child participates in or gives.	
18. Keep copies of any work that your child submitted for writing, poetry, etc. **contests** or documentation about any **competitions** they competed in.	
19. Include result copies of any **standardized tests** that they completed for that year.	
20. Keep a copy of their **affidavit** or other paperwork needed to show that you had legally designated them to homeschool that during that year.	

This page is left blank intentionally

Monthly Reading List

Reading List For: _____   Month: _____

Subject: _____   Grade: _____

Title	Code(s)	Author	Date Completed
WEEK 1:			
WEEK 2:			
WEEK 3:			
WEEK 4:			

R/A = Read-Aloud
I/R = Independent Reading
P = Poetry Selection

Ref. = Reference Only
Int. = Internet Resource
A = Audio Selection

FML = Folktales/Myths/Legends
HF = Historical Fiction
B = Biography

This page is left blank intentionally

Homeschool High School Coursework Transcript - Grade Level Format

Student Name: Joe Student

Student's Parents: Richard and Jane Student

Birthdate: 10/10/1999

Social Security #: 123-45-6789

Address: 123 Main Street

Anytown, State USA

Phone #: 555-555-5555

Grading Scale

A	90+	4 points
B	80-89.9	3 points
C	70-79.9	2 points
D	60-69.9	1 point
F	Below 60	0 points

Cumulative Summary

Graduation Date:	
Cum. Credits:	
GPA Credits:	
GPA Points:	
Cum. GPA:	

Testing

	Total Score	Percentile
PSAT		
SAT		
ACT		

Year 1 - Ninth Grade

Year	Course Description	Grade	Credit	Points

Year 1 Credits; Points
Cum. Credits
Year I GPA
Cum. GPA

Year 2 - Tenth Grade

Year	Course Description	Grade	Credit	Points

Year 2 Credits; Points
Cum. Credits; Cum. Points
Year 2 GPA
Cum. GPA

Year 3 - Eleventh Grade

Year	Course Description	Grade	Credit	Points

Year 3 Credits; Points
Cum. Credits; Cum. Points
Year 3 GPA
Cum. GPA

Year 4 - Twelfth Grade

Year	Course Description	Grade	Credit	Points

Year 4 Credits; Points
Cum. Credits; Cum. Points
Year 4 GPA
Cum. GPA

Our signatures attest that _____ has successfully completed the courses recorded above and that this document serves as his official high school transcript.

_____ (Father/Administrator) - Date

_____ (Mother/Teacher) - Date

Comments:

This page is left blank intentionally

Homeschool High School Coursework Transcript - Subject Level Format

Student Name: _____

Student's Parents: _____

Birthdate: _____

Social Security #: _____

Address: _____

_____

Phone #: _____

Cumulative Summary	
Graduation Date:	
Cum. Credits:	
GPA Credits:	
GPA Points:	
Cum. GPA:	

Comments:

Unweighted Grading Scale & Points		
90+	A	4
80-89.9	B	3
70-79.9	C	2
60-69.9	D	1
Below 60	F	0
Testing		
PSAT	*Total Score*	*Percentille*
SAT		
ACT		

Subject Overview

Subject	Total Subject Credits	Course Titles	Grade Earned	Points Earned	GPA by Subject
Math					
English & Literature					
History & Government					
Science					
Electives					
Total Credits		**Total GPA Credits**			
		Cum. GPA			

Our signatures attest that _____ *has successfully completed the courses recorded above and that this document serves as his official high school transcript.*

_____ (Father/Administrator) - Date   _____ (Mother/Teacher) - Date

This page is left blank intentionally

Homeschool Plans Summary Sheet (Chapters 1 – 4)

Family Vision Statement: _____

_____

_____

_____

_____

Why do I want to homeschool? _____

_____

_____

_____

_____

Will I have my child participate in standardized testing? If so, which one?

_____

_____

_____

Will I participate in a co-op or outsource part of my child's education? If so, who will I network with? _____

_____

_____

_____

What other concerns about socialization do I still have? _____

_____

_____

_____

What will my approach to home education be? _____

_____

_____

_____

What curriculum will I use to adequately address the "Four C's"? List by subject.

Bible:

Math:

History:

Science:

Literature:

English:

Spelling:

Handwriting:

Foreign Language:

Art:

Music:

I have these types of learner in my home: ML, SL, AL, or CL

I am homeschooling these seasons right now: Little ones, K-2, 3-6 G. or Jr./Sr. High

I will use the following tools and methods to teach, keep records and grades:

Appendix B:
Part II Forms

This page is left blank intentionally

Marriage Enrichment Summary Sheet

Marriage Principle	Positive Observations	Areas that Need Improvement	Steps We Will Take
Forgiveness			
Constancy			
Compassion			
Unity			
Intimacy			
Other:			

This page is left blank intentionally

Parenting Priorities for Our Children

I want to instill...	We will do this through these daily interactions and methods.

This page is left blank intentionally

Holiday Tradition Planning Sheet

Holiday or Significant Event	We will celebrate this occasion by establishing these traditions and practices.
Birthdays	
Our Wedding Anniversary	
Valentine's Day	
Easter	
Memorial Day	
Mother's Day	
Father's Day	
Fourth of July	
Thanksgiving	
Christmas	
New Year's Eve	

This page is left blank intentionally

Our Tithing Worksheet

Figure Descriptions	Operation	Annual Figures	Monthly Figures (Annual / 12)	Prayer Focus for Our Church
Our Annual Income	(Monthly Salary * 12)			
10% Annual Tithe Goal	(Gross * 0.10)			
(less) Current Annual Church Tithe	(Current Monthly Tithe * 12)			
Additional Annual Amount Needed to Meet the Tithe	(Goal - Current)			
Additional Monthly Amount Needed to Meet the Tithe (Annual / 12)	(Additional Annual Needed / 12)			

Our Giving Worksheet

Designated Organization or Missionary Doing God's Work	Program Description	Annual Donation Goal	Monthly Figures (Annual / 12)	Prayer Focus for This Ministry or Missionary

This page is left blank intentionally

Insurance Policy Summary Sheet

Policy Type	Policy #	Policy Description of Coverage	Company Contact Information
Term Life Insurance			
Umbrella Liability Policy			
Home Owner's Insurance			
Auto Insurance			
Medical Insurance			
Dental Insurance			

This page is left blank intentionally

Monthly Budget Planning Sheet

Income - Salary and Bonuses (Net of Taxes)	$	Other Income Sources (Net of Taxes)	$
		TOTAL INCOME (ALL SOURCES)	

Essentials Expenses

	$
GIVING	
Tithe	
Charity:	
Charity:	
SAVINGS	
College Fund - Total Monthly Contributions	
Short to Mid-Term Savings*	
Retirement Savings	
Other:	
Other:	
FINANCIAL MANAGEMENT	
Term Life Insurance Coverage	
Umbrella Liability Policy	
Safe Deposit Box - Annual Fee	
Annual Line of Credit Fee	
Sound Mind Investing Web Subscription	
Stamps	
Checks	
Other:	
Other:	
DEBT RETIREMENT	
Mortgage	
Other debt:	
Other debt:	
Other debt:	
HOUSEHOLD & UTILITIES	
Property Taxes	
Home Owner's Insurance	
Home Repair and Improvement*	
Yard Maintenance Expenses*	
Alarm Monitoring Service*	
Pest Control Expenses*	
Association Dues	
Electric Utilities Company	
Gas Company	
City Water Company	
Cable, Internet, and Phone Services*	
Cellular Phone Service	
Other:	
Other:	
AUTO EXPENSES (ALL CARS)	
Car Payment+	
Cost Co. Auto Insurance	
Car Registration	
Gasoline	
Car Repairs & Maintenance	
Other:	
Other:	
GROCERIES	
Monthly Health Food Store	
Monthly Warehouse Store	
Food Warehouse Membership	
Monthly Grocery Store	
Make Up and Beauty Products	
Other:	
Other:	
MEDICAL	
Medical Visits and Copays	
Family Medical Insurance Premiums	
Family Dental Insurance Premiums	
Regular Medical Prescriptions	
Medic Alert Membership	
Other:	
Other:	
Other:	
TOTAL ESSENTIAL EXPENSES	

Discretionary Expenses

	$
PERSONAL DISCRETIONARY	
Children's' Clothes and Shoes	
Parents' Clothes and Shoes	
Monthly Haircuts*	
Presents & Cards (Christmas, Graduations, Birthday, etc.)	
Professional Studio Photos	
Decorating, Office Supplies, other Household Expenses	
Other:	
Other:	
ENTERTAINMENT OR HOBBIES	
Eating Out Lunch Expenses for Work	
Entertainment (Meal, movies, etc.)	
Magazine Subscriptions (Parents)	
Photography and Digital Scrapbook Expenses	
Other:	
Other:	
EDUCATION, LESSONS AND CLASSES	
Homeschool Materials and Curriculum*	
Homeschool Supplies	
Standardized Testing Fees (IOWA)	
State, Conference, and Local Support Group Fees	
HSLDA Membership	
Magazine Subscriptions	
Music Lessons	
PE or Sports Classes	
Summer Swim Lessons	
Library Membership	
Other:	
Other:	
SPECIAL PROJECTS OR VACATIONS	
Vacation Account	
Other:	
Other:	
TOTAL Discretionary	

TOTAL INCOME	
(less) TOTAL EXPENSES	
NET BALANCE**	

**In a zero-based budget, the net balance would be "0" each month since the income is totally distributed across all categories, including savings.

If a balance is left, you can incorporate it into your short-term savings acccount or maybe a special savings account for vacation. Then start at "0" again the next month.

If, however, your balance is negative then it is time to examine your individual category expenses to see what expenditure habits or commitments are making you out of balance. Use the percentage chart below to see what your culprit may be and then take steps to address it.

	Percentage of Net Income
GIVING	
SAVINGS	
FINANCIAL MANAGEMENT	
DEBT RETIREMENT	
HOUSEHOLD & UTILITIES	
AUTO EXPENSES (ALL CARS)	
GROCERIES	
MEDICAL	
PERSONAL DISCRETIONARY	
ENTERTAINMENT OR HOBBIES	
EDUCATION, LESSONS AND CLASSES	
SPECIAL PROJECTS OR VACATIONS	
TOTAL	100%

This page is left blank intentionally

Expense Categorization and Audit Sheet

Expense Type & % Goal*	Expense Category	Expense Description	Is this expense under control? List problems.

*D = Discretionary; E = Essential; Write in goals as a percentage of income

This page is left blank intentionally

Medical Driving and Expense Log for _____

Date	Description	Purpose	Round Trip Mileage	Fees Paid

This page is left blank intentionally

Rotating Meal Planner - 3 Months

Meal Number	Protein Base (Pork, Chicken, Beef, Beans, Fish)	Main Dish	Side Dish	Recipe Location(s)	Beyond Basics Shopping List Needs
1					
2					
3					
4					
5					
6					
7					
8					
9					
10					
11					
12					
13					
14					
15					
16					
17					
18					
19					
20					
21					
22					
23					
24					

This page is left blank intentionally

Quick Fix Meal Options

Meal Number	Protein Base (Pork, Chicken, Beef, Beans, Fish)	Main Dish	Side Dish	Recipe Location(s)	Beyond Basics Shopping List Needs
1					
2					
3					
4					
5					
6					
7					
8					
9					
10					
11					
12					
13					
14					
15					
16					

Notes:

_____

_____

_____

_____

_____

_____

This page is left blank intentionally

Shopping List – Grocery Store

Produce:

Deli:

Meats:

Breads:

Breakfast Foods:

Coffee/Tea:

Baking:

Mexican Foods:

Canned Fruits:

Canned Veggies:

Pasta:

Boxed Foods:

Soups:

Cleaners:

Paper Products:

Condiments:

Drinks:

Snacks:

Dairy:

Frozen Foods:

Hygiene Items:

Medicine:

Misc. (Cards, etc.)

This page is left blank intentionally

Shopping List – Health Food Store

Hygiene Items:

Medicine:

Coffee/Tea:

Condiments:

Canned Fruits:

Pasta:

Canned Veggies:

Soups:

Spices:

Baking:

Boxed Foods:

Crackers/Cookies:

Drinks:

Cleaners:

Frozen Foods:

Paper Products:

Dairy:

Produce:

Meats:

Deli:

Breads:

Bulk:

Misc. (Cards, etc.)

This page is left blank intentionally

Shopping List – Warehouse Store

Breads:

Chips:

Deli:

Produce

Paper Products:

Frozen Foods:

Refridgerated Foods:

Drinks:

Baking/Spices:

Other Foods:

Canned Foods:

Snacks & Dried Fruit:

Breakfast Foods:

Food Wraps:

House Cleaners:

Clothes Cleaners:

Children's Items:

Hygiene Items:

Medicine:

Vitamins:

Misc.

This page is left blank intentionally

Daily and "One Other" Task Lists

Daily Task Example (Complete Entire list every day)	**"One Other" Activity Examples** (Select and complete ONE of these a day)
TOTAL HOURS SPENT ON DAILY ITEMS =	**TOTAL DAILY HOURS AVAILABLE FOR "ONE OTHER" ITEMS =**

This page is left blank intentionally

Daily Task Example *(Complete Entire list every day)*	"One Other" Activity Examples *(Select and complete ONE of these a day)*
	Working towards a long-term goal or project. (continuing education work, running a personal business, major home improvement project)
	Ministry or Community Involvement Work (preparation activities and fulfilling scheduled duties)
	Weekly House Cleaning and Yard Work Duties (dusting, sweeping, mopping, scrubbing, trash, mowing, gardening, tree/bush trimming, changing linens)
	Periodic Cleaning & Organizing Tasks (blinds, baseboards, dusting hard-to-reach shelves, ceiling fans, silk plants, windows, or touch up painting; organizing a room, drawer, garage, storage box, or closet)
	Business Correspondence (evaluating and answering e-mails, returning business calls, and going through the regular mail)
	Corresponding with Family or Friends (cards, sending video clips, e-mailing sample work, phoning, video conference calls)
	Homeschool Activities (researching new curriculum options and teaching concepts, weekly preparation, updating school plans, prepping new homeschool help tools and worksheets, or preparing grade cards)
	Grocery and Meal Preparation (inventorying pantry, preparing shopping list, researching new recipes, and going shopping)
	Outside activities (field trips, weekly Park Day, cleaning Grandma's house, or PE Class, sports programs, private lesson or class, planning a trip or vacation)
	Managing finances (budgeting, paying bills, managing investments, shopping insurance, shredding, filing)
	Health and Medical Activities (appointments, in-home therapy activities, physical training for boys, related phone work to physician's office or insurance company).
	Hobbies and Family Social and Activity Time (board game, Wii system, date night, Digital Scrapbooking, Photo Editing, etc.)
TOTAL HOURS SPENT ON DAILY ITEMS =	**TOTAL DAILY HOURS AVAILABLE FOR "ONE OTHER" ITEMS =**

This page is left blank intentionally

Daily Things to Do List

Today's Date: _____

Topic	Description	Done?
Personal Chores		
Other Chores		
Bible		
Character Training		
Math		
Spelling		
Handwriting		
Reading		
Grammar		
Art or Music		
Foreign Language		
History		
Science		
Physical Ed.		

Schedule Color Codes:	Complete before 9:30 a.m. - HIGHLIGHT YELLOW
	Completed between 9:30 a.m. and Lunch - HIGHLIGHT PINK
	Complete After Lunch - HIGHLIGHT GREEN
	Complete After Dinner - HIGHLIGHT ORANGE

This page is left blank intentionally

Weekly Schedule for: _____

Topic	Additional Instructions & Information	Monday	Tuesday	Wednesday	Thursday	Friday
A.M. CHORES						
BIBLE						
MUSIC						
MATH						
ENGLISH						
SPELLING						
FOREIGN LANGUAGE						
WRITING, LIT. &/OR HANDWRITING						
LUNCH						
HISTORY						
SCIENCE						
ART						
MORE MUSIC						
READING						
PE, SPORTS PROGRAM &/OR P.M. Chores						
DINNER						
CORRECTIONS						
ARTS SKILLS & APPRECIATION						
FREE READING						

Weekly Schoolwork Schedule for:

This page is left blank intentionally

Phase Allocation Time Needed by Subject

Topic	Phase 1 (Learn)	Phase 2 (Produce)	Phase 3 (Craft)	TOTAL TIME NEEDED	Comments
BIBLE					
MUSIC					
MATH					
ENGLISH					
SPELLING					
FOREIGN LANGUAGE					
WRITING					
HISTORY					
SCIENCE					
ART					
READING/ LITERATURE					

This page is left blank intentionally

Appendix C
Part III Forms

This page is left blank intentionally

Homeschool Support Group Interview Form

Group Name	Contact Name and Title	E-mail and Website Address

1. What is the purpose of your group and when were you formed? What is your group's "story of origin" and are you associated with a church? If so, what is the positional statement of that church?

2. What do you require of your members? Do I need to sign a statement of faith, code of conduct, or other such agreement?

3. What is the registration process, and do you charge an annual fee? If so, how much is it and how is that money used? How is money collected for participating in individual events?

4. What are the primary activities that your group does? How does one host or organize and event?

Program	Y or N?	Description
Park Day		
Field Trip		
Mom's Activities		
Family Activities		
Topical Workshops		
Student Clubs or Events		
Topical Workshops		
Other:		

5. How are leadership members selected and what are their responsibilities? How is accountability assessed?

6. What other processes or programs are unique about your group?

7. Bottom line: How would you say your group demonstrates unity of purpose, clarity of organization, and positive member commitment?

Other comments or questions: _____

_____

_____

_____

_____

_____

_____

_____

_____

_____

_____

_____

_____

_____

_____

_____

_____

_____

_____

General Sign-Up Form

Event/Program: _____

	Name	Phone Number	E-Mail	Other
1				
2				
3				
4				
5				
6				
7				
8				
9				
10				
11				
12				
13				
14				
15				
16				
17				
18				
19				
20				
21				
22				
23				
24				
25				

This page is left blank intentionally

Event Planner Form

Name of event:	
Name of Group/Person Coordinating this event: *(include phone number & e-mail address as this person will serve as the contact for inquiries and RSVP requests.)*	
Committee helping Group/Person above to facilitate this event:	
Event Description: *(Include a detailed description here including all of the points of interest to be experienced and any website information (i.e. URL address) that may provide more details about the event.)*	
Event Location: *(Include crossroads and directions and a description of exactly where the group is to meet upon arrival. Also, if a room is needed at a church or public facility, please allow at least two to three months' notice and complete the addendum section*.)*	
Event Date: *(Please note whether these are firm or suggested dates):*	
Event Time: *(Please beginning and anticipated ending times. Note set up times as well.)*	
What is the targeted age range of the attending children for this event?	
What is the expected attendance as well as the attendance limit (parents vs. children) if this event?	
What is the cost of this event that families will need to expect to pay? What additional budget funds are needed? *(Please describe on a per family or per child basis.)*	
What is the RSVP Process for this Event? *(i.e. via e-mail, phone call, via field trip website, etc. Please also include such items as contact information, payment requirements and RSVP deadline details.)*	
How will this event be promoted? *(i.e. postcard mailings, e-mail distribution to families, schedule of events at Park Day, church bulletin, etc.) E-mail your information to the proper person to distribute the message.*	
Any additional miscellaneous issues that need to be considered? *(List any other additional requirements or items of concern here regarding the coordination of this event.)*	

Event Planner Form*

Complete if public facility is required

Do you need a room or facility space at a church or other public venue? (specify your preferred space)	

Total time you need the room (set-up & clean-up):	*Beginning time:*		*Ending time:*	

Will you need a kitchen?		*Coffee Maker?*		*Refrigerator?*	.

Do you need tech support?

(Place an "X" in the Appropriate Spots)

	TV		Microphone		CD Player		PowerPoint		Large Screen

	Projection		Other: *(Please specify)*

Will you need chairs or tables set-up?

(Please use space below to draw the desired configuration of the room(s).)

Appendix D:
Holiday Tradition Planning Information

This page is left blank intentionally

Holiday Tradition and Planning Information

As mentioned previously in chapter five, I have included in this section some suggestions that you may want to incorporate into your family's traditions that we have found to be meaningful in our home. There, you will find useful ideas and "food for thought" on how to plan special moments and traditions into your family's celebration for birthdays, your wedding anniversary, Valentine's Day, Easter, Memorial Day, Mother's and Father's Days, Fourth of July, Thanksgiving, Christmas, and New Year's Eve and Day. You will see that it is not so much about what you do as it is about being consistent with your family's traditions. Remember that if you are interested in using a planner sheet, I have included one for you in Appendix B.

1. **Birthdays**: Make birthdays special by first seeing if your husband can arrange to take the day off. We do not really do school on any of their birthdays, and we try to plan some special activity. When our oldest was young, we started having parties for him at the age of three. However, that got a bit too expensive to do, especially as we started having more children. So, we changed to making sure that we did a big party for them when they were five years old, and other "milestone birthdays" with their friends. Then the rest of the time, it is pretty much just the family or an occasional outing with one or two other families. Here are some ways to make the day fun.

   ➤ **Make a note leading up to their birthday about any significant item or toy that they like and have been saving for consistently.** Often, it is like getting two presents when we purchase the item that they are working towards for their birthday, and then they find that they still have all of their money available that they had worked hard to save that they can now use for something else. We do not do this with everything that they are working towards, but it is fun to do it when we can!

   ➤ **Decorate the house** the night before so that they can have a fun environment when they wake up the next morning. It is surprising to see how much pleasure they can get out of a few balloons and streamers. We also allow them to have a candle in whatever breakfast item they are having as a build up to their cake.

   ➤ Rather than having them open all of their presents at one time during the evening when the day is practically gone and they are tired, **have your child open gifts throughout the day.** Even if it is just a couple of small items, it is much more fun for them. That way they can play with them throughout the day with their siblings rather than waiting "forever" to open them all at once.

   ➤ **Make a special cake for them**. When our oldest was going to turn one, I took a cake decorating class at the local craft store so that I could make him an "Elmo" cake. That was the first of dozens of specialty cakes that I have made so far, and the kids have absolutely loved being part of that decorating process. Although the cakes take a few hours to make from start to finish, it is another type of gift you can give your child that is both appreciated and memorable.

➢ **Make their favorite dinner for them**. Regardless of whether it is steak, macaroni and cheese, or pizza, ask them in advance what they would like for their birthday dinner and serve it.

➢ **Have each family member say a kind word about them at dinner**. Go around the table during meal time and ask each person to say what they really appreciate about the birthday child. These words of affirmation are great deposits into their emotional bank account.

2. **Your Wedding Anniversary**: Although most years my husband and I have gone out to nice restaurant or outing with just the two of us, we recently did something different. Instead of going out, we decided to make a special dinner at home and included the children. Then we spent the rest of the evening viewing our wedding video with them. They had seen wedding photos before, but not much of anything else. So, we showed them the video of the beginning "montage" of pictures of each of us growing up as well as the wedding ceremony itself. My husband and I reminisced with each other throughout the evening while the children asked a lot of different questions that we answered for them. They also had an opportunity to see photos firsthand of our loved ones who have since passed away. My husband had also purchased a special cake at the bakery so that we could have our own "wedding cake" with the kids that night. When all of that was done, we then went through a box of wedding and honeymoon memories with them. I also took my dress out and showed it to them—a thing I had not done in since the day it was put away! Fortunately, it had held up over time and they said repeatedly how much they loved looking at everything. Everyone had a happy and contented feeling when they went to bed and we realized that it is important we share these aspects of how our family began with them because they were not around to see it when it originally happened! I also made sure to have DVD copies made of our VHS wedding video to put in each of their keepsake boxes. Eventually, for our 25th anniversary, we recreated our wedding day for our family by having a progressive event starting with dinner at the same place we had enjoyed our rehearsal dinner. Then we took them to the church campus where we were married and toured that before ending up at the reception location.

3. **Valentine's Day**: This is one of those holidays that creeps up on me before I realize what is happening! My husband and I make sure to exchange our sentiments in front of the kids so that we continue to reinforce to them how their dad loves their mom. If we can, we go out to dinner. However, we have not been able to do that every year so sometimes we just make a nice dinner at home. For the kids, this is a fun time to work with your homeschool support group to put on an easy Valentine exchange at the park. Also, for younger ones, be sure to read *Saint Valentine* by Robert Sabuda in preparation for the day so that your child understands the significance behind all of the hearts and flowers.

4. **Easter or Resurrection Day**: This is a wonderful season in which to remember and honor the death, burial, and resurrection of our Lord, Jesus Christ. Make sure to set aside time during this busy weekend to pause with your children about the significance of what the holiday is all about. Although secular roots of the holiday relate back to the goddess of fertility (hence the eggs), we always emphasize that this is a time of year that focuses on rebirth and renewal. Birds and rabbits begin to have their babies and the spring flowers bloom while leaves return to the trees. Ultimately, however, you want to lead your child to the most important rebirth of all which is our own spiritual rebirth based on the work that Jesus did on the cross for us. You can begin preparatory discussions on Palm Sunday and lead your family to a time of remembrance on Good Friday. We like to read the account of the Easter story from the Bible and then watch *The Miracle Maker*, an excellent stop-animation movie released in 2000 that recounts the life of Jesus through his ascension. Then on Saturday morning after breakfast, we take time to go through our homemade set of Resurrection Eggs. You can either purchase a pre-made one at your local Christian bookstore or work with your child to just make your own. There are plenty of "how-to" instructions available online. Each egg is a different color with a different object in it telling about the experiences Jesus had in his last days, beginning with Palm Sunday and going on from there. You always end with a white empty egg to represent the empty tomb of Jesus. Later that afternoon, consider making "Resurrection Cookies" that again follow the Easter story and require you to leave them in the oven overnight.[347] Then they discover the "empty" cookies in the morning, along with a few other goodies before going to church. Then they can spend the rest of the day with family, enjoying a nice lunch, and then flying kites or hunting for eggs in the afternoon.

5. **Memorial Day**: Since 2002, we have gone together to our family's memorial park for a special time of remembrance. Since the passing of our so many loved ones, we have added the process of taking five balloons: a yellow one for Granddad (his favorite color), another yellow one for our oldest son (his favorite color too), a blue one for our second oldest son, a red one for my brother, and a white one to honor those who have served in the military and have given their lives to keep our country free. First, we visit my father's grave. We always clean the headstone thoroughly and have a time of remembrance about him. We may add a flag since he served in the military during the Korean War and freshen the silk flowers that are there if necessary. My husband says a special prayer and then we release the yellow balloon. Then we walk over to the niche area where our boys are laid to rest and follow a similar process for each of them—later releasing their balloons. You can also attach scripture or memory cards on the end of your balloon so that it can possibly minister to someone else eventually when it comes down. We finish with a time of walking around the cemetery talking about the importance of all of the

---

[347] There are many recipes on the Internet available for this egg-white base cookie, all with variations on the story and information you share with your child. Choose the one you feel is most suitable and have fun making them and discovering the "empty" cookies on Easter morning!

lives represented there, answering all sorts of questions the boys have about the different ways people are buried and about life and death in general. We then say a prayer of thanks for those who have served and given their lives in the military for our country and release the final balloon. It is a wonderful, quite time of reflection and so healthy for developing an accurate and positive sense of how life works from beginning to end. Even if you do not have loved ones buried locally, you can visit a nearby military or other cemetery on that day to have similar experiences.

6. **Fourth of July**: Leading up to this holiday, usually a day or two before, I liked to read the children the book titled *Fourth of July Story* by Alice Dalgliesh when they were young. It details our country's history in an easily accessible but informative manner through the signing of the Declaration of Independence through America's victory in the Revolutionary War. Jean Friz's books like *Shhh! We're Writing the Constitution* are also excellent resources for older children. One other title that is interesting is *So You Want to Be President?* By Judith St. George and David Small. On the day of the holiday, we put up our flag, and the kids like playing patriotic music before and after breakfast. However, unlike many families, we have not always made a regular practice of attending local fireworks displays. Although we enjoy them from time to time, we have found that the crowds, the late hour, and the noise level were largely unpleasant for the younger members of our family. Now that they are older, we go more frequently, but it is not always a given that we will do so. Instead, we have a barbeque at home and try to invite one or two families over to enjoy it with us during the day. Sometimes we make a special desert, like the standard flag cupcakes using white cupcakes, blueberries and strawberries arranged to look like one large flag. A Jell-O trifle is fun too with patriotic colors showing through a clear glass bowl. Then, after company leaves and the kids get washed up, we have a family time and watch most of the PBS presentation of *A Capitol Fourth* on the television to satisfy the need for fireworks. The children love the music and enjoy seeing all of the fanfare that goes along with this holiday first hand from the comfort of our living room. Sometime throughout the day, we also take time to remind our children how fortunate we are to live in this country and each person gives examples of what they appreciate about the freedoms that they have.

7. **Mother's and Father's Day**: Since "receiving gifts" is low on the list for my and my husband's love language, we always have to make special efforts to honor each other in this way during birthdays, Christmas, and Mother's and Father's Day. However, these holidays do not always mean that a personal gift is in order. Often, it is just the giving of time that it appreciated. Making breakfast for each other or completing that home project that has been bothering your spouse for many months can be a way to honor them with your time rather than racking your brain to buy them a "perfect" gift. I also marvel at how much money can be spent on greeting cards and believe that when children make their own cards to give out, it is just as special if not more so! If one of these days is approaching, also consider helping your child make a special craft for

them or picture frame for a special updated photo of the family that they can use for their desk at home or at work. Then during lunch, try to go around the table and have each person present say one thing that they appreciate about the parent that is being honored. Write them down on any cards received that day for a truly special memory.

8. **Thanksgiving**: Thanksgiving is one of my favorite holidays. The weather begins to shift to a more pleasant temperature in Arizona, and we know that my husband will have four whole days off from work to spend with us. In general, it is a very relaxed time, and everyone is in good spirits. Here are some ideas to consider when planning for this holiday.

   ➤ **Involve your child in the food preparations.** If you need to make a dish or tear up bread for stuffing a day or two in advance, involve your child in the preparations and just plan on taking extra time to do it.

   ➤ **Read** a book like ***The Thanksgiving Story*** by Alice Dalgliesh a day or two in advance for younger children. Prepare your child for what the holiday is for and how our nation was largely founded by people pursuing a place to live that would afford them freedom in their way of life and in their worship practices.

   ➤ **Have special guests come the night before to stay over**. Most years, my mother comes over the night before Thanksgiving so that she can have more visiting time to engage with her grandsons. The boys always look forward to this aspect of the day, and then we do this again on Christmas Eve.

   ➤ **Make a "thankful" card jar**. This can be done the night before Thanksgiving as a time where family members are given strips of colorful fall colors that they can then write on what they are thankful for. This jar can then be used during your special dinner as a discussion starter while each family member picks a "thankful" card from the jar, reads it aloud, and discusses it with the whole family.

   ➤ **Record and watch the Thanksgiving Day parades later in the day**. In this day and age of excessive commercialism, sitting through the morning parades on television can be an annoying experience. Sometimes they also have entertainment that is not that interesting or appropriate for children so having it recorded allows you to bypass these parts of the program as well as the commercials.

   ➤ **Look forward to decorating your home for Christmas the day after Thanksgiving**. Not to minimize Thanksgiving, but for many of us, it is a rare time to have our husbands off from work this long, so take advantage of that time by getting out the decorative items. If you do not have an artificial tree, consider investing in a good one during the after-Christmas sales that you can then use again and again in the years to come. Although real trees smell nice, you do not get to enjoy it as long, and condensed decorating time can rush the season.

> Later that weekend, **begin planning your holiday calendar for the remainder of the year**. Sit down with your husband and coordinate your calendars so that you can truly plan what you want to have happen rather than it just "happening to you". Do not forget to make time for any baking or shopping that needs to be done as well. If you shop online, be sure to also allow plenty of time for it to ship to you prior to Christmas.

9. **Christmas**: While this day is about Jesus, but we have some broader traditions as well. We do not ban stories about St. Nick from our home, but we do keep the reason for the day in perspective. Early on, we taught our boys that the generosity of Santa Claus is based on the historical figure of Saint Nicolas. When they were younger, we read about his life from a book like Diane Stanley's *Saint Nicolas* to understand the legends and what people mean when they refer to his good deeds, etc. Yet most of our communications just center around Jesus. One of the reasons that Christmas can be stressful is that so much emphasis is placed on the *date* of December 25th. Really you want to **make the Christmas *season* your focus and not just that one single day.** "Advent" means "coming", so consider implementing an advent process where you spend time during the four or five weeks prior to Christmas preparing as a family.

   Our season begins with the day after Thanksgiving by putting up the decorations and making plans for the coming month. It is a long weekend when my husband is available to build our artificial tree, and the kids all have their individual jobs that they love to do. The last thing we put on the tree is ***The Christmas Nail*** ornament, which you can find at most Christian bookstores. It is the size and weight of the type of nail that would have been driven into Jesus' hands and feet when He was placed on the cross. We place it near the inside trunk of the tree as a private reminder of our hope in Jesus and that He was born into this world to die for our sins. We then take the rest of that weekend to figure out our shopping and baking schedules and make plans for special seasonal events so that the kids can look forward to those things rather than just making last minute decisions here or there.

   Then over the next few weeks, we take time once a week to go through *The Advent Book* by Jack and Kathy Stockman. This is a wonderful, oversized book filled with intricate illustrations and twenty-five "doors" to open that tell the Christmas story and then some. We also have a special candle stand that holds five candles: three are colored purple, one pink and the last one white. We light one purple candle the on the first Sunday of December and then open all of the doors that are current to that date and take turns opening doors and reading each section. We follow the same process every week, lighting two the next week and then three the following week. After attending Christmas Eve services at our church, we then come home and finish all of the doors while lighting all of the purple and the pink candle. The final white candle is lit with all of the other four on Christmas Day at mealtime. It is really not an involved process, but it makes a statement all throughout December about where our focus is and the children all really enjoy participating in this tradition.

Here are Advent storybooks that are also interesting to use when your children are able to sit for longer periods of reading; all three were authored by Arnold Ytreeide.

> ➤ *Jotham's Journey; A Storybook for Advent*
> ➤ *Tabitha's Travels; A Family Story for Advent*
> ➤ *Bartholomew's Passage; A Family Story for Advent*

The other thing that we have done each year since the children were little is to make a **birthday cake for Jesus** a day or two in advance. This serves as our dessert on Christmas day and a great way to end the day. The cake is a three-layer round cake with a chocolate layer and two white layers that have been colored red and green, respectively. You can freeze the extra chocolate food layer for another time since you only need one. We then frost the entire cake white and decorate it by icing a yellow star and "Happy Birthday Jesus" on the top, red hearts on the sides, and holly leaves and berries all around. Then the day of Christmas, we place a large white candle in the middle star with other candles all around to represent our extended family. We use blue for the males, pink for the females, and yellow for those family members who have passed away. We then sing the "Happy Birthday" song and blow out the candles before cutting into the festive cake.

10. **New Year's Eve & Day**: I heard it said once that whatever you do on New Year's Eve is reflective of what you can be found doing throughout the rest of the year. It is definitely true for us! We incorporate a couple of movies, snack foods, and organizational projects into our day as we talk about and look forward to the coming year. We always have certain end-of-the-year organizational or paperwork processes we finish on that day. I also annoy the boys several times throughout the day by reminding them that they do not have to make their beds anymore this year or that we will not need to practice music again until next year, and so forth. They always roll their eyes and say, "Mom, tomorrow *is* next year!" By mid-afternoon, we are working on filing or maybe playing a board game while running the comedy "*Bachelor Mother*" with Ginger Rodgers and David Niven in the background. There is a "New Year's Eve" scene in the film, which is why we associated it with this day all those years ago! Later, my husband comes home from work and we get in our PJ's and get out our fun party foods that we have prepared that day. We then usually watch a special movie that they kids have selected and enjoy our food with that. We also always have a bottle of sparkling cider on hand, but no one ever stays awake to midnight to toast the New Year, so we just drink it early! Then in the morning, we usually have a full breakfast together and either spend the day visiting a special friend, enjoying family time, or just discussing our plans for the coming year. As you can see, our New Year's Eve and Day does not seem very unusual. However, there is a comfort and a happiness that settles in with the boys to know what to expect each year and they enjoy just "hanging out" together one last time before the year is gone. Remember, quantity time provides the necessary backdrop for quality moments to take place.

A Word About Halloween....

Perhaps you have noticed by now that **I have not included a section for Halloween.** Simply put, this is not a holiday we celebrate. Every Christian family must come to their own conclusion about this holiday, and I know that, as children, both my husband and I grew up in homes that participated in it. However, when we started having children of our own, we realized that we were not comfortable with the empty message that it had and could not biblically support why we would celebrate it. This was especially true for us after we researched more deeply into its origins and the meaning behind its images and practices.

My husband and I also do not think that the local church should bother with offering alternatives to it or trying to dress it up in an effort to somehow relate it to Christianity. Consider these verses: "Have nothing to do with the fruitless deeds of darkness, but rather expose them." Ephesians 5:11 (NIV) or "Have nothing to do with godless myths and old wives' tales; rather train yourself to be godly." I Timothy 4:7 (NIV)

So, for our family, we choose not to emphasize this holiday. I know that we rub many, including Christians, the wrong way for not celebrating it, but it really has not been an issue for our family to bypass it. At the same time, we do not condemn those who choose to participate. It is simply not a fit for what we want our family to spend time acknowledging, and we instruct our children to just say, "We don't celebrate Halloween", when they are asked the inevitable question of "What are you going to dress up as this year?"

Instead, consider spending time explaining to your children why you do not participate and, when they are older, share with them what the real origins are for images like Jack-o'-lanterns and the concept of "Trick or Treat". There are many good books available on the subject but the best and most accessible by far that I have come across is a lecture given by Pastor Mark Martin of **Calvary Community Church in Phoenix** called *Tricked by Treats*.[348] You can read the information at the footnoted link provided below, but also try to source the audio version of it as well in order to further research this topic.

Regarding your child, recognize that they are not typically interested in all of the spooky concepts associated with this day. Usually, children are just excited about the prospect of dressing up and getting candy. So, avoid all the commercial and media trappings of this holiday. Instead create other opportunities throughout the year for them to enjoy candy and play dress up in a way that is not associated with Halloween, and you will find that October 31st will come and go, and they really do not miss it at all.

---

[348] http://www.calvaryphx.com/portals/media/TrickedbyTreats.pdf

What are my other notes and ideas about holiday planning?

About the Author

Mrs. Carol Gary has been married to her husband Grant Gary since 1991 and they have been ardently homeschooling their sons in Phoenix-metro area of Arizona since the fall of 2000. They have four sons; two of whom they continue to homeschool and two of whom have gone home to be with the Lord. They faithfully attend their local church and are fully devoted followers of Christ. Their family is a member of a local homeschooling support group, and she enjoys digital photography/scrapbooking in her spare time. Most of all, she loves reading to her sons who especially love her range of "voices".

She served in the leadership of a large, local support group called "The Homeschool Ministry" for twelve years. Over this time, she interacted with hundreds of homeschooling families in various stages of the home education process and has a heart to help others succeed in teaching, discipling, and mentoring their children. She developed *The Balanced Homeschooler (TBH) Mentoring Program* to provide a unified resource for the common concerns and questions that she was called upon to regularly address about home education, discipleship, and home management. Recently, she has also authored *The Balanced High Schooler: Getting Parents and Homeschooled Teens "On the Grid" for College and Beyond.* She regularly presents at various homeschool conferences and events and joined the speaker lineup in 2016 for the Home Education Council of America. In addition, she and Grant have recently begun serving on the Board of Directors for MoezArt Productions, a local drama company specifically designed for homeschooling families.

Since 2013, she has served as the AZ State Ambassador and her husband as a Community Ambassador for HSLDA Compassion; the charitable department of Homeschool Legal Defense Association designed to help families continue to homeschool through hard times. She received their National Service

Award five times as she and her husband work with their team to meet a number of unusual and pressing needs in their local homeschool community.

She is active with her alma mater, Grand Canyon University, faithfully serving on the ALPHA Advisory Board to benefit AZ homeschoolers and also supporting the Evan C. Gary Memorial Scholarship administered through the Grand Canyon University Scholarship Foundation. She and her family also support the annual Run to Fight Children's Cancer organized by Children's Cancer Network's and hosted by Grand Canyon University.

Carol earned her B.S. in Marketing from GCU in Phoenix, Arizona in 1990, graduating Summa Cum Laude and earning the university's highest academic honor: the Ray-Maben Scholar award. She later earned her master's degree in Business Administration from GCU in 1998 as well as the distinction of being named GCU's "Outstanding Business Administration Graduate of the Year" award. She worked and advanced in the corporate environment in operational management and quality process consulting in both the retail and information technology industries for over thirteen years until 1998 when she transitioned into her favorite role of all: full-time mom.